CHARLIE SIRINGO'S WEST

1. *Frontispiece: Original cover of Charles Siringo's,* A Texas Cowboy, or Fifteen Years on the Hurricane Deck of a Spanish Pony, Taken from Real Life by Charles Siringo, an Old Stove Up "Cow Puncher" Who Has Spent Nearly Twenty Years on the Great Western Cattle Ranches *(Chicago: M. Umbdenstock & Company Publishers, 1885).*

Charlie Siringo's West

AN INTERPRETIVE BIOGRAPHY

HOWARD R. LAMAR

UNIVERSITY OF NEW MEXICO PRESS ～ ALBUQUERQUE

11   10   09   08   07   06   05   1   2   3   4   5   6   7

LIBRARY OF CONGRESS CATALOGING-IN-PUBLICATION DATA
Lamar, Howard Roberts.
Charlie Siringo's West : an interpretive biography / Howard R. Lamar.
p. cm.
Includes bibliographical references.
ISBN 0-8263-3669-8 (cloth : alk. paper)
1. Siringo, Charles A., 1855–1928.
2. Cowboys—Texas—Biography.
3. Texas—History—1846–1950. 4. Texas—Biography.
5. Frontier and pioneer life—West (U.S.)
6. West (U.S.)—History—1860–1890.
7. West (U.S.)—History—1890–1945.
8. Private investigators—United States—Biography.
9. Pinkerton's National Detective Agency—Biography.
10. Authors, American—Biography.
I. Title.
F391.S624L36 2005
976.4'092—dc22
2005013440

§ह

Book design and type composition:
Kathleen Sparkes

This book is typeset using Sabon 10/14; 25P6
Display type is Ramona and Copperplate

Contents

✖

Acknowledgments   vii

Preface   xi

CHAPTER ONE
Charlie Siringo and the Several
Worlds of Matagorda Bay   1

CHAPTER TWO
Civil War Comes to
Matagorda Bay, 1850–1867   17

CHAPTER THREE
Rites of Passage:
St. Louis and the Mississippi
River Experience, 1867–1870   35

CHAPTER FOUR
Shanghai Pierce and El Rancho Grande:
The Texas Cattle Industry from the
Open Range to Corporate
Enterprise, 1854–1900   45

CHAPTER FIVE
The Great Adventure: Charlie Siringo and
Billy the Kid on the Texas
Panhandle Frontier, 1877–1882   69

✖

Figures 2–19   91

CHAPTER SIX
"Queen City of the Border":
Caldwell, Kansas, 1871–1885   107

CHAPTER SEVEN
Rendezvous with Destiny:
Charlie Siringo, The Haymarket Riot,
and the Pinkertons, 1886–1890   129

CHAPTER EIGHT
Charlie Siringo Discovers New Mexico Politics:
The Ancheta Case and After, 1891–1898   157

CHAPTER NINE
The Bloody Coeur d'Alene Strike, 1891–1893   173

CHAPTER TEN
Chasing Butch Cassidy, the Sundance Kid,
and a Great Many Others, 1899–1903   191

Figures 20–43   211

CHAPTER ELEVEN
Two Victories and a Defeat: Alaskan Gold Thieves, Kentucky
Moonshiners, and the Haywood Trial in Idaho   231

Figures 44–60   252

CHAPTER TWELVE
The Trials of an Author, 1912–1922: Siringo's *A Cowboy
Detective* and *Two Evil Isms* Versus the Pinkertons,
and a Retreat Down Memory Lane—
Billy The Kid and *Lone Star Cowboy*   265

CHAPTER THIRTEEN
Recognition at Last!: Charlie Siringo
in Hollywood, 1923–1928   283

Figures 61–68   305

Notes   313
Bibliography   348
Index   363

Acknowledgments

My interest in writing a biography began in the mid-1970s when the Media Design Studio of Yale University invited me to write a film treatment of Charles Siringo's life for their projected *Westering* series about representative western figures.

Chief among those urging me to write a biography of Siringo was the late Ray Allen Billington of the Huntington Library, the recognized "dean" of western historians. Dr. Billington also introduced me to John Dunkel, a Hollywood writer for *Gunsmoke* and an expert on all things "western."

I am also grateful to the late Myra Ellen Jenkins for making available to me materials in the Historical Society of New Mexico and the Official Governors' Files of New Mexico in the New Mexico State Records Center, Santa Fe. In these early efforts I owe a similar debt of thanks to Professor Richard Etulain, then a faculty member at Idaho State University, Pocatello, for crucial materials on the Coeur d'Alene strikes in Idaho. Richard G. Magnusen, historian of the Coeur d'Alene region, not only provided access to local records, but generously granted me interviews when I was in Idaho.

From the beginning no one could have been more helpful in identifying and acquiring Siringo materials than Archibald Hanna, former curator of the Western Americana Collection in the Beinecke Rare Book and Manuscript Library at Yale University. His successor, George A. Miles, the present curator, has continued to acquire Siringo materials and has been an unstinting supporter of the study for two decades. I have also benefited enormously from the advice of former and present colleagues in the Yale History Department: William Cronon, now at the University of Wisconsin,

Madison; and Professors John Mack Faragher, David Montgomery, and David B. Davis, and Assistant Professor Jay Gitlin.

I am also deeply grateful to Peter J. Blodgett, curator of Western American History at the Huntington Library, for providing many materials relating to Siringo's life. Finally, I am equally grateful to David Grant Noble, independent scholar in Santa Fe, New Mexico, for locating and Xeroxing over one hundred letters between Siringo and his close friend and lawyer, A. B. Renehan, in the Siringo Papers at the Fray Angelico Chavez Library, Museum of New Mexico, Santa Fe, New Mexico.

Research grants from Yale University allowed me to secure the assistance of a number of former graduate students: Louis S. Warren, University of California, Davis; Guy Nelson, now a lawyer; Karl Jacoby, Brown University, Providence, Rhode Island; and most recently Jeremy Mumford, doctoral candidate in history, Yale University Graduate School.

It was my special good fortune that Dr. Paul C. Stone, lecturer in history at the University of Minnesota, with a joint appointment in the Hubert H. Humphrey Institute of Public Affairs, agreed to do research on Siringo in the summer of 2001 in Texas libraries, archives, and museums while conducting his own further studies of J. Frank Dobie, the subject of his doctoral dissertation in history at Yale. A specialist in Texas history, folklore studies, and western music, Stone went far beyond the call of duty to seek out Siringo records in Matagorda County, consult with archivist Mrs. Mary Belle Ingram, Matagorda County Historical Museum, and meet with John S. Runnells, II, a descendant of Abel Head (Shanghai) Pierce. In addition he consulted relevant documents in the Barker History Center in Austin, and with the help of Dulcinea Almayer, identified still more records in the Panhandle-Plains Historical Museum in Canyon, Texas, as well as Civil War maps in the Victoria College Library. Dr. Stone's information and personal insights have proved invaluable to me in the writing of this volume.

Among other Texas correspondents I have benefited from the advice of Ben E. Pingenot, author of the 1989 biography *Siringo*, and from Don E. Edwards, folksinger and historian of western ballads, who provided a copy of Siringo's *The Song Companion of a Lone Star Cowboy; Old Favorite Cow-Camp Songs.*

Finally I am indebted to Eliza Sherrod for patiently transforming my illegible handwriting into a finished manuscript. My greatest debt of gratitude, however, is to my family and especially to Shirley, my wife, who over the years has served as advisor, critic, editor, and proofreader during the completion of the biography. I am also grateful to my daughter Susan, who has sought out books and other western materials in New Mexico and Colorado relating to Siringo.

For any errors in the narrative and footnotes, I take full responsibility.

Howard R. Lamar
Yale University
New Haven, Connecticut

Preface

I FIRST CAME TO KNOW AND ADMIRE CHARLIE SIRINGO, THE TEXAS cowboy, Pinkerton detective, and author of seven books, nearly thirty years ago. That initial meeting came when the Yale University Media Design Studio asked me if I would identify ten representative western historical figures about whom a series of documentary film biographies could be produced called *Westering*. Of the ten figures it was obvious that one had to be a cowboy, whose image Americans and many persons all over the world think of as being quintessentially both Western and American.

It was immediately clear that one of the chief molders of the cowboy image was Charles A. Siringo, a small, thin, but fearless Texan, who was born on the Matagorda Peninsula in 1855. Thirty years later Siringo wrote *A Texas Cowboy, or Fifteen Years on the Hurricane Deck of a Spanish Pony* (1885). It was the first autobiography of a cowboy to be published, and it contained all the elements of the open-range cattle industry, and the cowboy saga that have become standard fare for western fiction and film for well over a century. But *A Texas Cowboy* was not fictional. J. Frank Dobie has called Siringo's account "primitive" but extremely valuable as to accuracy. Will Rogers, himself the son of an Oklahoma rancher, called it "the cowboy's Bible."

After recommending Siringo as a "representative cowboy" the Media Design Studio asked me to write a "treatment" for them to use in producing a film about him. That is when my quarter-of-a-century-long fascination with Charlie Siringo began. My positive response to Siringo then led the Media Design Studio to invite me to join Philip Garvin, a professional documentary filmmaker, who had achieved a national reputation in the field, to coproduce the film biography about

Siringo. Between 1975 and 1980 Garvin and I did produce a ninety-minute semi-documentary with professional actors.

That experience persuaded me to write a full biography of Siringo. My greatest research asset proved to be Siringo himself, for he had written seven largely autobiographical books during his lifetime. Moreover, he knew and corresponded with hundreds of western figures: cowboys and ranchers, businessmen, scholars, other writers about cowboys, including western novelists such as Andy Adams and Eugene Manlove Rhodes, and western artists such as Will James and Charles M. Russell. While the documentary was being made, much research was done in western libraries and museums, and the ranching and cowboy expert J. Evetts Haley of Canyon, Texas, was a great help. Descendants of Siringo's two children, Lee Roy Siringo and Viola Siringo, also provided valuable information.

There was never a dull moment as we learned more about Siringo's early life in south Texas, his cowboy days in the Texas Panhandle where he came to know Billy the Kid, and his years in the Kansas cattle town of Caldwell where, while running a successful cigar and ice cream store, he wrote his *A Texas Cowboy* in 1885.

Overjoyed by the generally favorable reception of his book, Siringo and his wife and daughter moved to Chicago where he thought he could write more books about the ranching west. But his life suddenly changed in 1886 when he was caught up in the violence and turmoil of Chicago's famous Haymarket Riot. Having developed a hatred of the anarchists accused of perpetrating the riot in which many policemen were killed or wounded, Siringo joined the Pinkerton National Detective Agency as an "operative," as their detectives were called, to track down the anarchists.

William A. Pinkerton, however, was fully aware of Siringo's experience in ranching, and as someone who had tracked down rustlers. Rather quickly he assigned Siringo to the agency's Denver office. There he served for twenty-two years on an incredible variety of cases involving ranching and mining frauds, labor strikes, railroad robberies, and chasing such notorious outlaws as Butch Cassidy and his "Wild Bunch." His assignments led him all over the West, up to Alaska and south to Mexico City. Siringo probably traveled a hundred thousand miles by horseback, stagecoach, and trains in the pursuit of his duties.

After many delays because of teaching and administrative duties at Yale, I was unable to resume work on my Siringo biography until my retirement. Since then, building on my older notes, I expanded my research to include more about the West in which Siringo lived. In the course of these further investigations I learned just how many well-known westerners had come to respect and admire Siringo during his lifetime. Besides historians like J. Frank Dobie, J. Evetts Haley, and Walter Prescott Webb, Siringo came to know Hollywood actors William S. Hart and Will Rogers. Indeed he moved to Hollywood in 1923 and soon came to know yet another distinguished coterie of Hollywood figures, such as Henry Herbert Knibbs, who wrote novels, poetry, and successful film scripts about the West.

It was this latest group of friends and admirers who persuaded the Houghton Mifflin publishing company in Cambridge, Massachusetts, to publish Siringo's last book, *Riata and Spurs*, in 1927. The irony was that Siringo, through his friendship with these Hollywood intellectuals, introduced me to a different, more complex and mature group of writers about the West—a score of figures who deserve further study and recognition.

My final efforts to tell the story of Siringo have been as personally rewarding as the first attempt was some thirty years ago. It has been a labor of love in my chosen field of western history. My hope is that the results will contribute to a fuller understanding of both Charles Siringo and the American West of his day that stretched from south Texas in 1855 to Hollywood in the 1920s.

Howard R. Lamar
New Haven, Connecticut

Oh, I am a Texas Cowboy, right off the
Texas plains,
My trade is cinchin' saddles and pullin'
Of bridle reins.
And I can throw a lasso with the
greatest of ease;
I can rope and ride a bronco any damn
way I please.

—Cowboy Song

The trail's a lane, the trail's a lane.
How comes it, pard of mine?
Within a day it slipped away
And hardly left a sign.
Now history a tale has gained
To please the younger years—
A race of kings that rose and reigned,
And passed in fifty years!

—Badger Clark Jr.,
The Passing of the Trail, *1915*

CHAPTER ONE

Charlie Siringo and the Several Worlds of Matagorda Bay

FROM THE TIME HE WAS FOUR YEARS OLD, THE SMALL, THIN BOY could be seen playing on the firm sand of the gulf-side beach of the Matagorda Peninsula, Texas. More often than not he rode a stick, which he pretended was a pony. Dressed only in a long shirt his mother had made from old flour sacks, he was engaged in his favorite game: chasing and trying to lasso beach crabs with a fish line that served him as a rope. Bursting with energy, quick and dexterous, this bright-eyed intelligent boy, whom everyone called Charlie, often succeeded in his goal.[1]

Sometimes his good friend, Billy Williams, the son of a neighbor who lived in one of the dozen or so houses that were known as Dutch Settlement, joined him in the game. When slightly older, the two tried to catch rabbits or went coon-hunting with the Williamses' dogs in the thick bush and swampy area on the bay side of Matagorda Peninsula. That ever-present brush, often mixed with small cedar trees, had led the early Spanish explorers to call the whole area—the peninsula, the bay, and the adjoining mainland—*Matagorda*, which in Spanish meant "thick bush" or "thick brush." At Caney Creek, where the peninsula was joined to the mainland, flourished some of the densest canebrake in the whole of Texas.[2]

But when on the beach astride his stick pony the youngster became a "cowboy" just like those boisterous men on horseback who rode over from the mainland to the peninsula each fall driving herds of cattle to forage on the luxuriant marsh and salt grasses that flourished there during the winter. In imitation of the cowboys, Charlie and Billy Williams, when a bit older, began to ride local calves as their "horses."[3]

An even more exciting time came when the cowboys returned in the spring to round up the cattle and calves. Shouting and yelling, they would chase down strays, sometimes lassoing wilder ones, or making sure unbranded yearlings stayed with the proper herd. The cattle were then driven back to the various ranches in Matagorda from whence they had come. Once the yearlings were branded, all the cattle would feed on the plentiful Prairie Coastal Plains coarse and grama grasses until roundup time, or they would be shipped as beef cattle to Galveston, Mobile, and New Orleans markets. Some were shipped to Havana as beeves for Cuban soldiers.[4]

By his own testimony later in his life, Charles Angelo Siringo, the young boy on the beach, declared that these dashing horsemen represented what he most wanted to be: a cowboy. Indeed, from the start, Charlie Siringo was attracted to all aspects of open-range ranching—already a major and ever-growing enterprise in Matagorda and adjoining counties, in large part because cattle, brought in by the Spanish mission fathers over a century earlier, had escaped and multiplied, creating many thousands of wild, unbranded cattle. Obviously, he dreamed of being a superb horseman, and an expert with the lariat. The outdoor life, the difficult task of herding or tracking down and lassoing wild steers who had taken cover in thick timbered areas in the more northern part of the county or in bushes or swamps, was also exciting, as was the noise and seeming chaos of branding strays and yearlings. As Charlie would later recall in a series of seven autobiographical accounts of his life on many ranches, or on the trail, or even night-herding in a thunderstorm, he thrilled to the challenge of danger while he sang to a restless herd, hoping the steady rhythm of the song would keep the cattle from stampeding. And afterward, as he also recalled, came that sense of companionship when the men were sitting around a campfire at night joshing and telling stories and sometimes singing. So taken was he by the songs, he wrote some of them down, and in his old age he published them in a small book.[5]

When he was only twelve years old, Charlie Siringo's dream came true. He persuaded his mother to let him work on a mainland ranch under the supervision of its owner, a Mr. Faldien, who knew the Siringos and had actually rented a portion of their cottage as a vacation spot in the hot summer months of the south Texas plains.

Siringo's love of the cattle business and the life of a cowboy were so great that in 1885 at the age of thirty, he published a vivid, rollicking, picaresque account of his experiences with the breezy title: *A Texas Cowboy, or Fifteen Years on the Hurricane Deck of a Spanish Pony— Taken from Real Life.*[6] *A Texas Cowboy* was the first full autobiography of a cowboy ever to be published. Many years later, the famous rodeo stage and film performer Will Rogers, in a letter to Charlie, recalled that when he was growing up on his family's Oklahoma ranch, Siringo's *A Texas Cowboy* was referred to as "The Cowboy's Bible."[7] Over time many thousands of copies of *A Texas Cowboy* were sold in Texas and in the Great Plains, and often hawked on trains for sale at a cheap price. J. Frank Dobie, beloved Texas teacher, folklorist, and writer, paid Siringo the supreme compliment when he wrote: "Charlie Siringo had almost nothing to say on life; he reported actions. He put down something valid on a class of livers, as remote now from the Atomic Age as Rameses II. His cowboys and gunmen were not of Hollywood and folklore. He was a honest reporter."[8]

We are indebted to Charlie Siringo for far more than a first cowboy autobiography, however. He gave an insightful history of open-range cattle ranching both on the south coast of Texas and later in the Texas Panhandle on the Great Plains during the 1870s and 1880s when that business was in its heyday. We are indebted as well for a fascinating and frank, if troubled, account of his twenty-two-year career as a Pinkerton detective. While he was still a cowboy he knew and liked Billy the Kid, with whom he had shooting contests at the LX Ranch. Many years later, as a Pinkerton, he tried to catch Butch Cassidy and the Sundance Kid, and did arrest and help convict scores of other outlaws and criminals.[9] Yet Siringo never forgot the men he had befriended in his cowboy days. He remained loyal to them and featured them in his seven books. Then in his old age, ill and poverty stricken, he moved to Hollywood, where he befriended Will Rogers and William S. Hart, the actor who made and acted in serious western movies. Hart even gave him bit parts in his westerns, so Siringo could earn some "eatin' money." Once settled in a little shack in back of a large house near Hollywood Boulevard, on Eleanor Avenue, Siringo continued to correspond and meet with his companions of ranching days, some of whom had succeeded and lived in the Los Angeles area. With the latter group he had a wonderful time "harkin' back," as he called their get-togethers.

It is the premise of this book that Charles Siringo's career and writings are significant enough to deserve a larger context—that is, to provide some account not just of himself but of the exciting world—one should really say *worlds*—in which he lived. His life coincided with what historians and the public call the last "Wild West." To the very end he knew he was writing about one of the most colorful and significant eras in the entire history of the American West—not just the brief heyday of open-range ranching but the story of one of the most popular and enduring symbols of America itself: the cowboy.

❧ ❧

How did Charlie Siringo come to be born on the fifty-mile-long and two-mile-wide stretch of land called the Matagorda Peninsula? And what was the world like in which he first found himself?

Sometime in the late 1840s or early 1850s, Antonio Siringo, an Italian immigrant to the United States, met and married Bridget White, the daughter of Irish parents who had come to settle in Matagorda County, Texas, to ranch and farm. The newlywed Siringos settled on Matagorda Peninsula at Dutch Settlement—really a German settlement of colonists who had come from Hanover, Germany, in 1846. The Siringos had two children, a daughter, Catherine, and Charles Angelo. The latter was born February 7, 1855, but a year after his birth, Antonio, his father, died suddenly leaving Bridget to raise her two children alone.[10]

From the scanty evidence we have about Antonio Siringo it appears that he was a vigorous, ambitious man who from the beginning tried to plan ahead. As early as December 1850, he recorded his cattle brand with Matagorda County authorities. In 1854, keenly aware that the town of Matagorda was booming as a mercantile and shipping center, he bought a town lot for $100 from one George W. H. Smith. A year later in October 1855, he registered a second cattle brand for his infant daughter, "Catherine Seringo [sic] and her children."[11] What brought a sudden end to his life remains a mystery. Charlie of course was too young to remember his father, but he was intrigued by his Italian and Irish heritage, exclaiming: "My father who died when I was only a year old, came from the sunny clime of Italy, while my dear old mother drifted from the Boggs of good 'ould' Ireland. Am I not a queer conglomerate—a sweet-scented mixture indeed!"[12]

By his own later account in *A Texas Cowboy*, Charlie remembered his mother as being constantly busy, cooking and washing, and seeing to her small herd of some twenty cattle, but especially to her milk cow, Browney.

One of Charlie's first memories was of her constantly asking him to bring dry driftwood up from the beach for the kitchen stove and her wash-day fire. Although the Siringos were poor and were sometimes reduced to a diet of mush and milk, Bridget Siringo was an enterprising religious woman who had ambitions for her children. When Catherine was only five and Charlie only four, she sent them to a school a mile away taught by a Mr. Hale, a Yankee schoolteacher.[13]

Later, Catherine was sent to school in Galveston, where she was undoubtedly looked after by Bridget's brother and sister, Nicholas and Mary White. But for Charlie formal school ended when the Civil War came and Mr. Hale departed to join the Union Army. Thereafter, recalled Charlie, "I was free and had a great chance to be mischievous."[14]

On occasion, Mrs. Siringo rented rooms in her cottage to visitors who came to the peninsula over the summer to avoid the intense heat and humidity—and the mosquitoes that plagued the mainland. In contrast, the peninsula always boasted a healthy sea breeze.

Then too, her sister and brother in Galveston sent them clothing and supplies. Young Charlie graduated from the flour-sack shirt when the relatives sent him a pair of trousers, which he promptly ruined by wearing them on a coon-hunt with Billy Williams on the bay side of the peninsula.[15]

A life of near poverty was made easier by friendly neighbors like the Williams family with their eleven children, and by John Zipprian and his family. Born in Germany in 1807, Zipprian came to Matagorda County in 1846 with 143 other German immigrants. Zipprian was a sailor, a chimneymaker who used burnt oyster shells, and a stonemason who also raised sheep on his 320-acre peninsula farm.[16]

What young Charlie realized almost from the start was that he was born, not on an unsettled frontier, but in an area destined to be Texas's first commercial cattle kingdom, dominated from the 1850s onward by famous ranchers like the Grimes family, by Abel (Shanghai) Pierce and his brother Jonathan, and the Kuykendall family. Seeing them as success models, he went to work for them while still in his early teens.[17]

❧ ❦

What young Charlie Siringo did not realize until later was that he had been born not only in the oldest and most historic region of Euro-American Texas, but in what had been the heart of one of the most unusual aboriginal Indian societies in the Southwest. The coastal plains and gulf-shore islands of Texas perhaps from present-day Galveston westward to Corpus Christi had been the home of the Karankawa and Tonkawa Indians, who had resisted would-be French, Spanish, Mexican, and American conquerors for nearly two hundred years until a remnant population was finally wiped out in 1858—when Siringo was only three years old.

The Karankawa Indians actually provide a turbulent but intriguing unifying theme to Texas history and especially that of Matagorda Bay from 1528 to 1858.[18] Who were these independent and always mysterious inhabitants of the Texas coastal plains, and why were they so fiercely resistant to white outsiders for nearly three centuries?

The Karankawas first encountered Europeans when four refugee Spaniards, who were survivors of the disastrous Narvaez expedition to Florida, appeared in their midst in 1528 while attempting to travel westward from Florida to Spanish northern outposts in Mexico. The four, three Spaniards and a North African Moor, were immediately enslaved by the Karankawas for nearly six years, and it was only through the leadership of Alvar Nuñez Cabeza de Vaca that they survived and eventually were allowed to make their way to Culiacan, Mexico, where they contacted Spanish soldiers.[19]

Cabeza de Vaca, an exceptionally able and intelligent man, published a remarkable account of his six-year stay with the Karankawas, which was not flattering. They were not only primitive, he wrote, but hostile and independent and truly bad tempered. Unlike the experiences of the Puritans in New England two centuries later, there were no charming Pocahontases or Massasoits among them willing to befriend the Spaniards. In a curious way the Karankawas may have been the first Texans to express a version of the now popular injunction, "Don't Mess With Texas."[20]

✢· ✢

After Cabeza de Vaca's six-year involuntary sojourn with the Karan-kawas and other coastal tribes, no Europeans bothered them until nearly 150 years later. The next intruder was Rene Robert Cavalier, Sieur de La Salle, who had come to Canada in 1663 at age twenty-three to make his fortune as a fur trader. Over time, however, La Salle became obsessed with the idea of exploring and occupying the vast Mississippi country. In 1677 the French crown awarded him a royal patent to realize his goal. After engaging in the fur trade in the Great Lakes region, he pushed southward into Illinois. Later, despite many business setbacks, he and his men reached the mouth of the Mississippi in April 1682. La Salle christened the whole valley Louisiana in honor of his patron, Louis XIV. A year later La Salle returned to France to recruit settlers for a colony he hoped to found in the Mississippi Valley.[21]

Luck deserted La Salle on his final expedition, however. Guided by misleading maps and his own mistaken idea of where the mouth of the river was, his fleet of four vessels with its 240 passengers sailed past the mouth of the Mississippi and, instead, entered Matagorda Bay on February 20, 1685, where he erected a fort on the northwest mainland side, again named for Louis XIV. But misfortune after misfortune plagued La Salle and his colonists from the outset. Having lost one of his four vessels to Spanish privateers at sea, his supply ship was wrecked in the strong current of Pass Cavallo. Then her crew and a number of colonists chose to sail back to France on the third ship, *Joley*. Many of the remaining colonists died from illness, malnutrition, exhaustion from building Fort St. Louis, and Indian attacks. Then at the end of the second year (1686) La Salle's only remaining vessel was wrecked on Matagorda Peninsula during a storm. Meanwhile, La Salle, rather than secure his colony's survival by friendly negotiations with the Karankawa Indians earned their enmity by hostile acts.[22]

La Salle himself was also absent a great deal of the time, exploring westward in the hope that he was near Spanish gold mines. Finally deciding to travel east to find the Mississippi and return to the other Fort St. Louis that he had established in Illinois, years before, he was mur-dered by a disillusioned member of his party.[23]

Meanwhile the remaining colonists at Fort St. Louis in Texas were busy trying to befriend the Karankawa, but the latter, having learned that

La Salle was dead, attacked the fort in late December 1688 and eventually killed all whites except for four children of the Talon family and Eustace Breman, a young boy. They were "adopted into the tribe" although one son, Pierre, had been living among the Hasinai Indians to the east, left there by La Salle to learn their language.[24] All were eventually "rescued" between 1689 and 1691 by Spanish authorities. Amazingly these five children survived and later were able to tell the incredible story of their experiences to both Spanish and, later, French officials.

The Spanish, greatly alarmed at the news of La Salle's colony in Texas, finally discovered the abandoned Fort St. Louis in April 1689. A year later, with the encouragement of Alonzo de Leon, governor of Coahuila, Franciscan missionaries came to east Texas to establish San Francisco de las Tejas in 1690.[25] Always feeling threatened by French claims to the Texas coastal area and occasional incursions, the Spanish founded a presidio and a mission near where Fort St. Louis had been located on Garcitas Creek. The missionaries at Espíritu Santo de Zúñiga hoped to convert the Karankawa to Christianity and to make them loyal subjects of Spain, but their efforts were not successful. The Mission soon came to be called La Bahía.[26]

In 1754 a second mission, Señora del Rosario de los Cujunes, was established on the San Antonio River north of La Bahía. Although it was more successful, the Indian neophytes kept deserting. In 1791 yet a third mission, Nuestra Señora del Refugio, was founded, and after several relocations was placed at Refugio, Texas, but by this time Comanche attacks on the few Karankawa and Coahuiltecans within its walls spelled failure for this mission as well.[27]

The fate of the Karankawa was finally sealed when the American financial panic of 1819 bankrupted a prominent Missouri lead miner, banker, and businessman named Moses Austin. Looking about for a new way to recoup his lost fortune, Austin decided to seek a land grant in the then Spanish, but soon to be Mexican province of Texas, and locate a colony of American settlers on it.

When he traveled to San Antonio de Béxar to seek the permission of Governor Antonio María Martínez in 1820, he was initially rebuffed, but an old acquaintance, the Baron de Bastrop, who was in San Antonio and was a friend of Governor Martínez, persuaded that official to reverse himself and endorse Austin's colonization petition and to send it to higher authorities for final approval. While returning home Moses

Austin became ill; and although he received the good news once back in Missouri that key officials had approved his Texas colony scheme, he knew he was dying. Through his wife he conveyed a deathbed wish to his son, Stephen F. Austin, then in Louisiana, to found the colony.[28]

Journeying to San Antonio in August, 1821, Stephen Austin secured his father's grant and explored the area between the San Antonio and Brazos rivers in search of an appropriate location for his American colony.[29] This included the very region where the Karankawas and Tonkawas had lived from time immemorial.

By this time Mexico had become independent of Spain and its new government had initiated its own program of awarding large land grants to qualified applicants, regardless of whether they were Mexican citizens or foreigners. In the next quarter century applicants successfully received grants in Texas, New Mexico, and Upper California.[30]

Although the details of the amount of land individuals and their families were to receive if they came to Texas as colonists were not settled until the mid-1820s, Austin was able to advertise extremely generous initial terms in New Orleans newspapers and throughout the Mississippi Valley. In the early years a man and wife together could be awarded 960 acres and their children 320 acres each, plus 80 acres for each slave belonging to the family. By the mid-1820s, however, a family or an individual could apply for a *labor* (a farm grant of 177 acres) and/or a *sitio* (or league) of ranch land 4,428 acres in size. Naturally most applicants petitioned for the sitio or ranching grant.[31]

The news of these favorable terms for the acquisition of land in Texas between the Brazos and Colorado rivers quickly spread throughout the Mississippi Valley, and by December 1821 the first colonists came, largely from the Trans-Appalachian region of the South, and consisted largely of planters and successful farmers. However a respectable number of Yankee colonists came from the northeastern states of Pennsylvania, New Jersey, and New York State. Some landed at the mouth of the Brazos River, the stream upon which Austin was to found his capital, San Felipe de Austin, situated on a beautiful bluff. Others disembarked at the mouth of the Colorado at the eastern end of Matagorda Bay. Still others came overland with their families, household goods, and slaves.[32]

Because Austin had agreed to bring in three hundred families, the early Austin colonists were soon called "the Old Three Hundred," and, indeed by 1825 nearly three hundred families and single adult men had come.[33] Meanwhile Mexican authorities had liberalized the terms by granting a married man 4,428 acres (a sitio or league) for a minimum charge. Settlers continued to come so that Austin himself eventually located some nine hundred families around his first colony at San Felipe in future Brazoria County. Austin and other colonizers called *empresarios* or agents were to receive some 67,000 acres of land as payment for each two hundred families they brought to Texas. Under the empresario system this region of Texas rapidly became more American than Spanish-Mexican. Altogether perhaps some ten thousand colonists now lived on the Brazos, Colorado, and other streams between the San Jacinto and La Vaca rivers. When Charlie's mother and her parents, the Whites, and his father, Antonio Siringo, migrated to south Texas, it was to an established Anglo-Texan world.

⚜ ⚜

Because Stephen F. Austin's empresario grants included the Matagorda Bay region, as did the empresario grants to Green Dewitt, Martin De Leon, and James Power and James Lewiston, some immigrants for the Austin colony had landed at the mouth of the Colorado at the eastern end of Matagorda Bay as early as 1822. One of the Old Three Hundred who showed an early interest in the Colorado River/Matagorda Bay area was Elias R. Wightman, born in Herkimer County, New York, in 1792. Trained as a surveyor, he had been attracted to Austin's colony, and as early as the summer of 1825 we find him working for Austin as a surveyor and land appraiser. Wightman quickly realized that it made sense to locate a town on the Colorado that could serve as both a base to protect incoming colonists from Indians and as a depot for supplies for colonists and for shipping local produce—soon to be cotton and cattle, to be sold to buyers in Galveston and New Orleans.[34]

As a surveyor he was aware that the channel of the Colorado River in prehistoric times had changed and that the old channel, now called Caney Creek, was a region of incredibly rich soil created by the silt from ancient river floods. Although the Caney Creek area was covered with dense canebrakes, he knew it could be cleared and burned and that the resulting ash itself would serve as an added fertilizer. Working through Austin, who got permission from Mexican authorities to found a town on Matagorda Bay that would protect immigrants, and serve as a fort, Wightman was also granted title to a sitio of land on Matagorda Peninsula east of Caney Creek.[35]

Meanwhile other members of Austin's Old Three Hundred group joined Wightman in petitioning for the establishment of the town of Matagorda. Hosea H. League, a Tennessean, not only joined forces with Wightman, by early January 1827, he was already back in Nashville busy recruiting twenty families to go to Texas with him.[36] Another one of Austin's Old Three Hundred colonists was William Selkirk, who was born in Selkirk, New York, the son of a Scottish immigrant. Trained as a surveyor, once at San Felipe de Austin, he, too, worked for Austin in that capacity, and served in the colonial militia, but he described his occupation as that of a goldsmith. On August 10, 1824, he too received title to a sitio of land at the mouth of the Colorado River. His grant, seemingly cut off from the mainland, was soon called Selkirk's Island and was still owned by his descendants in the 1970s. Selkirk helped lay out the town of Matagorda after it was finally founded in 1829.[37] Because Selkirk's Island was only a few miles east of where the Siringos lived, they must have known Selkirk's descendants.

In 1828, Wightman and another early colonist, David S. Burnet from a prominent New Jersey family, returned to the states to recruit colonists. Wightman himself managed to sign up some thirty-nine New York State residents to settle in and around his still to be built town of Matagorda. Among those he recruited were his own parents and two sisters—one married to Asa Yeamans. Their grandson Horace was one day to form a partnership with young Charlie Siringo to skin the hides of cattle killed in winter floods and storms and sell them to tanneries on the coast.[38]

What impresses one about the founding fathers is their intelligence, their shrewd business acumen, and their constant lookout for enterprises beyond mere landownership. All of them were at one time merchants or traders or owners of seagoing vessels. They knew the benefits of town building. Indeed, League, James Austin, and their partners, Duke and Selkirk, "each took a quarter interest in the town site." Their disparate origins—New York, Kentucky, and Tennessee—did not interfere with their ability to work together. And although some did not live to see their dreams fulfilled, Matagorda itself boomed from the start. Between 1840 and 1865 Matagorda emerged as Texas's second major port for immigrants and for shipping goods along the Gulf Coast all the way to

Mobile. When Mrs. Siringo and her neighbors referred to going to town, they meant Matagorda City. Many years later Charlie recalled in his *A Lone Star Cowboy* that Matagorda was "the first town I had ever seen," and noted that his father was buried in the old cemetery there.

It also became a social and cultural center for the planters on Caney Creek, who built elegant town houses in the town. The social elite held formal balls and centered other activities around Christ Episcopal Church, supported private schools for their fortunate children, and at the same time exhibited a ruthless awareness of what it took to succeed economically—that is a steady labor source in slaves. It is no wonder that Charlie and his mother referred to Matagordans as the "big bugs."[39]

Despite all of its northern settlers and merchants, Matagorda always remained a Southern town full of class and social awareness, and keenly devoted to using slave labor. There was always a mix of non-slaveowning farms and ranches, but black Americans were there in force. In 1850 the U.S. Census recorded 2,214 people there: 913 were whites, 1,208 were slaves, and only 3 free blacks were listed.

By 1856 the Anglo-American population had driven out the Indians and had almost expelled the county's entire Mexican population, despite the fact that Martín De León, a tall, impressive empresario from Mexico, had himself successfully established a colony in the area of present-day Victoria, Texas. The American colonists, especially those in Green DeWitt's nearby colony, contested De León's rights at every point regardless of the fact that the De León family had joined the Anglo-Texans in the 1835–1836 revolt against Santa Anna and Mexico.[41]

After the Texas Revolution, Matagorda County was organized in 1836 "as one of the first twenty-three counties of the Republic of Texas" and Matagorda became its county seat.[42]

✦ ✦

Charlie Siringo also did not realize until later that his own Matagorda Peninsula had been the birthplace of one of the most famous terms associated with open-range ranching—*Maverick*, named for a prominent Texas pioneering family. By the late 1850s *Maverick* had become a common term in south Texas for stray unbranded cattle, of which there were hundreds of thousands, if not millions who wandered on the open range of the coastal and prairie plains of Texas.[43]

Samuel Maverick, born in 1803, was the son of an aristocratic South Carolina family who, in addition to being successful planters with dozens of slaves, were also merchants and land speculators. Young Sam attended both Yale College and the University of Virginia Law School, but instead of choosing the legal profession for his career, he was attracted by land speculation and especially the promise of making a fortune in Texas lands. The famous—now almost legendary—story of Austin's colony at San Felipe de Austin on the Brazos, the subsequent Texas Revolution, and the rise of successful cotton and sugarcane plantations in Texas must have impressed every Southern landowner, and especially in South Carolina where farm lands were beginning to wear out.[44]

A year before the Texas Revolution, young Sam Maverick went to San Antonio to speculate in land. After the Texas Revolution of 1836, when Texas became an independent republic, Sam Maverick returned east in 1837 to handle family business, but he went by the way of Alabama to visit relatives. There he met and soon married Mary Adams, the impressive, charming, able daughter of a successful planter in Tuscaloosa, Alabama. Already obsessed with dreams of a fortune in Texas lands, Sam persuaded Mary Adams to move to Texas in the late fall of 1837. Their party of four whites and ten black slaves, after many misadventures with bad weather, arrived in Texas on New Year's Day, 1838.[45]

The newlyweds settled first in San Antonio, but Maverick had already invested in land at Cox's Point (Tres Palacios) on Matagorda Bay opposite La Vaca "with a view to possibly locating there." Besides boasting good land, it had promise as a port on Matagorda Bay, close to the Cavallo Pass, the only gulf entrance to the bay. For the time being, however, Maverick made San Antonio the base for his extensive land acquisition business. Soon he and his family did locate in La Grande, Texas, on the Colorado River, but the winter dampness and the oppressive heat of summer, with its mosquitoes, left Mary and the others in the family lonely and dispirited and in poor health. In her memoirs Mary wrote: "We concluded it would not do to live here any longer; the Colorado bottoms were too unhealthy. Mr. Maverick decided to take us to the Gulf coast where we could enjoy sea bathing."[46]

In December 1844, the Mavericks traveled by carriage, followed by two hired wagons filled with household furnishings and supplies, plus saddle horses and several cows, to Matagorda Peninsula, crossing at the mouth of the Colorado. From there they went down the beautiful hard beach—passing the site of future Dutch Settlement—to De Crow's Point at the western end of the peninsula. There the Mavericks lived until October 1847 when they returned to San Antonio.[47]

In one of his many real estate transactions between 1844 and 1847, Sam Maverick appears to have loaned money to a farmer, Charles Nathan Tilton, a New Hampshire–born immigrant who had spent some time at sea, whose property, called Tiltona, was twenty-five miles up the peninsula between De Crow's Point and Dutch Settlement. As collateral Maverick had taken a mortgage on the Tilton farm. It was an ideal piece of real estate for it boasted a large herd of cattle, vegetable gardens, orchards, dairy cattle, chickens, turkeys, and a small bay full of oyster beds. For some reason Tilton failed to pay off his loan, so that in March 1847 Maverick acquired Tilton's farm along with four hundred head of cattle at three dollars a head.[48]

Ironically, Sam Maverick's great interest was in land acquisition, not ranching or farming. And so he turned the property over to Jack, a trusted black slave, and his family along with a few other slaves to run the farm. Although Jack appears to have managed the farm successfully, given his limited authority as a slave, and Maverick's disinterest, Jack found that he could not control the cattle at Tiltona. Not only did they roam freely, so many remained unbranded that the unmarked cattle of the peninsula came to be identified as "Mr. Maverick's," and eventually just "Maverick's." Letters of complaint about the Maverick cattle came to both Sam and Mary. Indeed, at Jack's own urging, Mr. Graham, a white neighbor, wrote to say that without assistance Jack found it "impossible to pen and brand your cattle on the Peninsula and the stock is becoming more wild and unmanageable."[49]

Finally in 1854 Maverick went to Tiltona to move both slaves and cattle to a ranch forty-five miles below San Antonio called Conquista Ranch. But there again, lack of supervision allowed the Maverick herd to roam freely, mixing with wild free-range longhorn cattle and those from the herds of other ranchers. In time the name Maverick had come to mean any unbranded cattle and the term spread in south Texas, but did not become part of the lingo of the ranching world until after the Civil War. Eventually it also spawned the verb *mavericking*, which was applied to the already common practice of cowboys and ranchers putting their own brands on unmarked cattle at roundup or on the open plains.[50] Later, as a teenage cowboy, Charlie Siringo did his own full share of mavericking by placing his own $S2$ brand on strays while working for E. B. Grimes and the redoubtable Shanghai Pierce.[51]

To make a long story short, Charlie Siringo was born on one of the liveliest, most historic, controversial, and yet established areas in pre–Civil War Texas. It was no wonder that he himself developed a great ambition to get ahead in a world where he thought the key to success was the cattle industry. But before that could happen, the Civil War intervened in this young boy's life in the most dramatic way. It provided lessons in survival that he was to use, both consciously and unconsciously, for the remainder of his life.[52]

THE LONE STAR
(COMPOSED BY MRS. LEE C. HARBY)
OH, PRAIRIE BREEZE, BLOW SWEET AND PURE,
AND SOUTHERN SUN, SHINE BRIGHT,
TO BLESS OUR FLAG WHERE'ER MAY GLEAM
ITS SINGLE STAR OF LIGHT!
BUT SHOULD THE SKY GROW DARK WITH WRATH,
THE TEMPEST BURST AND RAVE,
IT SHALL FLOAT UNDOUBTEDLY—
THE STANDARD OF THE BRAVE.

—*Charles A. Siringo,*
The Song Companion of a Lone Star Cowboy, *3*

THE ONE GREAT CONTRIBUTION OF TEXAS TO THE
SOUTHERN CAUSE WAS MEN. . . . A QUARTER OF TEXAS'
MOST VIGOROUS MANPOWER WAS KILLED OR INCAPACITATED.

—*T. R. Fehrenbach,* Lone Star: A History of
Texas and the Texans, *354–56*

JEFF DAVIS IS OUR PRESIDENT,
AND LINCOLN IS A FOOL,
JEFF DAVIS RIDES A BIG GRAY HORSE
WHILE LINCOLN RIDES A MULE.

—*Sung by Charles Siringo during the*
Civil War, A Texas Cowboy, *75*

CHAPTER TWO

Civil War Comes to Matagorda Bay, 1850–1867

AFTER THE TEXAS REVOLUTION IN 1836 AND THE FORMATION OF THE Lone Star Republic, the settlers in the Matagorda Bay area had visions of a bright new future. There was prosperity despite the occasional dangerous incursions of Mexican military forces intent on retaking San Antonio de Béxar. In March 1842, for example, Mexican General Rafael Vásquez occupied San Antonio with seven hundred men, forced Texan defenders to evacuate the city, and raised the Mexican flag. But two days later Vásquez departed and crossed the Rio Grande back into Mexico.[1]

Later that year a second Mexican general, Adrián Wolle, attempted to seize San Antonio but was turned back by Texan troops at the battle of Salado.[2] Meanwhile Texan retaliatory expeditions, one led by Alexander Somervell, and a second, the Mier Expedition, proved to be disastrous, but these border exchanges did not really affect Matagorda Bay except to heighten prejudice against Mexico.[3]

In 1837 the town of Matagorda became the official county seat of Matagorda. It got its own newspaper, *The Bulletin*, that year and between 1840 and 1865 it continued to be Texas's second major seaport and port of entry for immigrants to that region of Texas, Galveston being the first.[4] Matagorda was the town in which Siringo's father had bought a lot, and where one registered cattle brands. It was the town young Siringo first learned about. He and his mother always referred to Matagorda City as "town."

Meanwhile the planters along Caney Creek were making money producing cotton, corn, sugarcane, and vegetables and raising cattle. James Boyd Hawkins, who had come from North Carolina to Lower Caney Creek in the mid-1840s with his family and a large number of slaves, was an outstanding example of the new prosperity. He raised cotton and sugarcane and constructed a large sugar mill, which produced brown sugar. He also raised corn and cattle, and by investing in a line of steamers, was able to ship his goods all the way to New York City.[5]

Hawkins and other planters, such as John Rugeley, a South Carolinian who had come to Texas in 1840, and had succeeded as a planter on Caney Creek, could now have their cotton ginned locally before sending the bales to Matagorda or Lavaca for shipment to buyers in Galveston or New Orleans to be transshipped to New York and Liverpool.[6]

⊹ ⊹

In the pre–Civil War era, the waters of Matagorda Bay and the rivers and creeks running into it were the chief means of transportation for all kinds of activity, personal and commercial. Individuals and families used small sailcraft to get from place to place inside the bay or to transport vegetables and fruits to port-town markets. Rather early on, Matagorda cantaloupes and peaches were popular in other Texas towns. Schooners went from bay ports to Galveston or New Orleans. Larger vessels, whether powered by sail or steam, came through Cavallo Pass to pick up produce or deposit supplies. After the Civil War young Siringo himself bought a boat, which he used to ferry passengers to various ports on the bay.

Although Matagorda boasted of an able set of merchants to handle goods, almost from the start the town was to experience competition from other would-be ports. DeCrow's Point on Cavallo Pass was an official port of entry, and Daniel DeCrow and his family made every effort to make it the place for transshipment of goods.[7] Some early immigrants to Texas landed at Cox's Point or Cox Bay and tried to make it a port. Tidehaven (later renamed Tres Palacios), located on the Tres Palacios River, was a stopping point for steamers in the 1840s where they picked up the usual Texas products of cotton, sugarcane, cattle, and hides—the latter from the Grimes Ranch tannery where Charlie Siringo once worked.[8]

The first real competition to Matagorda, however, came from the small village of Lavaca in Western Matagorda Bay, directly north of Cavallo Pass. As Claude A. Talley has noted, Lavaca succeeded because "the natural channel in the Bay passed within a few hundred yards of the town. So until 1845, Port Lavaca was considered the head of sea-going navigation for Matagorda Bay, and therefore prospered greatly from incoming passengers and freight traffic that moved through en route to Victoria, San Antonio and northern Mexico."[9]

By 1846 Lavaca had become important enough to be named the county seat of Calhoun County. Its future seemed further assured a year later when it "became a terminus for the ships of the Morgan lines," but that was only half the story. A stagecoach line ran between Lavaca and Victoria. It served as a base for the Morgan steamship line, whose business included forwarding goods to western Texas and northern Mexico. The size of Lavaca's export business is suggested by the report that in 1852 between ten thousand and twelve thousand bales of cotton were shipped from its docks.[10]

Lavaca soon experienced a challenge from another bay port, at first called Indian Point, but soon to be called Indianola. Indian Point got its real start in 1846 when Karl, Prince of Solms Braunfels chose it as the site to land German immigrants headed for his Texas German colony to the north. Savvy Anglo-Americans quickly envisioned a bright future for Indian Point, had the location surveyed, and began selling town lots. Indeed, it had a deeper channel and was suited for seagoing vessels, and by 1849 Indian Point had become Indianola and by 1852 had replaced Lavaca as the county seat of Calhoun County.[11]

It would be difficult to exaggerate the natural, geographical, and commercial advantages Indianola had as a Texas port. First, it was on a channel deep enough to take most seagoing ships. Second, it was the eastern end of the southern Chihuahua Trail on the military road to San Antonio, Austin, and Chihuahua, Mexico. It was also the trail to San Diego—"the shortest overland route to the Pacific from the Texas coast." Equally important, "it became the chief port through which European and American immigrants flowed into western Texas."[12] By 1849 the Morgan Steamship Lines, owned by Charles Morgan of New York and New Orleans, after some years at Lavaca, objected to Lavaca's high wharf fees and moved their operations to Indianola. The powerful Morgan lines guaranteed that Indianola would become the bay's most successful port for the next quarter century.[13]

In this heyday Indianola was a lively, prosperous town with an incredibly long-range and varied trade for its size. Indianola, like most port towns, was full of hotels and restaurants. It boasted the presence of a beginning dynasty of German-born merchants bearing such names as "Runge and Company," firms that have survived into the present. The town benefited from the 1849–1851 California gold rush when immigrants landed at Indianola before setting out on the overland trail across New Mexico and Arizona to the gold fields.[14]

In 1852 John Russell Bartlett, who headed the United States Boundary Survey to mark the border between this country and Mexico, came through on his way to El Paso, the Survey's headquarters. Then during 1856 and 1857 two shiploads of camels from North Africa landed in Indianola, part of a scheme by Secretary of War Jefferson Davis to find a suitable pack animal that could cross the arid southwest on the route to California. By 1858 plans for a railroad into the interior were underway.[15]

But there was an eastern flow of goods as well. Wells Fargo wagons brought silver bullion from Chihuahua, Mexico, there to be "shipped to the United States Mint at New Orleans." An overland stage also left twice a week for California. Indianola also had the advantage of having three hide and tallow factories located nearby, as well as three turtle packeries.[16] These towns deserve mention because after the Civil War, Charlie Siringo as a cowboy teenager, or a worker in Grimes's tannery, often found himself in Lavaca, Indianola, and Tres Palacios either loading cattle on steamboats or coming to town to celebrate at local bars.

Certainly Indianola owed much of its success to the remarkable Charles Morgan and his Morgan Steamship Lines. Born in Connecticut in 1795, he began his career at fourteen in New York where he soon distinguished himself as a shipping merchant who also managed sailing and steam packets that traded with the South and the West Indies. As early as 1837 he began steamship service between New Orleans and Galveston, and by the close of the Mexican War he had begun moving southwest along the coast to Matagorda ports and Brazos Santiago. When the Civil War broke out Morgan's line had a monopoly on the Texas coasting trade with Indianola as his chief port. Maintaining a strict business neutrality during the Civil War, he allowed both the Union and Confederate army and navy forces to seize his ships for their own use. By 1866, however, his vessels were back in service along the entire Gulf Coast. Always in search of a larger market, Morgan began investing in Texas railroad lines that would reach into the interior. Eventually he became a major railroad magnate in Texas.[17]

✢ ✢

The role of Texas and Texans in the Civil War is one of the most heroic and fascinating sagas of that tragic national conflict. As Ralph Wooster has noted in his fine essay on the Civil War in Texas, by 1860 the settled part of the state—the eastern two-fifths—was clearly Southern in its origins and its loyalties. Its inhabitants were largely farmers and planters, and their chief cash crop was cotton. Indeed, cotton and slaves, who constituted 30 percent of the population and were the workforce for the production of cotton, were the keys to Texas's economy in 1860, a year in which the state produced four hundred thousand bales of cotton.[18]

Hearing rumors of abolitionist plots, the news of John Brown's raid on Harper's Ferry, and an unfounded irrational fear in 1859–1860 that Texas slaves might rebel against their masters, Texans responded to the election of Abraham Lincoln precisely as the other Southern states did: they seceded from the Union and formed a committee of Public Safety, before electing Confederate state officers and planning a strategy of defense.

Texas had four clear strategic challenges: to seize military supplies from federal forts located in Texas; to send troops to the eastern front; to defend the state and especially its vulnerable four-hundred-mile coastline from federal blockading gunboats and possible invasion; and to keep the hostile Comanche Indians on the western and northwestern Texas frontiers at bay.[19]

Needless to say the Lone Star State responded enthusiastically to the outbreak of the Civil War. The number of volunteers, especially those joining cavalry units, was overwhelming. Governor Edward Clark, who succeeded Governor Sam Houston when the latter refused to take the oath of allegiance to the Confederacy, divided the state into six military districts—later increased to eleven—"for recruiting and organizing the troops requested by the Confederate authorities." By the end of 1861, twenty-five thousand Texans were in the Confederate Army, but before the war was over, some ninety thousand Texans had seen military service.[20]

Charlie, of course, was only six years old when the war started, and had no clue about what it was about, except that his mother and her neighbors were supporters of the Confederacy and rooted for Jefferson Davis. Yet it was the dramatic story of the coastal defense of Texas in which Charlie and all the residents of Matagorda Bay and the peninsula found themselves intimately, and on occasion, tragically involved.

As Alwyn Barr has noted, Texans organized coastal artillery units in the first year of the war. Volunteer companies along the entire coast were formed. In September 1861, for example, Colonel Joseph Bates was appointed commander of the Fourth Texas Volunteer Unit on coastal duty between San Luis Pass and Caney Creek. In the Matagorda–Corpus Christi area farther south, three more "companies of artillery were raised for coastal defense."[21]

During 1861 there were feverish preparations for future conflict. The Confederates rightly surmised that they desperately needed artillery guns for their shore defense. Thus there was a concerted and largely successful effort to capture federal guns from posts all over the state to be shipped to key defense points. The Texas Military ordered that Sabine Pass, Matagorda Island, Aransas Pass, and Port Isabel (on the Mexican border) were to be "entrenched"—that is defended. Captured heavy guns from the federal posts on the coast and from the interior were sent to these sites. The key port to be defended, of course, was Galveston. It was no surprise that the first Union action came when the federal vessel *South Carolina* appeared in July 1861 to "enforce the blockade" at Galveston.

Yet, in effect, this was a pseudo, sometimes even comic war. When Union commander James Alden shelled Galveston in early August 1861, ironically both sides were still so short of personnel, guns, and ammunition that neither could take effective action.

As elsewhere along the coast, Matagorda Bay residents responded to the challenge of war with enthusiasm. Edward S. Rugeley, Sr., a wealthy planter from Caney Creek, joined Reuben Brown's regiment and served throughout the war as a captain of cavalry. "Most of his time, however, was spent guarding the state coastline to repel invasion. His garrison was located in Matagorda. Other citizens founded reserve companies such as the Matagorda Coast Guards and the Caney Mounted Rifles."[22]

In addition some nine posts were established in the county. One Dr. E. A. Peareson, Matagorda's only physician, headed a volunteer unit in

1861 that created a temporary camp at the eastern end of the Matagorda Peninsula where they trained along the beach.

However, 1862 was another story. By July of that year there were Union-Confederate encounters along the entire coast—including Matagorda Peninsula—"between small boat crews and shore patrols." In August 1862, a federal naval force under Commander W. B. Renshaw was able to take Galveston, a success due in part to the pessimism of General Hebért, Confederate Commander of the Department of Texas, who had been convinced form the beginning that the federal blockade was "so superior, the Confederates would have to fight on shore or in the interior." By 1862 federal gunboats also began to shell Fort Caney, only a few miles from the Siringo home, with artillery fire and by landing shore patrols.[23]

❖ ❖

Our first evidence that Charlie was aware of the conflict came in one of his later reminiscences of when he met Jefferson Davis at a Houston fair in the early 1880s. That Davis was an old man shocked him for he had been told Abraham Lincoln was an old man and that Davis was a vigorous young hero. Clearly Bridget Siringo and her neighbors, as we shall see, were ardent supporters of the Southern cause.

Charlie was not personally aware of the conflict, however, until the summer of 1862 when he experienced one of the most dramatic—and to us, comical—introductions to war a young boy could have.

One Monday morning, which for Mrs. Siringo was washday, she sent a reluctant Charlie to the beach to collect dry driftwood for her wash pot. Once on the beach Charlie spied a cottontail rabbit, which took refuge in a hollow log. He had the bright idea that if he could roll the log into the shore water he could "drown the rabbit out." The hard work of digging the sand from around the log, plus the heat of a strong June sun, made him tired and sleepy. In his *A Texas Cowboy*, he claims that he dreamed of hell when the sun was out, and heaven when it went behind a cloud. Suddenly a huge noise awakened him. It was a large detachment of men carrying guns and "marching right towards me. The head ones were not over a hundred yards off, beating drums and blowing their horns."[24]

Believing they were after him, Charlie dashed for home, but ran into Mrs. Zipprian's drove of geese. An angry gander chased him and caught his shirttail for a time. When he finally dashed into his mother's yard he "ran against her, knocking her, tub and all, over in a pile, myself with them." Not comprehending what this was all about, Mrs. Siringo grabbed Charlie and began to beat him with her mush stick.

What had transpired was that the Confederate volunteer unit commanded by Dr. E. A. Peareson was training by marching and camping on the beach of Matagorda Peninsula and happened to camp near the Siringo house. Once Charlie had recovered from his initial terror, the friendly commander allowed Charlie to play soldier by giving him an umbrella stick as a gun and letting him march with the troops.[25]

⊱ ·⊱

Matagorda's worst war-time experiences were not to come until 1863. Although federal commander W. B. Renshaw, who had occupied Galveston in August 1862, sailed into Matagorda Bay and shelled Port Lavaca, he did not take the town. Meanwhile Confederate soldiers, commanded by Captain D. R. Shea, were busy constructing Fort Esperanza on the eastern end of Matagorda Island, for Shea had become convinced that he could not really defend the Cavallo Pass by occupying DeCrow's Point. Esperanza was finally completed in February 1863. During its building federal gunboats bombarded Indianola and occupied and looted the town, but withdrew a month later.[26]

Other actions along the coast to the east and west of Matagorda Bay took some pressure off the Confederate units. Among the most impressive was the recapture of Galveston on January 1, 1863, by the Confederates under Texas's new, imaginative and highly able commander, John Bankhead Magruder.

General Magruder, although a graduate of West Point and a distinguished officer who had served with General Winfield Scott in the Mexican War, decided to cast his lot with Virginia, his native state, by joining the Confederate Army in 1861. Magruder achieved an early fame in the war when he successfully deceived Union commander George B. McClellan by giving him the impression that he headed a large number of troops on the Virginia front lines. As a result an unsure McClellan delayed any action against the Confederates for three weeks. Magruder established an instant reputation as an able soldier and strategist. General Robert E. Lee, to the contrary, did not believe Magruder was aggressive enough and reassigned him to succeed Hébert as the commander of the District of Texas, New Mexico, and Arizona. He assumed his Texas post on November 29, 1862, making Houston his headquarters.[27]

Besides being a born soldier, General Magruder was personally popular with the Texans. Colorful, witty, energetic, he wrote songs, which he sang, and performed in amateur theatricals, a hobby that gained him the nickname "Prince John." Six feet tall with black mustache and looking truly resplendent in his regiment uniform, some contemporaries declared that he was the handsomest soldier in the Confederate Army.[28] Magruder deserves mention here because of two accomplishments that relate to Texas coastal defense and therefore to the Matagorda Bay region.

After federal commander Renshaw had captured Galveston in August 1862, the Confederates were determined to retake Texas's major port city. And no one was more determined to achieve this goal than Magruder.

Quietly laying his plans, he decided on a joint naval and land attack on Galveston Island, where the city of Galveston was located. For the naval attack on the four Union vessels in Galveston harbor, he converted two river steamers, the *Neptune* and *Bayou City*, by padding their gunwales and decks with bales of cotton, thereby turning them into "cotton clads."[29] On them he placed three hundred veterans of General Henry H. Sibley's New Mexico companies armed with rifles. This in itself was truly unusual—turning cavalry and infantry troops into "marines." Magruder then assigned two smaller vessels, also armed with riflemen, to join the *Neptune* and *Bayou City*.

Meanwhile Magruder had assembled more troops on the mainland opposite Galveston Island. At night on December 31, the mainland soldiers, using the railroad bridge that connected the mainland to the island, silently marched into the town of Galveston. While these troops were engaging Union forces in Galveston, Magruder's cotton-clads attacked the four Union vessels in the harbor.[30]

The results were astounding. Although the *Neptune* was sunk by Yankee gunfire, the *Bayou City* succeeded in getting so close to the federal vessels that the Sibley veterans were able to exact a deadly toll on Yankee soldiers with their guns. One federal steamship surrendered after all her officers were killed. Another vessel, having lost her tiller, ran aground, and the two remaining ships fled into the gulf. After these setbacks to the Union cause, Magruder forced the 300 Yankee soldiers from the federal garrison to surrender. In the fighting Union commander Renshaw was killed, and there were 150 naval casualties. Of Magruder's forces, 26 were killed and 117 wounded.[31]

Throughout 1863 gunboats and shore patrols never stopped harassing Fort Caney and Confederate boats in the bay. In effect, the citizens of Dutch Settlement experienced artillery shells passing back and forth over their heads. Meanwhile storms or accidents wrecked Union gunboats on the shore, with the result that the local residents became adept at salvaging clothes, food, and other goods from them. Mrs. Siringo, in fact, salvaged a set of fine china from a wrecked vessel. On one occasion Charlie and his sister came upon the corpse of a drowned Union soldier on the shore. But the salvagers had already preceded them. The drowned soldier was completely naked, his clothes having already been removed.[32]

These scavenging operations were becoming necessary, because in the spring of 1863, Confederate authorities ordered the removal of all cattle on the peninsula to the mainland so that federal troops could not seize them for food. Among those animals taken away was Mrs. Siringo's modest herd of twenty cattle. At her strong insistence her milk cow, "Old Browney," was left behind to supply milk to her and her son and daughter. On the mainland the cattle were turned loose to mix with the thousands of wild cattle already on the mainland.[33]

During the fall federal forces moved up from Brownsville, Texas, on the Rio Grande to take Corpus Christi, Aransas Pass, and to attack Fort Esperanza. The Confederates, convinced that they could not defend that post, spiked their guns, destroyed supplies, and retreated to Indianola. Supported by seven warships, General Cadwallader C. Washburn occupied Cavallo Pass. A detachment of soldiers "was ordered to march up the Peninsula and take Fort Caney some fifty miles away. Union gunboats were to accompany the soldiers and attack simultaneously." But curiously the federal troops never attacked Fort Caney, nor did the naval cannonading prove effective, but on December 26, 1863, Port Lavaca fell to Union forces and Union occupation of Lavaca and Indianola lasted until 1864.[34]

The news of Fort Esperanza's evacuation and the occupation of Port Lavaca obviously greatly alarmed the Confederate units in Matagorda and at Fort Caney and at Magruder headquarters in Houston. In late December there were rumors of a major invasion of Union troops on

Matagorda Peninsula, to which Commander Rugeley responded by ordering some forty-five soldiers to sail across the bay and engage the enemy. Tragically, a storm, a "norther," had come to the bay on December 31, just as the soldiers set sail. This ice had already formed on the waters of the bay. Once they set sail, a gale swept across the bay, capsizing one of the boats and twenty-two young soldiers, quickly overcome by hypothermia, were drowned.[35]

General Magruder was keenly aware that if a large number of federal troops could take Fort Caney, they could then march overland and retake Galveston. Therefore he ordered a number of Confederate units to concentrate at the mouth of Caney Creek to prevent that possibility and according to former Governor Francis Lubbock, Magruder himself went as far west as Victoria to assay Confederate defenses. Then he returned and established his temporary headquarters at Rugeley's plantation on the San Bernard River. Lubbock recalls that Magruder was "everywhere." "In this way, and in December, we traversed the old Caney country, stopping awhile at Hawkins' plantation and other places; and inspecting the works on the San Bernard."[36] On January 22 federal gunboats did land some 2,500 troops some ten miles from Caney, but inexplicably they moved down the peninsula away from the Confederate troops! Then over a month later, on March 13, 1864, they returned to their ships and sailed away.[37]

Meanwhile the residents of Dutch Settlement were, in effect, in the eye of the military conflict in 1863–1864. When a Union detachment of soldiers marched up the peninsula—presumably from Port Cavallo—in late 1863, they camped near the Siringo farm as had the Confederate troops a year before. This time the Union soldiers befriended Charlie Siringo and gave him hardtack to eat, which he found to be a great improvement over his largely mush and milk diet.[38]

Among the residents of Dutch Settlement who were ardent Confederate sympathizers was John Williams, the father of Charlie's best friend, Billy. During the time the Union forces were on the peninsula, Mr. Williams stole horses from them, which he turned over to the Confederate soldiers at Caney Creek. He was caught by Union soldiers, however, and strongly reprimanded. When he was apprehended a second time, the Union officers in charge sentenced Williams to be hanged, but a forgiving superior officer, saying that Williams was "an old man," ordered him released.[39]

Williams was fascinated by the war and at one point brought home what he believed was a spent cannonball. Assembling his family, he decided to drop a burning taper into the ball, thinking it would produce only a dramatic fizzle. Instead the ball exploded, fatally wounding Williams and seriously injuring a dog. Miraculously no other family members were hurt, nor was Charlie, who fortunately was watching from behind a fence.[40]

In the end Matagorda Bay was spared further federal invasions when larger military strategies on the eastern Texas front determined that both Union soldiers and gunboats were needed to invade Texas via a Red River route. Union troops withdrew from Indianola and Fort Esperanza was reoccupied by Confederate forces. Although all of Matagorda Bay had never been taken, the Union naval blockade had ruined the local planters and merchants, who could not sell or ship their cotton. In addition the rebel forces sometimes proved to be their own worst enemy. In their zeal to frustrate Yankee invaders, Confederate soldiers at Indianola destroyed wharves and tore up railroad tracks to the interior.[41] Whether or not the residents of Matagorda Bay realized it, militarily speaking they and Texans elsewhere had successfully defended their four-hundred-mile coastline. Whereas in 1863 most Texas ports were in Union hands, by 1865 they were back in Confederate hands. As the distinguished Texas scholar T. R. Fehrenbach has observed: "Historians generally regard the defense of the Texas coast and borders as one of the greatest military feats of the Confederacy."[42]

There were, of course, many prices to be paid, both real and psychological, by the warring combatants on both sides. Shelby Foote, in discussing the Union blockade forces, has noted that in 1863 the blockading of coasts accomplished little and suffered reverses at Galveston and Sabine Pass. "Boredom was the problem, especially for the crew of blockaders, who could not see that their day-in day-out service had much to do with fighting at all, let alone with speeding the victory which hard-war politicians and editors kept saying was right around the corner."[43]

On the Confederate side two factors deeply affected the morale of the mainland troops in the area between Galveston and Brownsville. First, by 1864 there was an unspoken recognition that the Confederacy had lost the war, once Admiral Farragut had seized the Mississippi and separated Texas, western Louisiana, and Arkansas from the rest of the

South. The prospect of defeat affected the incoming raw recruits in the Texas coastal areas. Officers claimed they simply could not train them well, or evoke an enthusiasm for the cause, an attitude undoubtedly reinforced by their being so far away from the real center of action east of the Mississippi.[44]

In his revealing "Reminiscences," Ralph J. Smith, who was stationed at Fort Caney in the winter and spring 1863–1864, records how the Second Texas Infantry skirmished with federal gunboats at the entry of Caney Creek, Matagorda County, when the latter shelled Fort Caney. The Confederates thought "this was it": they were going to land troops "to capture the garrison." But suddenly the shelling stopped and no troops appeared. Instead a federal gunboat had run "a Spanish sailing vessel in near the fort where she grounded. The crew, all Cubans, being much frightened, abandoned her and took to the woods. Our officers took possession of the boat and cargo, consisting of coffee, Irish potatoes, salt fish, calico, wash bowls and pitchers, bar iron and some few barrels, besides numbers of cases of various tonics, which we called soothing syrup, consigned to R. & H. Mills of Galveston."

The "soothing syrup," writes Smith, proved to be "overwhelmingly intoxicating." "In fact by twelve o'clock at night the whole command was stretched on the sands of the beach helplessly drunk, except Major C. George W. L. J. Fly, Sergeant Bill and myself." For the Confederate defenders at Fort Caney at least there were moments of escape and pleasure.[45]

Perhaps the epitome of Texas determination can be seen in the story of the legendary Texas hero Colonel John S. ("Rip") Ford during the Civil War. Already a veteran of the Texas Revolution and one of the first Texas Rangers as well as an indomitable Indian fighter, at the onset of the Civil War, Ford, who had been a member of the Texas secession convention, headed an expedition to Brazos Santiago (and Brownsville) on the Rio Grande Mexican border. There he seized Yankee artillery guns for the Confederacy, and was elected colonel of the Second Texas Cavalry. In double-quick time he negotiated a trade agreement between Mexico and the Confederacy, which allowed many needed goods and munitions to come across the border.[46]

Then in the fall of 1863 when the commander of Union troops in Texas, General Nathaniel P. Banks, decided to close this flourishing contraband trade by sending seven thousand troops under General Dana to occupy Brownsville, Confederate Brigadier General Hamilton P. Bee, commander of the lower Rio Grande district with his own headquarters at Brownsville, cleverly prevented key Confederate stores and cotton from falling into Union hands. Ford was also there to help on that occasion.[47]

But symbolically it was "Rip" Ford who led the last Confederate troops against the Yankees in the last battle of the Civil War, fought at Palmito Ranch more than a month after General Robert E. Lee had surrendered to Grant at Appomattox Courthouse in Virginia. In a complicated final action Ford and other Confederate officers defeated a federal force. But knowing the war was over, and satisfied after pushing the Union forces back, in the process having killed 111 men, capturing 4 officers and wounding others, he stopped and said to his men: "Boys, we have done finely. . . . We will let them well enough alone, and retire."[48]

That intrepid Texas determination was echoed in the actions of General Edmund Kirby Smith, commander of the Texas Military Department, who refused to sign a formal treaty of surrender at Galveston until June 2, 1865.[49]

⚜ ⚜

In his *A Texas Cowboy* Siringo recalls that "When the war broke up everybody was happy. We cheered for joy when Mr. Joe Yeamans [whose family were pioneer settlers in Matagorda] brought the good news from town."[50]

For the citizens of Matagorda City and the planters of Caney Creek, however, the end of the war meant the end of an era. They were shocked at federal reconstruction policies and even more so by the presence of African-American federal troops stationed in the town. During reconstruction many planters appear to have become so bitter against their former slaves that rather than adjust to their newly free status, they chose to concentrate on raising cattle rather than cotton. James B. Hawking, the largest slaveholder in Matagorda County, and the planter who had hosted General Magruder in 1863, continued to raise cotton and corn, but used convict labor to do so.[51] Ironically "the total slave population had increased by 35% during the war," one result being that "more than 200,000 Negroes were cast adrift in one of the greatest social revolutions of all time."[52]

Two unexpected developments regarding African-Americans occurred in Texas in the post–Civil War years. In Matagorda County in the

Caney Creek area, a community of free blacks formed, living on their own. At the same time a much larger westward movement occurred when ex-slaves went to work as cowboys on the great open-range ranches of south Texas. Although their presence was known, the large number who became cowboys or ranch hands was not really acknowledged until careful studies were made in the twentieth century. The most recent findings indicate that between one-fourth and one-third of the cowboys employed in the 1870s and 1880s were African-American.[53]

One reason for the swift turn toward ranching on the coastal plains of south Texas after the Civil War was explained by Siringo himself in *A Texas Cowboy*. He recalled that with the coming of peace "all of the men and boys that were large enough went over to the mainland to gather up the Peninsula cattle. On their arrival they found it a bigger job then they had figured on, for they had scattered over two or three hundred miles of country and [were] as wild as deer." Indeed, the cattle had mixed with wild cattle for nearly four years.[54]

> Billy and I thought it very hard that we could not go and be Cow Boys too; but we had lots of fun all by ourselves, for we had an old mule and two or three ponies to ride, so you see we practiced riding in anticipation of the near future, when we would be large enough to be Cow Boys.

At the time Siringo was twelve years old.

> After being gone about three months the crowd came back, bringing with them several hundred head of cattle, which they had succeeded in gathering. Among them were about twenty head belonging to mother.
>
> The crowd went right back after more. This stimulated Billy and I to become a crowd of Cow Boys all by ourselves, therefore we put in most of our time lassoing and riding wild yearlings, etc. We hardly stayed at home long enough to get our meals.[55]

Charlie and his friend Billy probably did not realize it, but Matagorda County residents were desperate for cash. Their one cash crop now was the incredible surplus of cattle roaming freely among them.

They could try to march them to one of the ports to be loaded on steamships for market in New Orleans, or they could kill them for their hides to be sold to booming tanneries in the bay area. In turn the Morgan lines profited from selling hides and tallow to New York and New England; therefore entrepreneurial ranchers were anxious to recruit cowboys wherever they could find them. Their sense of opportunity grew with rumors that one might drive cattle to railheads in Kansas and Missouri for the Chicago market.

Those expectations proved to be what Charlie thought was his salvation, for "in the spring of 1867, a cattle man by the name of Faldien brought his family over to the Peninsula for their health and rented part of our house to live in."[56]

"After getting his wife and babies located in their new quarters, he started back home, in Matagorda, to make preparations for spring work, he having to rig up new outfits, etc. He persuaded mother to let me go with him and learn to run cattle. When she consented I was the happiest boy in the 'Settlement,' for my life long wish was about to be gratified."[57] Charlie Siringo was to become a real cowboy at last!

Most runaways apparently did not turn to lives of debauchery and crime. . . . If these children defied parental authority, they also embraced many of Victorian America's most hallowed values, among them ambition, willingness to work, honesty, and self reliance.

Elliott West, Growing Up with the Country: Childhood on the Far Western Frontier, *155*

I do not know much about gods; but I think the river is a strong brown god.

T. S. Eliot, "Dry Salvages,"
in Four Quartets *(1941), I*

In 1882 Mark Twain, revisiting the river after an absence of 20 years, wrote "Mississippi steamboating was born about 1812; at the end of thirty years it had grown to mighty proportions; and in less than thirty years more it was dead. A strangely short life for so majestic a creature."

Mark Twain, quoted in
Lamar, NEAW, *1128*

CHAPTER THREE

Rites of Passage

ST. LOUIS AND THE MISSISSIPPI

RIVER EXPERIENCE, 1867–1870

WHEN MRS. SIRINGO GAVE CHARLIE PERMISSION TO WORK AS AN apprentice cowhand for Mr. Faldien on his ranch on Big Boggy near Lake Austin, Charlie thought his career as a cowboy had finally begun. Instead, the summer of 1867 proved to be not only a surprise, but a series of crises Charlie could never have predicted.

As he rode out to Faldien's ranch on the "grub" wagon with the "colored cook," older men on the ranch took him on a wild boar hunt. It was a savage introduction to a hunting lifestyle Charlie had not anticipated. The boars fought to the finish, so that some of the Faldien dogs were, in Charlie's words, "badly gashed up."[1] The next experience was, in its way, equally sobering. The cow ponies supplied by Faldien had not been used for a year, so that they were pretty wild. Witnesses tell us of watching young Siringo trying to ride the ponies and being thrown. But he was game and kept at it, despite his small size.[2]

Perhaps the real surprise was that one of Faldien's main goals was to round up unmarked cattle or mavericks and to put his own brand on them. Unlike the Matagorda Peninsula, however, the Lake Austin area was full of trees and swamps—a refuge for wild longhorn cattle of all ages. Siringo came to know just how ornery and dangerous these wild cattle could be. But Faldien was determined to round them up to sell. He told his men in effect, to brand everything in sight.[3]

Siringo probably would not have known it, but 1867 was the year entrepreneur Joseph G. McCoy chose Abilene, Kansas, as a railhead for cattle being driven up from Texas to be shipped by the Kansas Pacific Railroad to Chicago and points east. In short, there was a tremendous shortage of cattle in the United States after the Civil War, and Texas ranchers saw this market as their key to survival in the grim Reconstruction years.[4] McCoy himself had helped mark and advertise a trail from Texas to Abilene and later to other Kansas towns that came to be known as the Chisholm Trail—probably the best-known and most romanticized long-drive cattle trail in American history.[5] Faldien and hundreds of other ranchers in Matagorda and adjoining counties were determined to take advantage of this fantastic market opportunity. A dozen years later Charlie Siringo was to help drive cattle over the Chisholm Trail, and, as we shall see, gave us a rollicking account of his experiences in his *A Texas Cowboy*.

Charlie's participation in this first postwar cattle bonanza, however, was short lived. During the summer of 1867, he developed typhoid fever and was sent home, where he nearly died from the disease. Then came a second traumatic surprise: Mrs. Siringo was courted and won by a Yankee named Carrier, who claimed that he owned a farm in Michigan. After marrying her, Carrier persuaded Mrs. Siringo to sell her small ranch of 175 acres and her herd of sixty cattle to go north to Carrier's purported Michigan farm. They were to bring Charlie and his sister along as well.[6]

What appears to have been the most classic case of scam one could imagine then occurred. Once the Siringos and Carrier had boarded a ship at Indianola for New Orleans, Carrier began to drink heavily and appears to have done so all the way from New Orleans to St. Louis. Mrs. Siringo was soon bereft of the cash she had received from the sale of her farm and cattle. Soon she had even been forced by Carrier to give up her savings, which she had tried to keep secret from him. There followed a series of disasters in which she had to sell her own personal effects in order to rent rooms in St. Louis. Siringo reports that at times he and his mother and sister were on the verge of starving. Charlie himself got a number of odd jobs clearing winter sidewalks of snow and shoveling coal into cellars.[7]

But Siringo, while surviving and earning a bit of cash, was also consumed with anger at what had happened to him and his family. He was always ready for a fight, and an entire chapter in *A Texas Cowboy* recounts how he got into fights with other youths—whom he always saw as bullies. Things seemed to change in January 1868 when Carrier sent Mrs. Siringo enough money to get them to a farm in Lebanon, Illinois, east of St. Louis, where he said he was employed. But once there it became clear that Carrier was still squandering all his cash on drink. Once again, Siringo himself—now all of thirteen—had to take a job working for the local farmer on whose property they lived.[8]

Carrier eventually became such an obnoxious alcoholic he was driven out by the community. Mrs. Siringo found work in a private boarding house. Meanwhile Siringo himself tried working for Mr. Moore, the local farmer, but the wages were pitifully low. He was also often ill from what appears to have been malaria.[9]

At some point Mrs. Siringo and her daughter decided to move to St. Louis for better jobs, but somehow failed to send Charlie their new address. Still plagued by illness, Charlie worked for various employers, but, "as I had a chill every other day regular," I "therefore couldn't work much."[10]

Eventually Siringo went to St. Louis in search of his mother. Assuming that his dramatic account of being lost, nearly starving, and being truly "down and out" is more or less accurate, Siringo had a truly rough time during his second sojourn in St. Louis. He slept in dry goods boxes, and was treated as a street delinquent by a policeman. Even so, Siringo himself knew how to plead his case with kindly strangers who took notice of him. One of them eventually landed him a job as a bell-boy at the Planter's House, one of St. Louis's most elegant hotels. Miraculously he moved from rags to riches in a few days. Now he had decent clothes and benefited from generous tips, both from wealthy patrons and gamblers at the hotel.[11]

Siringo was still so keyed up and angry at the world, however, that at any challenge he would respond with his fists. Almost inevitably he got into a fight with another bellboy, whom he considered a bully, and was slapped by a hotel clerk as punishment. Furious, he quit his job and set out to buy a pistol in order to shoot the clerk, but became diverted by a street con game in which he lost all his money! It should be recalled that at the time Siringo was only thirteen or fourteen.[12]

Feeling that all was lost, Siringo decided that he must get back to his beloved Texas. He headed for the St. Louis levee, where he managed to talk his way onto the *Bart Able*, a riverboat bound for New Orleans, by persuading the purser to give him work while on board. Just when all seemed to be going well, as he helped sew up sacks of grain, Siringo slipped and fell into a hatchway and was knocked unconscious. But with incredible Siringo luck he was found, taken to the captain's cabin, and treated by a doctor. Yet he still could not stay out of trouble. Only a few days later, when his steamboat docked at Memphis, he allowed himself to be outwitted by some older boys and lost his pistol.[13]

After the *Bart Able* reached New Orleans, Charlie then tried to talk his way aboard a Morgan steamship bound for Indianola, but to no avail. In the meantime the incredible Siringo luck prevailed again. An older man named Mr. Myers found him almost unconscious from hunger and took him to his house to assist his wife with household chores. This time Siringo had won big. The childless Myerses virtually adopted him. They outfitted him with decent clothes and sent him to school. It was also the case that Mr. Myers was an agent for a shipping line, and promised to help Charlie get back to Texas.[14]

But here again Siringo's ferocious sense of independence ruined everything. Not only did he resist two of his teachers when they tried to discipline him, but he knifed a boy in a fight, seriously wounding him. Realizing what he had done, Charlie fled on a steamer upriver to St. Louis where once again he searched for his mother and sister without success.

Eventually he got up enough courage to return to New Orleans a second time, where he learned to his relief that the boy he had knifed had recovered and no charges had been brought against him. And once again the adoring Mr. and Mrs. Myers took him in and sent him to school. Using an excuse to leave the school to watch a nearby fire, despite his teacher urging him to stay in the classroom, he stowed away on a Morgan steamship and somehow got to Indianola. There the Siringo luck surfaced again when he was greeted by his old godfather, a Mr. Hagerty, "who stood for me when I was being christened by the Catholic priest." As Siringo recounts in *A Texas Cowboy*, Hagerty invited him to stay at his home "until I could find work."[15]

Within a short time Charlie got a job at one of the several packing houses located near Indianola. By this time Indianola boasted firms or "packeries" that shipped turtles, and tanneries that slaughtered wild cattle for their tallow and hides, the hides shipped east for shoes and leather goods. The remains of the cattle were then fed to hogs, and the hogs in turn were killed and their meat salted and packed for export. Apparently the stench of slaughtered cattle and that of the roving hogs was intolerable, but these firms represented jobs and a livelihood. Many of those employed to do the slaughtering, tanning of hides, and packing were Mexican workers and from them Siringo picked up a smattering of Spanish.[16]

Siringo, now about fifteen years old, had become, in effect, an experienced traveler up and down the Mississippi, had done a man's work on an Illinois farm, had easier work as a bell boy, and had done some work on steamboats, but he remained a boy at heart with an enduring love of cowboy life. Not surprisingly he used his first month's pay from the packing house to buy a pistol, and later wages to buy a "pair of star topped boots." At the time he also played monte with Mexican workers at the packing house. Most likely he borrowed from them the habit of wearing colorful sashes, just as Mexican vaqueros did. Later, after he became a full-fledged ranch hand, one of his first purchases was a bright red sash, which he wore for at least a decade.

❦ ❦

Siringo biographers have understandably tended to subordinate the story of his more than two years on the Mississippi River to his accounts of being a cowboy. Yet this was a crucial rite of passage for him. He lived these two years without a father or a male authority figure, and he was out of touch with his mother for at least that long. It is intriguing that Mark Twain's great novel, *The Adventures of Huckleberry Finn*, was about a thirteen- to fourteen-year-old boy, the same age as Siringo.[17] Both were trying to escape from extremely unpleasant situations: Huck Finn from his mean-spirited, abusive alcoholic father, Pap, and Charlie from his drunken stepfather, Mr. Carrier. In fleeing, both became, in effect, river orphans.

Both Huck Finn and Charlie also sought escape from being "adopted" by well-meaning adults. In Huck's case it was the Widow Douglas who wanted to raise him properly; and in Charlie's case Mr. and Mrs. Myers were determined to educate him even to the point of placing him in a school that stressed literature and foreign languages.[18] Also during their "adopted" periods, both resisted school and authority. Each teenager also possessed a gun, and while major violent events occurred throughout the experiences of Huck Finn—death, murder, lynching, and injustice to Jim, the slave who was Huck's companion on the river, Siringo had fights with no less than five different boys, or "bullies" as he called them, who were his own age or older.

Mark Twain brilliantly succeeded in entering a boy's world and let Huck tell his story in the form of a first-person narrative, while, as Alfred Kazin has noted, expressing Twain's own views of the "low life" types on the Mississippi River. Siringo's first-person narrative, although written fifteen years after he was in the Mississippi Valley, nevertheless reflected a boy's world. "Huck Finn's voice has many sides to it," writes Kazin, "but fundamentally it is the voice of a boy-man up to his ears in life, tumbling from danger to danger, negotiating with people and fighting back at things as necessity commands."[19]

Mark Twain's *Huckleberry Finn* and Siringo's accounts clearly have little in common as literature. *Huckleberry Finn* is full of profound insights about slavery, as seen though Jim's experiences, and the role of the river in the characters' lives. Siringo's narrative, as J. Frank Dobie noted, was largely about actions. For him the river was crucial as a highway. Even so, both are written in an American vernacular style and both demonstrate how youths dealt with adults while seeking not only to survive but to be free.

At times survival depended on getting food to eat. Both boys faced the threat of starvation, but were rescued by circumstance or kindly persons. For most of his trip with Jim down the river Huck let things happen. Siringo, on the other hand, had no mentor, as Jim the slave was for Huck. Siringo also practiced the art of being a victim, bursting into tears as he told his story to Mr. Myers and others. Huck Finn, as critics have noted, unlike Tom Sawyer, did not play games or maneuver people until the very end of the novel when he engaged in deception to help Jim be freed from slavery.[20] It seems no accident that for the rest of his life, Charlie, and especially as a Pinkerton detective pretending to be down and out or an outlaw on the lam in order to gain the trust of the person he was tracking, aroused the sympathy of his hearers.

At the end of his narrative Huck says, "I reckon I got to light out for the territory ahead of the rest, because Aunt Sally she's going to adopt me and civilize me, and I can't stand it. I been there before."[21] Similarly, Charlie fled school and the Myers to go back to Texas. "The next heard of me was on the 'rolling deep.' I had boarded a Morgan steamship and stowed myself away until the vessel was at sea, where I knew they wouldn't land to put me ashore." Like Huck Finn, Siringo was headed for his "territory"—Texas.[22]

The adventures of boys or young teenagers that have become literary classics are endless, but they also tell us much about youth on the American frontier. The Talon children who survived the disasters of La Salle's fatal Texas colony are a case in point. Davy Crockett, acutely unhappy at home because of an abusive father, hired out at age twelve to help drive cattle to Virginia. Crockett was on the move for the rest of his life until he died at the Alamo.[23] Kit Carson was apprenticed to a saddle maker in frontier Missouri at age fourteen, but ran away to New Mexico where he became a fur trader, mountain man, and famous guide for John C. Fremont.[24] After Buffalo Bill saw his father die from a fatal stabbing in 1857, when he was only eleven, he was a restless youth who became a teenage Pony Express rider.[25] Billy the Kid, fatherless and always on the move with his mother, was about eighteen when he is supposed to have killed his first man.[26]

Charles Morgan was fourteen when he began his career in the shipping business in New York.[27] The Texas orphan Wiley Kuykendall, whom we shall meet in the next chapter, set out to be a cowman at age nine.[28] Siringo's Mississippi River years echoed a common pattern of the experiences of rugged individual youths in nineteenth-century America. In *Huckleberry Finn*, Mark Twain had captured more than the story of a teenage boy. He had uncovered a world of American male youths that was larger and more significant than any American author had seriously explored in such depths, and with such profound understanding. Charlie Siringo was but another example of the adventurous boy-man who characterized that world.

Only in recent years has the story of children growing up on the frontier and its impact on them been explored; but thanks to Elliott West's seminal study, *Growing Up with the Country: Childhood on the Far Western Frontier* (1989) and other works, we are now beginning to see the West through the eyes of children.[29]

⚜ ⚜

Ever the sociable person with a deep affection for old acquaintances as well as a fierce nostalgia for the Matagorda area, Siringo soon quit his packing-house job so that he could visit the town of Matagorda and old

friends on the peninsula as well as his old homestead at Dutch Settlement. It was characteristic of his personality that he liked to "hark back"
to past happy events and experiences; indeed, he returned to Matagorda
periodically for the rest of his life to visit friends.

After a summer of trying to raise watermelons and sweet potatoes on
the peninsula in partnership with a Mr. Joseph Yeamans, a Baptist minister, he walked away from that latest experience in farming and headed for
Matagorda. There he learned that Tom Nye (which he spelled Nie), a representative of Shanghai Pierce and Samuel W. Allen, joint owners of the
"Rancho Grande" near Tres Palacios, was "hiring some Cow-Boys." With
an enthusiasm that must have amazed Nye, Siringo signed on with four
other youths, all in their teens.[30] Charlie Siringo was not only going to be
a cowboy at last, at Rancho Grande he would be working for one of the
most famous ranchers in Texas history. Its formidable chief owner, Abel
Head "Shanghai" Pierce, a Rhode Island–born entrepreneur who had
made Texas his home and ranching his profession, himself became one of
the most significant figures in the open-range cattle industry in the nineteenth century.[31] The Siringo luck had prevailed again.

MR. PIERCE WAS A LOUD TALKER AND NO MAN WHO EVER SAW
HIM OR HEARD HIM TALK EVER FORGOT HIS VOICE OR APPEARANCE.
HE WAS A MONEY MAKER, EMPIRE BUILDER, AND A
WONDER TO HIS FRIENDS.

—George W. Saunders, in J. Marvin Hunter, ed.,
The Trail Drivers of Texas, 924

I AM SHANGHAI PIERCE, WEBSTER ON CATTLE, BY GOD, SIR.

*—Abel Head Pierce to a hotel clerk at one of his favorite hotels,
in Chris Emmett,* Shanghai Pierce: A Fair Likeness *(1953), 11*

CHAPTER FOUR

Shanghai Pierce and El Rancho Grande

The Texas Cattle Industry from the Open Range to Corporate Enterprise, 1854–1900

I

Shortly after the Civil War had ended and during the harshest days of the Reconstruction period in Texas, Texas farmers and ranchers were desperate to find a market for the one product they had in abundance: the millions of longhorn cattle wandering freely on the prairies and plains of south and central Texas. Texans already knew how to round them up and brand them, but how to get them to market was the problem. Texas cattle had been driven overland to market in New Orleans, but that trail was replete with formidable obstacles with hundreds of streams to cross, bayous to skirt, and seemingly endless soggy swamplands to avoid whenever possible.

The quickest and most advantageous access to market was through the Matagorda Bay ports, especially Indianola, where the Morgan Steamship and other lines took livestock to Galveston or New Orleans (where they would be transferred to riverboats going upstream to St. Louis). Some cattle went to Cuba as well. But most small ranchers could not afford to send cattle to a port and be guaranteed early shipment. To resolve such problems cattlemen began to pool herds and to sell them to other cattlemen with connections to shippers.

The marketing of cattle in these early postwar days is epitomized by the meeting of Abel Head "Shanghai" Pierce and young George W. Saunders, a cattle man in a cow camp where various ranchers had congregated to sell their beeves. Saunders describes Pierce as follows.

> My first recollection of Mr. Pierce was just after the close of the Civil War when he sought fat cattle all over South Texas. I remember seeing him many times come to our camp where he had contracts to receive beeves. He was a large portly man, always rode a fine horse, and would be accompanied by a Negro who led a pack horse loaded with gold and silver which, when he reached our camp, was dumped on the ground and remained there until the cattle were classed and counted out to him; then he would empty the money on a blanket in camp and pay it out to the different stock men from whom he had purchased cattle. He would generally buy 200 or 300 head at a time. The cowmen would round up large herds at different times and Colonel Pierce would select what he wanted. We all looked upon him as a redeemer, and were glad to sell our cattle at any price, as money was scarce in those reconstruction days before the northern trail started.[1]

Who was Able Head Pierce, and how did he become one of Texas's most remarkable ranchers and innovative entrepreneurs? How did he acquire the nickname "Shanghai," a name he clearly relished? And how did he help shape the life of Charlie Siringo?

Abel Head Pierce was born in Little Compton, Rhode Island, in 1834, the son of hardworking parents. The father was a blacksmith and probably a farmer as well. The couple was quite religious. When he was only fifteen Abel's family sent this tall, lanky, energetic, restless, and ambitious youth to Petersburg, Virginia, to work in the store of his successful maternal uncle, Abel Head, for whom young Pierce was named.

It was clear that Mrs. Pierce greatly admired her brother and wanted him to give her son a good start in business. The uncle proved to be so pious and sanctimonious, however, that he and his nephew were in constant conflict, especially when the uncle repeatedly warned him that he would never amount to anything.[2]

When Chester Robbins, a young coworker in the Head store, whom Pierce had befriended, suddenly left for Texas to settle his father's estate (the father had been murdered in the Matagorda Bay area for a large amount of money he was carrying), Pierce felt more lonely and was unhappier than ever. Then his friend, Chester, returned briefly from Texas and raved to Pierce about Texas as a land of opportunity and especially praised the Matagorda Bay area.[3]

By the time he was nineteen, Pierce could stand his Bible-quoting uncle no more. He traveled to New York, where he walked the docks until he found a Texas-bound steamer. He managed to get on board as a stowaway, but when discovered by the ship's crew, he willingly agreed to pay his passage by handling cargo on board and at ports of call. When the vessel landed at Indianola and then at Port Lavaca, Pierce had more than paid for his passage by working zealously unloading goods. He himself disembarked at Port Lavaca in June 1854, and soon found a job with William Bradford Grimes, the most successful rancher and businessman in the area. Among other enterprises, "Bing" Grimes, as he was called, ran a packing or slaughterhouse where open-range cattle were slaughtered for their hides and tallow.[4]

Although Grimes's father, Captain Richard Grimes, a former Connecticut Yankee who lived in the county, persuaded his son "Bing" to hire the tall—now six feet, four inch—assertive Pierce to work for him, Grimes did not take a liking to the young Rhode Islander, and, as we shall see, over the next several years kept putting Pierce in his place by giving him menial tasks unconnected to the ranching business. Thus Abel's first job was to split rails rather than serve as a cowhand. Even so, Pierce's own determination to be a rancher and his obvious skills with horses and cattle eventually led Grimes to give him the more important job as a range wrangler and to increase his pay. What this really meant was that he could now brand wild cattle with the brands of Grimes, Grimes's sister Charlotte, and his own, for as soon as he could Pierce had registered his own brand, "AP," in Matagorda and began to acquire cattle for himself.[5]

As Chris Emmett so convincingly records in his fine biography, *Shanghai Pierce: A Fair Likeness*, Abel was smitten with Grimes's sister, Frances Charlotte, and dreamed of marrying her. Bing Grimes was not about to let that happen.

In 1860, six years after Abel had arrived in Matagorda County, his younger brother, Jonathan Edwards Pierce, came to Indianola, where he, too, found work with Bing Grimes. Jonathan was a sharp contrast to his tall lanky brother, who had such a long neck that friends said he reminded them of a boastful red Shanghai rooster. Indeed, friends began to refer to him as early as 1855 as "Shanghai" or "Shang." In contrast, Jonathan was a shorter, rather stocky individual who preferred farming over ranching. But he also proved to be good at keeping Grimes's business accounts in order and became, in effect, his secretary and accountant. Because Charlie Siringo was destined to work for both Pierce and Bing Grimes, the story of his employees and their personalities and accomplishments is worth telling.

Although they were Rhode Island Yankees, when the Civil War began, they both joined the Confederate Army. Pierce became a member of Augustus C. Buchel's Confederate Cavalry unit. His first enlistment, however, appears to have been with Dr. E. A. Peareson's unit that trained in the Matagorda Peninsula, where young Siringo encountered them. It would be intriguing to find that Siringo and Pierce unknowingly encountered each other on the beach in the early 1860s. Actually Abel Pierce only saw action in local guard and garrison duty in the Matagorda area until the last months of the war, when the unit was transferred to western Louisiana (still in Confederate hands) to defend Texas from invasion by General Nathaniel Banks's Red River Campaign. Although Texas troops successfully thwarted Banks's campaign, in the fighting Buchel was killed, but Abel Pierce survived to return to Matagorda and ranching.[7]

Jonathan Pierce went west instead of east to serve with Confederate troops in the Brownsville–Rio Grande area. He, too, returned without a scratch. Both brothers returned to Matagorda County to find that their cattle were gone and that they had to start over again. They were deeply angered by Grimes, who owed them money at the end of the war, but chose to pay them in worthless Confederate paper money! From then on they considered Grimes their enemy.[8]

With much more daring and ambition than resources, the two brothers agreed on a partnership and together established El Rancho

Grande to raise cattle, but as has been suggested earlier, more to collect cattle and ship them than to breed them. Indeed, the whole of south Texas was a paradise of surplus, unbranded cattle—or as they were now called, "mavericks." El Rancho Grande was not yet a specific piece of legally owned property, but a shifting territorial sphere of influence.

The intriguing maps found in Chris Emmett's biography of Shanghai Pierce list the "area of Shanghai Pierce's interest" as stretching from Matagorda Bay in the south, north through Matagorda County and into Wharton County. On the east the "interests" ran from east Matagorda Bay north to Richmond, Texas, and on the west from the Port Lavaca area north to the town of Edna (see map in Emmett, 120–21). It was no wonder that the never-modest Shanghai boasted that the Gulf of Mexico was his southern "drift fence" and that his cattle were actually "sea lions."

Generally speaking, the A. H. and J. E. Pierce Range was in Matagorda County north of W. B. Grimes's holding at Tres Palacios, and northwest of the city of Matagorda. (See Historic Matagorda County Map, p. 91, and Emmett, 120–21.) Over the years, however, Pierce allied with other ranchers and investors located in different areas of Matagorda, Wharton, Jackson, and adjoining counties, each of the alliances or ranges bearing different names. According to Chris Emmett at one point Pierce claimed that "me and Allen, Poole and Company must have owned more than 100,000 cattle and that he himself branded 18,000 calves or there about and 1,154 yearlings that year."9

His reference to Allen, Poole and Company actually provides the secret to his early success. This firm from near Houston had allied themselves with the Morgan Steamship Lines, which had a virtual monopoly on shipping cattle from Indianola to Galveston, New Orleans, and Cuba. Morgan Lines could guarantee weekly shipment of cattle from Matagorda Bay. Indeed, one of Charlie Siringo's first jobs with Pierce and his partner, Allen, Poole and Company, was to load cattle constantly onto vessels at Indianola until midnight twice a week. To put that another way, by having a guaranteed shipping arrangement, Pierce had an advantage over other shippers and thus George W. Saunders could exclaim, "we looked upon him as our redeemer." And far from abandoning the Morgan, Allen, Poole and Company partnership when the overland Chisholm Trail to Kansas opened in 1867, Pierce was still shipping cattle by sea in the 1870s.10

Pierce's actual ranch headquarters, El Rancho Grande, eventually came to be identified with the upper western part of Matagorda County where he made his home for the rest of his life. The final El Rancho Grande headquarters was east of the future town of Blessing near the upper reaches of Tres Palacios Creek and near the Hawley Cemetery where Shanghai was to be buried in 1900.[11]

At this point we should note the important presence and influence of his more silent brother, Jonathan Edwards Pierce. It is difficult to know how close the two brothers were, but Shanghai knew and respected his brother's quiet, shrewd assessment of events, and his "following up" with solutions to problems. Jonathan spotted both the major and small fallouts of Shanghai's blustering and sometimes thoughtless actions. The personal bonding and the "picking up" after a crisis never appears to have been articulated but it was there. It is important to note, for example, that when Abel married Fannie Lacy, the daughter of a neighbor, in 1865, later Jonathan quietly announced that he was marrying Fannie's sister Nannie. They both married well. Fannie and Nannie were the daughters of a distinguished Texas pioneer, William Demetris Lacy, a signer of the Texas Declaration of Independence who had also served in the army during the Texas Revolution.[12]

One of Jonathan Pierce's talents was to understand people, and especially wild young cowboys like Siringo. After Siringo went to work for Shanghai Pierce, he engaged in, as we shall soon see, putting his own brand on some of the mavericks supposed to go to his employer. He was discovered at this game and reprimanded by Shanghai. Although Charlie was in awe of the formidable Shanghai, he was never afraid of him—indeed of no man. It looks as if he and Shanghai talked easily and frequently, because they saw a lot of one another. When loading cattle on steamers for Pierce, Charlie recalls that Shanghai would come down and help; and if it was stormy with a cold norther or if the cattle were pummeled with sleet, Pierce would sing to the cattle with his extraordinarily strong voice.[13] Jonathan, on the other hand, was quiet but affable, and as we shall see, more than once played the role of a father figure to Siringo.

During the time that ranchers were avidly putting their brands on mavericks, inevitably gangs of professional raiders or rustlers decided to cash in on the mavericking frenzy by seizing already branded cattle, butchering them, and selling their hides illegally. It proved to be a complicated story in the Matagorda area that almost replicated the later classical accounts of western cattle rustling, resulting in blood feuds and sheer malice.

In these uncertain times the five Lunn brothers, in alliance with suspected ranchers in Jackson County, began to seize both Pierce's cattle and those of neighboring ranchers. The first complication was that the Lunns did not operate alone but had as their partners in crime members of the Sutton family. But the Suttons themselves were having a blood feud with another ranching family, the Taylors. To make a long story short, any rancher who identified with the Suttons or the Taylors was certain to experience reprisal by the enemy side. The feud has been described as "the longest and bloodiest in Texas."[14]

At first Shanghai Pierce believed that the Lunn brothers were friends, but eventually discovered that they were hijacking his and his neighbors' already branded cattle for slaughter in order to sell their hides and tallow. Forming what was a vigilante gang of friendly ranchers, Pierce and his allies caught three of the Lunns; one "All Jaw" Smith, a known "bad man"; and a stranger, red-handed while the latter were hijacking and slaughtering cattle. Moreover, they found them in possession of branded hides. In very much the style of a Ku Klux Klan format, the ranchers hanged the three Lunns, All Jaw Smith, and the stranger from the limbs of a dead tree.[15]

Of course the news of their action along with the evidence of the dead bodies got out. Indeed, a surviving Lunn brother brought charges against the lynch gang in Matagorda County Court and implicated Shanghai Pierce, who was summoned as an alleged witness of the hangings.

Knowing that he was in serious trouble, Pierce quickly converted his assets into gold by selling his ranch to Allen, Poole and Company for $110,000, and transferring the management of El Rancho Grande to his brother, Jonathan. He himself traveled northward to Kansas City and several other Kansas cattle towns—more often then not, the railroad towns to which his cattle were being sent from Texas. Ever the boastful controller of his own image, Pierce declared that he had gone north to Kansas City to "hunt society." Even given his great height and enormous booming voice, which he confessed was not appropriate for talking indoors, Pierce further confounded the public by appearing in sartorially resplendent suit and carrying an elegant walking stick. In short, as intended, he was a local sensation.[16] Although Siringo watched these events closely and noted that Pierce had fled Matagorda, he did not tell us what he knew.

Pierce, meanwhile, was actually as nervous as he would have been in Matagorda County awaiting a court summons, for by a twist of fate, John Wesley Hardin, the youthful well-known killer, turned out to be a kinsman and ally of the Suttons. This meant he was a friend of the Lunns. Indeed, Hardin often visited the very cattle towns in which Pierce had expected to do business. Moreover, Ben J. Thompson, the well-known Texas gambler and gunman, with an established reputation as a mankiller, had migrated to Abilene in 1870 where he and Phil Coe operated the Bull's Head Saloon. He, too, was a friend of John Wesley Hardin. Pierce truly feared that if Hardin chose to accost him, he was as good as dead. Fortunately Pierce managed to stay clear of Hardin, Thompson, and Coe but his eighteen-month exile in Kansas was not a relaxing time.[17]

Meanwhile Pierce remained incredibly active in the cattle business. He ordered Jonathan to send their herds north, first to Abilene, but then diverted them to Ellsworth, where there was neither John Wesley Hardin nor Ben Thompson. Instead he found an able man, Thomas Jefferson Hamilton, who wintered Pierce's cattle outside Ellsworth. Pierce was also busy in making financially rewarding friendships. Early in his career as a rancher, he had befriended an older Irish-born merchant, Daniel Sullivan, who ran a general store in Indianola but had money to loan. He and Shanghai had hit it off at once, and after Sullivan's death he continued the mutually rewarding relationship with Sullivan's heir and nephew, "Little Danny." The general store eventually evolved into a bank in Indianola, and the two became mutually engaged in the cattle business as the Pierce-Sullivan Pasture and Cattle Company, along with other enterprises.[18]

While he was on his "hunt for society" in Kansas, however, Pierce was also after bigger game. He journeyed to Omaha to meet Herman Kountze, one of the four remarkable Kountze brothers whose banking activities extended from New York to the Midwest and west to Omaha and Denver. Their two western offices were deeply involved in making loans to cattlemen. Pierce and the Kountze brothers found that they had many speculative interests in common—among them acquiring ranch lands by buying cheap railroad land-grant certificates that would allow them to buy whole sections in south Texas. Herman Kountze himself later came to visit Pierce in Texas, and together they inspected thousands of acres that might be bought with the railroad certificates or Republic of Texas land warrants owned by old Texas Revolution veterans who wished to sell them. After many complications and near ruptures, the Kountze brothers did purchase ranch lands adjacent to Pierce's holdings. Once allied with the Kountze brothers, Pierce abandoned his older New York financial agents without regret, and sadly in his old age broke his longtime association with Little Danny Sullivan in a truly bitter court fight.[19]

⚜ ⚜

Before we consider Shanghai Pierce's tempestuous evolution into a modern property-owning scientific cattleman during the 1880s and 1890s, we should look at the everyday workings of El Rancho Grande and Charlie Siringo's experience there as a brash young cowhand.

Let us start by noting who helped Shanghai and Jonathan operate the ranch. Somehow both, but Shanghai especially, identified and hired a cadre of truly loyal men. Two of the first and most enduring were Thomas C. F. (Tom) Nye, who recruited Charlie for the ranch, and Asa Dawdy. Both were local men who joined Shanghai early in their lives, branding maverick cattle and particularly the truly wild ones that retreated to woods and swamps in the daytime to escape maverickers. But Nye and Dawdy, as Siringo attests in his *A Texas Cowboy*, were innovative and ruthless in the ways they rounded up these mossyhorns.[20]

Siringo initially liked both men—Tom was decent and thoughtful and Dawdy was unceasingly good natured and talkative. On at least one occasion Pierce said in an affectionate way that Dawdy was "one of those happy-go-easy fellows who was always sticking his nose in everybody's business. He was as full of wind as myself, only a good deal more windier than I am." Pierce respected Dawdy as a trail boss but not in the selling of beeves. Dawdy eventually branched out on his own, but Shanghai knew he could always count on him.[21]

Tom Nye was loyal in more subtle ways. It was Nye and other ranchers who discovered that a local gang, dominated by four Lunn brothers, was hijacking their already branded cattle, killing them, boiling down the fat for tallow, and then selling the hides and tallow. He remained silent when the vigilante ranchers hanged the Lunns, All Jaw Smith, and the stranger, when they were caught red-handed with the hides bearing the brands of Pierce, B. Q. Ward, and Grimes. That was when, as we have already noted, Pierce suddenly departed for Kansas to "hunt up society."

Years later, when Pierce felt strong enough to encircle his old enemy Bing Grimes's holdings, and freeze him from access to unbranded cattle, in maneuvers too complex to describe here, Nye helped bring down the once large and affluent Grimes cattle empire. Grimes had insulted and cheated Shanghai when a young man, so the latter was determined to ruin Grimes. Although Grimes fought back, and at one point tried to encircle Pierce, he was bested by Shanghai both on the prairie and in court cases. In time Grimes accepted defeat and began a ranch in the Indian Territory.[22]

As suggested earlier, the open-range cattlemen did not legally own their spreads, and, of course, were engaged in a ruthless competitive free-for-all for the millions of unbranded cattle. But by the late seventies and early eighties, the big ranchers initiated what amounted to a modern version of the English enclosure movement by buying tracts of land, encircling the property of small farmers and ranchers, and forcing them to sell. Tom Nye, and, of course, friendly lawyers and judges were crucial to the success of this questionable operation. Nye even bought property elsewhere in the state for Pierce to use for holding cattle before shipment. Nye sometimes made shaky financial deals in Pierce's behalf that infuriated Shanghai, but he accepted Pierce's reprimands with humility and made restitution for his mistakes. To the end, Nye began his letters and messages to Pierce with "Dear Friend," and always sent his regards to Pierce's wife and daughter. Nye and Dawdy were not high-ranking staff, but Shanghai entrusted them to carry out many a questionable deal. Their loyalty was never in question.[23]

The most unusual and independent of those working closely with Shanghai for many years was Wiley Martin Kuykendall, one of the most happy men in the history of south Texas. Wiley Martin Kuykendall's grandfather, Robert H. Kuykendall, Sr., born in Kentucky but from a North Carolina family, was one of the first settlers to join Stephen F. Austin's colony, and was therefore one of the Old Three Hundred. Indeed, Wiley's grandfather preceded Austin, having already moved to the east bank of the Colorado when Austin's colony began. He was active as a fighter against the Karankawa Indians and of so much help to Austin, that in 1824 Austin granted him two leagues of land, one on either side of the Colorado. A severe head injury in an Indian fight eventually led to his death at age forty-two.[24]

The Kuykendall name was not about to disappear, however, for not only did Robert, Sr. have six children (among them Robert H. Jr., Wiley Kuykendall's father) but two of his brothers, Abner and Joseph, and several of their children qualified as members of Austin's Old Tree Hundred group.[25] Wiley's uncle, Jonathan Hampton Kuykendall (1815–1880) had studied law with William B. Travis for a time and along with his brother, Gibson, played a key role in defending Texas during the Texas Revolution. Jonathan Kuykendall became a journalist and newspaper editor; but the combination of being fluent in Spanish and being an attractive, outgoing public figure, with a keen interest in Texas history, archaeology, and anthropology, led him to publish insightful essays on Karankawa Indians and the minerals of Texas, and to attempt a history of Texas from Austin's colony to statehood. Unfortunately it was never published.[26]

All this is by way of saying that Wiley Kuykendall's credentials as a "genuine Texan" were not only impeccable, they were overwhelming. But this family past sat lightly on the young boy, born in Fort Bend County in 1839, who had lost his mother in 1846 and his father soon thereafter. A family descendant, Marshall E. Kuykendall, has provided us with an arresting summary of Wiley's early ears. At age ten Wiley left his home in Fort Bend County, riding on a mule behind a black servant, Lark, who eventually brought him to Matagorda, where he lived for a while with his grandmother, Susan T. Tone. Much like Charlie Siringo after him, he was enamored with cattle and ranching and was already punching cattle at age ten. Two years later twelve-year-old Wiley was trailing cattle to Missouri for cattleman Bill Hurden. When he was fifteen he again trailed cattle from Matagorda County to Missouri but the outfit he was with encountered so much hostility from Indians in the Indian Territory that they had to be escorted by United States soldiers.

These were the days before the Texas fever tick, which Texas longhorns carried, was known in Missouri and, of course, no quarantine laws existed. In 1857 Kuykendall found himself trailing a herd of six hundred head to Quincy, Illinois, a full decade prior to the opening of the Chisholm Trail to Kansas in 1867.[27]

Soon after Shanghai and Jonathan established El Rancho Grande in 1865, Wiley Kuykendall was one of their first recruits. He went to work for them as a range boss. Already experienced in trail driving, between 1869 and 1879 he made ten trail drives to Kansas. During those years not only did he handle the Pierce's cattle but herds for Bing Grimes as well. When the Civil War came, he joined the Confederate Army and like Jonathan Pierce, he too was sent west to the Brownsville area. His unit, Captain James C. Borden's Company D, Yagers Battalion of Texas Mounted Volunteers, also included his well-known uncle, Jonathan Hampton Kuykendall.[28]

"Mr. Wiley," as all members of the Pierce Ranch addressed him, was a workaholic when it came to the cattle industry. "As a boss," writes Chris Emmett, "he was harder than Shanghai." He rose early, had coffee and a pipe, and then went to the sleeping cowboys whether in the bunkhouse or in camp, and exclaimed: "come, boys, come. Get up and hear the little birds singing their sweet praises to God.' Then continuing in a loud and harsh voice, he shouted 'ALMIGHTY DAMN YOUR SOULS! GET UP!'"[29]

In those earlier years, Shanghai, Jonathan, Wiley, and Neptune Holmes, Shanghai's Black servant, worked as a team. Wiley himself took a liking to the Pierces' sister, Susan, who had been persuaded to leave Rhode Island and join her brother in Texas. When Shanghai learned that Wiley might join the family, he was furious, but Wiley and Susan, who appear to have been as strong minded as Shanghai, prevailed. They were married in 1869. Indeed, the two maintained their independence on the Colorado River until 1902 when they bought another ranch and property elsewhere. Wiley subsequently made other trail drives with other partners. In 1884 he helped the Pumphrey Brothers drive twelve thousand cattle to Wyoming Territory, and three years later headed a drive to Kansas.[30]

That "Mr. Wiley" was his own man was recalled by Charlie Siringo, who greatly admired him and became a lifelong friend. When branding cattle for Pierce, Kuykendall encouraged Siringo to put his own brand on some of the cattle "as a nest egg for the future." This "in house" conspiracy against Shanghai absolutely delighted Charlie.

When Shanghai was much older, he and Susan became so bitter toward one another that she took him to court over the disputed ownership of a cow. In the end, however, the Kuykendalls remained members of the family and were buried in Hawley Cemetery, near Deming Bridge, as Emmett writes, in the shadow of Shanghai Pierce's ten-foot statue of himself over his own grave.[31]

In time at least three other assistants became Pierce's trusted employees: two nephews from Rhode Island, George S. Gifford and Abel Pierce Borden, and Clay McSparrin. George Gifford was a lawyer who handled many of Pierce's legal and financial problems along with Pierce's able lawyer from Victoria, Fred C. Proctor. The clear favorite, however, was Abel Pierce Borden—named for Shanghai of course—who was always thinking ahead. He knew Pierce could be so set in his ways that he would resist intelligent change. It appears that Borden helped him move toward scientific breeding of cattle, to adopt barbed wire for fencing, and to use cedar trees on some of his property for fence posts—not just for himself but to sell. Borden also saw that rich bottomlands owned by Pierce should be farmed, and before Pierce had died, he was raising farm products with convict labor on a plantation in northeast Matagorda County. It was Borden who realized that well-watered flat low-lying property could produce rice, and today one of the major crops in Matagorda County is rice.[32]

In concert with Shanghai's intense support, Borden's greatest accomplishment, however, was to find an alternate breed of cattle that would be immune to Texas fever, which Texas cattle carried but were not affected by. But the ticks on them could spread to non-Texas cattle and kill them. As a result Texas cattle were eventually forbidden to enter the state of Kansas. After trying many alternatives, Pierce and Borden found the solution to be the importation of Brahma cattle from India. Brahma cattle, which had also been imported and bred by other Texas ranchers, became a success, and helped perpetuate the ranching legacy of the Pierce estate, along with the discovery of oil on the property. In effect A. P. Borden carried on the Pierce name into the twentieth and twenty-first centuries.[33]

Another member of the loyal Pierce team was J. Clay McSparrin, who worked his way up from trail boss to top trusted friend. In Shanghai's later years, "Mr. Clay," as McSparrin was called, was with Pierce constantly. According to Emmett, it appears that he, with A. P. Borden, were both really in charge of ranch operations. Perhaps symbolic of the friendship was the fact that when Mrs. McSparrin appealed to Pierce to donate a beef for a barbecue to raise money for a church, Pierce himself paid for the building of the church, at which his own funeral was later conducted.[34]

As we have already seen, Pierce had an uncanny talent for spotting able, trustworthy people. One of these was certainly Fred C. Proctor, a young lawyer in Victoria whom Shanghai always called "my counselor," followed by the sarcastic comment that "I am his most lucrative client." Proctor handled Pierce's legal affairs until his death and was involved in settling the extremely complicated Pierce estate.[35]

It must be clear by now that Shanghai Pierce ran a modern business using a patriarchal system: he and his partner brother were married to the two Lacy sisters. His ranch boss, Wiley Kuykendall, was married to his sister, Susan. His nephews, Frank Gifford and A. P. Borden, were an intimate part of the El Rancho Grande operation. He was sustained by Black workers in the home, on the ranch, and on the trail. In effect, it was a brilliant adaptation of the earlier entrepreneurial plantations of pre–Civil War Caney Creek southern planters.

El Rancho Grande's resemblance to a large Southern plantation becomes even more striking when one sees how many Black Americans were in residence. Elvira Miller, called "Old Vi," was the cook for the Pierce household. Ida Malone was the cook in nephew A. P. Borden's home. Neptune Holmes, Shanghai's loyal servant, who traveled with him on horseback for thirty-five years, lived on the ranch with his wife and nine children. Holmes's family tradition says that Neptune's mother, Sarah, worked for one of the Pierce brothers.[36]

In addition at least seven other Black Americans worked on Pierce's holding. As Teresa Palomo Acosta has noted, "Black cowboys predominated in ranching sections of the Coastal Plains between the Sabine and Guadalupe rivers."[37] Pierce, in fact, bought the fine pre–Civil War plantation of John Duncan and appointed a trusted friend, John McCroskey, to run it. If the clues are accurate, it was very much an operation with Black workers. Cotton and sugarcane gave way to cattle, and they in turn were supplanted by farming, rice, and oil.[38] Shanghai Pierce was lucky; he had few of the emotional hang-ups of the Southerners in Matagorda. Although he was contemptuous of Black Americans and constantly made racist remarks, he used Black workers, Mexican vaqueros, young teenagers, and Civil War veterans to keep his business going. Moreover, the operation was big time—it involved huge financial outlays, dealing with banks and railroads, and the legal system. Reconstruction woes hit Texas as much as any Southern state, but Reconstruction politics did not stop the cattlemen, whose chief market ironically was the Yankee North via the pack-ing houses of Chicago. Pierce's attitude was the equivalent of the hardheaded railroad builder, or of John D. Rockefeller or an Andrew Carnegie mixed with a high percentage of family paternalism.

What is so impressive is that Pierce had his equals in other ranchers: Samuel W. Allen and his early partner, Allen Poole, operated a ranch and cattle business south of Houston that lasted as a family business for over a century (1840–1945). George W. Littlefield, Dillard Rocker Fant, and George Saunders himself were big-time successes. Given these people and the booming of the cattle industry, the grim postwar picture of Texas needs some adjustment. Moreover, the romantic images of open-range ranching with the cowboy as the centerpiece of the story, calls for a broader, less romantic, perspective.

Certainly a major example of Shanghai's modern approach to ranching was his lobbying to get a railroad through his property. Finally in the early 1880s, a line with the imposing name "the New York, Texas, and Mexican Railway," which never made it to New York or Mexico, was built between Rosenberg Junction (with a connection to Houston and Galveston) and Victoria to the west. It ran through Pierce's property, where he insisted there be at least three depot stops: Borden, Shanghai, and Pierce Stations. He paid for the latter himself. According to Emmett, Pierce's relations with the railroads were always crisis-ridden, but the line did provide a way to ship cattle to Galveston, Houston, and north.[39]

Ironically, it was that quintessential cowboy, Charlie Siringo, who has given us an insight into the practical, hardheaded workings of the Texas cattle industry from the inside. It was a ruthless business characterized by danger, hard work, and heroic feats—of which the cowboy was a vital but not the only crucial player.[40]

II: ENTER CHARLIE SIRINGO

When Charlie Siringo was hired by Tom Nye to work at El Rancho Grande, he was sent first to "Palacios Point where the firm had an outside ranch and where they were feeding a large lot of cow ponies for spring work."[44]

Later the new hires moved on to the ranch headquarters on Palacios Creek. It was there that Siringo first saw Shanghai Pierce returning from Mexico with about three hundred head of wild Spanish ponies, destined to become cow ponies, which the teenage new hires tried to break and tame.[42]

Pierce soon sent three parties of cowboys to a different area for a period of two months to brand and round up wild cattle. It cannot be overemphasized that wild cattle in the Texas coastal plains reproduced so rapidly that their number doubled in size every four years. In short, there were mavericks or unbranded and wild cattle as far as the eye could see. Siringo was in Tom Nye's outfit, which was sent to "work west in Jackson and Lavaca counties," west and northwest of Matagorda County. The outfit had been ordered to gather a herd of "trail" beeves by branding mavericks for sale to a Mr. Black, an unsuspecting Kansas cattle buyer who planned to take them to a Kansas railhead. Charlie reports that while they gathered some 1,100, Black lost them all on the trail long before they reached Kansas because they were so wild and unmanageable. It was here that Charlie learned one of the first tricks of the trade. Once a herd was sold, you were no longer responsible, even though you knew the cattle would run amok and probably come back to their home area—in some cases to be sold again. This did not bother Siringo, who had a contempt for Kansas buyers—indeed, Charlie derisively called Black a Kansas "short horn." It seems likely that Kansans were seen as Yankees and therefore deserved tricking.[43]

When Nye's outfit returned to ranch headquarters in August, Siringo learned that the Pierce brothers had sold out their interest to the huge Galveston-based firm of Allen, Poole and Company for $110,000 in gold. Allen and Poole had shipped cattle for the Pierces from Indianola to New Orleans and Cuba ever since the close of the Civil War. Although he does not mention it in his *A Texas Cowboy*, Siringo must have found out that Shanghai had fled to Kansas City to avoid being called as a witness to the hanging of the Lunn brothers. The ranch itself had been moved down the Tres Palacios Creek and was now run by John Moore, who was a no-nonsense boss.[44]

Two weeks later, Siringo and a crew pulled out for a new assignment. This time the outfit's boss was Wiley Kuykendall, which pleased Charlie greatly. The strange mix of teenagers, Black Americans, and Mexican vaqueros that made up these outfits inevitably led to confrontations and fights. Siringo, still a wild youth himself, was punished by Tom Nye on his first job for attacking a Black cowboy with a club and for getting into knife fights. This time the outfit was sent out in September to Lavaca County to brand and round up cattle. There were Blacks in Mr. Wiley's outfit, too, but this time Siringo had reason to be grateful to

"Jack," a Black cowboy who rescued him after Siringo's horse got tangled up in his rope and fell on him. "I couldn't free myself until retrieved by 'Jack,' a Negro man who was near at hand."[45]

The rounding up of cattle in Lavaca County proved to be about as dangerous and brutal as one could envisage. The wild cattle came out of woods and thick brush only at night to feed on the lush prairie grasses; at daybreak they headed for the woods for safety. Kuykendall's strategy was to place his cowboys between the cattle on the prairie and the brush and head them off, roping the lead steers and tying them down until other cattle could be diverted. In some cases a tough bull might get loose from the roper and go through the herd toward the brush, followed by the herd, and endangering the cowboys. Siringo reports that sometimes they sewed the eyelids of fierce bulls together, so they could not see to lead. By the time the threads had become loose or rotted, the animal had become manageable and stayed with the herd.[46]

The fall and winter were also lively times for Siringo. Just before Christmas, John Moore sent Kuykendall's outfit to ship cattle at Palacios Point where, as Charlie recalls, "a Morgan steamship landed twice a week to take on cattle for the New Orleans market." The loading often kept them busy until midnight, when the outfit would repair to George Burkheart's "store," really a saloon, and fill up on "red eye."[47]

Moore must have considered Kuykendall's outfit one of the best, because after it had loaded cattle all winter, he sent them up the Colorado River to Wharton and Colorado counties to brand mavericks. Once done there, they returned to the home ranch in July, only to be ordered west to Jackson County again. One can guess that after a full year with a congenial, able veteran boss like "Mr. Wiley" the outfit had come to be a team. Kuykendall himself put his own brand on some of the choicest mavericks, and then allowed his men to brand a few. It is clear that no one was happier doing this than Charlie Siringo.[48]

Inevitably John Moore found out what Kuykendall was doing and fired him. At that point Siringo also decided to leave, but when he went to settle up at the ranch store, run by a very business-minded Irishman called Hunky-Dorey Brown, he learned that while he had earned $300, he had bought so many things "on tick" that his bill was $299.25!! Taking his remaining 75 cents Charlie splurged on a can of peaches, and went to work at the W. B. Grimes slaughterhouse, where some two hundred cattle a day were killed for their hides and tallow.[49]

The mass killing of cattle, skinning them, and boiling their meat for tallow was probably even a bit too much even for tough young Charlie. When Grimes asked him to take care of his stock horses away from the packinghouse, Charlie readily accepted the new job. It also gave him some time to skin dead cattle and to put his brand on a few mavericks. But being unable to keep his cattle together, he quit Grimes's employ and moved up to Tres Palacios Creek to live with Horace Yeamans, whom he had known since he was a boy on Matagorda Peninsula.

Clearly Charlie was searching for some base and stability when he retreated to the Yeamans' farm. He promptly fell in love with the Yeamans' youngest daughter, Sally, who was only fourteen, but the strict, religious household not only made Siringo behave, he tells us he "got broke of swearing."[50] Moreover, Siringo struck up a close friendship with Horace Yeamans, Jr., with the result that the two of them became partners "in the skinning business." During the harsh winter of 1872–1873 cattle had died by the thousands. Siringo, already used to animal deaths and slaughter, described the scene without emotion. He reported that cattle on the bay shore moved southward to find warmer weather, but having reached the north shore of the bay could go no farther; they died by the thousands, so thick that you could walk on top of their bodies. In other parts of the county, cattle seeking to cross a bayou got stuck in the mud and died, thus forming a bridge of carcasses that other cattle walked across to get to solid land.[51]

Siringo, always practical, took advantage of the thousands of unclaimed dead cattle by skinning them and selling the hides in Indianola for a princely sum of $114. Again, typical of his well-meaning, if sometimes fragmented impulses, he bought a good saddle and sent his mother $25, having finally learned her St. Louis address from an old peninsula friend who had received a letter from Charlie's sister. Feeling flush with his $114, he decided to become a horse trader but that endeavor was not a success. He returned to the skinning business with Horace Yeamans, Jr., during the winter of 1873–1874 while continuing to put his brand on mavericks.[53]

By now, Siringo appears to have had every experience a cowboy could have in the local cattle business, but still curious and restless, in the spring of 1874 "I hired to Leander Ward of Jackson County to help gather a herd of steers for the Muckleroy Bros., who were going to drive them to Kansas. I also made a contract with Muckleroy's boss, Tom

Merril to go up the trail with him. . . . My wages were thirty-five dollars per month and all expenses, including railroad fare back home."[53]

Siringo's first Chisholm Trail experience was not a happy one. A storm came up soon after they were on the trail, and despite trying to calm the cattle with songs, they stampeded. Moreover, the men of the Muckleroy Brothers outfit consisted mostly of "short horns" from Kansas, which to Siringo meant that they were naïve and incompetent. Mistakes were made, and a second stampede, due to a storm, occurred. Siringo and several of the cowboys exhibited such a contempt for Jim, one of the Muckleroy Brothers, that Siringo, Tom Merril, Henry Coats, and George Gifford were all fired. It was characteristic of Siringo, however, that while hating Jim Muckleroy, he liked the other brother, Charlie, and became fast friends with Charlie's son, Pat, who was a member of the outfit. When Charlie was fired, Pat not only joined him on the railroad trip back to Texas, he invited him to his home in Columbus, Texas, on the Colorado River some seventy-five miles north of Tres Palacios. Celebrating with Pat's friends, Siringo soon ran out of money and only got home after he encountered Asa Dawdy, who was at Columbus loading cattle on cars to ship to Galveston, and agreed to help him.

Like many other young cowboys, Charlie Siringo at age nineteen was not sure about who he was or where he was going. As J. Frank Dobie said of him, he was never thought but all action. Once back in the Tres Palacios area, he worked briefly for Grimes again, before deciding that his future lay in buying a schooner and using it to ferry merchandise or passengers in the Matagorda Bay area. Always fascinated by quick get-rich schemes, he took his schooner down to Matagorda Peninsula, bought melons from an old friend, and sold them outside of the Grimes packing house to workers just coming off their shift. Then in oyster season he repeated the scheme, selling bay oysters to Grimes's factory hands for "a dollar a barrel in the shell."[54]

By then Siringo had developed a far more ambitious scheme; he would take his boat overland to the Colorado River, and sell tobacco, jewelry, and knickknacks to the ex-slave communities living along both sides of the river. In return he would swap his wares for hides, pecans, and other goods produced by the Black residents. In a series of hilarious miscalculations, Siringo found himself and his boat marooned on the prairie west of the Colorado with no money to hire oxen to pull it farther. Anthony Moore, whom Siringo described as "a gentleman of color," agreed to buy the stranded schooner "right where she lay on the open prairie."[55]

Always going back to persons he respected and liked, Siringo then hired once again to Wiley Kuykendall, "who was busy buying and shipping beeves at Houston." Kuykendall agreed to pay him $25 a month. Abandoning Mr. Wiley after New Year's, Siringo began skinning cattle and branding mavericks at Cash's Creek close to his old friend Horace Yeamans. Siringo's aggressive mavericking angered at least one prominent rancher, who appears to have hired one Sam Grant, a professional killer, who was known to have murdered Blacks, and it was also rumored, illegitimate maverickers, of whom Siringo was certainly one. One night while out on the prairie Grant accosted and shot Siringo after making sure Siringo's pistol was not close to him. Grant aimed at Siringo's heart, but fortunately Charlie had his knee in front of him and the bullet hit and lodged in the knee instead. It looks as if Grant was preparing to shoot Siringo a second time when a Black cowhand named Lige appeared. Grant lamely explained that his gun had unexpectedly gone off and rushed away saying that he would send a doctor to aid Siringo from the Deming's Bridge Post Office, at the old Rancho Grande Headquarters. A doctor finally came late at night and cut the bullet out of his knee. Somehow Lige got Siringo to the Yeamans' ranch. His recovery was slow, but once he was able to move around on crutches, he went to Tres Palacios to board.

At this point, Jonathan Pierce, that thoughtful benefactor of Siringo, asked him to come to his ranch to complete his recovery. Pierce then made him a proposition: attend school while you are recovering and in return be paid to take care of my eight-year-old boy; Shanghai's twelve-year-old daughter, Mamie; and an older cousin, by taking them by horseback to the school several miles away. Inevitably, as he had in New Orleans, Charlie had a fight with the schoolmaster and left the Pierce ranch.[56]

Still adrift he decided to go to Houston to attend the Texas State Fair and to look up his aunt Mary White in Houston, where she now ran a boarding house. Her husband, James McClain, took Siringo to the State Fair, where he saw Jefferson Davis, showed him the sights of Houston, and loaned him his house and buggy to use. Later, Siringo also visited his uncle Nicholas White in Galveston, who gave him a Spencer Carbine, which he said he had "captured from a yankee while out scouting during the war."[57]

Of course by this time Siringo was out of money, and so he went to the Allen, Poole and Company on Simms Bay and hired to a Mr. Joe Davis, who had "the contract furnishing beef to the Gulf, Colorado and Santa Fe R.R. which was just building out of Galveston." One assumes he identified himself to Davis as a former cowhand of Allen's one-time partner, Shanghai Pierce.

When Charlie went back to Tres Palacios, having recovered from his wound, he discovered that his mother, after having learned from Charlie that he had been shot, had returned to Texas to care for him. Undoubtedly thrilled to see his mother again, he decided to build a home for her; but just as the project was underway, the famous 1875 hurricane struck Indianola and the entire bay area. The ferocious storm not only wrecked the entire city, but destroyed the Morris house in which the Siringos were staying as guests. The Morrises and the Siringos found themselves floating in waist-deep water. Undaunted, the Morris family moved farther up Cash's Creek, started a new ranch, and Siringo built his mother a shanty nearby. For lumber he used the remains of an old torn-down house that "I bought from Mr. John Pierce on 'tick.'" Once again Jonathan Pierce had come to Siringo's rescue.[58]

Realizing that he had better find regular employment, Charlie hired to W. B. Grimes to go "up the trail" at $30 per month. He must have been pleased at the prospect because the trail boss was his old friend Asa Dawdy. The outfit consisted of a cook and twenty-five riders, each with "six head of good horses to the man." They were to drive 2500 head of "old mossey horn steers" to Wichita, Kansas.

Everything seemed to go well except for swollen streams. The first ones were successfully crossed, but when they reached the Salt Fork of the Canadian River close to the Kansas state line, it was storming and the river rose so rapidly that although the cooks and the two chuck wagons got across the river, the cattle could not. Indeed, the river did not go down for several days, which meant that Dawdy and his outfit had no food for a week except fresh-killed unsalted beef. Finally, Asa Dawdy, Siringo, two cowboys, and "Negro Gabe" spotted an army unit across a nearby smaller stream, also waiting for the Salt Fork to subside. The Dawdy outfit and the soldiers shouted to one another over the small wild stream about food. The army officers said they could help if the Dawdy outfit would come and get it.

Siringo, being an expert swimmer, was named to make the crossing, keeping on his underwear because wives of the officers were in the army camp. Meanwhile soldiers threw biscuits over to Dawdy and his group. Siringo took flour, salt, and coffee in a washtub borrowed from the wives and landed a half-mile downstream, so swift was the current. Siringo wrote that the desperate men cooked dough on a stick over the fire, so anxious were they for bread. Finally on the eighth day the men and cattle got across the Canadian River to find that "the cooks had been having a soft time."[59]

On July 4, 1876, after three months on the trail, Dawdy's outfit reached the Ninnescah River some thirty miles west of Wichita. From there most of the boys went on to Wichita to take the train to Houston as the quickest way to get home. But for some reason Siringo decided to take a job with one of the three herds of eight hundred cattle each that Grimes decided to hold until the fall. Each herd had a cook and a chuck wagon, four riders, a boss, and five horses to the rider.

Siringo soon discovered that his own herd was near a family where two young women—from the East, "damsels" he called them—were visiting. Not only did he call on them constantly, he proposed to one as she was shucking fresh ears of corn. Apparently his words were so shocking to the young lady that she barraged him with ears of corn, one of which gave him a black eye. To make matters worse, he received a letter from his Texas girlfriend, whom he thought he loved, saying that she "was married to my old playmate, Billy Williams"![60]

Feeling completely rejected, Siringo considered migrating to the Black Hills, then the scene of a huge gold rush, but had no money to do so. He then drifted west to Kiowa County on the Medicine Lodge River where he took a job guarding 2500 Texas steers. Still dissatisfied, he decided to spend the winter trapping furs, but after investing in traps, he had no success, and every dugout he built for himself collapsed on him. Finally he decided to move south along the Cimarron River until he could turn east to intersect with the Chisholm Trail. Between making small cash by running his horse, Whiskey-Peat (Siringo's various spellings of the horse's name were numerous) in races, and cadging food and shelter from friendly army camps, Indian agencies, and hospitable settlers, he got back to Texas.[61]

In May 1877, however, he landed a job with Captain George W. Littlefield of Gonzales, Texas. Littlefield was one of the most impressive and successful cattlemen in the history of Texas and New Mexico. Littlefield was sending 3,500 head of "stock cattle" to Dodge City, Kansas. The outfit reached Dodge City on July 3, 1877, where Siringo went on a royal drunk, as he put it, to "whoop em up Liza's Jane."[62]

Whether it was by accident or deliberate decision, Charlie did not choose to return to Matagorda County. Instead on July 5, he "hired" to David T. Beals of the Boston firm of Bates and Beals to help drive a herd of 2,500 steers to the Texas Panhandle. Bates and Beals had already established a vast open-range ranching operation in eastern Colorado, but felt that they must move out of the path of the encroaching line of settlers. Colorado had become a state in 1876 and in 1877 silver was discovered in Leadville. It was boom time for the new state. Looking around they knew that in 1876 the warring Comanches in the Texas Panhandle had gone onto reservations and, further, that the vast southern buffalo herd there had been largely slaughtered by professional hide hunters. Those two developments had opened the Texas Panhandle to cattle ranching. There the nutritious mesquite grass was as ideal for cattle as it had been for bison. Not only was it a fine forage for cattle in the spring and summer, in the winter, though turning to yellow hay, it retained all its nutritious qualities. Here in the Texas Panhandle the last great era of open-range ranching would take place.

Although the saga of cowboys and ranchers in the open-range cattle industry has been told in thousands of books and articles and hundreds of novels and films, not many twenty-two-year-old cowboys had experienced so many facets of the industry as Charlie Siringo. He had rounded up and branded wild cattle, been in the hide and tallow trade, started his own herd by mavericking, had loaded cattle onto steamships and driven them up the Chisholm Trail three times; he had worked for four notable cattlemen, Shanghai and Jonathan Pierce, W. B. Grimes, and now George Littlefield. He was acquainted with the vast operation of Allen, Poole and Company, and had been shot by a would-be assassin. His early years had focused on the everyday operations of the open-range cattle industry of coastal Texas rather than on the saga of going up the Chisholm Trail. By acquainting us with the movers and shakers, as well as the cowboys, Siringo, in his *A Texas Cowboy*, has rendered a great service.

Yet Charlie Siringo's greatest adventures as a cowboy were yet to come. These action-packed years began in 1877 when he "hired" to Bates and Beals and went to work for them on the vast LX Ranch. So extraordinary were his experiences on the Texas Panhandle frontier that the Texas cowboy began to be a Texas historian, a side profession that occupied him for the rest of his life and produced no less than seven autobiographical books.

MOST OF THE TIME WE WERE SOLITARY ADVENTURERS IN A
GREAT LAND AS FRESH AND NEW AS A SPRING MORNING,
AND WE WERE FREE AND FULL OF THE ZEST OF DARERS.

—*Charles Goodnight*

SIRINGO, "THE SENIOR FOREMAN," ONE OF THE MOST EXPERT
COWBOY RIDERS, ROPERS, AND GUNMEN IN THE PANHANDLE,
TAUGHT ME THE TRICKS OF THE TRADE, AND A FRIENDSHIP WAS
FORMED THAT WAS CONTINUED TO THE DAY OF HIS DEATH IN 1928.

—*Dr. Henry F. Hoyt,* A Frontier Doctor, *108–9*

I WILL PAY $500 REWARD TO ANY PERSON OR PERSONS
WHO WILL CAPTURE WILLIAM BONNY, ALIAS [BILLY] THE KID,
AND DELIVER HIM TO ANY SHERIFF OF NEW MEXICO,
SATISFACTORY PROOFS OF IDENTITY WILL BE REQUIRED.

—*Lew Wallace, Governor of New Mexico*

IT WAS NATURAL . . . THAT EASTERN AND FOREIGN CAPITAL ON
A LARGE SCALE SHOULD SEEK A SHARE OF PROFIT FROM THIS
LUCRATIVE CATTLE TRADE. NO SECTION OF COUNTRY OFFERED
GREATER OPPORTUNITY THAN DID NORTHWEST TEXAS. THE BUFFALO
HAD JUST RECENTLY BEEN KILLED OUT AND THE INDIANS HAD BEEN
REMOVED TO THE RESERVATIONS AND, AS RUMOR HAD IT, THERE WAS
FREE GRASS IN ABUNDANCE AND LAND COULD BE BOUGHT FOR A SONG.
CORPORATIONS WERE FORMED IN THE NORTH AND EAST, BONDS
AND DEBENTURES WERE SOLD IN ENGLAND AND SCOTLAND AND . . .
MANY LARGE CORPORATE CONCERNS HAD ENTERED INTO THE
BUSINESS OF CATTLE RANCHING IN NORTHWEST TEXAS.

—*L. E. Sheffy, "British Pounds and British Purebreeds," 59–60*

CHAPTER FIVE

The Great Adventure

CHARLIE SIRINGO AND BILLY THE KID

ON THE TEXAS PANHANDLE

FRONTIER, 1877–1882

BETWEEN 1870 AND 1890 THE TEXAS PANHANDLE FRONTIER WAS probably the most classic example of all western nineteenth-century frontiers. It was the scene of a brutal Indian war between unconquered Comanches and the United States Army from 1871 to 1875. During those same few years, professional buffalo hunters wiped out most of the great southern buffalo herd of millions of beasts, creating a faunal void into which ranchers moved with hundreds of thousands of cattle. Overnight the Texas Panhandle Frontier came to epitomize the popular romantic image of the Wild West at its wildest and most colorful. Again, with startling speed, it became the center of the largest cattle ranches in the United States.[1] Their owners included famous cattlemen like Charles Goodnight and George W. Littlefield, and incredibly successful Chicago businessmen like the John V. Farwell family of Chicago, owners of the XIT Ranch, the largest in the Panhandle and possibly in the world. W. H. "Deacon" Bates and David Beals, two Bostonians, bought and developed the LX Ranch on the Canadian River area some twenty miles north of the future town of Amarillo. One of the first cowhands they hired in 1877 was Charlie Siringo.

The Panhandle was an international frontier in that English and Scottish investors bought some of the ranches. Many of the cowboys who drifted into the area came from all over, and more than a few had a violent past. William C. (Outlaw Bill) Moore of Bates and Beals's LX Ranch, having been a brilliant manager of the huge Swan Land and Cattle Company in Wyoming, had fled to Texas after having killed his Black coachman there; and before that, had killed his brother-in-law in California.[2]

On the LX Ranch alone could be found two cowboys who were future authors: Charlie Siringo and Dr. Henry Hoyt, and a future sheriff, Jim East, who was to become famous for chasing and helping capture Billy the Kid. And last and soon to be the most notorious was William Antrim (alias Billy Bonney), soon to become known as Billy the Kid, who spent a summer at the LX. Although reputed to be a killer and cattle and horse thief, this youthful boylike teenager had an affable but temperamental nature. He and his small group of friends, who had drifted over from New Mexico, made for lively times on the LX and in the saloons and dancehalls of Tascosa, the nearest town. It was only after the Kid and his companions (they were not yet a gang) had stolen cattle from the LX and other nearby ranches that Jim East and Siringo, along with other cowboys, were ordered by Bill Moore to track down the Kid and recover the cattle. But more of that saga later.

The dramatic history of the Panhandle Frontier has also inspired three of Texas's most famous historians to write about the Great Plains and the Panhandle. In 1931 Walter Prescott Webb's classic *The Great Plains* appeared. It so seized the imagination of historians and the public about this last frontier that it has been called the most influential book in western history in the twentieth century! Meanwhile Webb's good friend J. Frank Dobie had already written a charming story of ranching on the plains in his delightful *A Vaquero of the Brush Country* in 1929, which helped launch his career as Texas's most popular historical and literary figure. Yet a third friend of Webb and Dobie was a cattleman turned historian, J. Evetts Haley, Sr., who published articles on cowboys, wrote a splendid history of the XIT Ranch in 1929, and later a compelling biography, *Charles Goodnight: Cowman and Plainsman*, in 1936, thought by many to be "the best biography about a cowman ever written." Although pursuing his career as a rancher, Haley helped found the Panhandle-Plains Historical Society and the Panhandle-Plains Historical Museum at Canyon, Texas, in 1932.[3] To anyone interested in cowboys or cattle ranching, the museum is an invaluable resource. All three men recognized Siringo as an authority on the cowboy; Dobie and Haley interviewed him and wrote articles about him.

Up to the 1870s the Texas Panhandle was the domain of the Comanche Indians and their allies the Kiowa-Apache, who had so successfully held off American conquest, and had accepted reservation life in Oklahoma only after the close of the bitter Red River Indian War of 1874–1875. They were forced to do so because ruthless white and Indian buffalo hunters had killed millions of bison for their hides; but that savage butchery had also wiped out the Comanches' main source of food. The hunters operated out of Mobeetie near Fort Elliott. The latter, originally established as outposts against Indians in 1867, had become the headquarters for the hide trade with army officers and soldiers operating as middlemen and shippers of the skins east. It has been estimated that in 1877 between one hundred thousand and two hundred thousand hides came through Fort Griffin alone.

The historian J. Frank Dobie, quoting John Young, described Fort Griffin in 1878 as

> the worst hole I have ever been in. The population at
> this time was perhaps five thousand people, most of
> them soldiers, murderers, wild women, buffalo hunters,
> altogether the most mongrel and the hardest-looking
> crew that it was possible to assemble. The fort proper
> and a big store were up on a hill. The "Flats" where
> every house was either a saloon, a gambling den, or a
> dance hall, generally all three combined. No man who
> valued his life would go here unarmed or step out alone
> into the darkness. If about daylight he walked down to
> the river he might see a man hanging from the cottonwood
> trees with a placard on his back saying, "Horse Thief
> No. 8"—or whatever the latest number was.[4]

The defeat of the Comanches in the Red River War in 1875 allowed Spanish Americans from New Mexico, some of whom had known the Texas Panhandle for many decades as *comancheros*, or traders with the Comanches, to expand their pastoral sheep industry onto the Staked Plains and to found Tascosa, originally a peaceful Spanish-Mexican village boasting the presence of Casimero Romero, José Tafoya, and others. With the coming of the Anglo cattlemen, however, Tascosa was to become a major supply town, full of freight wagons from Dodge City, Kansas, or Springer, New Mexico, along with cowboys, merchants, saloons, and a redlight district.5

But the Panhandle's real heyday came when large ranchers and their cowboys moved their cattle in from Colorado and south Texas to create the truly classic open-range cattle industry that has remained the popular symbol of the "era of the cattleman" in American history to this day.

The Panhandle cattle frontier blossomed after the famous Kansas cattle towns of Abilene, Wichita, Ellsworth, Dodge City, and Caldwell had been receiving cattle from south Texas for nearly a decade, and thus did not use the Chisholm Trail. Instead the Panhandle ranchers pioneered their own trails from Tascosa to Dodge and Caldwell, and sent other cattle westward into eastern New Mexico to Springer, where they could be shipped on the Atchison, Topeka and Santa Fe.6 Still other routes moved vast herds to the northern cattle ranches of Wyoming and Montana in the 1880s and 1890s. It was on these lesser-known trails to Dodge City and Caldwell that Siringo was to herd cattle going to market over and over again between 1877 and 1882.

A word of caution: local, western, and national historians understandably have been taken with the dramatic story of the Chisholm Trail and the other south-north trails, with the often harrowing experiences of heroic young cowboys, and the violence in the cattle towns where Bat Masterson, Wild Bill Hickok, and a host of known gunmen congregated. As a result, with some notable exceptions, they have put less stress on the fascinating story of the development of the ranching industry in the Great Plains by brilliant businessmen, ranchers, bankers, and trail contractors who were the initial movers and shakers, whether on the ranch, in the cattle towns, in banks at Abilene, Topeka, Omaha, St. Louis, or in Chicago, New York, and Boston. Although Charlie Siringo was totally fascinated by the story of fellow cowboys, Billy the Kid, and other outlaws, he also came to know and appreciate the lesser-known business history of the cattle industry. Hence his accounts are not only valuable, they provide a broader context—even an explanation for some of the most colorful and violent episodes in the turbulent history of this last Old West.

✦   ✦

As a prologue let us begin with the career of a shrewd and successful Hispanic sheep rancher from the Las Vegas area of New Mexico: Casimero Romero (1833–1912), who was the son of a Spanish immigrant to Mexico in 1801. Somehow Casimero made his way north into Mora County, New Mexico, where he became a comanchero—that is, a person who traded with the Comanche Indians by going out to the Texas Staked Plains to designated locations with goods to exchange for horses, buffalo hides, or even children taken captive on raids into Mexico. With his profits Romero invested in New Mexico's traditional major industry—sheep ranching.

Always watching for new opportunities, Romero realized that with the removal of the Comanches to reservations, the Panhandle was open to white settlement. Thus in the fall of 1876 Romero gathered his family, friends, and other families to pioneer in west Texas. "Their caravan," writes H. Allen Anderson, "included twelve ox-drawn freight wagons, 100 peons, 3,000 Romero sheep and another 1,500 sheep belonging to Agapito Sandoval who accompanied them."[7]

After choosing a site on Atascosa Creek—soon to be called "Tascosa," Romero built a large adobe house, which boasted carpets from Dodge City and furniture from Las Vegas. Far more than just a sheep rancher, he raised crops through irrigation and acquired a herd of longhorns, and later dairy cattle. Romero's was a traditional Mexican hacienda set in the vast lonely Panhandle.

Always willing to engage in new ventures he not only drove his sheep and cattle to Dodge City, he became a freighter on the trail to Dodge as well. As H. Allen Anderson has noted, he actually moved to Dodge City in the 1800s and established the St. James Hotel there—an establishment at which Shanghai Pierce stayed when in Dodge. When the freight business began to decline, Romero cut his losses and hauled goods to local ranches, while continuing to operate his own ranch.[8] However, Tascosa itself began to decline after the railroad bypassed it for the town of Amarillo to the south and increasing pressure from Anglo cattlemen during the 1880s pushed the hundreds of early Hispanic sheep men out, many of them returning to New Mexico. Indeed, that is what Romero himself eventually did, although he did not sell his Panhandle ranch until 1896. After returning to Bard, New Mexico, he started yet another sheep ranch on land he had purchased three years before. There he lived until his death in 1912.[9]

⨦ ⨦

One of the legendary figures in the era of Anglo cattlemen was Charles Goodnight, who established his JA Ranch in Palo Duro Canyon. Born in 1836 of a pioneering farm family in Illinois, when he was only nine "he rode bareback from Illinois to Texas." "He was hunting with Caddo Indians beyond the frontier at thirteen, launching into the cattle business at twenty, guiding Texas Rangers at twenty-four, blazing cattle trails two thousand miles at forty, establishing a ranch three hundred miles beyond the frontier at forty, and at forty-five dominating nearly twenty million acres of range in the interest of order."[10]

Totally at home on the frontier, he first ran cattle in the rough Cross Timbers region; and when the Colorado gold rush began between 1860 and 1861, he joined a neighboring rancher, Oliver Loving, to send cattle to the hungry gold miners in the Denver area. Thus began a lifelong collaboration with Loving, who was as bold and intrepid an entrepreneur as Goodnight.[11]

On the eve of the Civil War Goodnight joined the Texas Rangers to fight hostile Indians and helped rescue the white captive Cynthia Ann Parker, mother of Chief Quanah Parker, from the Comanches. During the war Goodnight served with a Texas frontier regiment charged with maintaining a set of stations along the frontier of settlement between the Red River and the Rio Grande. Meanwhile, Loving, who like Goodnight was an ardent Confederate, was commissioned to drive cattle to Confederate troops along the Mississippi.

By the end of the Civil War, both men were desperate for a market for their cattle. Rather than look east to the Kansas railheads and Chicago, they turned west to Fort Sumner, New Mexico, where the federal troops under General James Carleton had located eight thousand Navajos and Indians of other tribes at what was really a prisoner-of-war camp at the Bosque Redondo. Loving and Goodnight drove their cattle to Fort Sumner, forging what came to be known as the Goodnight-Loving Trail. The trail began in Young County, Texas, followed the Butterfield Overland stagecoach route, then ran southwest to Horsehead Crossing on the Pecos River where it turned north to Fort Sumner. Later it was extended further north to Colorado.[12]

Once at Fort Sumner the two men sold their cattle for $12,000 in gold. Knowing that they were on to a good thing, Loving then drove stock cattle up to Denver while Goodnight returned to Texas to gather another herd. The two men decided to establish a ranch in New Mexico south of Fort Sumner. In the process they came to know John Chisum— himself a cattle king in New Mexico. From there they continued to supply cattle both to Fort Sumner and Santa Fe.[13]

In 1867 the two men returned to Texas for yet another herd, but while on their third trail trip west, Loving unwisely pushed ahead accompanied with only one scout. He was attacked by Indians and seriously wounded. Somehow Loving made it to Fort Sumner, where he died. Goodnight delivered the cattle to Colorado, but upon his return claimed Loving's body and took it back to Texas for proper burial by Loving's family. It was characteristic of Goodnight that he continued to share the profits of his sales with the Loving family.[14]

While continuing to work with John Chisum and moving cattle up to Colorado, Goodnight contracted with the future cattle baron John Wesley Iliff to deliver beeves north to Cheyenne, Wyoming, the town that the Union Pacific Railroad had reached by then. Iliff himself sent cattle farther north to stock ranges in Montana. All the while Goodnight explored for shorter, easier routes and developed yet another ranch on the Arkansas River near Pueblo, Colorado, to which he brought his bride, Mary Ann Dyer, to live when he married in 1870. Goodnight's trail was used by many other cattlemen until the 1880s when the coming of the railroads throughout the Southwest made the south-north trails unnecessary.

During his years in Colorado, Goodnight constantly engaged in new enterprises: he farmed, planted an apple orchard, started a bank, and founded a stockraiser's association. In 1873, depression in the cattle industry, however, persuaded him to think about moving his ranch to a new unoccupied region. Knowing that the Texas Panhandle had recently been cleared of Indians he decided to look there for a new spread. Accompanied by Panchito, a Mexican ranch hand, he located his future range in Palo Duro Canyon, the site where Colonel Ranald Mackenzie had burned a key Comanche-Kiowa camp and slaughtered their large horse herd in 1874. Palo Duro Canyon could not have been a more dramatic location. Set deep below the Plains surface on the Prairie Dog Town Fork of the Red River with adequate water, timber, and grasses, it was ideal for Goodnight's purposes. Once he decided to move there, he visited the future site of Tascosa, where he and Casimero Romero agreed that the New Mexican sheep ranchers, or *pastores*, would confine their operation to the Canadian River and its tributaries while he would center his operation on the Palo Duro Canyon area and on the tributaries to the Red River.[15]

Then in 1876 Goodnight moved his 1,800 head of Durham cattle from Colorado to the Canyon. He and the Bugbee Brothers, who came at the same time, were the major pioneer stockmen to settle in this region of the Texas Panhandle. Knowing that he was in one of the best locations for open-range cattle raising in the entire west, in 1877 he joined John G. Adair, a Colorado broker who had made big loans to Goodnight to form a huge operation called the JA Ranch. In time their endeavors resulted in assembling a herd of 100,000 cattle occupying more than seven hundred thousand acres of land. In 1878 Goodnight began to march his cattle north and east to Dodge City, Kansas, thereby blazing yet another trail—the Palo Duro–Dodge City Trail, which was later used by other Panhandle ranchers.

It was at the halfway point in Goodnight's remarkable career that Charlie Siringo, newly recruited by the large ranching outfit of Bates and Beals, who also moved their operation from Colorado to exploit the lush plains grasses, was to meet and admire the already legendary Charles Goodnight.[16] Part of Charlie's admiration, it must be confessed, was that the JA Ranch not only welcomed all visitors, Mrs. Goodnight served the most delicious meals to all comers.

❧　❧

As we have noted earlier Charlie Siringo helped deliver George W. Littlefield's herd to Dodge City on July 3, 1877. He was ready to celebrate the Fourth of July in a big way, and Dodge City seemed the appropriate place. As Siringo himself recalled in his book, *Riata and Spurs*, Dodge City in 1877 was the wildest of the cattle towns—with buffalo hunters, whom the cowboys hated, end-of-track railroad drifters, gamblers, cowboys, and soldiers from nearby Fort Dodge. As he and his friend "Wes" Adams tanked up on whiskey in the Lone Star Dance Hall, the almost inevitable fight developed between the unkempt rough and ready buffalo hunters and the cowboys. The result was that his pal, "Wes" Adams, was severely stabbed by a hunter. Knowing they would be arrested in a bar presided over by Bat Masterson, who hated violence in his saloon, Siringo and Adams fled to a Bates and Beals holding corral outside of Dodge. The next day, with good reason, Siringo "hired" to David T. Beals to help drive a herd of steers, 2,500 head, to the Panhandle of Texas, where he intended starting a new ranch.[17]

Charlie Siringo was lucky. Beals's partner, "Deacon" Bates, liked him and took him to hunt for a range, "one large enough for at least 50,000 cattle" in the Canadian River valley.

As Siringo recalls: "After being out three days we landed in Tascosa, a little Mexican town on the Canadian. There were only two Americans there, Howard and Reinheart, who kept the only store in town. Their stock of goods consisted of three barrels of whiskey and a half a dozen boxes of soda crackers." The Bates party then moved farther down the Canadian and near a small store kept by a man named Pitcher, who sold whiskey and tobacco to buffalo hunters, "they being mostly indians and mexicans." There Bates chose the location for the LX Ranch. The area was still full of deer and antelope and, as Siringo put it, "black with buffalo." He felt he was truly in the "western wilds."[18]

Who were "Deacon" Bates and David T. Beals, who hired Charlie in Dodge, and what was the character of their soon to be famous LX Ranch in the Texas Panhandle?

One should say the mastermind of this corporate ranching operation was David Thomas Beals, born in North Arlington, Massachusetts, in 1832. He was the son of a boot and shoe manufacturer. He had a public school education, then for a short time became a clerk for a Boston merchant at fifteen, before returning to Arlington to join his father in what appears to have been a very profitable business, the shoe trade.[19]

By the time he was in his mid-twenties, Beals saw broader opportunities in the West and in 1859 established a boot and shoe business in Missouri. In the 1860s, after silver and gold discoveries in Colorado, Montana, and later in Idaho and Utah, he set up stores in the booming mining towns that had sprung up overnight.

The hide business was to come full circle in David Beals's career. Texas hides had undoubtedly been used in his father's boot and shoe business. Then he sold his products to western customers, which led him to invest in the cattle business itself. Indeed in 1873 he returned east to seek capital and partners to enable him to start a ranch in Colorado on the Arkansas River. One of his partners was the fellow Bostonian W. H. Bates, who proved to be the quiet, loyal, on-the-spot lieutenant to Beals, for the latter was often in the cattle towns, in Chicago, or in the East.

Although Beals prospered as a rancher, when Colorado achieved state-hood in 1876, homesteaders attracted by the promise of fertile Colorado land began to flood into the new state. Beals, like all ranchers, hated the "fool hoe" men and determined to move his operation elsewhere. Like Casimero Romero and Charles Goodnight, he realized that the Texas Panhandle would be an ideal place to relocate. Four years later, in July 1877, he formed the Beals Cattle Company in Dodge City, Kansas. His able, loyal hardworking partner "Deacon" Bates—so-called by the cowhands because he seemed such a straight-laced Boston puritan—was ordered to take a herd of cattle to a site on the Panhandle range.

Bates chose a twenty-five-mile stretch on the Canadian River running southward to the future site of Amarillo, Texas, and from the north of the west-east-flowing Canadian some thirty-five miles to the headwaters of Blue Creek. Eventually the area embraced all or parts of no less than five counties. The ranch headquarters and a warehouse were located two miles east of Pitcher Creek. The nearest town was Tascosa, consisting, as already noted, of Hispanic residents and a general store run by Howard and Reinheart. Charlie Siringo was incredibly lucky. For the next five years (1879–1882) he was to serve as a cowboy on one of the pioneer ranches in the Panhandle.

The Bates and Beals ranch was soon an impressive, large-scale operation. In addition to the Kansas cattle Bates had driven from Dodge City, for the next two years, Beals sent down herds of cattle from his Granada, Colorado, ranch, along with his carefully bred herd of horses—a cross between fine mares and trotting and racing sires—whose offspring soon became known as superb saddle horses. By 1879, the LX Ranch did indeed hold fifty thousand cattle on its vast acreage.[20]

From the beginning Beals wanted to secure his range by buying it outright. As Anne B. Hinton has explained, Beals succeeded in his goal by buying twenty-three thousand acres from the Houston and Central Texas Railway, which had sections of right-of-way land grants in the region to sell. Later Beals purchased one hundred thousand acres from Joe Gunter and William B. Munson, two shrewd state surveyors who had acquired huge tracts of land as payment for their services to the state of Texas. Beals or his manager continued to buy sections of land from the Texas government throughout the 1880s.[21]

Beals himself was really an absentee owner who assigned duties to Deacon Bates and to a series of very capable managers such as Bill Moore and John Hollicott, about whom we shall soon hear more from Siringo himself. Beals's own approach to the cattle business was to make it efficient and profitable at every stage. To improve his herd he imported Durham and Hereford bulls to breed with his western cattle. He also insisted that his herds be moved slowly to market so that they would not lose weight; and once near Caldwell, Kansas, which replaced Dodge City as the nearest shipping town, he acquired a number of "feeding" ranches where the cattle could be fattened before sale. Sometimes Charlie Siringo was placed in charge of a Bates and Beals feeding ranch in Cherokee Strip in the Indian Territory just across the Kansas state line, where Caldwell was located. And when Siringo was put in charge of an LX horse herd near Caldwell, he considered it an honor.

Beals also continued to pay the same careful attention to his horse herd at the LX, seeking to upgrade western mustangs with blooded sires. The pride of westerners in their horses, whether they were ranchers or cowboys, was reflected in Siringo's praise of his own horse—"Whiskey-peet"—and his participation in occasional races, which he often won. It was no accident that westerners adopted the Spanish custom of rodeo festivals with horse races and roping contests on their own ranches and in cattle towns. These local events soon evolved into the famous institutionalized form with Buffalo Bill Cody's Wild West show after Cody had witnessed a July 4, 1882, cowboy celebration in North Platte, Nebraska, which featured cowboy skills with riding, racing, and roping. Beginning in 1883 the Wild West show became an American icon that continues today in rodeos all over the American West. It tells us something about the deep personal excitement and drama of being a cowboy when we realize that the rodeo is the only national sport to evolve from an industry—that of ranching.[22]

⁑　⁑

Late that fall, Bates and Beals hired a new ranch manager, William Moore, the former manager of the huge Swan Land and Cattle Company in Wyoming. Despite the rumors that he had killed two people, Bill Moore proved to be a splendid ranch boss with an iron will. Ironically, he proved to be one of the most vigorous defenders of law and order in the entire Texas Panhandle. No sooner had he arrived than a set of thieves ransacked Pitcher's store. Moore immediately formed a posse of nine men, including Siringo, to pursue the thieves, who were promptly caught. Siringo decided to celebrate their success by getting dead drunk off Howard and Reinheart's "bug juice." Charlie was so hung over and miserable afterward that he swore he would never get drunk again, but, as he later confessed, there was one exception: that being when Grover Cleveland was elected president, the first Democrat to win the White House since the Civil War.[23]

With the first ranchers also came cattle thieves, which meant that the cattlemen had to post guards to protect their herds. Indeed, Charlie's first assignment on the LX was to man a line camp, with a young cowboy named John Robinson, south of the Canadian at the base of the Staked Plains. Having built a small stone house at the head of a canyon, the two had, as Siringo called it, "a hog killing time all by ourselves." The buffalo were still so plentiful that they were a "solid string from one to three miles wide," moving so slowly that they took "three days and night to cross the Canadian River. And at other times I have seen them so thick on the plains that the country would look black just as far as the eye could reach."[24]

Moore was equally determined to recover all stray LX cattle, and in the spring he assigned Siringo and Robinson to a scouting outfit accompanied by a chuck wagon to ride over the plains to track down drifters. The trek was full of surprises. They encountered thousands of Comanche Indians from Fort Still, Indian Territory, out hunting. Badly frightened, they pointed out where they had seen buffalo. Next, they ran into a band of Pawnee Indians, and then a large band of half-starved Cheyenne, who had been unable to find buffalo. Although Siringo's outfit found only eighteen head of LX steers after an absence of seven weeks, Bill Moore sent them out again on another scout for strays until the following April, when Siringo was sent to Fort Bascom, New Mexico, to participate in a huge spring roundup.[25]

This was the first general roundup ever held in the Panhandle. From the LX went Moore, twenty-five cowboys, and "two well-filled chuck wagons," first to Tascosa, where they were joined by several other outfits. As Margaret Sheers notes, when they left Tascosa for the upper Canadian, "there were a dozen chuck wagons and more than a hundred cowpunchers." From Fort Bascom they "worked the whole Canadian River Valley down to the line of the Indian Territory, probably a distance of two-hundred miles. Their roundup which ended in June, netted the LX thousands of cattle."[26] In the middle of June Moore sent Siringo to take charge of a herd of 2,500 steers which, had been placed on the grasses of the south

Staked Plains to fatten. Moore wanted them "close herded" all summer so they would be tame before being sent to market in the fall. This time Siringo had a chuck wagon and a cook and four riders with five horses for each man. Once again Siringo thought he was in a cattleman's paradise for the rich buffalo grass was nearly a foot high, there was plenty of fresh water from frequent rains, and an abundance of wild game. "If ever I enjoyed life it was that summer," he later recalled.[27]

Siringo undoubtedly enjoyed himself in part because Moore kept giving him added responsibility. Toward the end of summer Moore put him in charge of four close-held herds on the north side of the Canadian. As their boss, Charlie rode his horse from herd to herd checking on things and making sure no cattle were missing.

That fall Siringo and a fellow cowboy, John Farris, got permission from Moore to catch up with an LX herd of eight hundred steers being driven to Dodge City, and once they were loaded on the railroad cars, to continue on to Chicago with them. Siringo had earned $350 that summer and was clearly raring to celebrate. Despite an Indian scare, Siringo and Farris made it to Dodge, arriving even before the LX herd. There he met Erskine Clement, a partner of Beals (who was also his son-in-law). Clement made immediate use of Siringo by ordering him to board the train carrying four hundred of the steers while Clement would follow with the second four hundred on a later train. When the train reached Burlington, Iowa, Siringo was met by Mr. Beals and the two spent the day there feeding and watering the cattle.[28]

As a young kid Siringo had lived in St. Louis and New Orleans and had visited Houston, but he was now a naïve, excited Texas cowboy in Chicago. Beals recommended that he stay at the Palmer House, but after paying a dollar for a meal there, Charlie, describing himself as a common clod-hopper, retreated to the Ervin House, a much cheaper hotel. Dressed in the fancy cowboy outfit he had bought in Dodge, he took in the town, squandering about fifteen dollars on child boot-blacks who flattered him by calling him "our Texas Ranger." By the end of the third day Charlie was broke and had to borrow money from Beals. Penniless but happy Charlie ended his six days in Chicago and, along with Beals and Clement, returned to Dodge where he picked up his horse "Whiskey-peet" and rode the 225 miles back to the LX Ranch.[29]

When he arrived at the stone and adobe headquarters of the LX he found that William Bonney, already known as a young outlaw, and his companions were there trying to sell a herd of ponies that they had stolen from enemies in Lincoln County, New Mexico, where a lethal feud between two contending merchants, each with cattlemen and politicians as allies, had been going on since 1875. By the summer of 1878 four participants had been killed and Billy the Kid had been identified as a partisan and possible killer allied with the Tunstall-McSween faction.[30]

When Billy and his friends, Tom O'Folliard, Henry Brown, Fred Waite, and John Middleton came to the Panhandle in late September 1878 with their stolen horses to sell, they frequented Tascosa, where a young physician, Dr. Henry Hoyt, newly arrived from Minnesota and in love with the Wild West, befriended Billy. Hoyt described him as

> a handsome youth with smooth face, wavy brown hair,
> an athletic and symmetrical figure, and clear blue eyes that
> could look one through and through. Unless angry, he
> always seemed to have a pleasant expression with a ready
> smile. His head was well-shaped, his features regular, his
> nose aquiline, his most noticeable characteristic a slight
> projection of his two upper front teeth.

Hoyt went on to say that Billy spoke Spanish like a native Mexican, while others said he was a favorite among women. Hoyt bought a stolen horse from Billy, who gave the naïve young doctor false papers of ownership. The horse had been stolen from Sheriff William Brady, who had been killed in the Lincoln feuding.[31]

Charlie Siringo was as attracted to and intrigued by Billy as Dr. Hoyt was. They engaged in shooting contests with their Colt 45s both at ranch headquarters and in Tascosa. Charlie proved to be as good as Billy in hitting the target but found to his chagrin that Billy "could get in two shots to my one." The two visited Tascosa together but since Billy did not drink, there were no barroom sessions. Before the Kid departed for New Mexico again, Siringo gave him a meerschaum cigar holder as a present. The Kid gave Charlie a finely bound novel bearing his autograph. Although the fall of 1878 appears to have been the only time Siringo saw the Kid in person, he maintained that in that short time they had become intimately acquainted. Clearly obsessed by Billy's violent career, Siringo started interviewing people who knew the Kid immediately after he was killed by Sheriff Pat Garrett in July 1881. Decades later Charlie not only published a sympathetic *History of Billy the Kid* in 1920, he also mentioned him at length in three of his other books.[32]

Meanwhile Charlie was busy with now familiar ranching tasks, among them training young Dr. Hoyt to rope, tame broncos, and drive cattle. Hoyt found him to be a splendid teacher and praised Charlie when he wrote his own memoirs many decades later. The two were to correspond with one another for the rest of their lives. Siringo also continued to watch for cattle thieves and participate in roundups. Later he drove steers to Nickerson, Kansas, on the Arkansas River where he was met by "Deacon" Bates, who had already driven several herds to Kansas, but had held the poorest ones back in a camp south of the town. Bates promptly ordered Siringo to search for cattle that Bates's outfit had lost on the trail. For Charlie this was like a vacation. He and his fellow cowboys spent a month hunting for cattle in an area of Kansas that had already been partially settled by grangers. Charlie's outfit somehow always managed to wind up at a farmer's cabin at mealtime! "We had a soft trip," he recalled, "as most of our hard work was such as buying butter, eggs, etc. . . . " At the end of the month Charlie had found only eighteen strays, but now had a bill for purchases of food that amounted to over $1000! Bates was so furious with Siringo that he said Charlie must go to Chicago and present his bill to Mr. Beals himself.[33]

Before leaving Nickerson, however, Bates received a letter from Bill Moore at the LX stating that two more herds were on the trail for Nickerson, but were so late they might be hit by an early winter storm. To speed things up, he ordered Siringo and a friend to rush back, meet the herds, and have them head for Dodge City, which was nearly 120 miles closer to the LX Ranch than Nickerson. Siringo and Joe Hargrove set out to turn the herds to Dodge City. After this delay, Siringo finally boarded the train to Chicago, where Beals, unlike Bates, did not seem to be shocked by Charlie's expenses. Charlie had already decided to go back to Texas for the winter and visit his mother, when Beals told him that he was planning to purchase a lot of southern Texas cattle for his Panhandle ranch and asked if Charlie would be ready to boss one of the trail herds.

Charlie then took the train to Nickerson, retrieved Whiskey-Peet and his pack animal, and bought supplies for an eleven-hundred-mile hunting and camping trip to Texas. Short of money, Siringo raced Whiskey-Peet in order to raise cash, sold his expensive saddle for a cheaper one, but after a month's time arrived at his mother's home in Cash's Creek where she gave him a rough time for having waited four years to visit her.[34]

In early March Charlie received word from Mr. Rosencrans, yet another one of Bates and Beals's several partners, inviting him to serve as trail boss for a herd of cattle that Beals had purchased from Charles Word, a prominent Goliad rancher. Charlie was to drive the herd to the LX ranch. Saying goodbye to his mother and his beloved horse, Whiskey-Peet, Charlie traveled to Goliad and then to Beeville where the cattle were located.[35]

Charlie soon discovered to his dismay that being associated with a Panhandle ranch, he was thought to be a youthful "Yankee." Over the course of several days Charlie had to prove once more that he could rope and brand cattle—for the Word cowhands were busy putting a road brand on the cattle under wet, muddy conditions. Charlie then demonstrated his skill in breaking wild Mexican ponies that Word had bought for the use of the trail outfit. It was slow going, because a storm had scattered the cattle at the outset; but when the final herds of some 3,700 steers were all collected at the Red River, Charlie took over 2,500 destined for the LX, while the remainder with a separate boss headed north to Wyoming. Siringo's herd, moving in a northwesterly direction, finally arrived at the LX on July 1. Moore immediately ordered him to take the herd out on the Plains and hold them there until the fall. After two months, Moore released them for the fall and winter, and Charlie was given an outfit charged with branding calves found on the range. Moore then sent Siringo to drift on the Plains watching for rustlers just as he had in previous winters.[36]

Charlie was just settling in to his "drifting" routine when he received word from Moore to return to the ranch and "to bring three of my picked men along." Undoubtedly mystified by this change of orders, Charlie learned upon his arrival at the ranch that Billy the Kid had stolen a large number of Panhandle cattle, LX brands among others, and had taken them to New Mexico. Moore had already sent Jim East and other cowboys to overtake the Kid and the stolen herd; East demanded their return, to which Billy responded, "You will take a heap of hot led before you do." They returned empty handed to the ranch and reported to Moore.[37]

Moore then sent five men including Siringo as boss with a cook and chuck wagon to track down the herd. They were joined by five men from the LIT Ranch and three more cowboys from the LS. Loaded with six shooters, ammunition, Bowie knives, and "Winchesters on our saddles," these thirteen men set out to New Mexico. From the start the whole episode proved to be a fiasco. Once in New Mexico Siringo went off to Las Vegas with $300 to buy supplies. While there he gambled it all away, while his men celebrated so wildly in the little town of Anton Chico that its inhabitants were soon on the verge of running them out of town. Upon his return Siringo moved his party to White Oaks.[38]

At White Oaks another more serious action was underway, guided by Sheriff Pat Garrett, whose main task was not to rescue cattle but to arrest and jail Billy the Kid and his gang for Lincoln County murders as well as for thievery. Garrett gathered all of the posse at White Oaks and chose the best men from each to track down the Kid. Among those chosen were Jim East, Lon Chambers, and Cal Polk of the LX, but not Siringo.

In a swift series of events, Billy's companions, Tom O'Folliard and Charles Bowdre, were shot and killed, and Billy was captured, tried in court at Mesilla, New Mexico, declared guilty of his crimes, and remanded to Lincoln to be held in jail until "hanged by the neck until dead." Once in Lincoln, however, the Kid managed to obtain a gun, kill both his jailers, and ride out of town. One can imagine Pat Garrett's fury at learning of the Kid's escape. But patience, determination, and effective use of spies were dominant features of Pat Garrett's techniques of detection. Led by tips, he and two deputies tracked the Kid to the home of the well-known rancher, Pete Maxwell. There on July 14, 1881, in Pete Maxwell's bedroom, Pat Garrett killed Billy the Kid; and from that moment on the legendary Billy the Kid took over, captivating writers, novelists, and filmmakers down to the present.[39]

What were Siringo and his men doing all this time? Siringo's own outfit finally made it to White Oaks, New Mexico, two days before Christmas, 1880. They "rented a large log house near lower end of town," again persuaded merchants to supply their needs on credit, themselves rustled a stray beef or two as their meat supply, and decided to wait for those of their outfit who were with Sheriff Garrett to return.

Some of Siringo's men showed up shortly after New Year's Day with the news that the Kid had been captured and was being taken to Las Vegas to jail. Finally the remaining members of the LX and LIT outfits returned, and the reunited group moved out into the hills where they could find grain for the horses and live more cheaply. There around the campfire, Lon Chambers, who had been with Garrett—and in Siringo's words, was "a splendid single-handed talker"—told the story of Billy's initial capture by Garrett.[40]

Lon Chambers finished his account by voicing the hope that he and his fellow cowhands would share the reward money as Garrett and Stewart had promised—a promise that was not kept. Disgusted and homesick, all but five men from the LX and LIT outfits voted to return to the Panhandle. That left Siringo, Tom Emory, Lon Chambers, Frank Clifford (Big-foot Wallace), and a cook with the chuck wagon to continue the search for the stolen LX cattle.

Siringo was greatly relieved when he received a letter from Moore enclosing $300 and expressing approval of Siringo's decision to remain in New Mexico. Having paid off his creditors in White Oaks, he promptly asked Moore for an additional $300, which also arrived. He and his party then set out to confront Pat Coghlan, who had bought the stolen Panhandle cattle from the Kid.

As he recounts in *A Texas Cowboy*, Siringo rode to Fort Stanton, where Coghlan maintained a slaughter pen; there he found hides of cattle bearing the LX brand, got witnesses from the fort to testify as to the accuracy of that theft, and moved on to confront Coghlan in person, but did not find him. By this time most of Siringo's men had given up and gone home, but he vowed to find the LX cattle if he had to go all the way to Arizona to achieve this. Although Siringo finally met Coghlan, who reluctantly promised to return the stolen cattle the Kid had sold him, Siringo soon learned, as he put it, that Coghlan was giving him "taffy."

At that point Siringo turned into a real detective, seeking out information at Mexican dances, adopting an assumed name, and telling people he was "on the dodge" for a crime he had committed in southern Texas. When someone he knew blew his cover by greeting him by his real name in Las Cruces, where he had traveled, Siringo knew that he had better get out of town fast and decided to return to White Oaks. While passing through Coghlan's range, Siringo naively took the advice of a Mexican—he called them "Greasers"—and set out on a shortcut to White Oaks. As he tried to negotiate a wild, difficult trail, he was ambushed, but fortunately fell off his mule and over a precipice, where he was able to take cover between boulders. His would-be killers, thinking he was dead, rode off. Siringo found his slightly wounded mule and then limped into White Oaks.[41]

It began to look as if the Coghlan imbroglio would never end when Siringo learned that the wily rancher was getting rid of the LX cattle as fast as he could before the date he was supposed to return them.

Recruiting Big-foot Wallace, who had been waiting around in White Oaks for new orders, he and Siringo took off for Fort Stanton with Lon Chambers and Tom Emory following behind with the LX chuck wagon and supplies. Siringo did find LX cattle about to be driven to Coghlan's slaughter pen and using threats of force, he, Big-foot, and Emory finally cut out eight of their cattle and returned to White Oaks. So angry were they that they seized a Coghlan steer and once in White Oaks butchered it for their own use.

After weeks of frustrating searches, Siringo found only two more LX cattle. While at Roswell, New Mexico, he learned that Billy the Kid had escaped. Siringo himself had a close call when he and his little outfit arrived at Fort Sumner, where they attended a dance. One of the attendees was the attractive Mrs. Charles Bowdre, now a widow. Bowdre had been killed by Sheriff Pat Garrett's posse earlier that year. Charlie liked her immensely, and walked her to her room, but to his surprise, was not invited in. Later that year when Siringo returned to New Mexico to participate in the Coghlan trial and saw her, she confessed that she could not invite him in, because Billy was hiding in her room reading.[42]

On his lengthy trip back to the home ranch, Siringo and his outfit managed to rescue about 100 more head of LX cattle and eventually succeeded in rounding up nearly 2,500 head, but traversing unknown country, Siringo's outfit and the cattle got lost on the dry plains and came near to dying from lack of water. Siringo finally got back to the LX Ranch on June 22, with the 2,500 head of cattle, and as he records in *A Texas Cowboy*, "after having been absent just seven months, to a day."[43]

Things had changed at the ranch. Bill Moore had resigned and started a ranch of his own, consisting of cattle he had branded as his own. A former manager for George Littlefield, John Hollicott, was now the ranch boss while Beals's son-in-law, Erskine Clement, handled shipping and other business matters. Siringo spent an easy summer working on the ranch and celebrating in Tascosa until October when word came for him to come to Lincoln, New Mexico, to serve as a witness against Coghlan, whom Sheriff John Poe had arrested and brought to trial. With his fellow ranch hand Lon Chambers, Siringo made the five-hundred-mile journey, arriving in Lincoln a few days before the trial began. The ever-evasive Coghlan got a change of venue, setting the trial in Mesilla in southern New Mexico for the spring of 1882. Lon Chambers, not being important to the trial, went back to the LX, but Siringo, having been told by Hollicott and Clement to stay the whole winter if necessary, remained and rekindled old friendships in White Oaks.

During the course of his stay in New Mexico, Siringo met "Ash" Upson, who was not only a friend of Pat Garrett's but at the time was living on Garrett's ranch. With Siringo's encouragement, the talkative Upson recounted in great detail not only the events of the "bloody Lincoln County War," but a full sketch of "Billy the Kid's" life. Everyone knew Garrett was writing a history of Billy the Kid, and it is clear that Siringo was interested in doing the same. As he remarked to his old Texas neighbor and friend, Fritz Cornelius, later in 1882, he was gathering some notes and doing some writing.[44]

Billy the Kid's life history has been told so often, both in exaggerated accounts and in careful biographies of that troubled youth, it need not be repeated here. What is of special interest here, however, is why Charlie Siringo not only became obsessed with the story of the young killer, but over the years developed a real sympathy for him, so much so that in addition to devoting a chapter to the "Kid" in *A Texas Cowboy*, he published a romantic and inaccurate *History of Billy the Kid* in 1920.[45]

We might begin by noting that Siringo had encountered Billy the Kid at the LX Ranch in 1878 where the two young men became buddies. When sent to New Mexico to recover the LX cattle Billy had stolen, he met Sheriff Pat Garrett. Three of his own outfit, Jim East, Lon Chambers, and Cal Polk were with Garrett when he captured Billy, only to have him escape from jail. When Garrett finally found Billy at the Maxwell home in Fort Sumner and killed him, in 1881, John Poe, the marshal who prosecuted Coghlan and came to know Siringo, told Siringo more about Billy. He gained his fullest information when he talked long hours with Ash Upson, a former newspaperman who had known both Billy and his mother for many years and had actually rented rooms from Mrs. Antrim when she ran a boardinghouse first in Santa Fe and later in Silver City. Of course, there was Pat Garrett's own highly popular account of Billy the Kid, which Ash Upson helped him write. It was already in print by 1882.

Siringo's own account in *A Texas Cowboy* represents some of his best and freshest writing. Moving swiftly he traced Billy from the time he became a cowhand at John Tunstall's ranch in Lincoln, New Mexico. When Tunstall was killed by a renegade posse, Billy swore vengeance on his killers and with fellow pro-Tunstall cowhands and local citizens, some ten or more persons, began killing the original killers, but in the escalating

Lincoln County War between the McSween (pro-Tunstall) and Murphy factions, Sheriff Brady was killed and then McSween was killed, and several outlaws met their deaths. Siringo then traced the Kid's life to the end when Garrett killed him. Obviously sad and sympathetic, Charlie Siringo provided his own obituary for Billy, writing, "Thus ended the life of William H. Bonney, one of the coolest-headed and most daring young outlaws that ever lived. He had dwelt upon this earth just 21 years, seven months and 21 days."[46]

Unfortunately Siringo's 1920 biography of Billy the Kid did not have the vigor of his short account in *A Texas Cowboy*. The book was error ridden and accepted without question Garrett's and Upson's manipulating of the facts. Later historians have tended to dismiss Siringo's *History of Billy the Kid* as romantic or sympathetic, but he was the first one besides Garrett to write a version based on accounts by participants—or knowledgeable persons—Ash Upson, Pat Garrett, Jim East, John Poe, Lon Chambers, and Dr. Henry Hoyt, and he followed what others wrote about the Kid for the rest of his life. Yet Siringo so believed in his own version, late in life he accused Stuart Lake, a Hollywood biographer of the Kid, of plagiarizing his account.

What Siringo, as so many others, tried to do was to see Billy as the leader of a well-formed local gang. But two of the Kid's companions at Tascosa chose not to return to New Mexico. Many others were later killed, so Billy did not really have a "gang." He was a central participant in the Lincoln County War, in revenging Tunstall's death and afterward, but as Robert Utley writes he was never the leader. Utley feels that it was the legendizers "who have made him more important than he actually was," and could never prove "that more than three or four were actually killed by him." Billy the Kid is really significant, observes Robert Utley, as an exemplar of "the twin specters of corruption and violence that remain imbedded in American culture, periodically to surface separately or in tandem. Whether originating in the frontier experience or in some dark stain on the American character, they continue to find expression in the legend of the youth who lived both. More than a century after his death, Billy the Kid still rides boldly across America's mental landscape, symbolizing an enduring national ambivalence toward corruption and violence." "For a life that ended at twenty-one," concludes Utley, "that is a powerful and disturbing legacy."[47]

However strong Siringo's attraction to Billy the Kid and his daring exploits, the fact remains that Siringo returned to New Mexico in

1880–1881 to testify against Coghlan, who was guilty of theft and corruption. Without knowing it, by deciding to join Pat Garrett's posse to hunt down and kill the Kid and by serving as a witness in the Coghlan case, Siringo had unconsciously declared for peaceful law and order and was on his way toward becoming a Pinkerton detective, only to discover one day that some detectives in that agency, in their zeal, sometimes also embraced the twin specters of corruption and violence while fighting corruption and violence. As he waited to testify in the Coghlan trial, which was to take place in Mesilla, Siringo wandered about participating in turkey shoots, visiting camps of buffalo hunters, and spending the money drafts from the LX Ranch all too freely. While paying a visit to Colorado City, Texas, he developed a severe case of smallpox, had his horse stolen, and tried to have an affair with a Mexican girl. Meanwhile through bribery and clever maneuvering in court, Coghlan escaped prison by paying fines. Disgusted with the outcome, but having served as a witness for Marshall John W. Poe, Siringo returned to the LX after being away for nearly eight months.[48]

In July 1882, Siringo was put in charge of a herd of eight hundred steers and an outfit with orders to drive them to Caldwell, Kansas, the last, and in some ways the most enduring of the end-of-trail cattle towns. Caldwell, located west of the Kansas-Texas fever quarantine line, was literally on the border of the Cherokee Strip in Indian Territory. There shrewd cattlemen had rented land from the Cherokee Tribe, on which they established ranches where they could hold their cattle until cold weather killed the ticks that caused Texas fever, or could ship them directly without having to deal with homesteaders on the other cattle trails.

Siringo liked Caldwell, and after loading his cattle on the railroad cars destined for Chicago, he proceeded to explore the city and as he put it, "immediately fell in love with the town, also with a couple of young ladies, and therefore concluded to locate. I bought some lots and contracted a house built, with a view to going after mother."[49]

Siringo did more cattle drives for the LX, but by then he had already located his mother in Caldwell, and had fallen in love with a wonderful young woman, Mamie Lloyd, and married her after a whirlwind courtship. Leaving her in Caldwell only a few days after the marriage, he reluctantly set out for the LX, but eighteen days out, swore off being a cowboy, and returned to Caldwell to his wife, and to the life of a merchant and budding author.

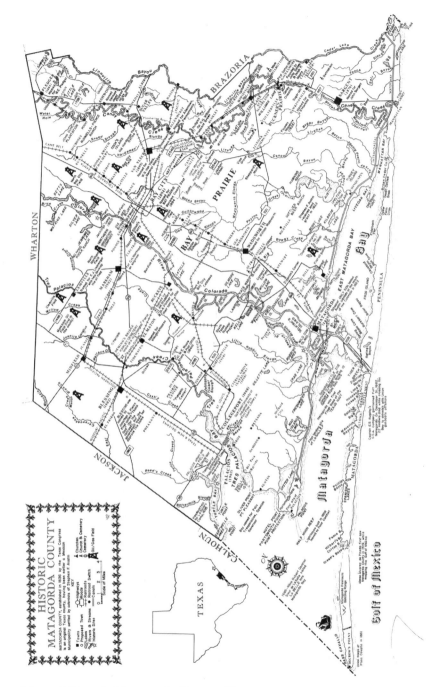

2. *Map of Historic Matagorda County, Texas.*
From the Matagorda County Archives.

3. Brand of Antonio Siringo. Taken from Matagorda Country Brands Book, vol. 1.

4. A photo of Charlie Siringo that he called "The Kidlet Author After He Became a Cowboy." From A Cowboy Detective *by Charlie Siringo (1912).*

5. *Shanghai Pierce as a younger man when visiting the Kansas cattle towns. From Chris Emmett,* Shanghai Pierce: A Fair Likeness *(Norman: University of Oklahoma Press, 1953).*

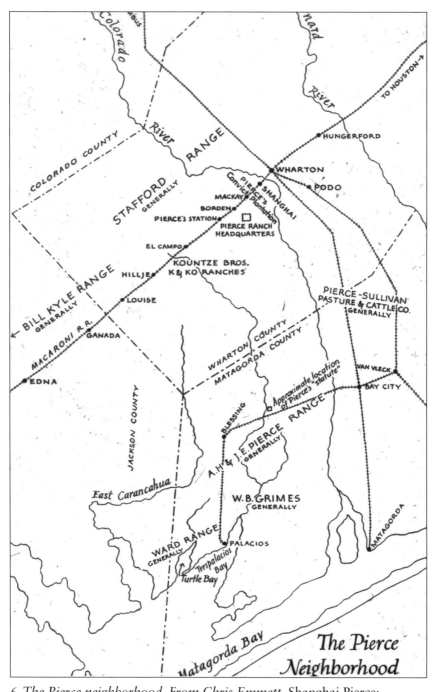

6. *The Pierce neighborhood. From Chris Emmett,* Shanghai Pierce:
A Fair Likeness *(Norman: University of Oklahoma Press, 1953).*

7. *Indianola, Texas, in the 1850s. Indianola was Matagorda County's most successful port. Virtually destroyed by a hurricane in 1876, it never recovered. From the Matagorda County Archives.*

8. *Charlie Siringo's cattle brand: S2 recorded May 19, 1873, as number 68 in old (second) Brand Book number 1. From the Matagorda County Archives.*

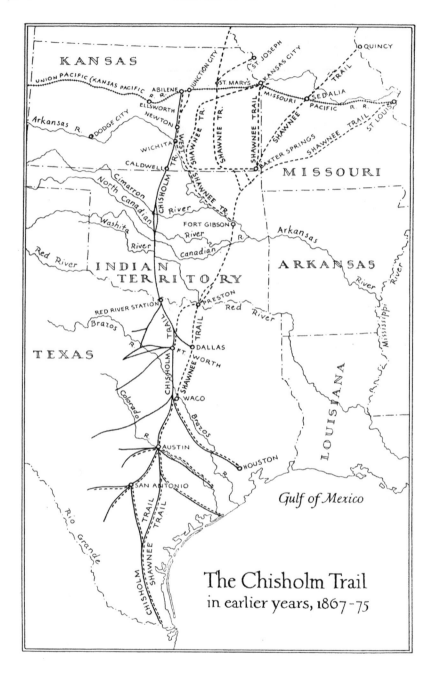

9. *The Chisholm Trail in earlier years, 1867–1875. From Wayne Gard,*
The Chisholm Trail *(Norman: University of Oklahoma Press, 1954).*

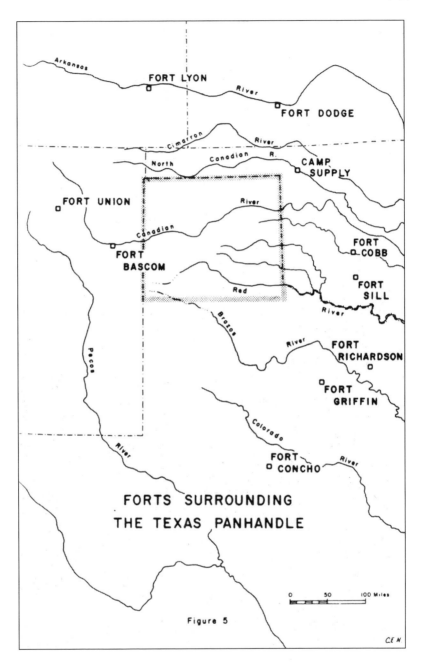

FORT LYON

FORT DODGE

CAMP SUPPLY

FORT UNION

FORT BASCOM

FORT COBB

FORT SILL

FORT RICHARDSON

FORT GRIFFIN

FORT CONCHO

**FORTS SURROUNDING
THE TEXAS PANHANDLE**

0   50   100 Miles

Figure 5

CE N

10. *Forts surrounding the Texas Panhandle. From Frederick W. Rathjen,*
The Texas Panhandle Frontier *(Lubbock: Texas Tech University Press,
1973; rev. ed. 1998).*

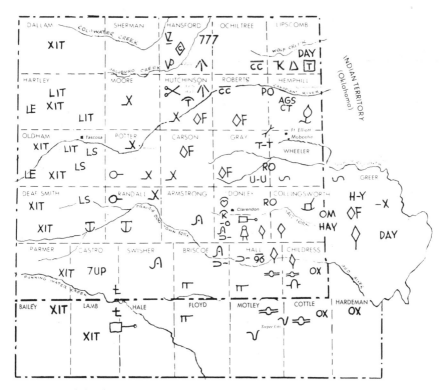

11. *Map of the frontier ranches in the Texas Panhandle, 1876–1887.*
From Pauline Durrett Robertson and R. L. Robertson, Cowman's
Country: Fifty Frontier Ranches in the Texas Panhandle, 1876–1887
(Paramount Publishing Company, 1981). The LX Ranch is identified
by its brand, _X, as seen in Moore, Potter, Randall, Hutchinson, and
Carson Counties.

12. *Outlaw Bill Moore, Manager of the LX Ranch.*

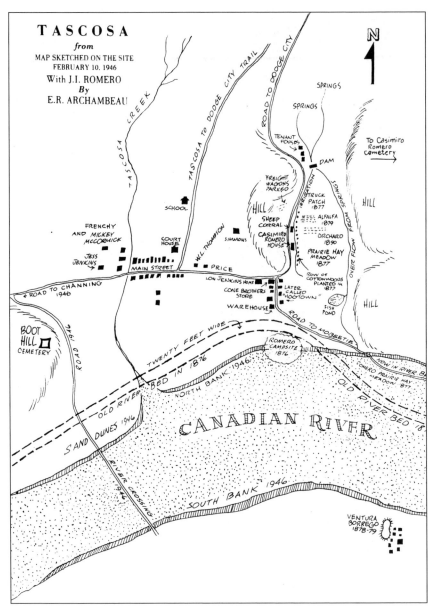

13. *Tascosa, "Cowboy Capital of the Panhandle." From John L. McCarty*, Maverick Town: The Story of Old Tascosa *(Norman: University of Oklahoma, 1946).*

14. *Inside the saloon at Tascosa LS Ranch. Cowboys drink at the bar. From the Erwin E. Smith Collection, Amon Carter Museum, Fort Worth Texas.*

15. *When first employed by the LX Ranch, Siringo lived in a "Line Shack," such as illustrated here. From the Erwin E. Smith Collection, Amon Carter Museum, Fort Worth, Texas.*

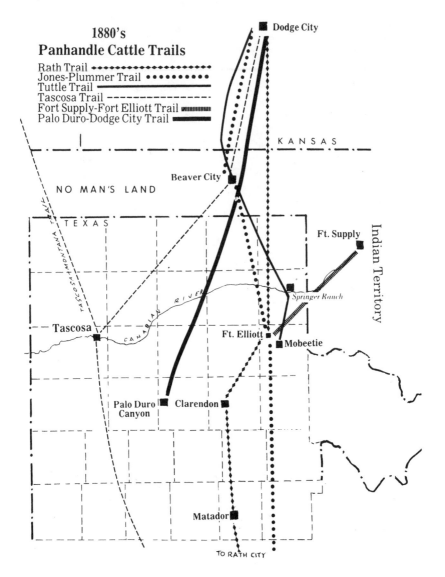

16. Map of 1880s Texas Panhandle cattle trails. Siringo used these trails to go to Dodge City and later to Caldwell. From Pauline Durrett Robertson and R. L. Robertson, Cowman's Country: Fifty Frontier Ranches in the Texas Panhandle, 1876–1887 (Paramount Publishing Company, 1981).

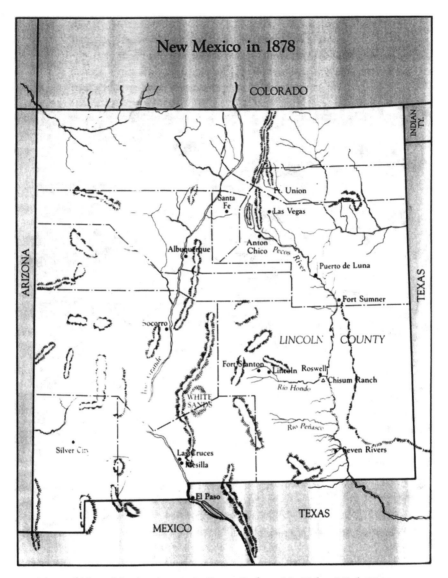

17. *Map of New Mexico in 1878. From Robert M. Utley,* High Noon
    in Lincoln: Violence on the Western Frontier *(Albuquerque:
    University of New Mexico Press, 1987).*

18. Pat Garrett, "Slayer of Billy the Kid." From George W. Coe, Frontier Fighter: The Lincoln County War by a Man who rode with Billy the Kid *(Albuquerque: University of New Mexico Press, 1934).*

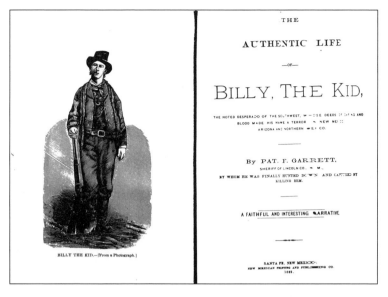

19. (above) Title page of Pat F. Garrett, The
Authentic Life of Billy the Kid (Santa Fe:
New Mexican Printing and Publishing Co.,
1882). Note line drawing of Billy the
Kid (detail at right).

BILLY THE KID.—[From a Photograph.]

BUSINESSMEN OF CALDWELL, TO YOUR POSTS! . . .
PUT YOUR SHOULDER TO THE WHEEL AND ROLL THE CHARIOT
OF PROSPERITY HIGH UP ON THE INCLINE TILL ALL THE
GREAT SOUTHWEST CAN BEHOLD THE GILDED CART.

— *Caldwell* Post, *April 20, 1882*

THE NEXT DAY I RENTED A VACANT ROOM ON MAIN STREET AND,
ROLLING UP MY SLEEVES AND PUTTING ON A PAIR OF SUSPENDERS,
THE FIRST I HAD EVER WORN, STARTED OUT AS A MERCHANT—
ON A SIX-BIT SCALE. THUS ONE COW-PUNCHER TAKES A
SENSIBLE TUMBLE AND DROPS OUT OF THE RANCH.

— *Charlie A. Siringo,* A Texas Cowboy, *197*

HIS INSIGHT IN THE CATTLE LIFE WAS NOT OBTAINED FROM
THE WINDOW OF A PULLMAN CAR, BUT CLOSE TO THE SOIL
AND FROM THE HURRICANE DECK OF A TEXAS HORSE.

— *Andy Adams, author of* Log of a Cowboy, *as a tribute to*
Charles Siringo's A Texas Cowboy, *cited in Wilson M. Hudson,*
Andy Adams: His Life and Writings, *32*

CHAPTER SIX

"Queen City of the Border"

CALDWELL, KANSAS, 1871–1885

I: THE CHISHOLM TRAIL AND CATTLE TOWNS

MANY THOUSANDS OF BOOKS AND ARTICLES HAVE BEEN WRITTEN about the open-range cattle industry, cowboys, the long drive from Texas over the Chisholm Trail, famous ranchers, and the colorful Kansas cattle towns of Abilene, Wichita, Ellsworth, Dodge City, and Caldwell. Thanks to the Hollywood westerns, the images of these events, persons, and places have been engraved on our psyche so deeply, they continue to help define the American character both for ourselves and the entire world. Like the Civil War saga, this popular last Wild West has been so romanticized and legendized that other significant and exciting aspects of the cattle industry in the United States have been neglected.

In his lifetime Siringo went up the Chisholm Trail to Wichita and Dodge City, and then on the Western Trail to Dodge City and Caldwell, Kansas. His colorful accounts, highlighted with stories of storms, attempts to kill buffalo, and hunting lost cattle fill many pages of *A Texas Cowboy*. And although true, they helped perpetuate the romance of the trail drive.

The books, articles, films, and television programs about the cattleman's world number in the thousands, many of them excellent, but they have tended to stress the wildness of the towns, their saloons and brothels, and shootouts between drunk cowboys and trigger-happy lawmen. We know more about Bat Masterson, Wyatt Earp, Calamity Jane, and Wild Bill Hickok than we do about the towns themselves, or most of their inhabitants.

Consider the remarkable television impact of *Gunsmoke*, originally a film but soon a nationally popular television series, which lasted twenty years, leaving the air only in 1975. Through *Gunsmoke* at least three generations of Americans have come to know Dodge City and with it the Lone Star Saloon; James Arness as Sheriff Matt Dillon; Dennis Weaver as Chester; Amanda Blake as Kitty, the saloon and dance hall proprietress; and Milburn Stone as Doc Adams. By 1959 "twenty-eight adult westerns played in prime time, nearly eighteen hours a week, the equivalent of 400 feature films a year, far more than ever produced during the golden age of the 'B' westerns of the 1930s."[1]

Ironically the story of these cattle towns—seemingly so distinctive, even unique—is also the larger story of other towns across the West—Tascosa, and Fort Griffin, mining towns in California, Nevada, and Colorado, and virtually all the other western states including Alaska. Lumber camps and towns in Oregon and Washington show similar patterns of boom, bust, and change. It is the saga of shrewd town builders, ambitious railroad leaders, merchants, and youthful, adventurous, restless, mobile people from every walk of life that made these settlements so interesting, and helped determine their ultimate success or failure. Together their experiences comprise a fantastic urban history of the Old West. Rest assured that this other side of the cattle-town story in particular does not lack color or drama. If desperate Texas cattlemen were anxious to find a cash market after the Civil War for their abundant cattle, so were buyers and entrepreneurs who supplied beef to the upper Midwest and the East. Missouri towns, Chicago, ambitious railroad leaders, and towns in the state of Kansas were equally avid to tap new markets.

The founding father of the first Kansas cattle town, Abilene, was Joseph G. McCoy, an Illinois businessman who, with his brother, were already wealthy as cattle raisers and shippers.[2] Indeed, ever since the 1850s, cattle had been marched from Missouri and Iowa to feeding lots in western Illinois to be fattened before being driven to the Chicago slaughterhouses. Even before the Civil War some Texas cattle were marched overland to Sedalia, Missouri, for sale; a good number came up the Mississippi by boat after having been shipped or marched to New Orleans. However, in the 1850s both Missouri and Kansas closed their borders to Texas cattle because they carried tick fever, to which regular farm cattle were not immune.[3]

It was McCoy, however, who in 1867 persuaded the Kansas Pacific Railroad to provide a railhead at Abilene, Kansas, just beyond the Kansas-Texas fever quarantine line. Then, he himself described and promoted a cattle trail up from Texas that could be an avenue for a fortune for himself, the railroads, town builders, and Texas cattlemen. McCoy himself advertised the availability of Abilene as a railhead in flyers and ads throughout Texas. The dramatic result came on September 5, 1867, when twenty carloads of Texas cattle were sent from Abilene on their way to Chicago, and by the end of the year some thirty-five thousand cattle had been shipped.[4]

How do certain names capture the imagination of Americans and become an enduring icon in American culture? The fabled Chisholm Trail was named for Jesse Chisholm (c. 1805–1868), a frontier trader whose father was Scottish and his mother a Cherokee. Chisholm went west at an early age and settled in a Cherokee community in Arkansas, where he became a frontier trader with tribes located in the future Indian Territory. His customers included the Osage, Wichita, Kiowa, and Comanche Indians.

Jesse Chisholm was a man of many talents. He not only knew the country, but claimed that he could speak fourteen Indian dialects! His language skills assisted Sam Houston in dealing with Plains tribes in the 1840s, and made him invaluable as an interpreter when federal officials were negotiating treaties in the Arkansas region. He was also a crucial player when white captives taken by the Comanches were being ransomed. During the Civil War Chisholm maintained a trading post near future Wichita, Kansas.[5] Immediately after the war he developed a wagon trail due south to the Red River to take trade goods to various tribes. It was his wagon route that became the Chisholm Trail, the name having been chosen by McCoy. Although the original trail did not run through Texas, eventually the entire extended trail from Abilene to the Rio Grande came to be known as the Chisholm Trail.[6]

Early herds from Texas usually followed the old Shawnee Trail that ran northward to San Antonio, Austin, and Waco, where the Shawnee and Chisholm trails divided. The Chisholm went on to Fort Worth, while the Shawnee went on to Dallas, and there to Preston on the Red River. There the Shawnee moved on to Fort Gibson in the Indian Territory, where it split again into five branches: the easternmost to St. Louis, another to Baxter Springs, and one from Sedalia to Quincy, Illinois. The next branch went due north to Kansas City. A more western one trailed to St. Mary's, Kansas, and to St. Joseph. A West Shawnee Trail landed up in Wichita.[7]

The Chisholm Trail veered from the Shawnee to go to San Antonio, and there to Austin where it reunited with the Shawnee as far as Waco. There it split, the Chisholm going on to Fort Worth and then north to Red River Station (on the Red River) and straight north to Abilene. It is easy to say straight north, but that meant crossing a daunting set of rivers: the Wichita, the Canadian, the North Canadian, the Cimarron, and after reaching Caldwell and Wichita, it crossed the Arkansas River before reaching Abilene. Most times the going was easy, but the Red River crossing, in Wayne Gard's words, was "made perilous by floods and quicksands." Other rivers that meant trouble were the South Canadian, the Cimarron, and the Salt Fork of the Arkansas where Charlie Siringo's outfit were detained for a week by floods.[8]

Ironically, in 1871, only four years after McCoy had made history by making Abilene the premier cattle-shipping town, it began to lose out in competition with the newer cattle towns of Ellsworth, Junction City, Newton, Wichita, and Caldwell. Naturally the route of the northern end of the trail varied with the destination of a particular town. The word *trail* suggests a specific well-defined route. In actuality the herds wandered on a wide swath, always hunting adequate grass and water but coming together at safe stream and river crossings.

Soon a classic system developed, so well described by Siringo and hundreds of others who participated in the long drives. Each herd was assigned a trail boss, twenty or more cowboys, a cook with a chuck wagon, and a horse wrangler—who took care of the remuda of horses, usually five or six for each cowboy. If weather conditions were favorable a herd could be marched from Texas to Kansas across the Indian Territory for between 60 and 75 cents per steer—a cost that was minimal compared to the cost of shipping by rail.

As has been noted earlier, ranchers with smaller herds often turned them over to a trailing contractor who would drive them separately or combine them into one larger herd and deliver them on a fee basis.

Donald E. Worcester has reported that one of the great trail contracting firms, the Pryor Brothers, agreed to deliver forty-five thousand cattle in 1884 by organizing them into fifteen separate herds. The Pryors realized a cool $20,000 net profit from this endeavor.[9]

Meanwhile other trails developed. The Western Trail ran to Dodge City, and those from the Panhandle followed more west to northeast routes, usually to Dodge, but later to Caldwell. The heyday of the Chisholm Trail lasted less than eighteen years, for in 1885 Kansas not only passed a new quarantine law against Texas tick fever, homesteaders had now occupied much of Kansas and fiercely objected to Texas cattle invading their farms. They sued for compensation—often successfully. The real end came with barbed-wire fences, making it impossible to march cattle north. But the traffic on the Chisholm Trail in its brief existence was truly awesome. More than five million cattle had gone up the trail, as well as a million mustangs. As Donald Worcester has observed, it was "the greatest migration of livestock in world history."[10]

Although the focus of this chapter is Caldwell, Kansas, where Charlie Siringo lived for three years as a merchant running a cigar store and ice cream and oyster store, each of the towns deserve attention.

As soon as cattle began to be shipped from Abilene in 1867, "hundreds of hopeful entrepreneurs, bankers, and land speculators" swarmed into the town. McCoy himself soon became mayor of Abilene, but shrewd businessman that he was, he allied himself with Shanghai Pierce, Charlie F. Gross, and Samuel N. Hitt in developing Abilene. By 1870 the town had segregated suburban brothel districts for Texas drovers, had enacted a civil code to govern cowboy behavior, and hired a marshal who controlled the entire police force of the town. He and his deputies made rounds, conducted routine arrests, and generally kept the town peaceful.[11]

From the beginning however, farmers objected to Texas cattle ruining their crops and grassland as they tramped past their farms, and exposing their own cattle to the dreaded Texas fever tick. McCoy had to promise farmers that he would compensate them for their losses. By 1871 land speculators anxious to sell farmland, and urban residents, tired of the gambling and corruption of Texas cattlemen and their associates, founded an effective anti-cattle movement that eventually pushed the cattlemen out. The drovers quickly turned to the next cattle town, Ellsworth, which was situated sixty miles to the Southwest. Not only was Ellsworth on the Union Pacific railroad line, it was the site of Fort

Harker, which had been established there in 1865 to control Indian raids. Despite floods and an outbreak of cholera, Ellsworth did attract Texas cattle trade for a few years. The Kansas legislature helped by laying out a cattle trail from Fort Cobb in the Indian Territory to the town. The drovers were assured that if they stayed on the trail and (by implication) in Indian Territory until cooler weather killed off remaining Texas ticks, Ellsworth would not have to observe the Texas fever quarantine. Even so, by 1872 the local farmers had formed a protective association and two years later, the quarantine law had been extended to include Ellsworth.[12]

Where would the next quarantine-free railhead be? This time it was Wichita, southeast of Ellsworth. Although the region had recently been the home of the Wichita tribe of Osage Indians until 1867, and land titles were still in a state of flux, town builders and speculators had moved in, in the hope that they could lure the AT&SF railroad to Wichita. Never one to admit defeat, McCoy himself, in alliance with Pierce, Gross, and Hitt, helped establish stockyards at Wichita. By 1872 the railroad had reached Wichita and the town boomed instantly with seventy thousand cattle being shipped in that year. Four years later, however, the Abilene and Ellsworth pattern was repeated when angry Grangers and anti-cattle settlers secured such an especially stringent herd law that Wichita's cattle business declined precipitately and by 1877–1878 the town had become an agricultural community.[13]

This time it was the Santa Fe Railroad that decided it made sense to establish a railhead for Texas cattle much farther west and thus safely beyond the quarantine laws at least for the near future. This newest cattle town, Dodge City, had a different beginning than its predecessor in that Fort Dodge, a federal army post, was situated there; it was also on both the Santa Fe Trail and on the Arkansas River. Moreover, like Fort Griffin in Texas, it had already served as a shipping point for buffalo hides. Indeed, during the winter of 1872–1873 some two hundred thousand buffalo hides were shipped from there. Among other things this meant that Dodge, with a full contingent of buffalo hunters, was a rough and ready town long before the cattlemen and cowboys began to arrive.[14]

Dodge was different in yet another way. Beginning at San Antonio, Texas drovers went up the Western Trail instead of the Chisholm. By 1877 the move was on and Dodge became the Santa Fe railroad's largest cattle shipping center. As has been noted before, by 1877 cattle were also being driven from the Texas Panhandle to Dodge. It also became a way station for cattle being sent north to Wyoming and Montana for summer grazing or as beeves for Indian reservations and federal forts, or even to establish year-round northern ranchers.[15]

To the nation Dodge City became the quintessential tough and violent cattle town with its saloons and brothels, its seemingly large number of shootings and murders, brought on by an enduring hostility between buffalo hunters and cowboys, or by Texas gunmen and outlaws. As has been noted earlier, Charlie Siringo and his friend Wes Adams had this experience when they got into a drunken brawl with buffalo hunters in Bat Masterson's Lone Star Saloon on July 3, 1877, and had to flee town to escape arrest. Here could be found Wild Bill Hickok, who was its town marshal for a time; and here Texas outlaws like Ben Thompson congregated. Dodge City could boast of nine murders in 1872 and 1873 alone—yet over the years the total number of homicides, writes Robert Dykstra, was only fifteen.[16] Dodge's great days ended in 1884–1885 when the governor of Kansas extended the tick quarantine law to the entire state. By that time, however, Texas cattlemen were already turning to shipping by rail lines that now crisscrossed their home state.

The last great cattle town was Caldwell, Kansas, 50 miles south of Wichita on the Chisholm Trail. Like its predecessor it was founded by shrewd town builders, in this case by Charles H. Stone, a land speculator, and James H. Dagner, a liquor dealer. Their biggest problem was that no railroad ran near the town. Between 1873 and 1880, however, local citizens and cattle interests negotiated for a railroad, promising subsidies to various lines, but not until June 1, 1880, did the Santa Fe Railroad reach the town. Caldwell knew that among other things it had the advantage of distance. It was 130 miles closer to Texas than Wichita.[17]

Then, ironically, the Kansas City, Lawrence and Southern Railway, seeing that it had lost the race to Caldwell, built toward Hunnewell some miles to the east. Hunnewell also had the advantage of being on the border of the Indian Territory. Its presence did have the effect of siphoning off some of Caldwell's cattle business. As we shall see, these two ambitious communities were to engage in a comic opera competition not only for the cattle trade but as a port of entry to Indian Territory lands if they should ever be opened up to white settlers.

Caldwell's unique advantage over the other cattle towns was that by being on the Kansas border, cattle coming up the Chisholm Trail could be held in the Indian Territory until ready for shipping, directly onto cattle cars, and thus avoid the Kansas quarantine law. That realization had already prompted Texans to arrange with Arapaho and Cheyenne tribes to rent their land as holding ranches. The Cherokee Strip—a six-million-acre region of future Oklahoma, also soon became the site of big Texas ranches, presumably temporary, but in actuality permanent with headquarters and a staff of ranch hands. Inevitably ranchers began to fence their rented lands with barbed wire, thus making it impossible for non-lease Texas drovers to trek their cattle through this portion of the Indian Territory.[18]

The Cherokee Strip ranchers were ruthless in their attempt to control these rented lands. When the Cherokee Tribe tried to collect grazing taxes, cattlemen tried to evade paying them and did so only after the fees were reduced. Then they proceeded to fence in the whole region with barbed wire and formed their own Cherokee Strip Live Stock Association with headquarters at Caldwell.[19]

With the coming of the Atchison, Topeka and Santa Fe, Caldwell also became a wild town almost overnight. The 1880 police register listed eleven saloons and twenty-five prostitutes, and later recorded that seven homicides had occurred between 1879 and 1881. To keep order, Caldwell chose to hire gunfighters as law officers. As one looks more closely at the homicides, however, they do not point to a clear pattern that the murders were associated with cattlemen and cowboys.[20]

One must admit Caldwell did all it could to promote the cattle trade. Not only did its businessmen travel to Texas to drum up trade, the city itself paid for ads and circulars to attract cattlemen. The Santa Fe itself engaged in a rate war with its rival, the Kansas City, Lawrence and South at Hunnewell.[21]

By 1880 most cattle trade was with large-scale customers: cattlemen living on some six million acres of leased land in the Indian Territory and those from the Texas Panhandle. That stability stemmed in part from the fact that Caldwell had become an informal headquarters for cattlemen permanently living in the Cherokee Strip, so much so that, as Robert Dykstra has noted, they not only sent their children to Caldwell schools, they started the Stock Exchange Bank, built their own hotel, the Southwestern, in 1883, and helped finance a huge civic auditorium a year later.[22]

Inevitably, factions representing the regional origins of Caldwell's citizens began to cause political and social problems. By 1885 over 88 percent of the residents were native-born Americans, of which over 41 percent were from the Middle West, while 26.4 percent were from the South. The 12 percent who were foreign-born were mostly from Ireland, Germany, Great Britain, and Canada, while a mere 5 percent came from New England or the West. Naturally, the southern 26 percent saw the 41 percent of Midwesterners as Yankees. Siringo himself had early believed all Kansans were Yankees. Regional tensions developed to the point that the south end of Main Street was seen as Southern with its own hotel and bank, while the northern end also boasted its own hotel and bank, the Leland and the Caldwell Savings Bank.[23]

As in the other Kansas cow towns, the Midwesterners tended to be reformers with a strong commitment to prohibition, so much so that they tried to close the Caldwell saloons in 1881 and 1882.[24] Meanwhile other dissident forces were at work. Speculators and early boomers, led by David L. Payne and William C. Couch, sought to open the Cherokee Strip to white settlers, even by invading the strip, only to be driven out by federal troops. For obvious reasons the Oklahoma Boomers, as they were called, strongly objected to the idea of a permanent cattle strip. Caldwell, still clearly dominated by cattlemen, became hostile to the Oklahoma Boomers.

With the passage of the total quarantine law against cattle in 1885, however, Caldwell had no option but to embrace the Boomers' movement. As early as February 1885, some four hundred Boomer supporters held a rally at the Caldwell Civic Center. Soon thereafter, George W. Reilly, a Boomer favorite, was elected mayor of Caldwell and a Boomer newspaper, the *Oklahoma War Chief*, began publishing in the town using enthusiastic spread-eagle promotional language. Indeed, Caldwell civic leaders, hearing that the Boomers, whose headquarters were at Arkansas City to the east, were unhappy with their reception in that town, sent a delegation, armed with cash and promises, and actually persuaded them to move their operation, which included two hundred supporters, to Caldwell! One of the key persuaders was none other but that one-time cowboy, now successful merchant, Charlie Siringo.[25]

⚜ ⚜

When Charlie Siringo returned to the LX Ranch after his seven months in New Mexico attending the Coghlan court case and wandering around southwest Texas and eastern New Mexico, he found a very different situation at the LX. Bill Moore, having illegally branded enough LX calves and steers to start his own ranch with some of his own cowhands, had been fired, and John Hollicott, an easygoing Scot who had worked for George Littlefield, was the new manager. Siringo himself had dreamed of becoming the manager, but was told by Beals that he was too wild and reckless for the job. This unwelcome information undoubtedly lessened his own sense of loyalty to the LX.[26]

Soon after his return, Charlie was asked by Hollicott to drive eight hundred fat steers slowly to Caldwell, Kansas, for shipping. With the usual outfit he reached Caldwell on September 1, where he turned the herd loose on the LX steer ranch on Turkey Creek in the Indian Territory. So numerous were the established ranches and their cattle in the western end of the Territory that he actually attended cattle roundups there, "gathering lost LX steers."[27]

When he had finished with the roundup, Siringo met David T. Beals in Caldwell, where he learned that the latter had purchased a farm on the Indian Territory line two miles southeast of the town on which he intended to winter the LX cowponies. Beals asked Charlie to take charge of the farm and the more than one hundred horses there. It is likely that Charlie volunteered for the job, for he was already taken with Caldwell, and, as noted earlier, decided to buy town lots there. Knowing Mr. Beals's fondness for Charlie, he may have loaned Charlie money for buying the town lots.

Whether he admitted it or not, Charlie was clearly finished with being a cowboy. He must have saved enough money to buy property and travel. Indeed, he chose to go back to Texas by way of St. Louis to visit his sister, now happily married with a family. While there he made peace with Jimmy Byron, the bellboy at the Planter's Hotel he had fought with many years before. Still feeling proud of himself, and decked out in proper clothes that his sister had chosen for him, he visited his uncle Nick White in Galveston before taking a Morgan steamship to the remains of Indianola, which was still recovering from the devastating hurricane of 1875. There he found two boyhood playmates, Johnny and Jimmy Williams, who took him in their sailboat to Matagorda, where many of his earlier acquaintances now lived. Then he went to Cash's

Creek to see his mother with the intention of taking her to Kansas, and hired Fred Cornelius, whom he had known on Matagorda Peninsula many years before, to take him in an ox-drawn sled to the nearest railroad fifty miles north. It was on this trip that Charlie confided to Cornelius that he was doing some writing.[28]

Charlie and his mother arrived in Caldwell a few days before Christmas, bought furniture for their house, and established, as he put it, "Home Sweet Home." He then "put in a winter" operating the Bates and Beals horse ranch before being ordered back to the LX Ranch in March.[29]

But before that happened he attended church with Miss May Beals, David Beals's niece, who introduced him to her fifteen-year-old friend, Mamie Lloyd, from Shelbyville, Illinois, whose parents had moved to Caldwell. Pretty, black-eyed Mamie was obviously a charmer, and Charlie instantly fell in love with her. Incredibly, six days later Charlie and Mamie married with both Siringo's mother and Mamie's parents in attendance. The wedding was held at the Philips Hotel in Wellington, a more established town than Caldwell. Charlie makes it seem so wonderfully sudden and romantic, but my twentieth-century perspective suggests that they may have known one another longer.[30]

Three days after his marriage, Siringo dashed to the LX, where he participated in a roundup of some three thousand head of cattle on the Red and Pease rivers in the eastern Panhandle. As soon as the ranch hands had sorted out eight hundred fat steers, Siringo set out for Caldwell, arriving around September 1. By this time the cattle drives from the Panhandle, only two hundred miles from Caldwell, were a routine business, so that as soon as he reached Caldwell and saw his beloved Mamie, Beals ordered him back to the LX to bring in another herd of steers. Charlie was infuriated by this latest order and fumed and fussed as he and his outfit made their way west. A few days out he became so angry, he turned the outfit over to his fellow cowboy, Charlie Sprague, and headed back to Mamie. As he wrote in *Riata and Spurs*, "Then I swore off being a cowboy. I hated to quit the LX outfit, as Mr. David T. Beals was the best man I ever worked for. He was an honest, broadgauge cattleman."[31]

Back in Caldwell, Siringo rented a storeroom on Main Street where he opened a tobacco and cigar store, to which he added a line of confectionaries. His first venture into the mercantile world proved to be so successful he rented an adjoining storeroom and cut an archway between the two. "In this I opened up an ice-cream and oyster parlour. Soon I had five clerks and attendants in my employ."[32]

Charlie's success was well-nigh inevitable. Contrary to the Hollywood image of cowboys rolling their own cigarettes using Prince Albert tobacco, they also liked cigars, especially when celebrating in a cattle town. Siringo himself enjoyed cigars. By 1882 Siringo probably knew some five hundred ranchers and ranch hands living in the Cherokee Strip who came to town to buy supplies and celebrate. Assuming that he did not yet have electrical refrigeration, some of those five attendants were undoubtedly endlessly cranking freezers! Oysters undoubtedly came in via the railroad packed in sawdust and ice.

Siringo's store benefited not only from the presence of cattlemen living in the Indian Territory, but also from U.S. soldiers stationed there both to keep order between the Indians and ranchers, and to prevent "Boomers" from opening up the Cherokee Strip to farmers. Indeed Caldwell's population had been augmented by groups of land speculators and "Boomers" hoping to use the town as a base from which to invade the strip.[33]

With the Boomers as yet another set of regular customers, Siringo had a sign painted whose ambivalent message suggested he was ready to welcome any factions. Mounted on the overhead framework of the iron bridge across Bluff Creek, "The painting showed a mounted cowboy with a long-horn steer at the end of a rope. Over this way my 'Oklahoma Boomer' cigar and advertisement." Although the sign was shot at repeatedly it was never torn down. Charlie now boasted that he was known as the "Oklahoma Border Cigar King." He ordered one hundred thousand cigars from an eastern firm, which obligingly printed "The Oklahoma Boomer" on the wrapper. Charlie tells us that they sold like "hotcakes."[34]

By 1885 Charlie was greatly enjoying his success as a merchant and his popularity with fellow citizens. When Caldwell held a grand cowboy tournament at the fair grounds (this was only a year after Cody had held a similar event in Ogallala, Nebraska, and after Dodge City had just held one), Charlie competed for prizes and won a lady's gold ring for Mamie. Later in the event he won a silver cup for roping and hogtying a steer in forty-four seconds. He was a cowboy again and wore his "high-heel" Texas boots, but since he could not find his red sash, which he had worn since he was a teenager, he had to wear suspenders. Later his wife confessed that she had been so embarrassed by the sash she had secretly burned it.[35]

⁘ ⁘

Siringo's joyous account of life in Caldwell must be countered by its darker, more violent history. On July 7, 1879, "two cowboys, George Wood and Jake Adams, rode into town armed with several six-shooters. Along with Johnny Nickelson, the pair had trailed cattle up from the Cherokee Nation in the Indian Territory. They were hot, tired, and ready for some excitement after their long journey."

Wood and Adams first had drinks in the Occidental Saloon on Main Street, then began to fire their revolvers and continued to do so after mounting their horses and riding up and down the town streets. Hearing the shooting, Caldwell's constable, W. C. Kelly, and John Wilson, his deputy, rounded up men to form a posse, which included George Flat, a fearless man known for his accuracy with a gun. By then the two cowboys were back at the Occidental, where Wilson and Flat encountered them. Words were exchanged, after which one of the cowboys fired at the officers. George Flat returned the fire, and as Douglas Lober has written, "Soon, both Wood and Adams lay dead in the streets of Caldwell." A few days later, a jury exonerated Wilson and Flat, saying that they had killed "while in the act of performing their duties."[36]

When Wood and Adams were shot, Caldwell was still in the process of electing a mayor and a city council and of passing an ordinance to create the office of city marshal.[37] As Douglas Lober has noted, however, Caldwell engaged in two systems of law enforcement. The first was the older frontier practice of vigilantism in which the criminals were hanged. "Eleven thieves and killers went before 'Judge Lynch' around Caldwell between 1871 and 1885," usually for two major crimes: "unjustifiable murder and horse stealing."[38] To control vice and crime generally, however, Caldwell adopted a most interesting if not original local legal system. It levied fines on prostitutes and madams, fines on gamblers—for gambling was illegal—and heavy fines on saloons for breaches of the peace, etc.[39]

The persons who upheld the law, arrested drunks, enforced a no-guns city ordinance with large fines, made arrests, and fined the "wicked," were marshals, often accompanied by a deputy, with fines being set by a police judge. The system looked all right on paper, but it was full of contradictions. The marshal's salary, for example, came in part from the income realized from fines; thus the more fines the better the salary. Given the fact that there was drinking and violence and guns were very much in evidence, there were shootouts. In short, a marshal's job was a dangerous one and there were few volunteers.

That led to the next contradiction: the town fathers hired gunmen, bullies, and sometimes outlaws and desperados to serve as marshals, based on the philosophy that was common in other cattle towns—hire gunmen to take care of gunmen. The results in Caldwell between 1879 and 1885 were extraordinary. As Douglas Lober has found, of the fourteen men who died in Caldwell during these years, five were marshals, one was an assistant marshal, one a policeman, and two were ex-mayors. Thus of the fourteen men killed in Caldwell, eight were so-called officers of the law![40]

There was, however, a reason for all these killings. Caldwell's police docket reveals that ten of its seventeen marshals were themselves arrested at least once for breaking the law. Nevertheless, they did keep order so that in a seven-year period there were only fourteen murders.[41]

Certainly the most dramatic crime in Caldwell's relatively peaceful existence occurred when Henry Brown, who had been a member of Billy the Kid's "gang" when they hung around the LX Ranch and Tascosa in 1877—was appointed marshal. His past was not well known although Siringo had met him at the LX, and knew that he had broken with the Kid and reformed.[42] Henry Brown was seen as a good marshal and won praises from the local newspaper. Siringo himself remained quiet about Brown's past.

Then one day Henry Brown and his assistant secured permission to leave town to chase a criminal in the Indian Territory. Instead the two men, joined by two more, went to Medicine Lodge, Kansas, some seventy miles away, where they robbed a bank, shot and killed the cashier, and fatally wounded the president, who died the next day. The enraged townspeople of Medicine Lodge killed Brown and hanged the other three robbers.[43]

What is so revealing about the homicides is that they occurred throughout the year and not just when cattle drovers were in town. In short, the old images of drunken cowboys shooting up the town needs some adjustment to the facts. It was true, however, that one key to the success of Caldwell's cattle trade was the presence of prostitutes, gamblers, and saloons. While all of these groups were constantly fined by city officials, when the fines threatened to drive them out, the city itself lowered fines when it seemed wise to do so.[44]

Caldwell was an exceptionally successful cattle town, but its days as such were numbered. In 1884 the last major drive over the Chisholm Trail occurred. With the coming of barbed wire, easy access to railroads that now crisscrossed Texas, and the imposition of a stringent statewide quarantine by the Kansas legislature, Caldwell quickly became both a farming community and an important supply center for Oklahoma Boomers seeking to open the Cherokee Strip to white settlers, an event which finally occurred in 1889.[45]

What is so intriguing about the Caldwell story is that while it had the usual quota of saloons, gambling houses, and brothels—the most notorious of which was the Red Light Saloon run by Mag Woods, a Wichita prostitute, and her husband, George—the majority of its population were law-abiding citizens. At least one authority has said the city never contained more than thirty-three "soiled doves," of whom at least five (Becky Banks, Lizzie Roberts, Belle Piper, Lucy Moody, and Mary Barbizi) were residents of George and Mag Woods's Red Light Saloon. Ironically we know their names because they were fined and thus their names turn up in the Caldwell police files.[46]

In contrast, the law-abiding citizens were busy establishing a public school as early as 1872. A decade later the school had become a seven-room brick schoolhouse. A school was a crucial institution because, according to the census of 1880, 22 percent of Caldwell's population was under ten years of age and 38 percent was under twenty. By 1883, the town had three churches, Methodist, Presbyterian, and Christian, two newspapers, two banks, two hotels, and a civic center.[47]

Even so, it was a curiously unbalanced population. In 1880, for example, 63 percent of its inhabitants were male, and 37 percent were women; but the 37-percent figure must be further clarified by the fact that over 30 percent of the females were under ten years of age and 56 percent were under twenty-one. Moreover, 96 percent of the women between thirty-one and forty were married and even 82 percent of the women between twenty-one and thirty were also married.[48]

"On the other hand," writes Douglas Lober, "almost 40% of the males were between twenty-one and thirty while nearly 60% were between the ages of thirty-one and forty."[49] But because seasonal cowboys were not included in the 1880 census figures the numbers and ages of males were not that accurate. What is stunning is that most females were either children or, if over twenty, married. No wonder Charlie Siringo found his bride in the teenage group. Mamie was only fifteen or sixteen when she married him.

Two events symbolize the passing of the cattle era in Caldwell. First, there had been a growing tension since 1882 between the prohibitionist and the whiskey forces in the city. In 1884 an outspoken prohibitionist newspaper editor, Enos Blair, had his house burned down by pro-gambling and pro-whiskey advocates led by a gambler named Frank Noyer. Irate citizens resorted to vigilante action and hanged Noyer.[50]

The second symbol of the passing of the cattle frontier occurred in 1887 when Caldwell's oldest saloon—the First Chance—burned. Its name came from the fact that it was located on the Kansas–Indian Territory border and advertised to Texas cowboys coming to Caldwell that it was their "First Chance," since liquor was prohibited in the Indian Territory, whereas a sign that greeted them on their way back to Texas claimed that it was their "Last Chance." An even more dramatic transformation occurred when the Red Light Saloon, the brothel run by George and Mag Woods, became a store selling, as Douglas Lober has wryly noted, "agricultural implements."[51]

II: THE BUDDING AUTHOR

In *A Texas Cowboy*, Charlie Siringo tells a charming story of how he came to write his first book. During the winter of 1882–1883 while running the Bates and Beals horse ranch in the Indian Territory just across the Kansas line from Caldwell, he and the eight cowboys at the ranch took a pledge to cut down on their swearing. So they "made an iron-clad rule that whoever was heard swearing or caught picking grey backs (lice) off and throwing them on the floor without first killing them, should pay a fine of ten cents for each and every offense. The proceeds to be used for buying choice literature—something that would have a tendency to raise us above the average cow-puncher."[52]

Charlie's pals must have been both a fine lot of swearers and lice-ridden for within twenty-four hours they had put three dollars worth of dimes in the pot. As self-appointed treasurer Charlie suggested that he "send the money off for a years subscription to some good newspaper." The problem was that two of the cowboys were Texans who "could neither read nor write." Nevertheless they had a vote and declared unanimously for a subscription to the *Police Gazette*. Why the *Gazette*? asked their companions. "Cause we can read the pictures," they said.[53]

When the *Police Gazette* arrived, Charlie himself became fascinated by the story of an old New York preacher named Pott who had written a sensational novel, which had earned him "several hundred thousand dollars," and so he was now "over in Paris blowing it in." Thinking how wonderful it would be to become a successful author by writing about a topic that was still an "untrodden field," Siringo, who was still very much a Texas Southerner, and whose boyhood hero had been Jefferson Davis, decided to write, as he put it, "a 'nigger' love story." Both hero and heroine were imagined as very dark in color and living in African Bend on the Colorado River. Siringo's frequent references to Black Americans when he was working for Grimes and Shanghai Pierce were always condescending unless a Black cowboy had done him favor. Happily for all of us, Siringo's Black romance soon got out of hand. The hero, Andrew Jackson, was sent to prison for hog stealing, and Patsy Washington, the heroine, eloped with a Yankee carpetbagger. Fortunately Siringo had enough sense to throw the manuscript into the fire. He then turned to "the idea of writing a history of my own short, but rugged life," still in the naïve hope that it would make him rich.[54]

As delightful as Siringo's anecdote about how he became an author is, several facts dispute its accuracy. When he was still employed at the LX Ranch in the late 1870s he was busy interviewing Ash Upson, Pat Garrett, Marshal John Poe, and his cowboy pals, who unlike Siringo, actually helped capture Billy the Kid the first time (before he later escaped prison and went on a second rampage). Obviously, Siringo had taken notes early on, for as he told Fred Cornelius during a visit to Texas in 1882, he was doing "some Writing." It also seems obvious that, like Pat Garrett, who had already published a volume on Billy the Kid, he, too, planned to cash in on the sensational saga of Billy the Kid's life.

Once Siringo settled in Caldwell he came to know the local newspaper editor, and later the editor of the Boomer newspaper, the *Oklahoma War Chief*. Both men must have complimented him on his spirited telling of his youthful experiences. Then, soon after he married Mamie and was feeling successful as a merchant, he invited Shanghai Pierce to dinner, where they talked of old times.[55]

Siringo's ego was further boosted when a blind phrenologist came to Caldwell to tell fortunes by "reading people's heads." Having attracted great attention and therefore a full house, he asked for volunteers who would let him analyze their heads. Appropriately, he predicted an unfavorable future for Marshal Henry Brown, who was soon to rob Medicine Lodge Bank.

Later, as he rubbed his hands over Mamie Siringo's head, he described her as a wonderfully sweet girl "who cannot tell a lie or do a wrong."[56]

When the audience asked Siringo to come forward, he recalls that after rubbing his head, the phrenologist said, "Ladies and gentlemen, here is a mule's head." After much laughter from the audience, he explained that Siringo had "a large stubborn bump but a fine head for a newspaper editor, a fine stock raiser, or a detective; that in any of these callings I would make a success."[57]

✢ ✢

While Siringo was writing *A Texas Cowboy*, he came to know a large, strong trailsman in 1883, when the latter delivered a herd of Texas horses to Caldwell. His name was Andy Adams. Born on an Indiana stock farm run by his pioneering, but cultured and educated Scotch-Irish parents, he grew up loving both the written word and horses and cattle. As Wilson M. Hudson, his biographer, writes: "Andy came to see cattle as man's companions through the ages, the ox as an agricultural helper and the cow as a provider of daily substance."[58]

Even so, Adams was especially attracted to horses, having seen herds of Texas horses being shipped while working in Arkansas. In 1882 he came to San Antonio, where a famous firm, Smith and Redmon, dealt in horses and mules. Although we have no clear evidence that he worked for this firm, we do know that he enjoyed driving herds of either horses or cattle to the railheads in Kansas. In 1883, the horse market was especially good at Caldwell, and he appears to have arrived there with a horse herd.[59]

Andy Adams was not as outgoing or boastful as Siringo, but this pleasant, good-natured man and Siringo made friends easily. Indeed, Adams had already befriended Frank Byles, J. Frank Dobie's uncle, a prominent Texas cattleman who was Dobie's lifelong hero and from whom he inherited his name "Frank."[60] Adams and Byles drove horse herds together to Caldwell and shared a hotel room while there. Once in Caldwell Adams must have listened to Siringo's stories about the cattle drives, his experience in the Panhandle, and his enthusiastic accounts of the fine horses he had owned and raced. He must also have mentioned that he had recently been in charge of the Bates and Beals horse ranch near Caldwell.

Although Andy Adams went back to Texas and brought herds of

horses and cattle north to Kansas and all the way to Montana ranches until 1890, and Charlie left Caldwell to live in Chicago in 1886, Andy Adams kept in touch with Siringo and admired his *A Texas Cowboy*. But not until he had retired from being a trail driver, a merchant in Rockport, Texas, and a miner in Nevada and Colorado did the easygoing Andy settle in Colorado Springs, Colorado, and decide to write about his own experience as a trail driver. Indeed, it appears that Adams decided to write only after reading Emerson Hough's *The Story of the Cowboy*, which appeared in 1897. Hough himself was an Iowa-born lover of the western outdoors whose writings glorified the West.[61]

After many attempts to write short stories, Andy Adams published his classic novel, *Log of a Cowboy*, in 1903, which the public immediately believed was his own true history—indeed his autobiography. It was a bestseller and gave him a national reputation.[62] Among those who praised him were Emerson Hough, Charlie Russell, Eugene Manlove Rhodes, Charlie Goodnight, George W. Saunders, Philip Ashton Rollins, and later, J. Frank Dobie, J. Evetts Haley, and Walter Prescott Webb.[63]

What is of particular interest is that Caldwell is the scene of one of Adams's early stories, "A Question of Possession," which is about how a crooked sheriff and his gang steal a herd of horses belonging to a Mr. Gray. But Gray, having formed his own posse of friends and other horse owners, stands the sheriff down and recovers his herd. As Hudson, Adams's biographer, has noted, "violence is threatened, but not a shot is fired. Gray wins the contest by moral courage." Many years later, "Andy told some friends in Colorado Springs, by implication, that he was riding with Gray's posse."[64]

Actually ten of Adams's stories in his book *Cattle Brands* (1906) were set "wholly or partly in the Indian Territory or Caldwell." Again, as his biographer notes, Andy made "liberal use of the material he had picked up while trailing through or staying in Caldwell to conclude his business." The fact was Andy had been in Caldwell many times and was there trading for weeks at a time. He came to know cattlemen in the Cherokee Strip and saw them in Caldwell.[65] One of Adams's stories, "Seigerman's Percent," is about a boastful man, Theodore Baughman, an army scout in the Indian Territory who made Caldwell his headquarters. Baughman appeared in Siringo's *A Texas Cowboy* as a boastful man whose head is examined by the blind phrenologist.[66] Another of Adams's stories centers on Marshal Henry Bown's attempt to rob the bank at Medicine Lodge.[67]

The evidence is circumstantial, but Siringo and Adams must have seen each other frequently in Caldwell, for not only did they correspond, after Adams moved to Colorado Springs, he asked Siringo, by then a Pinkerton Detective stationed at the agency's headquarters in Denver, to assist him to prevent a bequest to a children's orphanage from being seized by greedy local lawyers and policemen. Siringo also visited with Adams in Colorado Springs on other occasions.[68]

It is instructive that Adams concentrated on writing real western stories of tension and conflict—but with a minimum of shooting. In contrast Siringo was like the popular town merchant, glad-handing, telling stories, engaging in contests, and praising his wife, and reporting facts such as the Henry Brown bank holdup and death by a furious posse of citizens. Neither author focused on saloons and prostitutes in their accounts. Between Adams's Caldwell stories and Siringo's happy accounts of town life, cattlemen, and efforts to lure Oklahoma Boomers to Caldwell; and Dykstra's and Lober's accounts of politics and law and order, we begin to see a much fuller, and in the end much richer saga of the last of the Kansas cattle towns. In fact we get a fine example of western urban history.

Siringo, having written and published his *A Texas Cowboy* by 1885, had his eye on a career as a writer. In 1886 he moved to Chicago with his wife and child, naïvely thinking that he would be a successful writer about his particular American West. But things did not work out as he had hoped, and he was soon short of cash. As he looked around for work, he and his wife happened to be living near Haymarket Square in Chicago where on May 4, 1886, a bomb went off, killing one policeman and wounding many more, of whom seven later died. The policeman had been in Haymarket Square to control a labor rally organized by labor radicals—soon to be called anarchists—to protest the killing of two persons the day before during a strike at the McCormick-Reaper Machine Company, where workers were demanding an eight-hour day.

After the Haymarket bomb went off, the police responded with gunfire, killing seven or eight people and wounding about a hundred. The police shootout was so wild it injured perhaps as many as fifty of their fellow officers. The Haymarket Affair, as it came to be called, produced a national wave of fear, which led public officials and the press and even some local union leaders to blame and denounce foreign anarchists as the perpetrators. As a result in Chicago hundreds of men, both American and foreign, were arrested as socialists, anarchists, and labor radicals.

In the turmoil the Pinkerton National Detective Agency, whose main headquarters was in Chicago, was busily engaged in tracking down those suspected of the bombing. Inevitably the agency was also recruiting men with experience as detectives. Charlie Siringo saw his chance. Citing references to his detective work in rounding up stolen cattle, and in helping convict Coghlan in New Mexico while working for the LX Ranch, he applied to William A. Pinkerton and received a job as a detective.[69]

Had not the blind phrenologist predicted that he would make a good detective? Over the next twenty-two years, 1886–1908, he was able to prove that the phrenologist was right.

CRIME WAS A NATIONAL THREAT IN ALMOST EVERY LARGE
AMERICAN CITY FROM SHORTLY AFTER THE END OF THE
CIVIL WAR TO THE OUTBREAK OF WORLD WAR I.

—*James D. Horan,* The Pinkertons:
The Detective Dynasty that Made History, *ix*

THE EPISODE IS OF MAJOR SIGNIFICANCE IN THE ANNALS OF
AMERICAN LABOR AND JURISPRUDENCE WHILE THE BACKGROUND
WHICH MADE IT POSSIBLE AND GIVES IT MEANING CONSTITUTES
AN IMPORTANT CHAPTER IN THE SOCIAL-REVOLUTIONARY
MOVEMENT IN THE UNITED STATES.

—*Henry David,* The History of the Haymarket Affair: A Study in
American Social-Revolutionary and Labor Movements, *xix*

HAYMARKET DEMONSTRATED, IN MORE DRAMATIC FORM
THAN ANY OTHER EVENT OF THE POST–CIVIL WAR ERA,
BOTH THE INEQUITIES OF AMERICAN CAPITALISM AND
THE LIMITATIONS OF AMERICAN JUSTICE.

—*Paul Avrich,* The Haymarket Tragedy, *xii*

THUS THE WORLD MOVES ON AND WE ALL ACT OUT
OUR LITTLE PART ON THE BIG STAGE.

—*Charles A. Siringo,* A Cowboy Detective, *99*

CHAPTER SEVEN

Rendezvous with Destiny

CHARLIE SIRINGO,

THE HAYMARKET RIOT, AND THE

PINKERTONS, 1886–1890

I: THE HAYMARKET RIOT, MAY 4, 1886

CHARLIE SIRINGO, HIS YOUNG WIFE, MAMIE, AND THEIR BABY DAUGHTER, Viola, had moved to Chicago from Caldwell, Kansas, in the spring of 1886, where he hoped to promote the sale of his *A Texas Cowboy*, and write another book. The initial success of *A Texas Cowboy* made Charlie very boastful. Indeed, he claimed that Caldwell was too small for him, and Chicago was the kind of town where he could launch his writing career.

The Siringos were living in a boarding house on Harrison Avenue when a powerful bomb exploded in nearby Haymarket Square some blocks away during a labor protest rally. The bomb killed one policeman and injured sixty others, some so seriously that seven died in the weeks following. How many workers were killed or wounded remained unclear, and whether they fired back, killing a policeman and wounding others, was also unclear. It is argued, in fact, that in the chaotic moments after the bomb exploded, the police actually wounded one another in the confused shootout.

The labor rally was one of several that had been called in response to a violent confrontation a day earlier outside the McCormick-Reaper factory between striking employees and scab laborers who had replaced them in their jobs. The melee occurred when the scab workers came off their shifts in the afternoon and were greeted by jeering union workers. Police appeared on the scene, shots were fired, and at least two strikers—possibly four—were killed. Chicago was already in the grip of a potentially violent confrontation between labor and capital because of an intense union-backed campaign for an eight-hour day, in support of which Chicago labor leaders had scheduled a general strike on May 1, 1886. In addition there were already ongoing strikes, such as the one at the McCormick-Reaper plant and other firms. To everyone's surprise and relief, May 1 passed without incident, although both labor groups and police were geared up for a possible fight. That confrontation really began at the McCormick plant on the afternoon of May 3, 1886.

Every account of the Haymarket Riot—including Siringo's own version in his book *A Cowboy Detective*, begins with the assertion that it was an anarchist's bomb that killed or maimed the sixty or more policemen. Why was the bomb-thrower (who was never identified or caught) identified as an anarchist? Few union men in the United States, in Chicago or elsewhere, had ever embraced a philosophy of anarchism, which was seen as a European, and especially a German phenomenon in the nineteenth century.

In Chicago, however, a number of workers, many of whom were European immigrants, did embrace Marxist Socialism as a way of resolving capital-labor crises and creating a peaceful, ideal utopian society in America. In the years before the Haymarket Riot several highly intelligent, articulate labor leaders in Chicago, identifying themselves as "social revolutionaries," came forth to espouse the anarchist cause in newspapers—most of them German publications such as the *Arbeiter Zeitung*, but also in an English newspaper called *The Alarm*.

The evolving and often contradictory stands taken by the social revolutionaries were so numerous and complex that together they could indeed be called "anarchistic." Some were passive and peaceful, urging reform through education; others espoused reform through political action, while still another group wanted to create armed military units ready to fight with guns, arguing that the confrontation between labor and capital justified extreme actions.[1]

A number in the third group believed that using dynamite in the form of bombs would force industrialists and capitalists to accede to labor's demands. Alfred Nobel, the Swedish chemist who had invented dynamite in 1867, had continued to perfect this explosive so that by 1875 it could be handled in waxed paper cylinders of varying sizes and used for a thousand purposes, whether in blasting out dam sites, in quarries, dredging at construction projects, mining and, of course, in making homemade bombs. So taken were the more violent social revolutionaries with dynamite that they formed what labor historian Paul Avrich calls "the cult of dynamite."[2]

The three groups of social revolutionaries discussed their different philosophies endlessly in lecture halls, outdoor rallies, and newspaper articles, even to the point, in at least one instance, of publishing directions of how to make a bomb![3]

The Haymarket Riot was a national sensation. Every major newspaper in the country followed the search for the bomber or bombers. The Chicago police quickly rounded up perhaps two hundred persons from which they identified eight suspects: Albert Parsons, August Spies, Samuel Fielden, Michael Schwab, Oscar Neebe, George Engel, Adolph Fischer, and Louis Lingg, all of whom were tried and convicted of the Haymarket bomb throwing.

It would be difficult to find a more disparate group of social revolutionaries. Albert Parsons was not an immigrant but an Alabama-born American who could claim he was a Mayflower descendant. He grew up in Texas, where he became a journalist. While in Texas he married a Mexican woman, whom critics claimed was really an African American. Whatever the truth was, when he moved to Chicago he became a champion of Black Americans. A powerful speaker, during the great railroad strike of 1877 he attacked the capitalist press and railroad barons. Eventually he joined the social revolutionaries.[4]

August Spies, on the other hand, was a German-born immigrant. Perhaps the most able of the groups, this strikingly handsome thirty-one-year-old man could be caustic and wrote critical articles on the Pinkertons. He was a contributor to the *Arbeiter Zeitung*.[5]

Louis Lingg believed in the use of dynamite and followed the teachings of Johann J. Most, a German revolutionary who advocated the use of dynamite and violence, first in Germany and then in the United States, holding conferences and issuing manifestos in the United States to promote his views. Most worked in a dynamite factory in New Jersey, yet never was a bomb thrower himself.[6]

Samuel Fielden, an immigrant from Lancashire, England, worked as a laborer in Chicago but became so bitter about his poor income that he became a socialist. A gifted speaker, he became well known for his powerful appeal to working-class people. As Paul Avrich had noted, he was more emotional than intellectual in his approach to labor-capital issues.[7]

When Michael Schwab, a native of Bavaria, came to America in 1879, he was already an ardent trade-unionist and socialist. He was soon appalled at the lack of workers' rights in the United States, and in his own words, "by becoming an opponent to the order of things . . . was soon called an anarchist." Schwab was first a reporter for the *Arbeiter Zeitung* and then became its associate editor.[8]

Oscar Neebe was born in the United States of German parents who returned to their native land when Oscar was still a boy. Upon their return to the United States, Neebe wandered west as far as Chicago, holding odd jobs before joining a brother in Philadelphia. He moved there but returned to Chicago to a good job in a metal factory. When the famous railroad strike of 1877 occurred, however, Neebe, writes Paul Avrich, "joined the socialist movement and was dismissed from his job as an agitator." Thereafter Neebe had a hard time finding a job until his brother and some friends started a yeast firm, which was a success. Neebe's great talent proved to be his ability to organize other workers into small trade unions and to secure better wages and a ten-hour day for them. Neebe's particular group of social revolutionaries, "the American Group," was influential in the Chicago labor movement out of proportion to their number and played a key role in the events leading up to the Haymarket Riot.[9]

Of the eight men arrested after the event all had endorsed the use of dynamite, "retaliatory violence," and resistance to the repressive force of capitalism and government. Only Lingg, Engel, Fischer, and Neebe had actually handled or experimented with dynamite, and Neebe does appear to have lost some fingers from a premature dynamite explosion.[10]

George Engel and Adolph Fischer were editors of the *Anarchist*, a German journal, which like the *Arbiter Zeitung* was located in Chicago. They have been described by Paul Avrich as "anarchists of an implacable and ultra-militant stamp . . . devoted to armed insurrection and propaganda by the deed."[11]

While still a student in Bremen, Germany, Fischer, with the encouragement of his father, had embraced socialism. After immigrating to America, Fischer became a printer for newspapers and eventually got a job as a printer at the *Arbeiter Zeitung*. None of the eight was more devoted to the goal of a true social revolution. Although possessed of an affectionate, outgoing nature, and beloved by his friends, Fischer had no reservations about dying in the cause of social justice for the workers of the world.[12]

Most of the Haymarket anarchists were younger men under forty years of age, but George Engel, born in Cassel, Germany, was fifty years old. After many hardships as a struggling painter and craftsman in his native land he had come to Philadelphia with his family full of hope for a new life in a free country. When he witnessed striking miners being mistreated by state militia in Philadelphia, and himself suffering from ill health that almost cost him his eyesight, he moved to Chicago in 1874 where he took a job in a wagon factory. There he befriended a fellow worker, an ardent and highly articulate socialist, who introduced him to the works of Marx, Lassalle, and other socialist writers.[13]

Progressively disillusioned by the corrupt politics of Chicago, by mistreatment of laborers, and by constant disagreements among the moderate anarchists like Parsons, Spies, and Schwab, Engel and Fischer decided to publish their own journal, *The Anarchist*, in January, 1886.[14] The publication was short-lived, but in its four issues were calls for violent action against capitalists in which Lingg, Fischer, and Engel all agreed the use of dynamite was justified. Yet none of the three appears to have been the anonymous bomb thrower in Haymarket Square. What led to their arrest, trial, and conviction were their own printed words and the inflammatory language they used in their public addresses. It was also the case that they were seen as aliens—immigrants from Europe espousing un-American beliefs. It was inevitable that Chicagoans and the nation itself would demand scapegoats for so heinous a crime.

Eventually four, Parsons, Engel, Fischer, and Spies were hanged; Lingg committed suicide by blowing himself up with a bomb while in jail. The remaining three, Fielden, Neebe, and Schwab were sent to the Illinois penitentiary.[15]

The newspapers everywhere saw the whole affair as a treasonable act by aliens—German immigrants—against the United States. American labor leaders, such as Terence V. Powderley, Grand Master of the Knights of Labor, as well as the rank and file of labor, were quick to disassociate themselves from the use of violence and bombs.[16] Tragically, none of the eight "anarchists" appear to have been actually responsible for throwing the bomb at Haymarket Square, yet they were convicted in such an obviously biased trial that scholars and legal experts have condemned it as an act of rank injustice.

On the other hand, it is true that all eight men knew each other, wrote or were associated with the *Arbeiter Zeitung*, and were leaders in the union movements. All were outraged when two strikers were killed and others wounded at the McCormick plant on May 3. Indeed, August Spies was speaking nearby to a meeting of workers. After first urging his own audience not to interfere, when he himself saw the outcome he was so angered that he dashed off a leaflet in English originally entitled "Working Men to Arms," but a compositor in the printing shop added the word "REVENGE!" in capital letters. The powerful leaflet, soon distributed as a circular, listed the humiliations workers had suffered at the hands of "the factory-lords" and called for the workers to "destroy the hideous monster that seeks to destroy you. To arms we call you, to arms! YOUR BROTHERS."[17]

Spies then penned an even stronger circular in German, which exclaimed: "annihilate the beasts in human form who call themselves rulers!" While these circulars were being distributed to working groups, others called for a protest meeting at Haymarket Square on May 4. Meanwhile Spies continued to print bitter accounts of the McCormick confrontation in the *Arbeiter Zeitung* in which he asked the question: what would have been the outcome if the workers "had been provided 'with good weapons and one single dynamite bomb, not one of the murderers would have escaped his well-deserved fate.'" By using such language it is easy, as Paul Avrich notes, to see how those extreme words "drove another nail into his coffin" when he was on trial.[18]

Understandably another militant social revolutionary group called for armed intervention and used the password *Ruhe*, (German for "rest") to alert their followers to that possibility. The password "Ruhe" was printed without Spies's knowledge in the "Letter Box" column of the *Arbeiter Zeitung*, thus seeming to demonstrate that a conspiracy to commit violence was underway. That, too, was used as incriminating evidence in the Haymarket Affair court trials.[19]

II: SIRINGO JOINS THE PINKERTONS

Charlie Siringo's own response to the Haymarket Affair—as it soon came to be called—was identical to that of other Chicagoans, except that given his Texas belief in swift justice, he was active from the very night of the bombing through the trial and conviction of the eight anarchists. Indeed, when he and his wife heard the bomb go off, and the shooting that followed, he recalls in his *A Cowboy Detective* that "A young lawyer, Reynolds by name, ran to our room to tell me to get ready and go with him to the riot." Mamie Siringo, however, would not let Charlie go. Instead, Siringo gave his Colt's 45 revolver to Reynolds to take with him. When the police saw Reynolds with a pistol in his hand, they thought he was—in Siringo's words—"an anarchist." Somehow Reynolds fled the scene as bullets whizzed by him, and he returned to the boarding house. Giving Siringo's gun back to him, he said that "he had enough of the riot business."[20]

Siringo would have us believe that he went immediately to the Pinkerton National Detective Agency in search of a job with them to hunt down the anarchists, but it was not until June 29, 1886, when he, armed with a character reference from his Chicago bank, formally applied for a position with the Pinkerton Agency. Fortunately he did get to see William Pinkerton, the son of the legendary founder, Allan Pinkerton. William had taken over the head office in Chicago when his father died in 1884.

In the interview William Pinkerton asked Siringo for the name of persons who could recommend him. Very shrewdly Charlie listed David T. Beals, former owner of the LX Ranch and now president of the Union National Bank of Kansas City, Missouri; James H. East, former LX cowboy, but later sheriff in Tascosa, Texas; and Sheriff Pat Garrett, whom Siringo boastfully described as "the slayer of 'Billy the Kid.'"[21] It seems likely that Charlie played up his own role in capturing the Kid, which of course was misleading, although as we have seen, members of his own LX outfit, including Jim East, did chase Billy into New Mexico in pursuit of stolen LX cattle.

Charlie Siringo could not have been luckier that day for Pinkerton told him that the agency was opening an office in Denver and that "they would need a cowboy detective there, as they figured on getting a lot of cattle work." Siringo then cockily told Pinkerton that "the East is too tame for me hence I wanted a position in the West."[22] Siringo's positive references did the trick and he became a Pinkerton "operative," as they were called, and went to work on the Haymarket Riot case, and other assignments in Chicago.

Although he does not tell us what he did in Chicago, his brief references suggest that he soon learned how anxious the Chicago police were to convict the anarchists, and that the finger of guilt for throwing the bomb pointed toward a certain social revolutionary named Rudolph Schnaubelt, who after being arrested had escaped, fleeing first to London and then to Argentina. Siringo believed Schnaubelt was the guilty party, but modern students of the Haymarket Riot believe that there is not a shred of evidence that he was the bomb thrower.[23]

If Siringo was wrong about Schnaubelt, he did feel that the incredibly inflammatory literature put out by the social revolutionaries, and especially the "Revenge" circular, pointed to the guilt of the eight "anarchists" in fomenting violence and hence the bombing. Even so, he must have listened to the trial closely, because he came away convinced that Oscar W. Neebe, accused of writing and distributing the "Revenge" circular calling for violence on the very day of the Haymarket bombing, had only been the printer of the circular and not its author. Many years later, John Peter Altgeld, a reform governor of Illinois, pardoned Neebe, Schwab, and Fielden because they had been unfairly accused. Siringo himself later wrote, "I heard most of the evidence, but I couldn't see the justice of sending Neebe to the pen. All that he did was to set the type in the 'Revenge' circular which was circulated calling a mass meeting on Haymarket Square to revenge the killing of strikers in a late riot in the McCormick factory."[24]

Siringo also had mixed feelings about the remaining anarchists. Observing that although "a million dollars had been subscribed by the Citizens' League to stamp out anarchism in Chicago," he felt that "much of it was used to corrupt justice." What was most important to Siringo, however, was that we had sent a stern warning to all anarchists from foreign countries that Americans would not put up with the assassinations they had perpetrated in Europe.[25]

It is revealing to dwell on Siringo's views of the Haymarket Affair, for he spent the rest of his life hating anarchists. For his short, bitter book written many years later when he was fighting with the Pinkerton Agency over his right to publish the details of his experience as one of their detectives, he chose the title, *Two Evil Isms: Pinkertonism and Anarchism*

(1915). But before that when he tangled with the union leaders in the famous Coeur d'Alene strike of 1892, he reserved his fiercest hatred for George A. Pettibone, who was enamored of using dynamite, and did so to destroy one of the Bunker Hill and Sullivan mine buildings in Idaho. Again in 1903 a vengeful member of the Western Federation of Miners, Harry Orchard, encouraged by Pettibone and Big Bill Haywood, began to use bombs in labor disputes in Colorado, seeking to assassinate both mine owners and scabs, conducting what James D. Horan has called "an unbelievable tour of murder." The climax of his vicious career came when he claimed that he was ordered by Haywood to kill former Governor Frank Steunenberg of Idaho by planting a powerful bomb at the governor's front gate. Steunenberg was blown to bits. In a sensational trial that followed, Orchard, Haywood, Pettibone, and others were tried, and Orchard was sentenced to hang, but that was later changed by Idaho's governor to life imprisonment. Siringo himself was at this 1907 trial as assistant and guard to James McParland, his boss in Denver, who had miraculously persuaded Orchard to confess to all the crimes he had committed.[26]

Thus, from his first days almost to the end of his twenty-two years with the Pinkerton Agency, Charlie Siringo was involved in capital versus labor cases that featured the use of dynamite bombings. Indeed, Siringo's career is so replete with the violent struggle between industrial capital and organized labor, that his accounts of each, the Pinkerton policies, and his often conflicted feelings about corrupt labor leaders and the unjustly treated common laborers, had a major impact on his life.

Given these facts, it is important to understand what the Pinkerton Detective Agency was, what policies it pursued, and how they influenced Charlie Siringo's life because he worked for them longer than the time he had been a cowboy.

Allan Pinkerton not only created the first major private detective agency in the United States, it became so important in the mid-nineteenth century that it was called "America's Scotland Yard." Pinkerton's incredibly strong personality and his ability—for he was an exceptionally bright man—deserve attention because his agency reflected his views—which were embraced by his two sons, Robert A. and William A.—long after his own death in July 1884. His career, well presented in James D. Horan's fascinating book: *The Pinkertons: The Detective Dynasty That Made History* (1967), is one of the most riveting rags-to-riches sagas in American history.[27]

III: ALLAN PINKERTON

Allan Pinkerton was born in Glasgow, Scotland, in 1819 in a tenement to working-class parents located on the left bank of the Clyde River, a tough slum area. His father, William, had been a hand-loom weaver before becoming a trusty in the Glasgow City Jail. His mother worked in a spinning mill. Allan's father died when he was eight years old, and he became a mainstay for his mother and his siblings. He became a cooper who at age twenty joined the Chartist movement, whose purpose it was to give ordinary citizens full voting rights and electoral reform to achieve social equality. The Chartists, however, were made up of many diverse groups. Some sought their goals by peaceable means or "moral force," while others believed in using physical force and did not hesitate to engage in violent confrontations. Pinkerton himself became a "physical force" young Chartist in the local movement and was soon on a Glasgow police list as a troublemaker. Fearing arrest in the spring of 1842, he decided to go to America but not without Joan Carfrae, with whom he had fallen in love. They were secretly married and together embarked for the United States. Despite a harrowing shipwreck off the coast of Nova Scotia, and a brief sojourn in Montreal, where he found work as a barrel maker, Pinkerton decided to migrate to Chicago where Robbie Fergus, a Chartist and printer from his hometown, helped him find a job. Pinkerton, however, soon moved to Dundee, Illinois, a small town settled by Scots. There he set up his cooperage business.[28]

By accident while he was in Dundee, Pinkerton discovered a money counterfeiting ring in the woods nearby; he spied on them and quickly reported his findings to the local sheriff. When the ring was broken up, Pinkerton was given the credit. Soon he was called on to investigate other counterfeiting operations. Pinkerton's career as a private detective had begun.[29] Meanwhile he was engaged in a secret operation of his own. Pinkerton had strong antislavery views. At some point he met John Brown, and agreed that he would assist fleeing slaves as they made their way on the Underground Railroad to Canada.[30] In time, local feuds and religious debates in Dundee led Pinkerton to move to Chicago where, because of his reputation as a fearless law and order man, he got a job as deputy sheriff of Cook County. Within a short time, the mayor of Chicago appointed him Chicago's first detective, which was followed by his appointment as a Special United States Mail Agent of the United

States Post Office, which at the time was experiencing an epidemic of postal thefts of bank drafts and money orders.[31]

To solve these crimes Pinkerton adopted a technique he and all of his future agency operatives were to use endlessly. He got a job as a mail clerk, soon spotted the crooked clerk who was stealing, had him arrested, and searched the clerk's room for evidence of pilfered bank bills and money. It was after this success that Pinkerton and a friend decided to create their own agency. Their logo, a large eye over the words "we never sleep," soon became a well-known phrase in the United States, and especially in the *Police Gazette*. His decision could not have come at a more opportune time. Contrary to the usual perception that lawless men and robbers were concentrated in the American West, the eastern half of the United States from the Midwest to Massachusetts, New York, and Pennsylvania was plagued by bank robbers, mail thefts, outlaw gangs, or a miner's union often terrorizing a rural community.[32]

During his first few weeks as a Pinkerton detective in Chicago, Siringo posed as a bum in a Chicago slum, worked for the British by shadowing Irishmen who were allegedly conspiring to harm Her Majesty's government, and became a convivial friend of a high-living corrupt banker. This was, Charlie confessed, "My first experience in having a 'good time' at someone else's expense," a technique Siringo was to perfect in his twenty-two years as a Pinkerton.[33]

Allan Pinkerton was a highly articulate man who had worked with a printer. Early on he laid out a set of general "Principles," which all operatives had to obey. Siringo recalls that he had to study the rules and regulations of the agency, "which were in book form." Some of the rules were stern; for example, the end justified the means if the ends were "for the accomplishment of justice." Operatives were to be paid on a per diem basis only and not on a salary and had to submit expense accounts. Taking on marital problems and divorce cases was forbidden.[34]

With his headquarters in Chicago, Pinkerton found himself in the center of perhaps the most ambitious railroad building boom of the mid-nineteenth century. These roads needed protection of many kinds, especially since the local state authorities could not track criminals beyond their specific jurisdiction. The Pinkerton operatives could move across state lines. Gangs and thieves found railroads to be easy pickings. Gangs could descend on a construction crew, beat, and rob them; others focused on rifling railroad mail cars. After the Civil War still others penetrated the security of the famous express companies: Adams, Southern, American, United States, and Wells Fargo. Western Union found, to its dismay, that confidential business messages were being tapped so that speculators could buy up or sell stocks before the message coming from the West or elsewhere to New York or Philadelphia could reach its rightful recipient. Moreover, bank robberies in the Midwest and East appear to have increased dramatically after the Civil War.[35]

In dealing with the Illinois Central Railroad during the 1850s, Allan Pinkerton soon befriended and came to admire George B. McClellan, vice president of the Illinois Central, which firm retained Pinkerton's service for an annual fee of $10,000. Soon Pinkerton secured contracts with six other railroads (the Michigan Central, Michigan Southern and Northern, Indiana, Chicago and Galena Union, Chicago and Rock Island, and the Chicago, Burlington and Quincy).

His success in dealing with railroad executives led Pinkerton to favor railroads and industry over labor, a predilection that became even stronger in 1877 when the agency was called upon to bring an Irish-dominated miners union in Pennsylvania to justice. Nicknamed the Molly Maguires, the union was a corrupt, violence-oriented group that was terrorizing their communities. Eventually, through the tactics of Pinkerton operative James McParland, posing as a fellow hard-drinking Irishman for nearly three years, the Molly Maguires were arrested, tried and convicted, and nineteen of them were hanged. One can easily see why the Pinkerton name was anathema to working men and why they denounced the agency during the Haymarket Affair, calling them pro-police and pro-capitalist—which of course they were.[36]

So successful was the agency that by the 1880s they employed many hundreds of operatives and opened branch offices in New York, Philadelphia, and Boston. Allan's oldest son, William, headed the Chicago office while Robert managed the New York office.

As impressive as Allan Pinkerton and his operatives were, they experienced failure as well as success. When the Civil War began there were rumors that President-elect Abraham Lincoln would be assassinated as he traveled by train from Baltimore to Washington. Pinkerton was called on to foil the plot, which he did by having Lincoln arrive in Washington earlier and at night.[37] In July 1861, when Pinkerton's friend George B. McClellan was appointed commander-in-chief of all the Union armies, he cast his lot with McClellan, for he had formed a low opinion of Lincoln in his dealings with the new president. Pinkerton hoped that the dapper general would make him head of a secret service that would spy on the enemy, even to posting operatives in the Confederate capital at Richmond; meanwhile he was busy identifying Confederate agents in Washington. McClellan had ordered Pinkerton to send spies into the Confederacy, which the latter did from the "Secret Service Department" he had established in Cincinnati. Perhaps a score of operatives, headed by Tim Webster, went to various parts of the South, as well as several to Richmond. Within a year, however, Lincoln had replaced McClellan as head of the Union forces. Eventually Pinkerton's spies in the Richmond area were caught and Tim Webster was tried and hanged in Richmond. He was also partly outwitted by a charming Confederate agent in Washington, Rose O'Neal Greenow, who had her own spy ring. In sum Pinkerton's wartime efforts have been seen as ineffective.[38]

Pinkerton also met failure when invading a local area to track down and arrest outlaws or robbers, for the local police and sometimes the citizens conspired to defeat Pinkerton with biased juries and arranged escapes of the accused from jail. When Pinkerton tried to track down the Youngers and the James brothers, the latter not only evaded his operatives, they killed two of his detectives; indeed, at one point, they sent their own men to assassinate Pinkerton himself.[39]

As has been noted earlier, Pinkerton suffered a stroke several years before his death in 1884, so it was his son William who interviewed Siringo in 1886 and gave him a job. Siringo's experiences in Chicago, plus the charged atmosphere of the trial of Haymarket anarchists, led Siringo to accept Pinkerton's offer to join the new office in Denver. There in the mile-high city, however, Charlie Siringo was to learn that there were many other sides to the detective business.

IV: Denver and Archuleta County

When Charlie, Mamie, and little Viola boarded a Pullman car from Chicago to Denver in the fall of 1886, Siringo was full of hope about his new career in the American West. His first cases were urban ones, however, such as getting the goods on local crooks and breaking up a ring of streetcar conductors who had figured out a way to duplicate their punched tickets so that each could inflate their record of sales, and thereby earn themselves some extra cash.⁴⁰ Siringo does not tell us, but one of Allan Pinkerton's early lessons in disguise was how one of his operatives could pose as a streetcar conductor.

His first major assignment was not to track down cattle thieves but to resolve a violent political feud between Anglos and Mexican Americans in southwestern Colorado in Archuleta County, situated just above New Mexico's northern border. Its county seat was Pagosa Springs, located on the San Juan River, and the nearest railroad town was Amargo. In many ways the feud had comic opera aspects. Archuleta County was a part of southern Colorado that had once been part of New Mexico Territory, with a majority population of Spanish-American settlers. But after the Civil War and especially after Colorado statehood was achieved in 1876, Anglo-Americans, mostly ranchers, moved in, and soon claimed to be a major-ity of the voters in Archuleta County, whose county government had been traditionally controlled by Mexican-Americans.

Determined to break the Hispanic stronghold, the Anglos put up candidates for the 1886 election of local officials, but it appears that key Mexican-Americans living just across the state border in Amargo, New Mexico, and led by the Archuleta family, rounded up voters, who came to Pagosa Springs to vote and defeated the Anglo contestants. Furious at being denied office, the Anglo residents literally ran the elected com-missioners out of the county, and promised to kill them if they tried to return. The exiled county commissioners knew that in order to keep their jobs, they must meet within sixty days or forfeit their right to office. It was they who retained the Pinkerton Agency to prove that the Anglo insurgents had acted illegally, had burned their property, and under threat of violence had driven them from office.⁴¹

In the perspective of time, the Archuleta County case was not a very important one in Siringo's long career, but the methods he used and the way he handled life-and-death situations coolly, illustrates nearly every technique he was to use as a detective. They were, in fact, classical methods used by all Pinkerton operatives and therefore deserve some explanation.

Siringo was assigned the case because he spoke Spanish and could relate to the deported county commissioners, but when he went south to Archuleta County he first identified himself to the Anglo insurgents as Charles Anderson, a Texas outlaw who was fleeing with a price on his head. Having bought a horse and saddle in Durango, Siringo cunningly stopped at the ranch of one of the insurgents—one Gordon G.—who himself was known to be a "bad" man from Texas. Siringo confided to Gordon G. that he had killed three Mexicans in Texas and therefore was on the run. Gordon G. then told Siringo of his own trouble in Texas! How Siringo managed to make an almost total stranger confide in him remains one of his most impressive and mysterious achievements.[42]

Because the Archuleta feuds had been fully aired in the Denver newspapers, in which the county was said to be in a state of anarchy, Siringo knew the names of the "revolutionaries," as they called themselves. Upon arriving at Pagosa Springs he immediately went to the home of the insurgent county clerk, E. M. Taylor, and by the end of the day, had confided to Taylor that he was an outlaw from Texas and did not dare stay at a hotel. Instead he said that his "friend," Gordon G., had recommended that he seek lodging with Taylor. Despite the reluctance of Mrs. Taylor, Siringo was invited to board with them![43]

Meanwhile the exiled county commissioners attempted to return to Pagosa Springs from New Mexico backed up by an armed escort of "sixty mounted and well-armed Mexicans," but they were stopped by the revolutionaries at a bridge over the San Juan. Despite parleys under a flag of truce, no progress was made. After nightfall the revolutionaries concocted a plan to slip around the armed Mexican-American guards and commissioners and set a haystack on fire, which would then ignite the house in which the officials were staying, and as they ran out they would be shot. Siringo, knowing that he had to save the commissioners, who after all had hired him, himself slipped across the river at night to warn the commissioners. But when the revolutionaries saw the commissioners dash to the safety of their guards, who were sleeping in an old barracks, they wondered who had warned them. Siringo was not present, and therefore became a suspect, but immediately on his return, he denied their accusations, and was backed by Taylor, the local sheriff, Dyke, and Gordon G. Even so Siringo was now distrusted by the mob, and the next night when he was spotted going to the house of a commissioner to deliver a message via the latter's wife, Siringo was openly accused of treachery. He denied this with vehemence and pulling out his Colt revolver, said, Bring the person who told you this and I will confront him face to face. That was done, but Siringo was still so fierce that the young man weakened and said he was not sure it was Siringo he saw.

Deciding that Siringo was after all one of them, the "revolutionary" sheriff Dyke made him a special deputy at a salary of $4.00 a day.[44]

The revolutionaries next hatched a plot to allow the commissioners to come to town and organize if both their men and the insurgents would stash their arms and allow matters to proceed; but then the insurgents would dash in and kill the commissioners. Siringo managed to warn a key commissioner of the plot and the assassinations did not take place.[45]

After a four-day impasse, the insurgents and the commissioners agreed to a truce whereby in the future, the county offices would by equally shared by both sides. Meanwhile Siringo knew that he had to "get the goods" on the revolutionaries, for they had broken the law. So trusted was he by the Taylors that when he was alone in their house, he rifled Taylor's desk, where he found "piles of political letters and receipts for votes bought during past elections." Eventually Siringo appeared before a grand jury in Durango in adjoining La Plata County and presented his evidence. The result was that sixteen of the revolutionaries were indicted. Before he could be spotted and most likely killed by the insurgents, Siringo "sneaked" onto an eastbound train for Denver.[46]

Siringo's next cases resembled those Allan Pinkerton himself had handled twenty years before. The first was to recover $10,000, which an "Atchison, Topeka, and Santa Fe Railway brakeman had stolen from the Wells-Fargo Express Company at La Junta, Colorado, during the excitement of a train wreck." Acting on information that the brakeman had fled to Mexico with the cash, Siringo patiently followed his quarry there by taking the Mexican Central Railway to Mexico City, where, true to his penchant for covering his own tracks in the previous Archuleta County case, he wrote E. M. Taylor in Pagosa Springs to say that his brother in Texas had warned him to flee because a grand jury there had returned an indictment for murder against him. Again Siringo "confided" in Taylor by giving him his new "assumed name." Three weeks later Taylor wrote him about the outcome of the jury trials and the continued suspicion that Siringo was the informer. But then Taylor added that both he and his wife continued to trust him, and offered to help him with money if he needed any! Here another example of Siringo's ambivalent and tolerant nature is illustrated, for in his *A Cowboy Detective* he confesses to the reader that the Archuleta insurgents "had good cause for revolting, as politics in that county were rotten. Most of them were honorable citizens, though a little rough and wild. Of course I felt 'sore' at them for wanting to hang me up by the neck."[47]

Meanwhile Siringo did manage to locate the brakeman who had stolen the $10,000, who, like Siringo himself, was living under an assumed name. To Siringo's dismay under Mexican law the brakeman could not be extradited to the United States, so Siringo quietly waited until the latter returned to the States and to his home in Leavenworth, Kansas, where he was finally arrested. While in Mexico City, Siringo learned that the brakeman had used his stolen money to invest in the purchase of diamonds there. Somehow Siringo managed to secure evidence of the purchase, and this helped in the brakeman's arrest and conviction.[48]

Siringo's next case involved recapture of the well-known Bassick Mine in Querida, a little village south of Canon City, Colorado, for its owner David Bryan, a Minnesota millionaire. The mine had been occupied by local laborers, who threatened to kill anyone who tried to reclaim it. Siringo and three other Pinkerton operatives, armed to the teeth, broke a window and slipped into the Bassick hoisting works in the middle of the night.

The next morning they confronted a former sheriff named Schofield, whom the miners had made custodian of the building, and asserted that they were in control. With many threats and much bluster Schofield promised to dispossess them if it "cost all the blood in Roseta [sic]" (another nearby mining town). A mob did approach the mine building, but its members were so drunk and in such fierce disagreement as to what to do, that eventually they returned to Rosita without taking any action. As seemed always to be the case, Siringo befriended Schofield, the custodian, and they swapped drinks. But when Schofield tried to get Siringo to come to his cellar, promising him a bottle of whiskey from a demijohn stored there, Siringo made Schofield stay ahead of him at all times, and once he had his bottle of whiskey he backed out of the door and up the steps. Schofield had intended to trap Siringo in the cellar and to retake the mine, now being held by only one Pinkerton. The crisis ended when the court appointed a legal custodian and the mine was once more controlled by its proper owner.[49]

His next major case involved apprehending Bill McCoy, an outlaw who had killed a deputy sheriff in Lusk, Wyoming, and had been caught and slated for execution but had escaped. McCoy was thought to be hiding at a Wyoming ranch called the Keeline located on the Laramie River.

The ranch itself was said to be run by tough ex-convicts from Texas. Once again Siringo pretended to be a Texas outlaw on the lam. Using this pose, in a remarkably short time he learned the location of the ranch from a hard-drinking saloon keeper named Howard, and his wife, by drinking heavily with them. Knowing that he was up against not one but a whole outfit of hostile and likely criminal cowboys, Siringo took elaborate measures to make the Keeline outfit accept him. On his way to the ranch, he shoved his horse off a rocky bluff onto soft sand in an arroyo some twenty feet below. The horse was not injured but left a huge impression in the sand. Siringo then proceeded to make an impression with his own body in the sand to make it appear that he had fallen with the horse.

When he got up, he dragged his leg in the sand as if he had broken it. Then he removed his left boot, ripped his pants' leg, and tightened his underdrawers around the leg to make it red. In addition he "rubbed the knee with dry grass" and poured some of Howard's "rattlesnake juice" (whiskey) on the area. Properly disguised as a man with a broken leg, he rode up to the Keeline ranch house. Once the twelve men there, almost all of whom were escaped convicts from Texas, realized Siringo was injured, their suspicions of him turned into concerned sympathy.

When the cowboys asked him why he had wandered into such cold country on the eve of winter, Siringo gave his usual answers: he was a Texas outlaw and was being hunted down. Some members of the outfit believed Siringo's tale; others were suspicious and double checked his story with Howard, the saloon keeper. Soon, however, Siringo learned that Bill McCoy, the man he was after, was known to the Keeline outfit. Indeed, they had helped him escape from jail. He was now on his way to South America.

Siringo's stay was punctuated by constant drunkenness and fights among the Keeline cowboys, and by visits to local dances where he befriended a young girl. The dances took place in a small community near Fort Laramie. One night when the cowboys at the dance were hopelessly drunk, Siringo made it to Fort Laramie, checked in at a hotel, wrote reports to his agency, and rushed back before dawn. Siringo did persuade the leader, Tom Hall, to confess to various crimes before saying he was going to visit his girlfriend again, who conveniently lived near the terminus of the Cheyenne Northern Railway. Instead he sold his horse and saddle and took the train to Cheyenne. There he reported his findings to a grand jury that was in session. Acting on Siringo's reports the sheriff and a large posse surrounded the Keeline Ranch and arrested Hall and his gang. Somehow the case was mishandled by the local district attorney and all were freed. Secretly, Siringo was pleased because he had come to like, even admire Tom Hall and another Keeline cowboy, McChesney, and was glad they did not have to go to prison.[50]

Siringo's next large case was a Denver and Rio Grande Railway robbery in which two Smith brothers and a man named Rhodes were prime suspects. In cooperation with "Doc Shores," the sheriff of Gunnison County, Colorado—who was in charge of the case—Siringo found out that the Smiths had come from a small farm in northwestern Kansas. Without hesitation Siringo went to the farm; got a job with the owner, the father of the suspect; and was soon romancing the farmer's pretty daughter, who soon innocently told him that her brothers were living in Price, Utah. With that information Sheriff Shores got Utah law officers to arrest the Smiths and Rhodes and bring them to Montrose, Colorado, where Shores and Siringo would take them to the Gunnison jail.

Both Shores and Siringo knew that they did not yet have a confession from the men. To secure a confession they decided that Siringo would pretend to be a prisoner as well. Sheriff Shores put handcuffs and leg irons on a sullen, wild-looking Siringo and not only had him march with the three robbers to the Gunnison jail, he put all four into the same cell! It proved to be a hell-hole with blood on the walls from a previous prisoner who had cut his own throat and died there. In addition, the Smiths were "alive with vermin," to use Siringo's words. One of the Smiths also had a bullet wound through his head, which had occurred when they were fighting among themselves while hiding in Utah. Siringo himself confided to the Smiths that he was an outlaw wanted for murder in Wyoming. In turn, the Smiths told him everything about their robbing the Denver and Rio Grande train. Then two weeks later Siringo was taken away "by a supposed officer from Wyoming, who was taking me there to be executed for murder." With their confessions in hand, Sheriff Shores brought the Smith brothers and Rhodes to trial, where "they were each sentenced to a term of seven years in the Colorado penitentiary."[51]

Although Siringo had already solved an impressive number of cases, and was pleased with himself and his job, he was deeply troubled from his first days in the Denver office by the activities of his superior, Superintendent Eams, who had hired a bunch of thugs for his detectives.

They took bribes, padded their expense accounts, hired themselves out to merchants as security guards, and bilked clients. Under Eams's orders, they accepted second assignments at the same time, but charged each client for a full day's work when, in effect, they were handling only one case a day. The Denver agency bookkeeper, Lawton, was on the take as well.[52] Siringo himself was threatened by Eams if he refused to cooperate, even to the point of saying some harm might befall Mamie and Viola.[53]

As Siringo notes in his *Two Evil Isms*, he discovered that two of the operatives, Doc Williams and Pat Barry, were beating up a suspect "to make him confess to a robbery that Siringo knew Barry himself had committed. Siringo was so incensed that he drew his Colt 45 and burst into the room to order the beating to stop. He then read the riot act to Superintendent Eams, telling him that he had seen detectives Pat Barry and Doc Williams commit the robbery that they were now trying to accuse an innocent victim of doing."[54]

From that point on, Siringo knew that Eams, Williams, and Barry were out for revenge. Indeed, Eams urged William Pinkerton to fire him for insubordination, but Pinkerton, knowing how able Siringo was, refused to do so. Pinkerton learned about the state of affairs in Denver after he sent his trusted operative, James McParland, to Denver to investigate. Pinkerton was so outraged he came to Denver himself and threw out the whole group, except for Siringo, and sent a new crew from the East. As Siringo recalled, "I being the only one of the old 'bunch' left. This swelled my head, of course."[55]

This event marked another professional and personal turning point in Siringo's life, for in Eams's successor, James McParland, he found another enduring father figure, the last having been David T. Beals, owner of the LX Ranch. James McParland was none other than the determined, redheaded Irish-born detective who had broken up the Molly Maguires in Pennsylvania. William Pinkerton now sent him to head the reconstituted Denver office. Happily, McParland and Siringo instantly formed an abiding friendship. Each respected, where possible, the tactics and approaches of the other. As Pingenot has observed, "for the next twenty years he would serve as McParland's principal troubleshooter."[56]

Siringo's first case after McParland arrived, involved an all-too-common form of robbery in the American West: ore-stealing from successful gold or silver mines. This type of theft, plus the "salting" of mines by conmen, occupied his time over and over again in the next two decades. "Salting" a mine can best be described as planting rich samples of ore in a mine that actually contained a mediocre or minimum amount of ore; then having an expert take samples and declare it a valuable property. With the expert's endorsement, the mining property was then sold to an unsuspecting buyer for a fancy price. Only the most classic and/or important cases will be treated here.

Siringo's first big case was to ferret out ore-stealing at the Aspen Mining and Smelting Company located in the mining boomtown of Aspen, Colorado. Again Siringo assumed a fictitious name and got a job in the mine to find out who the culprits were. He soon discovered that one Paddy McNamara was the leader of a gang of ore thieves and quickly joined them. In a sense McNamara was the middleman for he handled "ore stolen by the miners and bosses of pack trains." Siringo finally got the goods on McNamara when he persuaded the general manager Fred Rucklan and D. R. C. White, a banker who owned the mines, to secret themselves in vacant freight cars or in an upstairs room near the tracks to watch the ore being delivered to samplers late at night. Siringo himself was busy helping "Paddy Mack" make these deliveries. At one time the ore was loaded onto burros. On another occasion other ore thieves delivered ore to a man who had a "false cellar" under his house. After he had accumulated a wagonload, he "would then hire a wagon and team and deliver the ore in brood daylight to the samplers. When the thieves were finally arrested, Siringo was among them. While Siringo did his work well, the cases against the thieves were so delayed that eventually all were freed "with the understanding that they sell out and quit the county." Although Siringo reports that "'Paddy Mack' died from a broken heart, soon after being arrested," others who had been ore-stealing at Aspen were soon plying their trade at other Western mines.57

Siringo's next big case, which came in 1888, was a classic example of mine salting. No less a person than the Lord Mayor of London was persuaded to invest $190,000, in cash for the Mudsill Silver Mine at Fairplay, Park County, Colorado. He also contracted to build an ore-treating plant at a cost of $40,000 and to give the sellers of the mine (identified only as Dan V. and Matches) $75,000 in stock in a new company called the Mudsill Mining and Milling Company. The Lord Mayor was not a complete naïf, however, and so asked a New York mining expert named McDermott to examine the property. Even after McDermott gave a highly favorable report on the available ore, the Lord Mayor asked an English expert to examine the ore. The second expert was even more enthusiastic than McDermott about the value of the ore. Reassured, the Lord Mayor signed a contract and then paid Dan V. the cash. Shortly thereafter Parson and Ayllers (actually Frazier and Chalmers) were given a contract to build a $40,000 mill on the property. Construction had already begun when McDermott, the original ore assayer, discovered that the silver in the samples he had reviewed did not match the Mudsill ore. He cabled his suspicious findings to the Lord Mayor, who responded by asking McDermott to hire the Pinkerton Agency to investigate.

Siringo was flattered when Superintendent McParland asked him to take on the case. But this time there was a catch. William Chalmers (alias Mr. Allymers), one of the mill contractors, was married to Joan Pinkerton, Allan Pinkerton's daughter, and sister to William and Robert Pinkerton! McParland warned Siringo that if humanly possible he should avoid having to recommend voiding the Frazier and Chalmers Mill contract.

As usual Siringo went directly to the mining town of Fairplay, caroused with the tough element in the town's two saloon–dance halls, where he let it be known that he was a Texas outlaw named Charles Leon. One of the saloon keepers, an ex-cowboy, knew Siringo in Texas, but assuming the latter was in trouble, carefully used only Siringo's assumed name.

From the outset McParland and Siringo believed that Dan V. had salted the Mudsill Mine and so Siringo's task was to locate the man Dan V. had hired to do the salting. He soon learned that he was called Jacky and set out to befriend him. The serendipitous Siringo's luck once more smiled on him. He happened upon Jacky, who had bought a wild bronco, but was afraid to mount him, having already been thrown once, as Siringo reports.

> Here was my chance; so stepping up, I inquired if my
> services were needed. Taking hold of the rope I volunteered
> to take the wire edge off the bronco for him. He (the bronco)
> was a wiry Texas four-year-old and he gave me a ride, as he
> bucked pretty hard at times. Even after I had taken off the
> wire edge, Jack, was afraid to mount him, as he still had a
> lame leg caused by the fall from the horse. The result was
> that I promised to break the bronco gentle for Jacky, and

that night he and I went on a glorious drunk together.
We wore pistols strapped to our waists and ran the
dance halls to suit ourselves.[58]

During the course of the evening Jacky and Siringo got into a fight
with a gang of toughs who, with reinforcements, were determined to
beat them up if not kill them. The dance-hall girls locked Siringo and
Jacky in a room and told the toughs that they had "gone to bed." By this
time Jacky and Siringo were "bosom friends, and ever afterwards in
Fairplay, I was regarded as a dangerous man to 'monkey' with."[59]

Soon Jacky had boasted to Siringo that he had helped other people
salt mines, which convinced him that Jacky had indeed salted the
Mudsill for Dan V. He reported to McParland that the Mudsill mine was
a fake. One result was that the mill contract was cancelled. Siringo then
made a quick trip to Denver where he met McDermott, who had come
out from New York. He urged Siringo to continue to investigate the case
"regardless of expense."

After weeks of more carousing with Jacky, he did get a partial confession about how Jacky "had spent three years salting the Mudsill
mine." On the recommendation of McDermott, Siringo now went at the
case "whole hog" as it were, by actually bidding to explore the lower
workings in the mine. When he received the contract to do so, he made
Jacky his foreman! Eventually Siringo got a full confession from Jacky.[60]

Meanwhile Siringo, never happy to be away from his beloved
Mamie, arranged for her and Viola to spend time at a nearby hotel in
Alma as the niece from Kansas of a trusted Siringo friend living there.
Siringo was soon "courting" Mamie, who meanwhile was hearing from .
local women that she must avoid that tough outlaw Texan![61]

Finally Siringo lured Jacky to Denver, still without giving himself away
as a detective. Then Jacky found himself in McParland's office, where he
was confronted with the fact that he was an escaped criminal who had
served time in the Nebraska penitentiary, after which Jacky confessed to
McParland about the Mudsill salting. In effect, McParland took over where
Siringo left off. Later, in a federal court case, Dan V.'s and Mr. Matches's
properties were attached and eventually the Lord Mayor of London recovered $150,000 of his unhappy investment on the Mudsill mine.[62]

⚜   ⚜

Charlie Siringo was a born Texas storyteller whose accounts of his extraordinary adventures always fascinated the reader. His accounts were always told in a good clear first-person vernacular style. You can not only hear Charlie talking, but pick up traces of his Texas accent. He was very good at timing—saving surprise to the end. His accounts were always tinged with humor, even satire, sentimentality, and an ironic sense. The latter feature came through when he admitted that the thief, robber, or even killer he had chased down had some good qualities as an excuse for having drifted into a life of crime. In the Mudsill case, for example, the prime conman, Dan V., had been fooled by a mine salter some years before he himself took up the dubious trade. Jacky, the salter, while admitting his crime to Siringo and McParland, did not want news of his arrest to get back to his friends in Fairplay.

Siringo's wonderful series of adventurous episodes are so compelling that they sometimes obscure a larger pattern of events taking place in the American West. His stories not only provide insight into the increasingly violent battle between labor and capital, but suggest how poor, desperate, disillusioned, and even lost some of the persons he dealt with were. They speak volumes about how extreme alcohol addiction affected many western areas, and indeed many eastern towns and cities. His stories also tell of the pervasiveness of political corruption, the general contempt for Black Americans and Mexican Americans, and the deep distrust of the forces of law and order. His narrative also explains how powerful railroads were both such an economic boom, and yet such a brutally tough industrial presence that they inspired both robberies and political reform, while providing the means by which criminals, business, and lawmen could move rapidly across the country. It is this larger context of Siringo's life that this volume attempts to portray along with the colorful narrative of his incredible adventures.

Siringo's next big case—a saga of bombing rich mine owners, bitter laborers, and outlawry in Nevada—provides telling examples of these larger issues while remaining an engrossing detective story.

V: The Pelling and Prinz Case

In the late summer of 1889, Superintendent McParland called Siringo into his office to meet a Mr. George Pelling from Tuscarora, Nevada, a small mining town located in the mountains about fifty miles northwest of Elko. Pelling was the co-owner, with C. W. Prinz, of a valuable mine and mill at Tuscarora. Pelling's reasons for seeking Pinkerton's help were, if one may pun, "compelling." During the previous spring someone had planted dynamite bombs under Prinz's and Pelling's respective residences and set them off. Siringo's laconic account of what happened to each is worth quoting in full.

> Mr. Pelling and his mattress went off through the roof and
> landed right side up with care in the middle of the street.
> He was still wrapped in quilts and blankets, and the shock
> put him out of business for a while, but otherwise he was
> not hurt. Not so lucky was Mr. Prinz. He was badly used up,
> but soon recovered. He, too, was blown out into the street
> but not on a feather bed.[63]

Pelling and Prinz, full knowing they were the targets of an organized gang of "desperate enemies," sought help from a detective agency in San Francisco, which sent two detectives in secret to Tuscarora. Meanwhile Pelling and Prinz had offered a large reward for evidence that could be used to convict the bombers. The San Francisco detectives failed to uncover any clues and appear to have been quickly identified as detectives by the locals. It was then that Pelling traveled to Denver to hire Pinkerton. McParland gave the case to Siringo. Not surprisingly Pelling himself warned Siringo in the sternest terms that it was a dangerous assignment.

Siringo was told by Pelling to take the Union Pacific to San Francisco and to await him there at the Palace Hotel until he arrived some days later. Siringo's assignment coincided with a crisis in his own family. His wife, Mamie, was experiencing a severe case of pleurisy, so much so that at the insistence of her father, she went back to his home in Springfield, Missouri, where she could be operated on by a trusted family physician. Siringo's expectations of a good time in San Francisco, which he had never visited before, were frustrated by his worry for Mamie.[64]

After talks with Pelling, Siringo boarded the train to Elko dressed as a cowboy and then took a stage to Tuscarora. Incredibly, once again the Siringo luck was with him, for on the same stagecoach was a man named Philip Snyder, whom Mr. Pelling had mentioned was "a possible friend to the dynamiters." Siringo and Snyder had chosen to sit on the seat with the driver. As they traveled, Siringo spotted a coyote. Quickly Siringo pulled out his Colt 45 and shot the animal dead. This made a great impression on Snyder, who, upon arrival in Tuscarora, introduced Siringo to his friends as a Texas cowboy who was "a crack shot with a pistol." And of course that reputation soon made him one of the boys with the tough miners.

That reputation was further enhanced when Siringo demonstrated to a suspicious Tim W., a bitter enemy of Prinz and Pelling, that he was a crack shot by shooting out a pine knot in a tree fifty yards away. Playing it carefully, Siringo chose to board at the ranch of the town butcher, which was some distance from town. After he had made more friends, Siringo moved into town. He reported on his progress when he had one meeting with Prinz in an old abandoned mine at night. Meanwhile he went on fall hunting trips with Phil Snyder. Slowly he learned who disliked Prinz and Pelling and cultivated them. One key enemy of the mine owners turned out to be a man called "Wild Bill" who maintained a hunting camp on Lone Mountain, although he was skilled as a craftsman working with steel. Indeed, Siringo learned that "Wild Bill" had created "his own plates to print counterfeit money."[65]

At this point Siringo's plan of action became much more elaborate. Siringo himself decided to "salt" a local mine in connection with a man named Harnrihan, who with him fleeced the butcher Morrison. Next he invited his chief suspect in the bombing, "Tim W.," to a prospecting and hunting trip in the Indian Territory where Siringo said there was strong evidence of gold. Despite "Tim W.'s" friends warning him that Siringo was probably a detective, even to the point of claiming that Prinz and Pelling had hired him, somehow Tim W. and Siringo got all the way to Wichita Falls without mishap, but in Wichita Falls he knew he had friends who might greet him and call him by his real name.

In a curiously halcyon set of days the two men looked for gold, feasted off turkeys, and through Siringo's manipulations, Tim W. never got mail from Tuscarora declaring that Siringo was a detective. Siringo even managed to keep Tim W.'s lover, who had traveled to Fort Sill, Oklahoma, from seeing him. Inevitably Siringo, in familiar cattle country, was finally recognized by a former cowboy, who called him by his real name. Siringo somehow bluffed this one out by finding his friend while Tim W. was sleeping, and explaining the circumstances. By this time Tim W. had already told Siringo of his role in the Pelling and Prinz bombings.[66]

Of course Siringo never did things by the halves. It just so happened that he and Tim W. were in Oklahoma when the first famous Oklahoma land run of 1889 occurred, in which the two participated. But yet another former acquaintance of Siringo managed to tell Tim W. that Charlie's real name was Siringo and that he was a detective. Although Tim W. told Siringo of the episode, he refused to believe it, and the two traveled back to Denver together. There Tim was arrested by McParland, and at the latter's office was confronted by W. C. Prinz, who had come from Nevada "to be at the wind-up." Siringo had spent nine months on the Tuscarora case. Tim's detailed confession, state's evidence in today's parlance, allowed him to go free! Meanwhile the guilty parties had fled the camp and Prinz and Pelling had by then sold the mine. Prinz now lived in San Francisco, in Siringo's words, "as a prosperous mining man." According to rumor, Mr. Pelling had married a San Francisco heiress, and "was now soaring high in society, quite a change from the time he soared high in the air through the roof of a house, with dynamite instead of dollars as the lifting power."[67]

Here again, however, guilty parties did not wind up in jail. Nor did Siringo tell us why Tim W. and others blew up the homes of Prinz and Pelling. A curious amoral game of violence had occurred in which neither side explained the reasons for their actions. One is left with a disturbing feeling that western labor and western capital had no respect for one another, that it was a ruthless game to the finish in which each side, whether right or wrong, was prepared to go to extremes. Such an approach and attitude go a long way toward explaining why the West, and, indeed, the whole nation was such a violent society in the nineteenth century. Charlie Siringo, caught in the middle, did what he could to resolve things. As he himself observed in 1889: "Thus the world moves and we all act our little part on the big stage."[68]

It is the curse of this country that
political prejudices run so high.

—*Governor L. Bradford Prince of New Mexico,*
to Victor L. Ochoa, July 22, 1892, Prince Papers

The democratic committee is getting ready
to use dirty little circulars and I presume
we must fight them the same way.
In every town we must have them distributed.

—*Max Frost to Judge A. A. Morrison,*
September 26, 1892, Catron Papers

CHAPTER EIGHT

Charlie Siringo

Discovers

New Mexico Politics

THE ANCHETA CASE

AND AFTER, 1891–1898

CHARLIE SIRINGO REALLY BEGAN HIS CAREER AS A "DETECTIVE" IN the 1870s tracking down stolen cattle. In the process he witnessed the hunt for Billy the Kid, and was on the edge of the political violence that we know as the Lincoln County War. That conflict resulted in the deaths of perhaps as many as fifty men, some law officers, some feuding citizens seeking economic and political control of Lincoln County, and a number of outlaws. Out of that experience Pat Garrett and Jim East became well-known sheriffs, Siringo eventually became a detective, and Billy the Kid became a legend.

Charlie's first Pinkerton case, it should be remembered, was to hunt persons involved in the Haymarket Riot, or in Chicago cases involving petty crimes. Once he had moved to Denver, his first big assignment was to bring political rebels who had illegally seized control of Archuleta County, Colorado, to justice.

During the fall of 1890 and the winter of 1891, however, Siringo had been given a break from big cases for a very sad reason: his beloved wife, Mamie, was now fatally ill with pleurisy in both lungs, and that winter she died in his arms at their home in Denver. Naturally Siringo was not only devastated by Mamie's death but deeply concerned about who would rear his daughter, Viola. As a detective who was often away from home weeks, even months at a time, he could hardly care for her. Fortunately Mamie had a loving aunt in Illinois who came out to nurse her niece in her last days and had become attached to Viola, perhaps especially so because she had no children of her own. The aunt, Mrs. Will F. Read, volunteered to take Viola with her back to Illinois and rear her as her own daughter.[1]

Once Siringo's family affairs were in order, Superintendent McParland assigned Charlie to another "big" political case—this time in Santa Fe, New Mexico. He was to work for the governor of New Mexico Territory, L. Bradford Prince, to track down the persons who had tried to assassinate J. A. Ancheta, a prominent Hispanic who was a much-respected political figure in the Republican Party. The would-be assassins—for it was believed there were at least two of them—fired shots into the window of Thomas Catron's law office in Santa Fe where Catron, J. A. Ancheta, and Elias Stover, a former lieutenant governor of Kansas now living in New Mexico, were holding a committee meeting concerning the creation of a public school system. The New Mexico legislature was in session at the time.[2]

Buckshot fired through the window seriously wounded Ancheta in the neck, while a rifle bullet barely missed Stover, who was now serving as a member of the Territorial Senate. Thomas Catron, the most powerful Republican in the territory, was standing at his desk, facing the window, and was in the direct line of fire, but fortunately he had a set of large law books in front of him. Buckshot had slammed into the volumes but missed Catron.[3]

What had provoked the attempted murder? The legislature had been contemplating the passage of a law establishing the first public school system in New Mexico. Up to this time all schools were maintained by the Catholic Church for the overwhelmingly Hispanic population. A series of complex feuds had developed between Anglo Republican political leaders and Hispanic political leaders, many of whom also voted Republican but opposed a secular public school system. Still another group of Hispanic Americans supported the Church's opposition not only to public schools but to threats to traditional Hispanic values and the

Spanish language. Tempers were running high. Ancheta, a much-respected Hispanic New Mexican, had come out in favor of the school bill. He was bitterly assailed for his views.

This was only one of many issues that further divided the political factions within both Republican and Democratic ranks. Governor Prince, for example, was an able appointee from New York State and was determined that New Mexico schools be more progressive. Thomas Catron, a Missourian, on the other hand, had been in New Mexico for many decades, had been a hugely successful lawyer, and by aggressive means had gained control of millions of acres of land. Indeed, he was the largest controller, if not actual owner of land in the territory. Catron's political genius lay in creating combinations that reached beyond the Republican Party to include key Democrats, leading Hispanic leaders, key court and county officials, and allies in Washington. This extraordinary coalition came to be called the Santa Fe Ring. For several decades it dominated the legislature, and occupied nearly all the key elected and appointive officers of the territory. It is no exaggeration to say that it was a western version of the famous Boss Tweed Ring in New York City.[4]

In 1890, the year before Charlie Siringo came to Santa Fe, Catron and his allies had actually initiated a statehood movement and had written a constitution, which fortunately for New Mexico, was so conservative and partisan that it was defeated by an overwhelming vote of 16,000 to 7,496. The sheer dominance of Catron's views in its provisions led the public to call it the Tom-Cat Constitution.[5]

No one was more appalled at the rough-and-tumble, cynical methods of Catron than Governor Prince, and by 1891, the two men were each engaged in a ruthless struggle to control the Republican Party. At the time of the Ancheta shooting, in fact, many observers felt that the bullets and buckshot were intended for the controversial Catron, who was standing and a very obvious target. It was indeed ironic that the "law"—in the form of books—may have saved his life.

The outcry over Ancheta's attempted murder led Governor Prince and the legislature to appropriate $20,000 to be used to apprehend the would-be killers. As Siringo himself reminds us, however, the committee appointed to handle the fund consisted of Governor Prince, Attorney-General Edmund L. Bartlett, and territorial senator Thomas B. Catron! Although all three were leading Republicans, Prince and Catron despised one another.[6]

The first pieces of evidence Siringo got from the committee, once he had arrived in Santa Fe, was that one of the horses ridden by one of the shooters had a crooked hoof and had left a peculiar track in the snow and slush outside Catron's office. John Gray, city marshal, and several citizens had followed the tracks of the horsemen out of Santa Fe to a fork in the road. One road led to Las Vegas and the other to Cow-Springs, but by then traces of the peculiar hoof mark were no longer visible.[7]

Complicating the incredible internecine feuding in New Mexico was the presence of a secret anti-Anglo group of poorer Hispanic New Mexicans calling themselves the *Gorras Blancas* or the "White Caps," who had organized to protect themselves from Anglo land takeover in northeastern New Mexico. They particularly resented Texas ranchers who had invaded their traditional sheep raising area with large herds of cattle and had brought with them the hated barbed-wire fencing. Still more ranchers and Anglo settlers had come after the Atchison, Topeka and Santa Fe reached Las Vegas in 1879. The line furnished a swift, cheap way to ship cattle directly to the Chicago stockyards.[8]

What made the New Mexicans so angry was that there had been a huge 496,000-acre Las Vegas land grant, which had always been regarded as a "community grant," "open to anyone who wanted to use its water and pasture land." "When many of these new settlers with their Anglo concepts of land tenure began to claim absolute ownership of certain portions of the grant and to fence their claims, hostility erupted."[9]

The White Caps got their name from the fact that in their night raids they wore white caps on both their own and their horses' heads. On occasion even their horses were clad in white sheets. The White Caps were soon rumored to be cutting fences, scattering the stock of the intruders, and "even killing stockmen who had fenced in large tracts of land." They were as hostile to the railroads as they were to the ranchers, and tore up tracks to express their anger.[10]

In 1887 a local court actually awarded a native claimant his land right over that of an Anglo buyer in the case *Millhiser vs. Padilla*, in San Miguel County. The decision led to a three-hour joyous demonstration when the ruling was announced. More lawsuits occurred, however, which led to ongoing protests by Hispanic New Mexicans. These conflicts finally led to the formal organization of the White Caps in 1888. By 1889 Governor Prince was already being badgered by Anglo ranchers to curb the White Caps. Prince actually took the complaints of nearly thirty ranchers to Washington, where he urged the federal government to take action. Upon his return he issued a proclamation in English and Spanish to the citizens of San Miguel County, center of White Cap activity, stating that "further disorder would not be tolerated."[11] When Prince himself called a public meeting of the local leaders in Las Vegas to discuss matters, he was stunned to learn that "four-fifths of those in attendance proved to be in sympathy with the 'fence cutters.'"[12]

Meanwhile the White Caps had begun to befriend the local representatives of the Knights of Labor in the hope that they might become their allies. When Prince learned this he was so agitated that he wrote Terence V. Powderley, the Grand Master of the Knights, urging him to disassociate his association from that of "the terrorists." The local Knights themselves began to have misgivings when there was a new upsurge of local violence. To complicate matters even more, in San Miguel County the Hispanic wing of the Republican Party proved to be so corrupt in office that the more proper (Anglo?) Republicans founded their own Peoples Party. Meanwhile, Felix Martinez, a Democratic leader, had assumed control of the New Mexican Populist party, which in 1892 fused with the Democratic Party. This group eventually joined the National Peoples' party—the Populists. In turn, the local Knights of Labor, now disaffected with the White Caps, gave their allegiance to the Populists.[13]

In short a whole new set of disaffected leaders in San Miguel County had emerged who greatly upset both Governor Prince and the Santa Fe Ring. But the greatest shock came when Pablo Herrera, brother of Juan José Herrera, the founder of the White Caps, ran for and won a seat in the Territorial House of Representatives in the 1890 elections![14]

The complexity of the election of 1890 in New Mexico almost defies analysis. Republicans accused the Knights of Labor of allying with the White Caps. They also pilloried the Democrats for being secret supporters of the White Caps. The Republicans themselves were accused of buying White Cap votes with money from Tom Catron! The result was that the Democrats profited from all the political discontent and won control of the lower house of the Territorial Assembly. Two new faces from San Miguel County were T. B. Mills, a Republican turned independent, and the colorful White Cap, Pablo Herrera.[15]

A reform spirit was in the air in Santa Fe. T. B. Mills and young Joseph A. Ancheta, a twenty-five-year-old Republican legislator from Silver City, joined to propose educational reform bills. Ancheta, a graduate of

Notre Dame University, was determined that there should be a public school system in New Mexico. Educational reform measures were passed; Prince himself was very pleased. But it was when the education committee was meeting to discuss implementation of the measures on February 5, 1891, that the unknown assassins shot through Catron's office window wounding Ancheta in the neck, face, and shoulder.[16]

When McParland briefed Siringo before he left for Santa Fe, he opined that the White Caps were Western Molly Maguires. Siringo himself soon decided that Francisco Chavez, the local Santa Fe sheriff, was behind the shooting and that Catron, not Ancheta, was the intended victim. The reason was that in recent local elections, Catron had supported Francisco Gonzales y Borrego for sheriff, a bitter rival of Chavez. The shooting was designed to get rid of Catron.[17]

Meanwhile Prince and others believed the shooting was inspired by hostility to the creation of a public non-Catholic school system. Because Prince was so obsessed with the White Caps, who stood for traditional Hispanic values and Catholic control of education, he was determined to pin the shooting on the White Caps and their supporters. As the brother of the founder of the White Caps, Pablo Herrerra's presence in the legislature must have especially bothered Prince.

It was into this incredible political nightmare that Charlie Siringo walked during the spring of 1891, and it was undoubtedly Prince who urged him to investigate the White Caps and especially Pablo Herrera. Siringo also soon learned that Francisco Chavez, the popular Democratic sheriff of Santa Fe County and a bitter enemy of Catron's, was a member of the White Caps, and appears to have believed, for a time at least, that it was Chavez and the Tecolote White Caps who had shot through the window with the intention of killing Catron.

As one who knew Siringo could almost predict, he decided to befriend the convivial Chavez, and through him he managed to meet Representative Pablo Herrera, who was in Santa Fe attending the closing session of the legislature. Soon the three were busy carousing together in bars and saloons almost nightly. Using his assumed name, Charles T. Leon, Siringo successfully cultivated Herrera's friendship, so much so that the latter invited Siringo to visit him in Las Vegas, once the legislative session had ended.[18]

Siringo must have told Herrera of his own earlier whoop-em-up visits to Las Vegas some twelve years before while in New Mexico hunting for stolen LX Cattle. Once in Las Vegas, the affable Herrera introduced Siringo to his "White Cap" friends, two of the most impressive being Pablo's strikingly handsome brothers, Juan José and Nicanor Herrera. As Siringo tells us in his *A Cowboy Detective*, "Days passed into weeks and Pablo and I became inseparable. We consumed much bad liquor and ate many fine meals in swell society at the Montezuma Hotel, six miles from Las Vegas, at the Hot Springs."[19]

At last the time came when Herrera felt comfortable enough with Siringo to invite him to a White Cap evening meeting outside of town. Although many members, whom Siringo described as rough looking, ordered Siringo, who was clearly a "Gringo" who spoke Spanish poorly, to leave the hall, Pablo made an impassioned, truly eloquent speech in support of "Gringo" Leon, with the result that Siringo was not only allowed to stay, but initiated into the order! The meeting turned out to be one where other new members were being initiated as well. As noted earlier, the White Caps had tried to affiliate with the Knights of Labor. Indeed, some of the initiation ritual appears to have been adopted from that of the Knights of Labor, but Siringo believed that they "pretended to be a branch of that organization merely for effect."[20] Robert W. Larson, an expert on New Mexico Populism, feels that there is some question as to whether this was a White Cap meeting or a Knights of Labor meeting.[21]

While Siringo was appalled at some of the cruelties practiced by the White Caps, he finally concluded that Herrera and the White Caps had nothing to do with the Ancheta shooting. This was not to say that the Herreras were nonviolent law-abiding citizens, however. Pablo, who had already served a jail term before he was elected to the legislature—a time that he described as infinitely less boring than being in the lower house— became an outlaw and a killer, and was eventually fatally shot by a law officer. Meanwhile his brother, Nicanor, was convicted of killing a man and sent to the penitentiary, but was eventually pardoned. And as if seeking to salvage a tragic story, Siringo tells us that Juan José Herrera, founder of the White Caps, "died a natural death."[22]

While Siringo was busy following leads in Las Vegas, Santa Fe City Marshal John Gray was pursuing his own investigation on the Cow Springs road and had managed to identify two men, Victoriano and Felipe Garcia, whose horses fitted the description of the Ancheta attackers. Taking up where Gray had left off, Siringo traveled to Cow Springs, and found both Garcias and eventually their horses.[23] As usual he culti-vated the friendship of the Garcias, but while there, Siringo, who had once had a nearly fatal case of smallpox, and therefore thought he was immune, volunteered to help bury a Mexican woman who had died of the disease. To his astonishment and dismay, he himself contracted small-pox, and only by the greatest effort did he finally reach Santa Fe, where he nearly died from the disease. With a doctor's help and that of several nurses he somehow survived. Siringo's description of his illness is truly dramatic: at one point in his slow recovery he tells us that the sores over his whole body "seem to have melted and all run together forming one solid scab from head to foot." Later photos of Siringo suggest that facial scars from the smallpox were visible for the rest of his life.[24]

Siringo's failure to find any guilty parties in Las Vegas angered Governor Prince, who began to complain to McParland in Denver that the Pinkertons were charging expenses for many drinks and lavish meals at the Hotel Montezuma. To the governor it looked like deliberate padding of the expenses account. Yet when Siringo finally told Prince that the guilty parties were the Garcia brothers at Cow Springs, the gov-ernor, to his chagrin, found out that far from being White Caps, they were good Republicans and hence he did not want to arrest them for fear of causing yet another split in the Republican party.[25] Ironically, after all his efforts, Siringo was told "to drop the matter and discontinue the operation." Thus the whole Ancheta case came to an inconclusive end, and although Siringo himself had already secured a partial confes-sion from one of the brothers, he never found a clear motive as to who were the intended victims.

Besides learning more than he wanted to about the corrupt, rough-and-ready politics of New Mexico, Siringo came away from his experi-ence there with a true sympathy for the White Caps as poor Mexicans trying to protect themselves. They were not the anarchists of the Chicago brand, nor the dupes of the Knights of Labor; they supported the Populists because they saw them as possible reformers; and they were certainly not a western version of the Molly Maguires.[26] To his surprise he had fallen in love with Santa Fe and New Mexico, so much so that he decided to buy a tract of land near Santa Fe, which he christened Sunny Slope Ranch. One day it would be his home.

❧ ❧

In the perspective of time it was probably inevitable that Siringo would fail to find those really responsible for the Ancheta shootings. Indeed, New Mexican politics continued to be so full of racial, religious, and partisan factions, plus ongoing family feuds, that those guilty of corrupt acts and violent crimes more often than not escaped punishment. In 1892, a year after Siringo had left Santa Fe, the territorial capital was burned mysteriously, and other politically inspired killings continued to occur.[27]

The delegate election of 1892 laid bare the seamy side of New Mexican politics as never before. The election of a territorial delegate to Congress was always a key event, for the delegate had access to the president, Congress, and heads of departments and federal agencies, more than any other official in New Mexico. In 1892 intrigues began when Governor Prince decided to prevent Thomas Catron not only from becoming the Republican delegate candidate that year, but from controlling the territory's delegation to the National Republican Convention of 1892.

A word about the source of this enmity seems necessary at this point. By 1892 both Prince and Catron were avid supporters of statehood for New Mexico Territory, but their approaches were as different as night was from day. When a move to call a state constitutional convention was passed by the legislature in 1889, Catron and his allies made sure that it would produce a conservative document. Moreover, once the convention was held, the dominant Republicans gerrymandered the Democratic counties out of full representation in the legislature, and although they endorsed the goal of a public school system, they also adopted a "proposal that no one could vote or serve on a jury in the future state who did not understand the English language without the aid of an interpreter." This proposal boldly guaranteed that the new state government would be controlled by Anglo-Americans. Both mining and land tax clauses were included to benefit the large mine and landowners. From the outset the "Tom-Cat constitution," as it was soon nicknamed, was subject to fierce criticism. After a long and bitter campaign the constitution was overwhelmingly defeated—as noted earlier, on October 17, 1890, by a vote of 16,000 against to 7,493 for.[28]

There were almost as many unspoken reasons for the constitution's defeat as public ones. In Washington, key Congressmen, including Antonio Joseph, New Mexico's own territorial delegate, were lukewarm. Meanwhile, back in New Mexico the Democrats denounced the constitution as too partisan Republican, but their real reason was that they thought New Mexico was not ready for statehood, and feared that if it became a state, it would be dominated by Spanish Americans, a fear confirmed by the fact that the Catholic Church opposed public schools, as did most Hispanic citizens.[29]

No one was more angry at how the Catron Republicans had botched the statehood movement than Governor L. Bradford Prince, who had great hopes of "Americanizing" New Mexico and perhaps becoming a senator once statehood was achieved. In an address to the legislature in December 1890, Prince "presented that body with a stinging recital of New Mexican faults." He reminded them that they had never devised an effective system for conferring land titles, still had no public school program, suffered from corrupt taxes, and had an antiquated court system.[30]

By 1892 Prince at least was ready to have another try at statehood for New Mexico. The often ambivalent Delegate Joseph had just succeeded in persuading the U.S. House of Representatives to pass an enabling act for New Mexico statehood. Prince thought he also had a friend in President Benjamin Harrison, whom he supported. Since Catron was anti-Harrison, that is why Prince was so anxious to prevent Catron from controlling the New Mexican delegates to the Republican convention, where Harrison hoped to be nominated for a second term.

As usual, Catron, still anxious for statehood, had a very different agenda. He was a close friend of Stephen Elkins, who was once New Mexico's territorial delegate, but then had moved back East to become a powerful senator from West Virginia, and from that office had moved to become Harrison's Secretary of War. Elkins had always been Catron's ally, and New Mexican Republicans, seeing that alliance, allowed Catron to control the territory's delegation to the national Republican convention in Minneapolis.[31]

While Catron was in Minneapolis, however, he received a telegram informing him that a gang of assassins had ambushed and killed Francisco Chavez, the former sheriff of Santa Fe County, whom Siringo had so assiduously cultivated while working on the Ancheta case a year before. What made Chavez's murder a true sensation, however, was that Sylvestre Gallegos, the police chief of Santa Fe and a close friend of Chavez, had also been killed shortly before Chavez was ambushed; later other murders followed these. Since both had been leading Democrats, the rumor started that the assassins belonged to a gang called the "Alliance League," which specialized in "doing professional dirty work for politicians."[32] Thus when Catron returned from Minneapolis he assumed that he would run for the position of territorial delegate against the Democratic incumbent, Antonio Joseph, but the rumor mill suggested that the Republicans had had these popular Democratic politicians killed and that Catron may have been involved. The situation began to look much worse when Prince's new appointee as sheriff of Santa Fe County proved unable to find the killers. The result was that Catron was on the defensive throughout the campaign and despite spending much money, lost the election to Joseph, who was, after all, one of New Mexico's most able Spanish American politicians.[33]

The 1892 campaign revealed that New Mexico was full of gangs and secret societies, some of which Siringo himself had gotten to know while in Las Vegas. The Penitentes, a religious society, for example, on occasion banded together to influence elections in New Mexico's northern counties—the Rio Arriba. Others were outlaw gangs using robbery, vengeance, terror, and political control to dominate a locality. The most notorious of this group was Vicente Silva and his "forty bandits," who robbed and beat people in the Las Vegas area. The forty bandits, incidentally, included no less than three members of the Las Vegas police force! The White Caps, a branch of whom Siringo had joined in Las Vegas, had spread into other counties such as Colfax and Mora "to organize the vote, cut fences, harass the railroad, or drive out homesteaders." Meanwhile the Alliance League, operating in Santa Fe, included an ex-chief of police and his brother among their members.[34]

Something had to be done. Fortunately for New Mexico, Grover Cleveland had been elected president in 1892, and upon returning to the White House, he appointed a Democrat, William T. Thornton, to replace Prince as Governor. Thornton was not only a good lawyer, he had the reputation of being honest and fearless. Nor surprisingly he made it his priority to track down the gangs and murderers. The supreme irony, however, was that Thornton was a law partner of Thomas Catron, whose firm, in the good old Santa Fe tradition, made sure both Democratic and Republican leaders were law partners.[35]

In effect Thornton became a crusading district attorney, and during his time in office, members of the Alliance League were arrested and five others were eventually tried for the murder of Gallegos, and, by implication, for the death of Sheriff Chavez. Because two of the five were the Borrego brothers (whom Siringo, with his penchant for phonetic spelling, always wrote as the "Barreago brothers"). After their arrest and trial, all the other trials came to be called the Borrego case. And as if to demonstrate what a curiously incestuous polity New Mexico was, Thomas Catron chose to defend the Borrego brothers while his partner, Governor Thornton, was prosecuting them! Back in Denver, Siringo appears to have followed the trial closely.

The case did not come up until 1895, but in a dramatic, near-violent trial lasting thirty-eight days, the jury, on the third anniversary of Sheriff Chavez's death (May 29, 1895) brought in a verdict of guilty. Despite many appeals all the way to the U.S. Supreme Court, the convictions were upheld and in 1897 the five prisoners were executed. Catron's court performance during the trial was so rough and tumble that the presiding judge cited him for contempt and he was temporarily disbarred.[36]

Intrigue and violence in New Mexico politics did not end with the Borrego case, but it served as a symbol that things were changing, and that the old Santa Fe Ring, dominated by the likes of Catron and politicians from both parties, was giving way to a new generation and new political forces. By 1890 a territory-wide Farmer's Alliance had come into being, and its members, many of them new immigrants to New Mexico, followed the fortunes of the National Alliance. And from the local Peoples Party groups of 1890 arose the Populists. Similarly the new national interest in free silver and currency reform was reflected in New Mexico's silver-mining towns. By 1894 the silverites had become active members of the national and local Populist Party. Governor Prince described the new attitude in a letter to Secretary of the Interior John W. Noble, saying that the old way was "rule by coercion, threats and 'bulldozing.' That seemed to succeed until the railroad came. But conditions have changed and modern and American systems are needed. The native people will not stand what they did fifteen years ago. The new population will not stand it at all."[37]

The new era was dramatized by the national presidential election of 1896, when almost everyone in New Mexico politics became involved in the silver controversy. The local Democratic party had endorsed the free coinage of silver as early as 1890, and by 1894, a Populist Party had been formed and chose its own candidate, T. B. Mills, to run for the office of territorial delegate. Mills did not win, and by taking away votes from the Democratic candidate, helped Tom Catron win the delegateship. By the time of the national election of 1896, however, the silver issue had split both major parties into gold and silver factions, and a reformer Democrat from Albuquerque, Harvey Fergusson, won the delegate election that year.[38]

A further symbol of change came when the newly elected president, William McKinley, ignored the advice of the old Republicans in New Mexico and appointed a young Spanish American, Miguel A. Otero, to succeed Governor Thornton. Otero was the first native-born governor of New Mexico. The son of a leading New Mexican Hispanic family, whose father had twice served as territorial delegate and had helped bring the Atchison, Topeka and Santa Fe to New Mexico, Otero had been educated in St. Louis and New York. His mother was an Anglo-Southerner from St. Louis. In short, Otero was at home with both the Anglo and Hispanic peoples of New Mexico, and he soon had an efficient political machine of his own in operation. He was so successful, in fact, that he remained in office for nine years (1897–1906). Miracle of miracles, Otero responded to the Spanish-American War in 1898 with such enthusiasm that he persuaded both Spanish and Anglo-Americans to join the armed force, despite the fact that Hispanic New Mexicans would be fighting their spiritual and cultural mother country—Spain. Under Otero New Mexico became more a part of the nation, so that after the turn of the century nearly all parties began to clamor for statehood, which finally came in 1912 along with statehood for Arizona Territory.[39] Yet who was chosen as one of the first U.S. Senators but Thomas Benton Catron?

How does our friend Charlie Siringo fit into this narrative? It was he who sensed in the Ancheta case just how flawed politics were in New Mexico. And it was he, a "gringo" who personally got to know poorer Mexican Americans, who was initiated into the White Caps order, and realized the political importance of the Penitente Brothers. It was he, an outsider, who was so intrigued with New Mexican events that he predicted that the "Borrego gang of 'bad' men—five of whom were hanged for murder in Santa Fe a few years later—had a hand in the Ancheta shooting." Indeed, Siringo recalled that when any of the Cow Spring suspects (the Garcias) visited Santa Fe they would always call on the "Borrego boys." As Siringo wrote, "there seemed to be a deep friendship between the two families."[40]

❧ ❧

Santa Fe and New Mexico made an unexpected deep and lasting effect on Charlie Siringo during those months in the territory: he fell in love with the landscape, the lifestyle, the Mexican-American people, and the dry clear climate. As he himself writes:

> It was early fall when I took my departure for Denver. I hated to leave, as I had found the climate of Santa Fe the finest that I had ever been in. The summers can't be beaten anywhere, and the winters are better than most places. In fact, I liked it so much that I made up my mind to build a permanent home there, and with that end in view I secured a tract of land a short distance form the outskirts of the city and christened it the Sunny Slope Ranch.⁴¹

Siringo recalled, too, that during his eight months in New Mexico, "I saw much of the Mexican people, especially of the lower classes. I like them as a whole, and would like them still more if the blood of their Spanish sires could be eradicated so as to do away with their cruelty to dumb animals." Siringo's great disappointment was that they "fill up on the rotten poison liquors which are manufactured in local cellars cheaply for this class of trade by Jews and so-called Americans of the money-grabbing races."⁴²

It is worth noting that while Siringo herded cattle ruthlessly and slaughtered them for their hides as a teenager, he was always an admirer of horses, and despite being a bronco-buster, he tried to get people to respect horses and dogs. In his second edition of *A Texas Cowboy*, he included an appendix urging humane treatment of horses. His entire life is highlighted by stories about the horses he owned and loved, especially "Whiskey Pete" (originally spelled Whiskey Peet). In later years his Sunny Slope Ranch was a refuge for older horses and dogs such as the wolfhound, "Eat 'Em Up Jake." Indeed, he hired local men to look after his animals while he was away on a case.⁴³

Siringo had reason to feel this way for in nearly all his narratives he was on horseback moving cattle great distances, or carefully stalking a suspect, or tending the LX horse herd at Caldwell. To him the great cattle drives could not have occurred without trained horses. In describing a drive he always gave his readers facts about the remuda, the horse wrangler, and the outfit's equestrian experiences. As has been noted earlier, while living in Caldwell, Kansas, Siringo befriended Andy Adams, author of *The Log of a Cowboy*, thought to be the first fictional account of the long drives written. But many of Andy Adams's drives were of horse herds, and his affection for and understanding of horses was at one with Siringo's, all of which is to say that Charlie Siringo was indeed, a true cowboy.

When Siringo left the Pinkerton Agency he retired to Santa Fe and lived there until his age and poor health forced him to move to California to be near his son and daughter. But he left his mark, for today, although Sunny Slope Ranch no longer exists, two Santa Fe streets, Siringo Road and Siringo Drive, perpetuate his name in the city he came to love.

BROTHERS, YOU HAVE ALLOWED A SPY TO ENTER YOUR RANKS,
AND NOW HE SITS WITHIN THE REACH OF MY HAND.
HE WILL NEVER LEAVE THIS HALL ALIVE. HIS FATE IS DOOMED.
YOU KNOW YOUR DUTY WHEN IT COMES TO TRAITORS TO OUR
NOBLE CAUSE FOR THE UPBUILDING OF TRUE MANKIND.

— *Gabe Dallas (alias Tim O'Leary),*
quoted in Charles Siringo, A Cowboy Detective, *145*

OH, MR. ALLISON, RUN FOR YOUR LIFE. MRS. WEISS
SAYS THE FRISCO MILL IS BLOWN UP AND MANY SCABS
KILLED AND WOUNDED. NOW THEY ARE COMING TO
GET YOU AND BURN YOU AT THE STAKE AS A TRAITOR.

— *Mrs. Kate Shipley to Siringo,*
Riata and Spurs, *171*

SIRINGO WAS ONE OF THE FEW MEN IN AMERICA TO
WITNESS THE TWO COURTROOM DRAMAS
(THE HAYMARKET AND THE COEUR D'ALENE TRIALS)
MOST IMPORTANT TO THE LABOR CAUSE OF HIS TIME.

— *Michael Boudett, "Charlie Siringo*
and the Anarchists," 44

CHAPTER NINE

The Bloody
Coeur d'Alene Strike,
1891–1893

I

LET US BEGIN BY FOLLOWING THE CAREER OF THE REMARKABLE merchant, steamboat owner, and investment capitalist Simeon G. Reed, born in 1830 at East Abington, Massachusetts.[1] An incredibly bright and ambitious young man, always on the lookout for wealth, he and his wife, Amanda, migrated to gold-rush California in 1852, but they soon moved on to the thriving frontier town of Portland, Oregon, which was already experiencing its own boom by shipping grain, meat, foodstuffs, and lumber to San Francisco. Reed could see that Portland, though an inland port, not only had access to the Pacific Ocean, but was on the Columbia River, one of the greatest and longest navigable streams in the United States. Steamboats on the Columbia were the means to ship supplies upriver to mining camps all the way to future Idaho Territory. On the return trip they could bring down ore and lumber for transshipment to San Francisco. Moreover, steamboats could also go up the navigable Willamette River and collect agricultural products from the lush, fertile farms in the Willamette Valley.

Allying himself with banker William S. Ladd, a former Vermonter, Reed invested in three steamships and soon formed the Oregon Steam Navigation Company in 1860. In partnership with Captain John C. Ainsworth and Robert R. Thompson, the company not only became Oregon's most successful enterprise, it established a virtual monopoly on the river traffic when mines were being opened up in the interior.[2]

After selling the Oregon Steam Navigation Company to the Villard Syndicate in 1879 for five million dollars, Reed invested in mines in eastern Oregon and Idaho. Of particular interest to him were the mines in the Idaho Panhandle where gold had been found, but it was soon obvious that the real fortune to be made was from the extensive silver and lead deposits in the district. Without delay, in 1887 Simeon Reed bought the Bunker Hill and Sullivan Mine, "one of the richest properties in northern Idaho."[3]

To manage the Bunker Hill and Sullivan, Reed hired one of the most remarkable mining engineers in the West, Victor Clement, from Grass Valley, California, who soon urged Reed to make a greater capital outlay to develop the property. Again, with his uncanny knack for hiring the best, Reed commissioned John Hays Hammond to find $300,000 for this purpose. Hays, a graduate of Yale's Sheffield Scientific School, and both a brilliant engineer and entrepreneur, got half the sum from David O. Mills and William Crocker of California, more from a Chicago group that included Cyrus McCormick, and some from various mining engineers around the country.[4] Later, in his role as a mining engineer involved in the Bunker Hill and Sullivan strike of 1892–1893, Hammond met Siringo, praised his actions in the strike in an article, and kept up a correspondence with Charlie for the rest of the latter's life.

It is no exaggeration to say that Reed and his colleagues knew every mining engineer in the nation. Many, in fact, were trained at the Bunker Hill and Sullivan and became managers there. Among the most noteworthy was Frederick Worthen Bradley, who had been born in 1863 in Nevada County, California, where his father was a civil engineer. Mining was Bradley's chosen career from the start. At age nineteen he entered the University of California, where he took a mining engineering course. Although he never graduated, having left because of his father's early death, Bradley was so talented, he was soon in charge of several California mines, and proved to be so efficient he managed to mine and mill ore for only sixty-five cents a ton.[5]

Not surprisingly, after three years he was hired by Victor Clement to be his assistant at the Bunker Hill and Sullivan. When Clement resigned in 1893, Bradley became the mine's manager, but he soon became its president. Bradley's ambition was matched by his acuity and energy. During his tenure as president, he enlarged the scope of the BH and S operations, was active in developing Alaskan gold mines, in gold dredging in California, and in directing the fortunes of the famous Consolidated Copper Mine. "By the time of his death in 1933, Bradley had been president of sixteen different mining and smelting companies in the West and Alaska."[6]

Like Clement, his predecessor, Bradley became an expert on legal problems troubling the BH and S. He was careful to acquire federal patents to mining claims, and negotiated with the Northern Pacific for the purchase of additional lands. The firm hired the best legal experts, often choosing Rossiter Raymond and John Hays Hammond to handle their court cases. As Clement put it, they must down both the opposition and local opinion: "we must prepare to give them a squasher."[7] By "squasher," he meant complete defeat.

Victor Clement and Fred Bradley did not like being overcharged by the railroad lines and thus saw them as an enemy; but if their battle with the railroad was in the cause of good business, they hated the rise of the miners unions with a deep passion. Inevitably they and other mine owners and managers felt that the answer to these two problems was to form a Mine Owners Protective Association—soon to be called the MOA. This "confederacy" of mine owners was formed in 1891 and lasted to approximately 1916. They "fought the railroads and smelter trusts for a quarter of a century." Because of their connections, they were, writes John Fahey, "a dominant force in Idaho and the interior Northwest." And who would emerge as the leader of the MOA but the BH and S owners and managers?[8]

When the owners began organizing in 1889, Victor Clement explained their goals, saying the "objective is mutual benefit and protection—we will act in a body if necessary when dealing with the Smelters and Railroads for incoming and outgoing freight—we'll also endeavor to regulate many abuses in the labor question."[9]

It is clear that the "labor question" arose in part because their mineworkers were so diverse in origin. Among the 329 employees of the BH and S in 1894, for example, 84 were Americans, 76 were Irishmen, 27 were Germans, 24 were Italian, 23 were Swedes, 19 came from

England, and of the remaining, 14 were Scots, 12 Finnish, 11 Australians, 8 Norwegians, 7 French, 5 Danish, 2 Swiss, and one each were Spanish, Portuguese, and Icelanders. Many of these thus came from European countries where unions existed, or from backgrounds in which socialist, even anarchist ideas were known. This diversity in national origin was common to workers in all the Coeur d'Alene mines.[10]

Actually, miners were busy organizing at the same time the MOA was forming. Between 1887 and the fall of 1891, four local unions came into being in the Coeur d'Alene region. The four then formed a central committee in 1891. The fiercest opponent of the unions was the BH and S. As John Fahey had noted, other mine owners blamed the BH and S for causing their labor troubles by being so rigid and hostile.[11]

Of the twelve original members of the MOA three deserve mention because they greatly affected Charlie Siringo's role when he became a Pinkerton spy for the MOA in the Coeur d'Alene district in 1892–1893. They were: the Bunker Hill and Sullivan, the Gem (owned by the Milwaukee Mining Company), and the Frisco (whose official name was the Helena and San Francisco Mine). A fourth mine company, the Bear, does not appear to have played a central role in the troubles.

Virtually all industrial labor-capital conflicts in late nineteenth-century America centered on wages and hours disputes and the Coeur d'Alene troubles were no exception. Indeed, when the BH and S announced a reduction of wages for shovelers to $3.00 a day (down from $3.50 a day), and an increase in hours for the underground workers from nine to ten hours, but with no raise in wages, and then said it would "deduct one dollar a month from miners' wages for the company doctor," the miners struck. To the workers' surprise, after fifteen days, the company gave in, but for a secret reason: they needed time recruit nonunion workers "in Spokane and other cities." The other mines had continued to work during the BH and S strike.[12]

Meanwhile the MOA had moved against the Northern Pacific and the Union Pacific after the latter raised rates for hauling concentrate. In retaliation, the MOA announced that they would close their mines, thus depriving the railroad of all their business. Indeed, they did stop production January 16, 1892, "throwing about sixteen hundred men out of work." This time it was the railroads that gave in after two months of no revenue from the mines. They restored their lower rates with the understanding that the mines would reopen in April 1892.[13]

The MOA had another trick up its sleeve, however. Once again the MOA announced that because of depressed lead-silver markets they were reducing wages to $3.00 a day for a ten-hour day. This time all the local mine managers joined to support the MOA wage reduction. By this time, the MOA had also recruited nonunion labor from elsewhere. One of the most avid supporters of importing non-union labor was Charles Sweeney, promoter of several nearby mines, who brought in men under armed guard. These men opened the Gem and Union Mine, managed by John A. Finch and A. B. Campbell. Meanwhile the MOA had hired professional detectives to penetrate the union as spies—and among the most famous (soon to be infamous)—was Charles Siringo from the Pinkerton office in Denver.[14]

II

James McParland and Charlie Siringo had such mutual respect for one another that they negotiated Siringo's assignments. One of the most revealing of these exchanges occurred when McParland asked Charlie to go to the Coeur d'Alene mining district in the Idaho Panhandle where a strike by the local Miners' Union due to a cut in wages had occurred. The strike had so alarmed the mine owners that they had asked the Pinkerton Agency to send a good operative to join the Miners' Union "so as to be on the inside of the order when the fast-approach eruption occurred," for they were convinced there would be violence.[15]

Siringo initially declined the assignment saying, "My sympathy was with the labor organizations as against capital." McParland reluctantly accepted his decision but warned him he might have to order him to go. Meanwhile Siringo went off to handle a railroad case. A month later, however, he received a telegram ordering him back to Denver at once. This time McParland was firm, saying:

> Now Charlie, you have to go to the Coeur d'Alenes. You're the only man I've got who can go there and get into the Miners' Union. They are on their guard against detectives and they became suspicious of the operative I sent up there, and ran him out of the country. We know the leaders to be a desperate lot of criminals of the Molly Maguire type, and you will find it so. I will let your conscience be the judge,

after you get into their union. If you decide they are in the right and the mine-owners are in the wrong, you can throw up the operation without further permission from me.[16]

Given this option, Charlie accepted and journeyed to the Coeur d'Alene area. He soon found that the center of the controversy was in the three towns of Wallace, Gem, and Burke. The Northern Pacific had crossed the region in 1880, but in 1884 one of the wildest stampedes in the history of America's mining took place there when prospectors discovered rich silver-bearing quartz. Tough miners came in from all over the West, but especially from the famous copper-mining town of Butte, Montana. Butte was already known throughout the West as "the Gibraltar of Unionism." At the same time corporations took over the mining operations, so it was a labor-capital crisis from the start, as has already been suggested by the brief account of the BH and S in its formative years.

As soon as he arrived Charlie had a secret meeting in his hotel room in Wallace, where he met with Mr. Hawkins, a representative of the Mine Owners Association, and with John A. Finch, the MOA secretary, associated with the Gem Mine. In this briefing they explained that the price of silver was so low they could not pay the $3.50 a day asked by the striking miners. To break the strike they had imported scab labor and planned to starve the workers in the camps by periodically closing the mines. Declaring that they had to "down" the strikers, they asked Charlie to find out who the troublemakers were and to keep the MOA posted as to the miners' next move.[17]

Siringo was not sure he liked these explanations, but agreed to go to work in the Gem Mine. The Gem mining superintendent, John Monihan, was told who Charlie was, but no one else knew. Charlie then applied for a job, which he got a few days later. Now calling himself C. Leon Allison and clad in miner's clothes, he was to work two weeks on the day shift and two on the night shift. Siringo was told to join the union shortly after he began his job as a miner. He was sworn in by George A. Pettibone, "a rabid anarchist" in Charlie's eyes, in an empty building. According to Siringo the union oath was virtually that of the Molly Maguires. Among other demands he was warned never to turn traitor, for if he did, death would be his reward.[18]

After working for a short time Charlie managed to shirk his duty as a miner and got fired. He then went on a spree, telling his fellow miners that his Texas father had sent him money "to carry him through the winter." Some five hundred miners and several hundred surface workmen lived in Gem, a camp of two or three stores and a half a dozen saloons. The saloons ran half the night, and as usual, Siringo patronized them and, in his own words "made myself a good fellow among 'the boys.'"[19]

At this point we should introduce Mrs. Kate Shipley, a remarkable woman whom Siringo had befriended in Gem. Mrs. Shipley ran a boarding house where Siringo had a room. Just why she and her young son were in Gem while her husband was proving up a farm in Dakota is left unexplained. From all accounts she was an intelligent, practical, fairly young and pretty woman who had an instinct for getting along with people. It seems likely that Siringo had an affair with her, but both were aware that Gem presented business opportunities and decided to join forces. Siringo used his "winter money" to set up, or buy into, a store and to expand the rooming house over the store. Mrs. Shipley agreed to run the store. Happily for all, Mrs. Shipley's son soon became extremely fond of Siringo.[20]

Meanwhile, Pettibone recognized that Siringo was an extremely intelligent man, and asked him to go around with him to tell scabs to leave Gem. The union would then hold a special meeting "to resolve on running certain ones out."

Siringo's description of what happened afterward was truly graphic.

Often many as half a dozen "scabs" would be taken from their homes, sometimes with weeping wives and children begging for mercy, and with tin pans and the music of bells, they would be marched up and down the streets to be spit upon and branded as scabs before the public eyes. Then, half clothed and without food, the poor devils would be marched up the canyon, a few miles beyond the big mining camp of Burk [sic] three miles distant, and told to "hit the road" and never return at the peril of their lives. Pistols would be fired over their heads to give them a good running start.[21]

Because this driving out of scabs "was kept up all winter," Siringo confessed that his mind "had taken a regular 'flop' on the union question." Henceforth Siringo was persuaded that the leaders of the Coeur d'Alene Union were "a vicious, heartless gang of anarchists."

Over the winter capital-labor relations went from bad to worse. Late in 1891 the various miners' unions in the area formed a Central Organization group to coordinate their activities. Pettibone boasted to Siringo that the Central Organization had selected the worst men to "put the fear of Christ into" the scabs.[22]

During the winter of 1891–1892 events approached a violent climax. Siringo himself was now so trusted he became a messenger boy for the union. He got to know both the officers of the Central Union and those of the local Gem Union, of which he became its recording secretary! Pettibone, already the financial secretary of the Gem Union, also became a justice of the peace in the area. Later, Siringo learned that Cunningham, the county sheriff, was pro-union and had probably been paid a large sum to support the workers.

When the MOA arranged to send in a trainload of "scabs" at Wallace, the union leaders decided to waylay them. But Siringo tipped off the MOA of this plan, and the train barreled through Wallace to Gem and unloaded a hundred scabs directly at the mine. The Central Organization was furious. Joe Poynton, secretary of the Central Union, and Pettibone, among others, begged Thomas O'Brien, president of the Central Union, to let them blow up the scabs. But other trainloads of scabs under guard came in to furnish workers for the Gem and Helen-Frisco mines.[23]

During this crucial period Siringo had been having a nightmare of a time getting his reports to Pinkerton headquarters in St. Paul, where they immediately went to the MOA. Because the postmaster in Gem was pro-union, Siringo had to go four miles under cover of night to Wallace to mail his reports. These went to St. Paul, then to the MOA there, and then back to the MOA officials in the Coeur d'Alene district. When some of his reports got printed in the Coeur d'Alene *Barbarian* in nearby Wardner, which was a mine owners' newspaper, the local union began to suspect that there was a spy in their midst and imported their own trained union spies to ferret out the informer.[24]

It was soon clear that local union officials suspected Siringo. One of the union imports from Butte, one Dallas by name, bluntly warned Siringo that "Hell is going to be turned loose in the next few days or weeks. You won't be safe even though you might be innocent." To which Siringo replied that he was innocent, and "I will be a true soldier by sticking to my guns."[25]

As things began to approach a climax, we can imagine Siringo talking to Mrs. Shipley, who had learned that the miners did not trust him. She begged him to stay away from the next miner's meeting. Yet even after alarming her by telling her of Dallas's threat, he said he would stay and attend. He probably did not reassure her when he showed her his gun under his arm and his knife hidden in his trousers.

At the miners' hall, on the scheduled day, Siringo read the minutes of the previous meeting to a packed hall. The union president, Oliver Hughes, then called upon Dallas to speak. Looking at Siringo, Dallas said: "Brothers, you have allowed a spy to enter your ranks, and now he sits within the reach of my hand. He will never leave this hall alive. His fate is doomed. You know your duty when it comes to dealing with traitors to our noble cause for the upbuilding of true manhood."[26]

Even Siringo admitted that it had been a fine speech and he joined in the clapping. The president then declared a recess of ten minutes in order to examine the records of the secretary. Hughes, Dallas, Pettibone, and Eaton examined Siringo's record book. "Oh, we have got you now," Dallas declared. Siringo reports that he stepped to the platform and asked, "What's the matter gentlemen, you seem to be puzzled?" Dallas responded: "Here's a leaf out of this book. We want an explanation." Siringo replied that "Mr. Hughes ordered me to cut that leaf out."

Hughes jumped up, claiming that was a lie! Siringo replied: "Mr. Hughes, you remember when the members of the Burke Union came down to hold a joint meeting with us. At that time we voted to pull up the pumps of the Poorman and Tiger Mines at Burke, and flood the lower workings of these deep properties. I wrote the resolution down and read it at the following meeting. You then ordered me to cut out and burn it, as nothing of that kind should be put in the minutes to be on record in case the book fell into the hands of the enemy." Hughes then admitted that he had ordered Siringo to cut the page out, and told the union members that they would take no action on identifying the spy. The irony was that Siringo had not burned the page but had sent it to St. Paul.[27]

Siringo went home to bed, but kept his Winchester at his side along with one hundred cartridges. The next morning while Siringo was eating breakfast with Mrs. Shipley, she told him that there was a man sitting on a box in front of the post office. Siringo quickly recognized him as someone he had known on a case in Nevada. It was "Black Jack" Griffin, who had been implicated in the bombing of two mine owners

(Prinz and Pelling). From that point on Siringo knew he was a marked man. He handed in his resignation as secretary to the Gem Union, and found that men shunned him on the street.[28]

Siringo now began to plan his escape for if he stayed in Gem he was as good as dead. He climbed down a ladder, which he had put up against a side second-story window in the narrow alley between his house and the Nelson Hotel next door, and crept to the sixteen-foot-high fence that surrounded his backyard. He had already loosened a board in the fence and crawled on his stomach between two fallen trees into swampy brush that led to a creek. Looking up, he saw three armed men on a bridge surveying the area. (Some weeks before Siringo had learned from Pettibone that the union had imported a hundred rifles to use when necessary.)

Siringo crossed the stream under some spruce branches. Once on the other side, he ran to the Gem Mine and told Superintendent John Monihan that he had learned that the union members planned to beat two scabs to death when the lights went out at a local saloon. At that point the town constable also arrived to report that the two men had already been beaten. One had managed to flee while the other lay nearly dead beside the bridge. At the requests of Monihan, Siringo and a Gem miner fetched a doctor from Wallace to treat the badly wounded man.

Siringo then boldly returned from Wallace on the night train on which Pettibone and a number of union officials were also riding. He told Pettibone he had resigned as secretary. Pettibone's response was to ask him why he was carrying a rifle, to which Siringo replied: because he was attacked last night. Pettibone then said: "That's all very well, but you can't go into Gem with that rifle," but Siringo defied him by detraining and walking up to Mrs. Shipley's store without being challenged.[29]

Siringo then told Mrs. Shipley that he would slip out again to the mill to tell Monihan that he believed the riot of miners against the mills would start the next day. Siringo then returned once again under cover to Mrs. Shipley's in order to glean more information. By this time Mrs. Shipley was in an extraordinary state of agitation, and was even more horrified when Siringo knocked on her door to say that he was back. She told him that the attack on the scabs and the mining properties was about to start and that "they all know you are a detective. You must get out. They plan to kill you as soon as the trouble starts."

The next morning firing did start. MOA guards were killed, perhaps a dozen men were hunting Siringo, and shooting began in Gem and at the Frisco Mill. Seeing no way to escape over his old route to the Gem Mill, Siringo realizing that he was trapped, returned to Mrs. Shipley's house, sawed a hole in her floor, got rid of his Stetson and familiar raincoat, and put on an old leather jacket and a slouch hat. He squeezed himself into the hole under Mrs. Shipley's floor, where he was handed a cup of coffee and a sandwich before she put the carpet back on her floor and pulled a trunk over the hole.

Under the house Siringo saw that he might make it to a raised board sidewalk that ran next to the street. Through the cracks he saw his would-be nemesis, Dallas, standing above him with a rifle. At that moment the miners blew up the Frisco Mill and Mrs. Shipley moved the trunk and shouted down the hole: "Oh Mr. Allison, run for your life. Mrs. Weiss (a neighbor) says the Frisco Mill is blown up and many scabs killed and wounded. Now they are coming to get you and burn you at the stake as a traitor." The Frisco Mill, incidentally, had been blown up by none other than George Pettibone.[30]

By this time nearly a thousand men had gathered in front of Mrs. Shipley's store hunting for Siringo. Although she had closed her store, Dallas shouted, "Open the door or we'll break it down." According to Siringo, Mrs. Shipley said, "Break it down then . . . you'll suffer for it." Dallas and others broke in the door and the store filled with angry cursing men. When Mrs. Shipley denied that Allison (Siringo) was there, Dallas called her a liar. But she stood her ground and after searching the house they finally left.[31]

Siringo, truly desperate, decided to crawl under the raised sidewalk toward the union hall. Since there was no room to crawl, he wiggled his way forward, dragging his rifle. As he inched along he heard the miners just above him on the boardwalk talking about the blowing up of the mill. He heard an Irish voice wonder why they couldn't find the traitor Allison and saying, "I want to smash his face in." Meanwhile Siringo finally got to a saloon, which he found he could crawl under toward the back of the building. Here he was overjoyed to see daylight streaming through another opening in the rear. Fortunately for Siringo, the saloon was over a brushwood swamp with enough height in bushes to allow him to walk in a stooping position. But then he saw three men posted to guard the back of the saloon.[32]

To make his escape Siringo knew he would have to crawl up and over a railroad embankment in order to get to the Gem Mine. But then he faced the possibility that he would be shot by the mine-owner guards (his own allies) as a union enemy. Here again the fantastic Siringo luck came into play. Charlie spied a boxed culvert through which the fast-flowing water of the creek passed under the railroad embankment. After getting to the culvert with only one shot having been fired at him, he made it through the culvert only to hear a voice shout, "drop that gun or off goes your head." Siringo shouted back that he was a friend; in response to which the guard ordered him to take off his hat, after which the guard asked "if I was Allison the detective." Siringo answered "yes," and was quickly led to the Gem Mill.[33]

There he found Monihan and a crowd of others congratulating Fred Carter, a cowboy who had been the only man to escape from the Frisco Mill after the explosion. Although he had lost a knuckle and was wounded in the heel, he was all right. It was from Carter that they learned the strikers had sent powder down a Frisco Mill tramway to blow the building up. Siringo told Monihan he thought they would use the Gem tramway to do the same. At Siringo's suggestion Monihan's men placed heavy poles across the Gem tramway.

At this point the union men sent a man under a flag of truce to Monihan to say that if he and his men surrendered they would not blow up the Gem Mill. A half-hour later Edward Kenney, John A. Finch's secretary, arrived under a second flag of truce with a message from the MOA to surrender and thus prevent the loss of the mill. When Monihan agreed to obey Finch's order, Siringo decided that he must escape again for he knew the union men would kill him if they caught him.[34]

Accompanied by a young non-union miner named Frank Stark, who also feared for his life, Siringo crawled up the mountainside and under cover watched Monihan surrender. Siringo recalled that as the Gem men lined up, the union men looked into each face hunting for Siringo.

Stark and Siringo headed toward the town of Mullan on a footpath only to find three men with rifles blocking the trail. But rather than go over the mountain they decided to trick them. Siringo then said in a loud voice: "You shoot the one on the right; I'll kill the fellow on the left!" His shout so startled the men that "all three jumped as if they had been shot, and next instant they were tearing down the canyon for their lives; dropping their rifles, and even turning somersaults over fallen trees in their eagerness to get away." Stark and Siringo then had a good laugh.[35]

Stark and Siringo finally got to Wallace, the major town in the area, after successfully evading four more armed men. There they slipped into the back of the Carter Hotel, where they found two MOA officials, A. D. Goss and Monihan, who told them to leave at once for they themselves would be murdered if they were caught talking to Siringo! After retreating to the hills again, Siringo and Stark were hidden by friendly miners where they watched how the strikers treated Monihan, the scabs, and pro-MOA merchants and clerks. Many of these were forced to walk to the state of Washington border some hundred miles away.

Naturally once the strike became violent the mine owners had called for territorial and federal assistance. The governor of Idaho Territory responded by declaring martial law, and from Washington, with President Benjamin Harrison's approval, the Secretary of War ordered Colonel William P. Carlin, commander at Fort Sherman, in Coeur d'Alene City, to take troops to Wallace and stop the violence. Their arrival was delayed, however, because the Central Union had blown up the railroad bridges leading to Wallace. Other troops were sent immediately from Montana but they, too, were delayed. On July 14, however, once the troops had arrived, Siringo came down from his hiding place, made himself known to Colonel Carlin, and reported his adventures in full. That night he and Stark slept at the Carter Hotel. As Siringo writes, "It was the first peaceful nights rest I had since I had resigned from the Gem Union."[36]

III: AFTERMATH

Life was very different for Siringo once the U.S. troops were there. In sharp contrast to being a hunted man, he had now been made a deputy by Colonel Carlin, and was ordered to identify union men and put them in a "bull pen."

Siringo was now engaged in a more familiar task: he was rounding up stray union members as if they were Texas cattle. As he and a detail of soldiers picked up some here and there, in the process he returned to Gem where he saw Mrs. Shipley again. Upon seeing Siringo, her little boy—in Siringo's words—had "duck fits" for he thought "the man" was still down the hole under the floor. He then met Monihan, who described the robbery and the killing of scabs when they were waiting at the Coeur d'Alene Catholic Mission for transportation elsewhere. Monihan himself barely escaped from them.[37]

Siringo's next task was to testify in the trials of the miners at Murray, Idaho, then Shoshone County seat; but he was threatened so often by angry miners, he slept on the mountain above the town, and always went from one place to another by an unusual route so that he would not be ambushed. Given Siringo's talent for clear facts and detail, the Idaho newspapers reported that he had "stunned" the defense with his testimony.[38]

As usual Siringo distinguished between the good guys and the bad guys. He felt that while some mine managers were OK, Victor Clement and A. M. Esler, both of the BH and S, were violently hated. Esler was something of a soulless efficiency expert who applied the same "starve 'em out" tactics he had used on the railroads to the union men. The miners also hated R. E. Brown, the pro-MOA editor of the *Barbarian*, and the pro-MOA Doctor Simms, whom they later assassinated.

On the union side Siringo seemed to like and respect Oliver Hughes and Thomas O'Brien, Gem union officials, but he hated George Pettibone and Joe Poynton. In the last round of trials, eighteen union men were convicted, among them Pettibone, O'Brien, and Poynton. Meanwhile anti-Siringo persons took their own vengeance by burning his store and rooming house in Gem, in which he had invested $3,000. He had bought out Mrs. Shipley and gone into partnership with Mr. and Mrs. Will Read, Mamie's uncle and aunt from Illinois who were raising his daughter, Viola. Siringo appears not to have understood that as one of the most hated men in Gem, sooner or later his property would be attacked.[39]

The Coeur d'Alene experience was the most traumatic of Siringo's colorful and often dangerous life as a detective. How did he come out of it? What did he learn? As we have just noted, Siringo came to hate the cruel union tactics of driving scabs out of the district, of dynamiting buildings, and instances of killings by trigger-happy union leaders. Undoubtedly it brought back memories of the Haymarket Riot, which was his introduction to deadly industrial labor–capital conflict in which ideological anarchists praised the use of dynamite as a weapon to be used in the cause of justice. In his accounts Siringo called the Coeur d'Alene union leaders anarchists, and as in Chicago, foreigners. He came to hate the Irish union leaders such as Dallas, sent out from Butte. And as we already know, he had developed an obsessive dislike of George Pettibone, who did believe in bombing with dynamite.

Yet Siringo could not dislike the average union worker. He knew they had reasons to protest against the MOA policy of wage cuts, starving them out by closing the mines, a favorite tactic of A. B. Esler and the BH and S, and the introduction by importation of scab labor. He was, in fact, deeply disturbed by the union attitudes of some of the MOA leaders—especially Victor Clement. It seems safe to say that in time he must have wondered at the justice of his own actions as a Pinkerton detective.

Although Siringo left the Coeur d'Alene district after his testimony against union leaders in 1893, only a year later mine and railroad workers and many businessmen and ordinary citizens in Montana, Idaho, and Washington were so disaffected that they supported the newly formed industrial union formed by Eugene V. Debs in the strike against the Pullman Palace Car Company. Labor discontent, already exacerbated by the financial panic of 1893, and the resulting national depression during the mid-1890s, was expressed in the Pacific Northwest when these groups supported Populist Party candidates for public office in local and state elections.[40]

A far more significant consequence of the Coeur d'Alene strike and its outcome, however, was the decision of the western labor leaders to found the Western Federation of Miners (WFM) in 1893. Meeting in Butte, Montana, the new union was headed by Edward Boyce, who served as president of the WFM from 1896 to 1902, and gave it strong leadership. He was succeeded by two even more dynamic figures: Charles H. Moyer as president, and William D. (Big Bill) Haywood as secretary. They became a major presence in new strikes in Cripple Creek and Leadville, Colorado, in 1894, and in the Coeur d'Alene area in 1899 where once again the Bunker Hill and Sullivan silver-mine complex was the target of a unionization drive that became violent when the WFM blew up the company's concentrator at Wardner, Idaho. Once again U.S. troops came in to restore order, and, as before, put strikers in the hated bull pens. So great was the tension in Wardner that the troops remained there until 1901![41]

During 1903 and 1904 a whole new series of violent strikes occurred in the Colorado mines at Cripple Creek and elsewhere. As labor historian Richard Maxwell Brown has written, the sense of outrage was so great that, "Eventually a campaign of mine owners, state authorities, and a vigilante-type citizens alliance subdued the WFM with what has been called the most systematic use of violence by management in American labor history."[42]

To recover from their major defeat in Colorado, the WFM leaders now joined the Industrial Workers of the World, a radical union in Chicago, which it helped found in 1905.[43] In that same year former Idaho governor Frank Steunenberg was killed by a bomb fastened to the front gate of his house. In 1899 Steunenberg, who had been pro-labor, had sent in troops to quell the 1899 Coeur d'Alene troubles, and the WFM had never forgiven him. Surprisingly, a man known as Harry Orchard admitted to planting the bomb. His confession, extracted by none other than Siringo's boss, James McParland, implicated WFM officials Haywood and Moyer, and a WFM ally and Siringo's old enemy, George Pettibone.

All were arrested in Colorado and sent, illegally, across state lines to Idaho where they went on trial in 1907. The trial attracted even more national attention when the famous Chicago lawyer Clarence Darrow defended Moyer, Haywood, and Pettibone and won their acquittal, for the prosecution could not connect Orchard to the three.[44] Ironically, Charlie Siringo was to find himself once again involved with the Coeur d'Alene troubles because his own boss, James McParland, had persuaded Harry Orchard to confess, not only to the killing of Steunenberg, but to lethal bombings in Colorado killing scores of persons. Now an old man, and nearly blind, McParland was so hated by union men that he, too, was targeted for assassination. Thus when he was called to Boise, Idaho, to keep Orchard, now in jail there, as a witness in the Moyer, Haywood, and Pettibone trial, McParland asked Siringo to serve as his bodyguard.[45]

Although not involved in the trial itself, Siringo was present in court and heard the eloquent arguments between Darrow and the Idaho prosecutors—James Hawley and Senator William E. Borah—in 1907. Clarence Darrow's brilliance had a great impact in Siringo and may have changed his life, as we shall note later, for Darrow had lambasted McParland and detectives in general. But back in 1893 Siringo could not foresee that his life would be affected by future Coeur d'Alene troubles. Instead, after a rest, he was assigned to track down the most colorful bank and train robbers in the West, Butch Cassidy and the Sundance Kid. His adventures in that operation comprise one of the most extraordinary chases in his entire career. And that, dear readers, is the topic of the next chapter.

JUST WHEN THE WILD WEST SEEMED READY TO BOW
TO THE INEVITABILITY OF LAW AND ORDER, A LARGE BAND
OF OUTLAWS BEGAN A CRIME SPREE THAT RANGED ACROSS
SEVERAL WESTERN STATES. THE OUTBURST WAS THE LAST
GASP OF THE COWBOY-CRIMINAL-BADMAN TO PLY HIS TRADE
BEFORE CIVILIZATION HAD HIM COMPLETELY HEMMED IN.

—*Ben E. Pingenot, speaking of*
"The Wild Bunch," in Siringo, *59*

BUTCH CASSIDY... "WAS THE SHREWDEST AND MOST DARING
OUTLAW OF THE PRESENT AGE, THOUGH NOT OF THE
BLOOD-SPILLING KIND SUCH AS KID CURRY AND BLACK JACK."

—*Charles A. Siringo,* Riata and Spurs, *238*

THIS REMARKABLE STRANGER SUCCEEDED IN JOINING THE RANKS
OF THE WILD BUNCH AND SO INGRATIATED HIMSELF INTO THE
TRAIN ROBBERS' INNER CIRCLE THAT HE MANAGED TO LEARN
ALL THEIR SECRET CODES AND PLANS AND THEN HE VANISHED
AS MYSTERIOUSLY AS HE HAD COME. HE WAS PINKERTON OPERATIVE
CHARLES A. SIRINGO, OF THE AGENCY'S DENVER OFFICE, AND THIS
INFORMATION HE OBTAINED, TOGETHER WITH THE SECRET CODES
HE HAD LEARNED, WAS SOON IN THE HANDS OF THE GANG'S
INTENDED VICTIMS. THE LEAKAGE OF THIS INFORMATION HELD
UP THE PLAN OF THE GANG FOR NEARLY A YEAR.

—*Excerpt from Pinkerton Agency files on the Wild Bunch,*
cited in James D. Horan, Desperate Men, *209–10*

CHAPTER TEN

Chasing Butch Cassidy, the Sundance Kid, and a Great Many Others, 1899–1903

I

IT IS AN EXTRAORDINARY COINCIDENCE THAT CHARLIE SIRINGO MET and befriended Billy the Kid, the best-known and most written-about of the nineteenth-century western "bad men," with the exception of the James Brothers and the Youngers. Then nearly two decades later Siringo spent four years chasing Butch Cassidy (George Leroy Parker) and the Sundance Kid (Harry Longabaugh) and other members of their gang called the Wild Bunch.

It seems equally extraordinary that Billy the Kid, Butch Cassidy, and Charlie Siringo all wound up in Hollywood: Billy the Kid and Butch Cassidy and his pals in films, and Siringo in person as a friend of two famous western film actors, William S. Hart and Will Rogers. Then, ironically after Siringo's own death in 1928, he, too, was portrayed in bit parts in several films as a mysterious detective, and in a fictional version of his own life. Then in 1978, the Media Design Studio of Yale

University produced a semi-documentary with professional actors called *Siringo and the West.*[1]

Yet, while hundreds of authors wrote about Billy the Kid in the nineteenth and twentieth centuries, including an admiring, but romantic and inaccurate biography by Siringo himself in 1920, no one wrote about Butch Cassidy and the Wild Bunch beyond many newspaper accounts of them as very successful train, bank, and company payroll robbers. In the second half of the twentieth century, however, because of George Roy Hill's brilliant 1968 film, *Butch Cassidy and the Sundance Kid*, these two outlaws, respectively played by Paul Newman and Robert Redford, became the best-known and most liked western "bad men" in the eyes of the general public in our time. They diverted the attention from the outrageous killers Bonnie and Clyde, whose violent, sordid careers had been made famous by director Arthur Penn in his film, *Bonnie and Clyde*, produced in 1967, starring Warren Beatty and Faye Dunaway.[2]

Butch Cassidy and the Sundance Kid has now been listed by the American Film Institute as one of the hundred most influential films of the twentieth century. It received three Academy Awards, made the song "Raindrops Keep Fallin' on My Head" enduringly popular, and in 1969 grossed over $30,000,000. At this point, however, we face a multiple set of ironies. George Roy Hill's portrayals of Butch Cassidy and the Sundance Kid do not jibe with the facts about these men. Although they themselves were not killers, others in their gang were. They were pictured as "good" badmen, helping people in trouble and robbing banks and trains to pay lawyers to get their friends out of jail. As was the case in most of the Billy the Kid films, *Butch Cassidy* was full of nostalgia and romantic fiction, yet it turned out to be one of the first major anti-westerns, showing the dark side of western corruption, portraying railroad barons as heartless, and federal government policies as destructive. Critics say George Roy Hill used Butch Cassidy and his group obliquely to express protest at the time of the Vietnam War against corporate and government authority.[3]

Fortunately, we have a revealing documentary by Hill himself, *The Making of Butch Cassidy and the Sundance Kid*, in which his, Newman's, and Redford's interpretation of the chief characters are discussed. Newman, for example, "kept the character of Butch 'very loose'; . . . He admitted to putting a 'good deal of myself in the part.'" "Sundance on the other hand was portrayed by Redford as 'aloof, a loner.'" As Robert Murray noted: "He was as quiet and brooding, and nervous as Newman's Butch Cassidy was outgoing, spontaneous and fun-loving. Together, the two formed a recognizable pair of friends, as opposites often unite to form that most basic human molecule."[4]

In the nearly thirty-five years after Hill's remarkable film made Butch Cassidy and the Sundance Kid known to most Americans, awareness of them has undoubtedly been kept alive by Paul Newman's continuing fame as an outstanding actor, and as the sponsor of the Connecticut Hole-in-the-Wall Camp for children with cancer, the name itself coming from Hole-in-the-Wall, Wyoming, where Butch and his pal hung out on occasion.[5]

Equally important, Robert Redford has kept alive the name "Sundance" with his own Sundance Film Institute in Salt Lake City, Utah, which holds an annual Sundance Festival in Park City, Utah, in January, at which previews of the works of independent filmmakers are shown. Periodically, the general public also receives catalogues from Redford's Sundance, a firm featuring western clothes, jewelry, and furniture.

It is Redford's deep love for the wild areas of the western slope of the Rocky Mountains and his fierce crusades to preserve the rugged terrain of the Colorado Plateau, however, that have made him a national hero to environmentalists. These are the very regions in which Butch and his men hid out from the law so successfully, especially in the Robbers Roost area of Utah's high desert country. In 1995 when President Clinton signed an executive order "creating the new 1.8 million acre Grand Staircase-Canyons of the Escalante Monument" in the region, Frank Murary notes that Robert Redford, one of its key promoters, "was nearby."[6]

II

Curiously, it was thirty years after the debut of Hill's film before a truly serious, fully documented and readable biography of Butch Cassidy was published. But in 1998, after many years of exhaustive research, Richard Patterson's *Butch Cassidy: A Biography* appeared. It seems logical that we might follow Patterson's own version of Cassidy's unique career told, as it were, by an objective, fact-oriented reporter.[7]

Patterson attests at the outset of his biography that Butch and his Wild Bunch gang were well-known—perhaps infamous would be a better word—for their exploits throughout the 1890s and well into the first decade of the twentieth century. Dozens of successful western train, bank, and company payroll robberies were attributed to him and his gang whether they had perpetrated them or not. Indeed, federal, state, and local law officials and the Pinkerton Agency became so paranoid about the amazing feats of the gang, but especially about Butch and his partner, the Sundance Kid, whose real name was Harry Longabaugh, that long after the two had fled to Argentina, and even after they had died in a shootout after robbing a mining camp payroll in Bolivia in 1911, that some said they were still alive and had returned to the United States to commit more crimes. Rumors of their survival even led some imitators in the 1920s and 1930 to claim that they were either Cassidy or Longabaugh in disguise!

Because the Cassidy saga has now been so well researched and reported by Patterson, and their careers seem so unique when compared to those of the James Brothers or to the violence of Bonnie and Clyde, it seems logical to follow their fascinating story first, rather than see them through the eyes of Charlie Siringo, who pursued the Wild Bunch for over four years. In the telling we shall see just how brilliantly the shrewd and professional Butch outwitted the equally shrewd and professional Siringo, but that his failure to catch Cassidy was probably due more to the Pinkerton Agency's bureaucratic hang-ups and mistakes than to wrong moves by Siringo. Because Siringo followed the Butch Cassidy group for over four years over much of the Rocky Mountains West, Wyoming, Utah, and Arizona, it seems logical to describe where Cassidy and the Wild Bunch went in their series of robberies.

Let us begin with Butch Cassidy's personality. According to Patterson, Cassidy himself was not a psychopathic misfit or villain at war with the world—as Jesse James was reputed to be—but was "quick-witted and good humored." He enjoyed a good time and did not like killing. He sought the company of women and occasionally gambled and drank. To him robbing banks and trains was simultaneously a game, a sport, and a serious business. He was, in fact, an adept professional who planned each robbery with attention to every detail.[8] Paul Newman's version of him in the film is sometimes strikingly accurate.

Robert Leroy Parker, the future Butch Cassidy, was born in 1866 in remote Circle Valley, Utah, to Mormon parents. The Parkers lived a hardscrabble life trying to support fourteen children on a small farm. As a young teenager Bob Parker hired out as a hand on a nearby ranch, where he soon came under the influence of a lively older ranch hand, Mike Cassidy, who was probably already into horse and cattle stealing. Cassidy became Parker's hero and rebel role model, so much so that he later adopted the name "Cassidy" as his own.[9]

In 1884, at age eighteen, Bob Parker left home to help deliver a bunch of stolen horses to the mining boomtown of Telluride, Colorado. There he met other colorful figures, often on the wrong side of the law, among them Matt Warner, who was already involved in both stealing horses and running horse races in nearby towns. The rest is history; Parker was committed to stealing and armed robbery for the rest of his life.[10] It is not clear what he did between 1884 and 1887, but in 1889 Matt Warner and Cassidy were joined in Telluride by Tom McCarthy, a third outlaw with whom Warner had already boldly robbed the prominent Denver Colorado banker David Moffat of $21,000.[11]

Returning to Telluride in 1889, the two, with Cassidy, decided to rob the San Miguel Valley Bank located there. Because Matt Warner, who wound up in prison many years later, told his story to Murray E. King, a reporter, who published Warner's memoirs as *The Last of the Bandit Riders* in New York in 1938, we have an accounting of how the robbery took place. The three rode into Telluride on June 22, 1889, all dressed up as recently paid cowboys on a spree. Hitting the bank at the noon hour, when business was slow, they took some $20,000 and fled the town.[12]

Although the local sheriff quickly formed a posse and gave chase, Warner and Cassidy had organized a set of relay horses along their escape route so that they would always have fresh mounts. Willing confederates and relay horses were to be a standard feature of all of Cassidy's robberies, whether it was a bank, train or company payroll heist.

Taking zigzag routes north they eventually wound up in Brown's Park near the Utah-Colorado border. The Green River ran through the park. As Richard Patterson tells us, Brown's Park had been a fur trappers' paradise until beavers became scarce. It was then abandoned until occupied by ranchers in the 1870s. The isolation of the park "made it a popular hiding place for stolen stock which cowboys from Texas had cut out of herds being driven north to summer pasturage in Wyoming." "From the beginning, the area became a general hangout for rustlers and eventually outlaws of all kinds." Matt Warner himself already knew the area because he had once raised horses in the Diamond Mountains, which constituted the southern boundary of the park.[13]

Brown's Park also boasted what every western hideout seemed to have: a local resident, quite often a rancher and/or a saloon and general store owner, who was willing to assist robbers and rustlers. Matt Warner knew just such an individual in Brown's Park: Charlie Crouse, who had a ranch on the Green River. Undoubtedly for a price, he directed the three Telluride robbers to a remote cabin, which he owned. Crouse's reputation as a go-between was so well known, a few days later a posse showed up at his ranch in search of the Telluride fugitives. Forewarned, Warner, McCarthy, and Cassidy then fled south to Robbers Roost, an almost impenetrable region of deep canyons and steep cliffs, located, as noted earlier, in eastern Utah's high desert country. It was their "Sherwood Forest," desert style.[14]

Sometime in 1889, Robert Leroy Parker changed his name to George Cassidy (the nickname "Butch" was to come later). But with his share of the stolen cash, "George Cassidy" joined a fellow cowboy, Al Hainer, to buy property near Dubois, Wyoming, which they turned into a horse ranch. Again the action was very characteristic of Cassidy, for, as Patterson had noted, "He has a special way with horses; they became his life: stealing them, raising, racing them and selling them—and eventually escaping on them with other peoples' money."[15] During his stay near Dubois, Cassidy, this handsome, blue-eyed, good-natured youth, easily made friends with his neighbors.

After a short while, however, Cassidy sold his herd, closed the ranch, and moved to Johnson County, Wyoming, located some 250 miles northwest of Cheyenne. Johnson County had just boomed in the 1880s as the center of large cattle ranching operations. It soon became obvious that former employees of the ranchers would take up homesteads and develop their own small cattle operation, often with animals rustled from the big ranchers. It was said that ranchers were cattlemen who farmed on the side and the homesteaders were rustlers who farmed on the side. Their lawless acts became so common that the ranchers demanded satisfaction from territorial law officers, but although many were arrested, the courts seemed incapable of getting convictions.

To make matters worse, the rustlers were active in long-distance horse-stealing, an "industry" that had grown up in which horses were stolen, quickly driven out of the area, and sold in other states or territories. The operation was so efficient, horse thieves in other regions would swap their locally stolen horses for the imported ones, and we even have evidence of Dakota Territory horses winding up in Wyoming. It was into tumultuous Johnson County that Butch Cassidy, Matt Warner, and Tom McCarty came to engage in cattle and horse rustling. Cassidy himself acquired nearly six hundred acres in the Blue Creek area. It was during this time that Cassidy, while working at a butcher shop in Rock Springs, Wyoming, acquired the nickname "Butch."[16]

It was also during his Wyoming stay that Cassidy befriended Douglas A. Preston, an able lawyer who was—for want of a better term—a negotiator between outlaws and the law; that is, he tried to keep outlaws out of jail, or if they were caught and convicted, to get them reduced sentences or pardons. Far from just practicing locally, Preston had legal ties with other lawyers and elected officials all over Wyoming and Utah. Given his friendship with outlaws and his considerable talent as a lawyer, Douglas Preston was thriving in Wyoming, and it was to Preston that Cassidy turned when in 1893 he himself was arrested for buying stolen horses.[17]

Meanwhile cattle rustling had become so dominant while the courts were proving to be so ineffective that the big ranchers hired detectives to track down and even ambush violent suspects, one of those being Tom Horn, a former Pinkerton turned vicious. That of course, led to more violence, the most notable event being the vigilante hanging of "Cattle Kate" Watson and her partner Jim Averill by six local ranchers in the Sweetwater Valley area of Wyoming. The ranchers, members of the powerful Wyoming Stock Growers Association, were convinced that two homesteaders, Watson and Averill, were dealing in stolen cattle and decided to lynch them. When the news of hanging a woman reached WSGA headquarters in Cheyenne, WSGA officials persuaded a local reporter for the *Cheyenne News Leader* to vilify the victims by claiming that Averill was a killer and rustler and that Watson was a prostitute running a bawdy house where cowboys swapped cattle for sexual favors. The reporter dubbed Ellen Watson "Cattle Kate," a name that was the nickname of a Wyoming prostitute, Kate Maxwell. The actual facts of the brutal lynching have finally been established by recent exhaustive scholarship, but the original "Cattle Kate" legend still persists.[18]

By 1892 conditions were so bad the ranchers, operating through the Wyoming Stock Growers Association, had compiled a list of known rustlers and outlaws whom they decided to kill. Then, at the conclusion of their annual spring meeting, the Stock Growers Association assembled forty-six vigilantes who boarded a special Union Pacific train at Cheyenne, the state capital, to go to Johnson County and wipe out the outlaws. In addition to nineteen cattlemen, and five of their stock detectives, they hired twenty-two gunmen, mostly from Texas. The special train included three baggage cars to hold horses, wagons, and gear to get them to Johnson County.[19]

Once they had reached Johnson County the invaders surprised and shot to death two men, Nate Champion and Nick Ray; but then the hunters became the hunted, because news of Champion's and Ray's deaths so angered the citizens of Buffalo, the county seat, that the local sheriff mounted a posse of two hundred men who surrounded the invaders at a ranch a short distance south of Buffalo. Now came the ultimate irony: the vigilante invaders had to be rescued from the citizen posse by a troop of United States cavalry sent in by the governor and Wyoming's two United States Senators, Francis E. Warren and Joseph M. Carey. Johnson County wanted to try the vigilantes in local courts, but instead the troops took the hapless group to Cheyenne for protective custody. Although a trial was eventually held, lack of witnesses and a bankrupt Johnson County resulted in dismissal.[20]

Butch Cassidy was not involved in the Johnson County War, but in 1893, he was arrested for possessing a stolen horse (although the law officers knew he had stolen many horses), tried, convicted, and sent to the Wyoming State Prison on July 15, 1894. Butch was pardoned before serving a full term, but his biographer, Patterson, believes that the prison experience set him onto a life of crime, a conclusion that seems to have been confirmed when, upon release from prison, Cassidy went to join Matt Warner in Brown's Park. Warner, now married, had a cabin on Diamond Mountain.[21] While there Cassidy became a close friend of Elza Lay, who also resided in Brown's Park. Lay, a handsome, tall, "dark-complected" man, was a professional counterfeiter. For a time Butch served as a "front runner," spreading out counterfeit money in the area, but was never caught while doing so.[22]

It was at this point that the legendary "Robin Hood to the Rescue" image of Butch Cassidy began. In 1896 Matt Warner and two other men were arrested for killing two prospectors in a shootout and charged with their murders. Warner, who had no money for a lawyer, appealed to

Butch for help. In turn Butch contacted Douglas Preston, who took on the case after Cassidy promised to pay his legal fee. Elza Lay and Henry "Bub" Meeks, the latter a Mormon who had become an outlaw, and had befriended Cassidy, probably also promised to help pay Preston.[23]

While it cannot be proven, it looks as if Butch, Elza Lay, and "Bub" Meeks robbed the local bank in Montpelier, Idaho, to get the cash to pay Preston. Possibly because Butch was a friend of Sheriff John Pope of Vintah County, Utah, who had been ordered to arrest Butch and Lay and failed to do so, the two were able to flee south to Robbers Roost, where they appear to have hidden out at a camp near "desolate Horseshoe Canyon in northern Wayne County about twenty-five miles east of Hanksville."[24]

What evidence we have suggests that Cassidy, Elza Lay, and possibly Harry Longabaugh (the Sundance Kid) managed to locate their camp on the eastern wall of Horseshoe Canyon. Far from seeming like desperate fugitives, Butch had a girlfriend (possibly Etta Place) with him, and Elza Lay's wife was there as well. Both women appear to have spent a mild winter there before returning to their respective homes in March 1897. According to Richard Patterson it was at this time that Butch had already begun to recruit members of his future gang. Meanwhile, he and Lay were also planning their next robbery: "the payroll office of the Pleasant Valley Coal Company at Castle Gate, Utah."[25]

Castle Gate was a company town a few miles north of Price, Utah, owned by the Denver and Rio Grande Railroad, which had a railroad spur running to it. Through assiduous research Butch's group discovered that they faced what appeared to be impossible logistical and image obstacles. The company payroll, for example, was delivered by train every two weeks, but deliberately on an irregular schedule to thwart would-be robbers. This meant that robbers had to hang around the little town of Castle Gate until the payroll train actually arrived; but located in a narrow valley and connected by train to the world, the company's miners had no need of horses. Cowboys on horses would stand out like sore thumbs, but at the same time the town's residents did enjoy seeing bareback horse racing. Stationing his men at a ranch outside of the town, Butch and a few of his men would ride in bareback, explaining to the curious that they were training their horses for bareback races in Salt Lake City.[26]

Butch was lucky. He and Elza Lay were in Castle Gate one day when the payroll train arrived. The train gave a signal, after which E. L. Carpenter, the paymaster, and his clerk, T. W. Lewis, started down the stairs from their second-floor office over a store. After they met the train and collected the payroll in several bags, they started back up the stairs to the company office. Butch was there with his gun and ordered Carpenter to drop the satchels. He complied, but Lewis, seeing what was happening, tried to get to the front door. A miner in the store came to see what was wrong when Lewis dashed in. Elza Lay ordered him to stay inside or he would kill him. Then the whole scheme threatened to fail when Butch's horse, frightened by the noise and Butch's tossing bags to Lay, broke away and ran down the street. Somehow Lay on his own horse got to the animal so that Butch could mount him. By then employees had figured out that a robbery had occurred, and began firing their rifles at Butch and Lay, but in the best Hollywood tradition the two got away.[27]

The paymaster, acting as efficiently as anyone could, tried to telegraph the county sheriff at Price, Utah, but discovered that the wires had been cut, obviously by one of Butch's gang. He then climbed into the cab of the train and "ordered the engineer to get him to Price as fast as possible."[28]

As usual Butch had planned a careful getaway route with fresh horses strategically located along the way. Unsure of the robbers' escape route, the several posses giving chase eventually gave up, and Butch and his group made it back to Robbers Roost, but later moved on to Brown's Park in northeastern Utah.[29]

At some point in the mid-1880s, Harry Longabaugh, a Pennsylvania-born youth, had come to Durango, Colorado, and then drifted up and down the Rockies, as far north as Calgary, Canada, and as far south as Robbers Roost. He was an expert in the breaking of horses. But by the late 1880s he was in trouble with the law for stealing a horse, a saddle, and a bridle from a cowboy in Montana. Tried and convicted, he had served eighteen months in the Sundance county jail, where he probably picked up the name the Sundance Kid. Longabaugh, with two or three others, had tried robbing trains, sometimes not very successfully. What we do know is that by 1896–1897 he had joined Butch's gang, which soon acquired the name the Wild Bunch, presumably because they would invade a town, celebrate at a saloon, and then shoot off firearms in the street when leaving. Patterson finds that the name Wild Bunch was in general use by 1902.[30]

Although the Wild Bunch seemed a lot more organized and threatening to citizens, businessmen, bankers, railroads, law officials, and detectives—whether the Pinkerton or some other agency—according to

Patterson the gang probably numbered no more than eight or nine members, some of whom came and went, while others, not so lucky, were apprehended, tried, and sent to prison. By the late 1890s those closest to Butch Cassidy were Elza Lay, Bub Meeks (a fellow Mormon), Harry Longabaugh, Harvey Logan, who was also called "Kid Curry" (whom Siringo initially thought was the gang's ringleader), and another, "Flat Nose" George Currie. Even so, some members attempted bank robberies without Butch, and on occasion without success.[31]

It was also the case that by 1898 the governors of Colorado, Utah, and Wyoming had joined forces to break up the various outlaw gangs.[32] Meanwhile railroad companies, and especially the Union Pacific under the direction of E. H. Harriman, had made mail and baggage cars almost impregnable to robberies. Seeing that things were closing in, Cassidy and Elza Lay fled first to Arizona and then to Alma, New Mexico, a town close to the Arizona line, where they got jobs as cowboys on the WS Ranch, run by an able, bright Irish nobleman named William French. Always in search of competent, loyal cowboys, French saw at once that Butch and Elza seemed to be both experienced and dependable. To make a long story short, Butch and Elza, using the respective names Jim Lowe and William McGinnis, went to work for French and his newly hired foreman, Perry Tucker.[33]

Observing that Lowe was a very capable, experienced cowhand, French made Butch Tucker's assistant, while McGinnis was assigned to breaking wild horses. French was even more pleased when he realized that petty cattle rustlers, who constantly preyed on his herds, had declined dramatically.

With no reason to suspect that Lowe and McGinnis were other then loyal hands, French did not object when the two men asked to take a week or two off in late May and early June 1899. Nor did he associate the fact that a train robbery had occurred at Wilcox, Wyoming, where the attackers dynamited the express car and, after blowing open the safes, took "mostly unsigned banknotes." Although the bandits escaped, this time law officers mounted one of the largest manhunts in the history of Wyoming, because in the exchange of gunfire, Sheriff Josiah Hazen was killed. Some suspected that members of the Wild Bunch, such as Harry Longabaugh, had carried out the robbery, but no one ever proved that Cassidy was there, although he appears to have been present later when the loot was divided. If he was the mastermind of the robbery, we have no definite proof.[34]

The Wilcox train robbery led railroad and other officials to call on the Pinkerton Agency to trace the Wilcox train bandits. Indeed, it appears that Robert Pinkerton himself assigned Siringo and his old friend and fellow agent, W. O. Sayles, to trace the fleeing bandits, who were reported to be driving thirteen horses from southwest Wyoming to Brown's Park before moving on to Robbers Roost.[35] Before we recount Siringo's and Sayles's frustrating chase of the Wilcox train robbers, however, let us follow the last years Butch and the Wild Bunch operated in the West.

With incredible aplomb, Butch and Elza Lay returned to the WS Ranch, but talked of leaving French's employ. A short time later a Colorado and Southern train was robbed near Folsom, New Mexico, and in a gunfight with a pursuing posse, Sheriff Edward Farr was killed, two deputies were wounded, and on the outlaw side, one Sam Ketchum had his arm broken by a bullet and Elza Lay (McGinnis) was shot in the shoulder and the back. Lay had been caught and was now in jail, charged with killing Sheriff Farr.[36]

Quite by accident William French learned of the Folsom robbery from a posse member who told him of his employee's (McGinnis's) role in it. As French learned more, he realized that his wrangler, Lowe (Butch), and some of his other cowboys were most likely outlaws who were involved in this and other robberies. Yet Butch, never shy, asked French if he would put up bail for Lay. French refused, and Lay himself was convicted for killing Sheriff Farr. Lay was sentenced to life in prison, although it appears that he did not fire the shot that killed the sheriff.[37]

Meanwhile, one of the most absurd episodes in Butch Cassidy's always dramatic career occurred when Frank Murray, a senior Pinkerton detective who was actually Charlie Siringo's immediate superior in Denver, had traced some of the stolen treasury bills, taken at Wilcox, to Silver City, New Mexico, and then to the town of Alma, near William French's ranch. In Alma Murray went to a saloon to find out who had circulated the bills. During his visit he had a good conversation with a man who appears to have been the bartender in the saloon. The would-be bartender said his name was Jim Lowe! The unsuspecting Murray had met the mastermind of Western train robberies without knowing it. A short time later Siringo and Sayles learned of their superior's naiveté from William French and others after they had already left the WS Ranch. Needless to say Siringo and Sayles failed to catch any of the Wilcox robbers.[38]

Meanwhile, two more train robberies, and possibly a third, occurred. The first was of a Union Pacific train in the area of the Continental Divide at Tipton, Wyoming. By chance, the mail clerk in the Union Pacific express car was C. E. Woodstock, the same man who had been in the express car at the Wilcox robbery. Not only did he recognize several of the robbers, one of them boasted about their previous success at Wilcox! Other witnesses also testified that one of the Tipton robbers was Butch, and several believed that they had recognized Harvey Logan (Kid Curry) and Harry Longabaugh.[39]

The Tipton robbery, which netted Butch's gang some $55,000, was soon followed by a second on September 19, 1900, when the First National Bank of Winnemucca, Nevada, was robbed of gold coins by three men who did not even trouble to wear masks. The Pinkerton Agency, already working on the Wilcox and Tipton heists, were also assigned to this robbery, but no one was ever caught.[40]

The third robbery symbolizes the reputed mysterious omniscience of the Wild Bunch and the fact that by 1901 the legends about them had almost replaced the truth about their actions. Rumors regarding their whereabouts, about who led the gang, and who were the actual robbers, led to fierce debates between state governors, Pinkerton detectives, and local law officers between 1898 and 1903.

As Cassidy's fine biographer, Richard Patterson, points out, these deep concerns were truly ironic, for it appears that after 1900 Butch and Harry Longabaugh had decided to give up their life of crime and to leave the United States to live in Argentina. Several factors undoubtedly influenced their decision. First, they had acquired quite a small fortune in cash and gold. Second, trains had become harder to rob, and third, Butch had explored the possibility of a pardon from the Governor of Utah by promising to "go straight." But that pardon was not forthcoming.[41]

Then there was the fact that Matt Warner, his first companion in crime, was in prison for life, as was his closest associate in the 1890s, Elza Lay, and the others like "Bub" Meeks were also in prison. But possibly the most compelling reason was that Butch Cassidy was always a careful planner who enjoyed life. Although he was not a killer, it was clear that Harvey Logan (Kid Curry) was, and the most recent robberies had resulted in the deaths of two sheriffs. Patterson's research also suggests that Harry Longabaugh was not a killer.[42]

Ironically it looks as if Cassidy, Longabaugh, and other gang members went to Fort Worth to celebrate and possibly to attend the wedding of Will Carver, a fellow gang member. Whatever the case they then journeyed to San Antonio, famous for its houses of prostitution. There the mysterious Etta Place, who may have been Cassidy's girlfriend back in Utah, became Longabaugh's lover and "partner"—to use our contemporary term for serious relationships. Before going to New York to take a vessel to Argentina, Longabaugh, Etta, and Butch visited Longabaugh's family in Pennsylvania. After arriving in New York they appear to have "frolicked" for three weeks before Harry and Etta sailed on the *S.S. Herminius* freighter to Buenos Aires. It is unclear but Butch appears to have followed them on a later vessel.[43]

His later departure has led scholars to suggest that Butch actually went west again to pull off the last express car robbery in the United States. This time a Great Northern Railroad train was held up near Wagner, Wyoming, on July 3, 1901. The take was a sum of $40,000. If he did stage this robbery it meant that he did not go to Argentina until late in 1901. And as if to confirm the Wild Bunch's legendary reputation, the perpetrators of the Wagner robbery were never caught.[44]

Once in Argentina, it appears that the trio bought a large ranch in a remote province near the foot of the Andes. By 1904, however, they had become restless. Etta Place returned to the United States and disappeared forever. Cassidy and Longabaugh robbed two local Argentine banks before they disappeared across the border to Chile.

The two next turned up working for a mining company in Bolivia. But once again they robbed payrolls, and in a shootout in the small town of San Vicente in 1911 local Bolivian authorities and soldiers killed Cassidy and Longabaugh. While some scholars and buffs believed they might have escaped back to the United States, Richard Patterson and other serious scholars believe they did die, until George Roy Hill, Paul Newman, and Robert Redford made them immortal.[45]

III

As has been noted earlier, after the Wilcox robbery, the Pinkerton Agency sent two of its most experienced operators, Charlie Siringo and W. O. Sayles, to track down the robbers. They soon heard that two men who fit the description of the train robbers had been spotted driving thirteen horses from southwestern Wyoming toward Brown's Park. Later a second report reached Siringo and Sayles stating that the two men and the horses had passed through Hanksville, Utah, several hundred miles to the south, in Robbers Roost Country.[46]

This was familiar territory to Charlie for he had been on many cases that had led him along both the eastern and western slopes of the Rocky Mountains. Sometimes it was a case of identifying miners stealing ore; others involved catching thieves who were stealing goods from railroad storehouses or baggage cars left on sidings. In still others he was told to catch individuals stealing goods from their employers. Less often it was rounding up hardened criminals who had killed someone. Siringo enjoyed these assignments because he could work on his own. As we have seen earlier, one of his techniques was to disguise himself as a fellow criminal on the lam who was put in the same jail cell with the culprit to gain his confidence and exact a confession from him. To do this he had to work closely with local law officers. The result was that he came to know some sheriffs and marshals intimately—many of whom were in the Rocky Mountain counties of western Colorado and eastern Utah.[47]

One of the sheriffs he came to know well was Cyrus W. "Doc" Shores of Gunnison County, Colorado, who also worked for the Denver and Rio Grande Railroad. Shores proved only too willing to assist Siringo and Sayles in their pursuit of the Wild Bunch.[48] Over the years Siringo had also established a confidential relationship with friendly saloonkeepers, hotel owners, and ranchers who were at home with both criminals and lawmen. Indeed, it appears that nearly everyone in the West had friends living on both sides of the law, and thus "informing" or "tipping off" was almost as common as passing the time of day. It is in this more subtle sense of having ambivalent loyalties that the West developed an "interchangeable" reputation for "rugged individualism" on the one hand, and an acceptance of "lawlessness" on the other.

In addition there was genuine dislike, often hatred for the soulless mining corporations with their brutal labor policies, the company store, and the bank that charged exorbitant interest rates. And when a family member had a run-in with the law, his family not only resented the charges, but set out at once to try to get a sympathetic official to grant a pardon or to pay a lawyer to maneuver to get a reduced sentence.[49] Butch Cassidy's own brother, Dan Parker, for example, was convicted of holding up the U.S. Mail and was given a life sentence in the Michigan

State Penitentiary. After many struggles his family got the sentence reduced. Thus when Siringo and Sayles began their pursuit of the Wild Bunch, there were scores, indeed hundreds of local residents whose ambivalent loyalties led them to whisper information to both sides.

In his *A Cowboy Detective*, Siringo includes an entire chapter entitled "On the trail of Union Pacific Train Robbers Through Utah, Colorado, New Mexico, Kansas, Indian Territory, Arkansas, Tennessee, Mississippi, Montana, and the Republic of Mexico." Having decided that the Union Pacific train robbery at Wilcox, Wyoming, was the work of the "Hole-in-the-Wall" gang (another name for the Wild Bunch), the two detectives were ordered to go to Salt Lake City and then to Brown's Park, which Siringo described as "a haven for criminals." While in Salt Lake they consulted "Doc" Shores, now working full time for the Denver and Rio Grande, and proceeded to buy horses, saddles, a pack animal, and food supplies for their long trek. Just as they were about to leave, however, Shores shared a letter he had received from one of his agents in Hanksville, Utah, which stated "that two men supposed to be the Union Pacific train robbers had just passed there going south" and "that they were driving thirteen head of good horses."[50]

At that time Siringo believed that Harvey Logan, alias "Kid Curry," had been the ringleader of the Wilcox robbery. He had not yet learned of Butch Cassidy's role in the Wild Bunch. It also took him some time to figure out that Kid Curry was not the same outlaw as "Flat Nose" George Currie. What he did know was that Kid Curry and his gang frequently engaged in horse rustling and he thus became convinced that he should pursue Kid Curry.

To reach eastern Utah in time to intercept the horsemen, Siringo persuaded Shores to furnish them a Denver and Rio Grande stock car that would take them east, but that plan was vetoed by the Pinkerton superintendent at Denver, who told them to follow the original instructions to go to Brown's Park. The result was that the two frustrated detectives rode some five hundred miles, often held up by rain and swollen creeks. Ironically in Price, Utah, they were themselves arrested as the suspected train robbers, which suggests just how widespread the news of the Wilcox robbery was.[51]

In the end the two detectives did turn south to Hanksville, where they learned that the two suspects and their horses had passed through ten days earlier. Then approximately a week later, the owner of the hotel at which

Siringo and Sayles were staying in Hanksville, reported that his brother had helped another man herding five horses get across the swollen Colorado River. The hotel owner's brother believed that the man fitted the description of "the notorious Kid Curry." Siringo tried to follow the trail but it was so steep and threaded through such impassible canyons, he had to give up the chase. A year later, Siringo learned from a resident of Bluff, Utah, that he had come within a half mile of Kid Curry's campsite.[52]

To his chagrin, Siringo discovered that his superior in Denver had also assigned two Pinkerton detectives from Flagstaff, Arizona, to the case and that they were two days ahead of them on the robber's trail. Furious at being seen as "bringing up the rear," Siringo and Sayles pushed their jaded horses to the nearest railroad and boarded a train for Durango, Colorado, where they caught up with the two rival Pinkertons "and left them so far behind, they returned to Denver."[53]

In the weeks that followed, Siringo and Sayles split up, each tracing conflicting leads. Siringo was the less lucky of the two. After following the "horse herd" into Colorado and New Mexico, and eventually to Dodge City, Kansas, and even to his old stomping ground, Caldwell, and then east to Fort Smith, Arkansas, he completely lost the trail. Later he followed other clues all the way to the Mississippi River, but the trail was so cold by then, the Denver office wired him to give up the chase and come home.[54]

Meanwhile Sayles had gone to Montana to dig up information on Kid Curry by interviewing his relations there. Sayles also discovered that some of the unsigned treasury bills from the Wilcox robbery had been cashed at a saloon at Harlin, Montana, an establishment belonging to Kid Curry's brother, Lonny Logan (also alias Curry), and a cousin, Bob Curry. Yet as soon as he identified them, the two Currys "sold their saloon and shipped out before Sayles had a chance to arrest them."[55]

At this point Siringo was ordered to meet Sayles in Helena, Montana; buy horses; and track down the Currys, who they knew by now were actually the Logan brothers, of whom Harvey Logan (Kid Curry) was, indeed, a member of Butch Cassidy's Wild Bunch. Wandering around in zero-degree winter weather, in a region called the Little Rockies, Siringo learned at Landusky, Montana, that Kid Curry had a half interest in a horse ranch with a partner called Jim Thompson. Together Logan and Thompson "owned about 500 head of good horses which ranged in the Little Rockies."[56]

With the usual Siringo luck, Siringo, using the name Charles L. Carter, and claiming he was a fugitive from Old Mexico, met Curry's partner Thompson, befriended him, and, as he put it, "paled around with the worst people of the community." Siringo then befriended the common-law wife of Lonny Curry, from whom he learned much. Meanwhile other Pinkerton agents had located Lonny Logan, who was in Missouri, where he was hiding out with a relative. In a violent confrontation the Pinkertons shot and killed him.[57]

Because the Pinkertons knew so much about Kid Curry (Harvey Logan), Siringo assumed Harvey would never return to the Little Rockies of Montana, but he did, and in an act of revenge killed a local rancher who had killed his brother, Johnny. By then Siringo learned that "Flat Nose" George Currie was hiding out in Mexico, and went south to track him down. But here Siringo was unlucky. While still in New Mexico he learned that "Flat Nose" had been shot and killed in Utah "while trying to resist his capture." The Pinkertons could not claim complete victory over the Wild Bunch, but two of the Wilcox train robbers, Lonny Logan and "Flat Nose" George Currie, had been killed.[58]

Upon his return from Mexico to Denver, Siringo learned of a new train robbery at Tipton, Wyoming, which authorities believed, had been carried out by Kid Curry, Bill Cruzan, and "a man who might be Longabaugh [sic]." As he probably expected to be, Siringo was assigned to this new case. Taking the Denver and Rio Grande to Grand Junction, Colorado, where his pal, "Doc" Shores, now lived, Siringo visited the Robbers Roost area, where he now asserted that "Butch Cassidy and the Wild Bunch had used as headquarters until Deputy Marshal Joe Bush, Sheriff Allred, and a posse of Salt Lake City officers made a raid in the Roost and killed some of the gang."[59]

Here Siringo was only half right. Deputy U.S. Marshal, Joe Bush, whom Patterson describes as a fearless, gruff bear of a man, did invade Robbers Roost and encountered a party, which fought back. Another posse under Sheriff Allred found Joe Walker, a member of the Wild Bunch, and he was killed. Another man was also killed whom Bush and Allred thought was Butch Cassidy, and a third, Elza Lay, was wounded and captured. The great elation over the "killing" of Butch Cassidy turned into dismay when witnesses who knew Butch stated that the second dead man was not Cassidy. Marshal Bush's raid did not force the Wild Bunch out of the Roost on this occasion.[60]

This time, the Pinkertons, convinced along with Siringo that Butch had robbed the train at Tipton, sent Siringo to Circle City, Utah, to interview Butch's family, the Parkers. This time he rode a thousand miles in search of Butch, and this was when he and Sayles wound up in Alma, New Mexico, where they learned his naïve superior had actually talked to Butch (the so-called bartender), who said his name was Jim Lowe. However frustrated Siringo was in his pursuit of Butch, he did learn a lot about the gang, and especially about Elza Lay (William McGinnis) whom he actually visited in the Santa Fe jail.

While Siringo was in Santa Fe interviewing Lay, Butch Cassidy, Will Carver, and Harry Longabaugh robbed the Winnemucca National Bank in Nevada of some $50,000 in gold. After the Winnemucca robbery, Cassidy, Longabaugh, and Will Carver, and other members of the gang, traveled to Fort Worth where Will Carver was to be married to Callie May Hunt, a prostitute from San Antonio. It was there that the famous photo of the gang was taken, a copy of which Butch sent to the Bank of Winnemucca as a thank you for their "contribution."[61]

Although Siringo never caught Butch or the Sundance Kid, with the assistance of his LX Ranch cowboy pal, Jim East, now a law officer in Arizona, he did track down Will Carver (also known as Will Casey).[62]

Siringo claims that he spent four years on the Union Pacific train robberies and in the process traveled twenty-five thousand miles. But the fact is that neither he nor anyone else ever caught Cassidy or Longabaugh, although all the other members of the gang were arrested or killed by other Pinkerton operatives or local law officers. It is also a fact that he did not recognize the two men until after he had been disabused of the belief that Kid Curry (Harvey Logan) was the leader of the wild Bunch, but as with Billy the Kid, he took advantage of the Wild Bunch saga to make a good story. The truth of the matter is that the Wild Bunch greatly impressed Siringo. He acknowledged their cleverness and professionalism and visited Cassidy's family in Utah to learn more about him. One of his longest chapters in *A Cowboy Detective*, forty-one pages, is about the Wild Bunch. In a later book, he acknowledged that Billy the Kid and Cassidy were two of the most daring outlaws in his experience.[64]

What can we salvage from Siringo's account that provides valuable insights? One is the prevalence of lawlessness in Wyoming, Utah, and in Rocky Mountain regions. A second is his description of the places he visited: the Little Rockies, Brown's Park, and Robbers Roost. He was, in effect a traveling reporter about regions now celebrated as the location of Dinosaur National Monument, Canyonlands National Park, and Grand Staircase—Canyons of the Escalante Monument.

Writers of western novels, and especially Zane Grey, in *Riders of the Purple Sage* (1912) and *Nevada* (1928), have exploited the theme of the thin line between lawmen and outlaws.[63] But few writers have given us such candid accounts of places and people and such varied and detailed information on the Rocky Mountain and High Desert West as Siringo. Siringo's reputation as an amateur historian of places, as well as of people—south Texas and the Texas Panhandle, Kansas, Montana, Nebraska, Colorado, New Mexico, Idaho, Utah, and Arizona—over a sixty-year period deserves scholarly attention and further research that will allow us to judge his incredible local knowledge more appreciatively and benefit from it.

20. *Joseph G. McCoy, who developed Abilene, Kansas, as a railhead for Texas cattle and conceived the idea of a clear trail from Texas, which he named after Jesse Chisholm. Courtesy of the Kansas State Historical Society, Topeka, Kansas.*

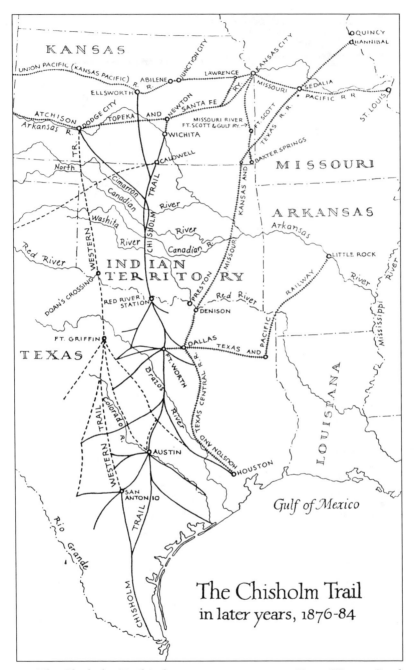

21. *The Chisholm Trail in later years, 1876–1884. From Wayne Gard,*
The Chisholm Trail *(Norman: University of Oklahoma Press, 1954).*

22. *Ellsworth, Kansas. Trains of cattle leaving for Kansas City. Kansas Pacific railway cattle buyers arriving from the East. Courtesy of Kansas State Historical Society, Topeka, Kansas.*

23. *Dodge City in 1878. Courtesy of Kansas State Historical Society, Topeka, Kansas.*

24. *Forty thousand buffalo hides ready for shipment from Dodge City.*
Courtesy of Kansas State Historical Society, Topeka, Kansas.

25a. A Dodge City dance house where George Masterson worked at the bar.

25a and b. One of Dodge City's most famous officers was "Bat"
        Masterson (25b, facing page), whom Siringo knew. His brother,
        George Masterson, worked at the bar of a Dodge City dance
        house, (25a, shown above). Reproduced in Floyd B. Steeter,
        Prairie Trails and Cow Towns: The Opening of the Old West
        (New York: Devin Adair Co., 1963).

25b. "Bat" Masterson.

26. *Cowboys in Indian Territory, 1883, Charles A. Siringo*, A Cowboy Detective *(1912)*.

27. *Mamie and Viola, Siringo's wife and daughter.*
From Charles A. Siringo, A Cowboy Detective *(1912)*.

28. *Above: Charlie Siringo's store and ice cream and oyster parlor in
Caldwell, Kansas. Below: the sign that hung over the bridge across
Bluff Creek, Charles A. Siringo,* A Cowboy Detective *(1912).*

29a and b. Southwestern Hotel and Stock Exchange Bank, Caldwell, Kansas. Courtesy of Kansas State Historical Society, Topeka, Kansas.

30. Andy Adams, author of The Log of a Cowboy, *whom Siringo befriended when both men were in Caldwell, Kansas, in the 1880s. From Wilson M. Hudson,* Andy Adams: His Life and Writings *(Southern Methodist Press, 1964).*

A TEXAS COW BOY

OR,

FIFTEEN YEARS

ON THE

Hurricane Deck of a Spanish Pony.

TAKEN FROM REAL LIFE

BY

CHAS. A. SIRINGO,

AN OLD STOVE UP "COW PUNCHER," WHO HAS SPENT NEARLY TWENTY YEARS ON THE GREAT WESTERN CATTLE RANGES.

31.
Title page of Charlie Siringo's
A Texas Cowboy *when it*
appeared in 1885.

32. Color drawing of "Life in a Cow Camp" from the 1885 edition of
A Texas Cowboy.

33. *Announcement of Haymarket meeting. Original from Chicago Historical Society. Reproduced in Paul Avrich,* The Haymarket Tragedy *(Princeton: Princeton University Press, 1984).*

34. *"The Haymarket Anarchists." They are, clockwise from middle to left, Albert Parsons, Louis Lingg, August Spies, George Engel, Oscar Neebe, Samuel Fielden, Adolph Fischer, and in center, Michael Schwab. In Charles A. Siringo,* A Cowboy Detective *(1912).*

35. *Stationery of Pinkerton's National Detective Agency bearing the famous logo, "We never sleep." Media Design Collection (Lamar Collection), Beinecke Library, Yale University.*

36.
James McParland, director
of the Pinkerton Ageny in
Denver, Colorado, and
Siringo's employer and close
friend. Courtesy of Idaho
State Historical Society,
Boise, Idaho.

37.
Pablo Herrera and his
brothers, whom Siringo
befriended during his
investigation of the
Ancheta Case in
New Mexico.

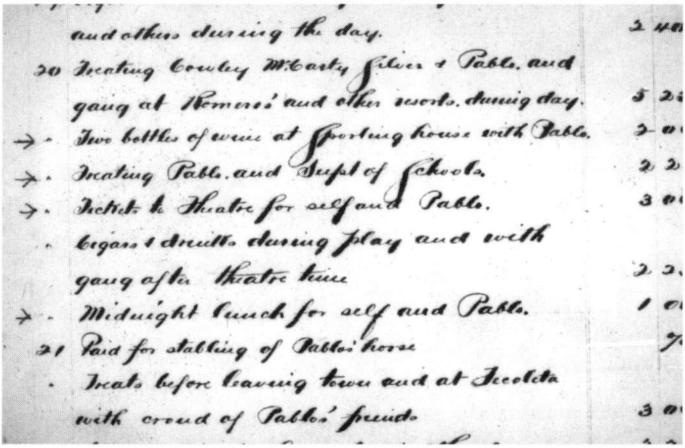

[handwritten expense account, partially legible]

and others during the day.   2 40

20 Treating Cowley McCarty Silver & Pable. and
    gang at Nemoros' and other resorts. during day.   5 25

→ . Two bottles of wine at Sporting house with Pable.   2 00

→ . Treating Pable. and Supt of Schools.   2 25

→ . Tickets to Theatre for self and Pable.   3 00

   . Cigars & drinks during play and with
      gang after theatre time   2 25

→ . Midnight lunch for self and Pable.   1 00

  21 Paid for stabling of Pable' horse   75

   . Meals before leaving town and at Jecolata
      with crowd of Pable' friends   3 00

38. Detail of Siringo's expense account sent to the Pinkerton Agency
    while investigating the Ancheta Case. Media Design Collection
    (Lamar Collection), Beinecke Library, Yale University.

39. *Gem, Idaho, where Siringo lived when investigating the Coeur d'Alene
    strike of 1891–1892. Siringo identified the buildings as: "A. the
    author's building where he sawed a hole in the floor to escape union
    men who wanted to kill him, B. Jenny Nelson's hotel, where [Siringo]
    escaped through a window, C. Saloon building where [Siringo] crawled
    from under the sidewalk, D. Miners' Union hall, E. where [Siringo]
    entered the culvert, F. House where [Siringo] emerged from culvert,
    G. Dawson's saloon, [and] H. Company store." From* Charles A.
    Siringo, A Cowboy Detective *(1912).*

40. *The wrecked Frisco Mill, which union forces destroyed with dynamite.*
From Charles A. Siringo, A Cowboy Detective *(1912).*

41. *Wallace, Idaho, where Siringo hid in the hills (X marks the spot) until*
federal soldiers arrived, and he reported to their commandant. From
Charles A. Siringo, A Cowboy Detective *(1912).*

42. *Siringo helped round up union men and served as a government wit-*
ness in their trial in Boise, Idaho. Above is a photograph of Siringo
during the trial. From Charles A. Siringo, A Cowboy Detective *(1912).*

43a, b, c, d, and e.
Photographs from a ninety-minute historical docudrama of Siringo's life,
coproduced by Howard Lamar and Philip Garvin and filmed by the Yale
University Media Design Studio in 1976. Entitled Siringo, *the film starred*
actor Steve Railsback as Siringo, actress Jennifer Warren as Mrs. Shipley,
actor Richard Venture as James McParland, and actor James Green as
George Pettibone. The film was made on location in Las Vegas and Santa
Fe, New Mexico. It was directed by Stuart Miller (coproducer of Little Big
Man*), with screenplay by Jack Gelber (*The Connection*) and John Dunkel*
(Gunsmoke). The film was based on a treatment written by Howard
Lamar and Philip Garvin. A grant from the National Endowment for the
Humanities funded Siringo. *From the Media Design Collection (Lamar*
Collection), Beinecke Library, Yale University.

43a. Steve Railsback as Siringo.

43b. Railsback and Richard
Venture as McParland.

43c.
*Jennifer Warren as Mrs.
Shipley with Railsback.*

43d.
*Railsback
crawling under
the Gem,
Idaho, board-
walk to safety.*

43e.
*Railsback and
a wounded
non-union
man in Gem
mine head-
quarters before
escaping to
Wallace,
Idaho.*

ON ARRIVING IN JUNEAU, A SWIFT LITTLE CITY BUILT
ON STILTS MOSTLY . . . , IT WAS AGREED THAT I APPLY FOR
WORK IN THE BIG TREADWELL GOLD MILL, THE LARGEST
IN THE WORLD, IN A REGULAR WAY.

—*Charles A. Siringo*, A Cowboy Detective, *199*

KENTUCKY: ON VIOLENCE IN APPALACHIA

COMMENTATORS, FOR EXAMPLE, USUALLY ATTRIBUTED THE
HATFIELD-MCCOY FEUD TO AN IRRATIONAL DISPUTE OVER A
HOG AND BITTER CIVIL WAR MEMORIES. IN TRUTH, IT GREW FROM
THE TRAUMATIC EFFECTS OF MODERNIZATION, INCLUDING THE
SHIFT TO A CASH ECONOMY AND INCREASED SOCIAL AND ECONOMIC
INEQUITY. DISAGREEMENTS OVER THE MERITS OF THE TIMBER AND
COAL INDUSTRIES AND THE OUTSIDERS ASSOCIATED WITH THEM
CONTRIBUTED MORE TO THAT AND OTHER FEUDS THAN ANYTHING ELSE.

—*Mark Banker, "Beyond the Melting Pot and*
Multiculturalism: Cultural Politics in Southern
Appalachia And Hispanic New Mexico," 22–23

WHEN A DETECTIVE DIES, HE GOES SO LOW THAT HE HAS TO
CLIMB A LADDER TO GET INTO HELL—AND HE IS NOT A
WELCOME GUEST THERE. WHEN HIS SATANIC MAJESTY SEES
HIM COMING, HE SAYS TO HIS IMPS, "GO GET A BIG BUCKET OF
PITCH AND A LOT OF SULPHER, GIVE THEM TO THAT FELLOW AND
PUT HIM OUTSIDE. LET HIM START A HELL OF HIS OWN.
WE DON'T WANT HIM IN HERE, STARTING TROUBLE."

—*Big Bill Haywood, 1911,*
cited in J. Anthony Lukas, Big Trouble, *9*

Two Victories and a Defeat

ALASKAN GOLD THIEVES,

KENTUCKY MOONSHINERS, AND THE

HAYWOOD TRIAL IN IDAHO

AFTER THE COEUR D'ALENE EXPERIENCE, CHARLIE RETURNED TO Pinkerton headquarters in Denver to handle more routine cases. There he met Lillie Thomas, a resident of Denver, with whom he fell in love. After a whirlwind courtship in the summer of 1894, he married her in November of that year. Lillie Thomas, described as "pretty and blue-eyed," was only twenty-one, while Siringo was thirty-seven. But he had a way with the ladies, regardless of their age, and for a time it promised to be a successful union.[1]

Even so, Lillie, who appears to have been close to her parents, who lived in Denver, was lonely when Siringo took her to another city to work on a case, and missed him terribly when Charlie was away for six months on the Alaskan gold robbery case, and left her in Denver. The birth of a son 1896, whom they named William Lee Roy, did not seem to reaffirm their earlier close relationship, especially after Charlie began to suggest that she move to his Sunny Slope ranch in Santa Fe—a tiny adobe house on the outskirts of that town. At this very time her parents decided to move to California. Moreover, as Ben Pingenot has pointed out, she was made very nervous by "unsavory characters coming to their home and asking for Siringo by name or by one of his aliases." In the end, "they agreed to disagree," got a divorce, and Lillie and their son moved to California. Charlie claimed that he and Lillie continued to be good friends, but he does not appear to have ever been close to his son, although Lee Roy did look after Charlie when the latter, by then old, ill, and poverty-stricken, moved to the Los Angeles area in the 1920s.[2]

ALASKA

Two of the most interesting, important, and geographically far-ranging cases to which Siringo was assigned were a gold bullion theft from the Treadwell Mill in Alaska in 1895, and an exceptionally dangerous case involving the kidnapping of the son of a wealthy Philadelphia business-man by Kentucky miners and moonshiners. Both suggest the extent of his varied experiences, the brilliant innovative tactics he used to survive, and what the state of outlawry was in two very different regions of the United States.

Sometime in February 1895 James McParland called Siringo into his office and "told him to get ready for a trip to Alaska." Siringo did not want to leave his new wife, but he was always thrilled at the prospect of a new adventure, and the possibility of solving the theft of $10,000 in gold from a refining mill in Juneau excited him. McParland's special pitch was that the new Pinkerton office in Portland, Oregon, had made a botch of the case by sending three inexperienced operatives to Juneau to investigate. The Pinkerton Agency, angry at the failure of their new Portland office, wanted a success story. Siringo was especially flattered to learn that Robert Pinkerton himself had urged that two experienced men such as Siringo and his friend, W. O. Sayles, who had worked with him on the Butch Cassidy case, be assigned to the job.[3]

To make a long story short, someone had stolen $10,000 in rough gold from the Treadwell Mill located on Douglas Island near Juneau. The mill officials had no clues as to who had done it or what the thief (or thieves) had done with the gold. On arriving by steamer from Tacoma, Washington, in Juneau, which Siringo described as "a swift lit-tle city built on stilts mostly," he met secretly with a Mr. Durkin (prob-ably a disguised name), the mine superintendent. Just as he had done in other mining cases, Siringo "applied" for work in the mine, this time as a machine oiler, a job that "took me to all parts of the mill where I could make the acquaintance of all the employees. Part of the time I was on the day shift, then I changed to the night shift."[4]

By the time his partner, W. O. Sayles, arrived three weeks later, Charlie had already gathered enough clues to suspect that about a month after the robbery two mill hands, Charlie Hubbard and Hiram Schell, had suddenly quit work at the mill and had purchased a small schooner and had sailed westward. No one seemed to know where they were going or what they were doing.

Siringo and Sayles soon decided that they, too, would imitate Hubbard and Schell by purchasing a large canoe to trail them by water rather than on horseback. In their case they posed as whiskey peddlers to the Indians by taking twenty-five gallons of whiskey on board. Meanwhile Siringo had quit his job by falling down a flight of mill stairs and claiming to have broken his arm. The mill doctor could not find a break, but because Siringo had deliberately rubbed his arm raw before his tumble, the doctor and sympathetic onlooking mill workers put him to bed. The next day he appeared at the place where the workers ate lunch, with his arm in a sling, and asked one of the men to cut his meat for him. He did this for several days, "then drew my pay and left for Juneau."[5]

Here again luck was with Siringo. He and Sayles found the Hubbard and Schell schooner moored in the Juneau harbor, and Sayles had a friendly conversation with the two owners, from which he learned that they had been visiting the west coast of Admiral Island, a large island due west of Juneau beyond Douglas Island, from which it was separated by the Stephens Passage (now part of the Alaska Marine Highway).[6] Siringo and Sayles then quickly completed the purchase of a forty-foot Indian canoe, rigged it with a sail, bought supplies and "twenty-five gallons of good Canadian rye whiskey." Two cowboys sailing a boat might seem madness, but as a youth Siringo had owned and operated a sailboat as a ferry on Matagorda Bay. One assumes Sayles thought this was a risky endeavor, but armed with a fine chart of the Alaskan coast, they set out to find where Hubbard and Schell were probably hiding the stolen gold.[7]

Despite storms and rip-tides, somehow the two seagoing detectives survived, and slowly learned from Indians they encountered that the two men in the schooner were indeed sailing westward. Some of the detectives' experiences bordered on slap-stick comedy. They mistook a sleeping whale for a small island, and after discovering it was a whale, Siringo tried to shoot it. The whale's response was to thrash so wildly their boat was almost sunk.[8] In a series of adventures and encounters with Indians as they sailed, for all the world they appeared to be—and were—naïve tourists in frontier Alaska.

At last they found Hubbard and Schell taking it easy in an Indian village (which Siringo called Chieke) with a white friend named Hicks, who was married to "the richest woman in the village, her wealth being in the form of blankets."[9] Hicks himself had decided to invest in hogs, chickens, and cattle, which Hubbard and Schell had brought to the village. Since none of the local Indians were familiar with these animals, they were understandably quite suspicious of them.

Knowing that they could not hang around peddling whiskey for long, Siringo and Sayles expressed a keen interest in finding the "Lost Rocker" gold mine, which was reported to be near a great waterfall in the vicinity. They moved their tent there and, as Siringo put it, "Then we began prospecting for the gold that was never there." At that point the "bait," as they called their rye whiskey, began to work. Charlie Hubbard loved the brew, but at first he had to pay for it; however, when he joined their prospecting effort, it was made free to him.[10]

Believing that Siringo and Sayles were real experts regarding gold, they finally asked the two what was "the best treatment for chlorination gold" (which was what had been stolen from the bottom of a tank at the Treadwell Mill). Inevitably, Hubbard and Schell, desperate to know how to capitalize on their stolen gold, confessed to the theft, and offered Siringo and Sayles "$400 if they would melt it into pure gold for them."[11]

After appealing to Siringo, who at this time was using the name Lee R. Davis as his alias, the latter explained that there were certain technical processes involving the purchase of "clay to make a furnace, and material to melt the gold." This meant that he had to go to Juneau to get these products. Of course Siringo reported to Superintendent Durkin what was transpiring. They arranged for a Deputy U.S. Marshal to come to their location and to make arrests at the appropriate time. Meanwhile Siringo did go through the charade of buying chemicals and a crucible for refining the gold.[12]

When Siringo got back to his prospectors camp, he sensed that something was amiss. On an excuse to retrieve something from their tent, Sayles slipped Siringo a note, which said, "It's all off. They are suspicious of us and say they won't dig up the gold." During Siringo's absence Hubbard had decided that Sayles was a "fly-cap—a detective." Siringo pretended astonishment at this news. Somehow, with his incredible charm, Siringo convinced Hubbard that he was an innocent friend of Sayles and that they should go ahead with the purification of the gold.[13]

After using various subterfuges for slowing the process of refining, their furnace did produce some handsome nuggets. Slipping away late at night, Siringo managed to reach Deputy U.S. Marshal Collins, who arrested Hubbard at breakfast time in their prospectors camp. Feeling totally betrayed, Hubbard confronted Siringo saying: "Davis, how in h__l can you ever face the public again, after the way you have treated me? I laughed and told him that my business was mostly with individuals, not the public, hence my conscience would not bother me on that score."[14]

Even so Siringo stayed with Hubbard until he signed a written confession. Hubbard and Schell were convicted and sent to prison, but with light sentences. Curiously Hubbard was another one of Siringo's victims who, while in jail, corresponded with Charlie regularly. Once out of prison he wrote Siringo that he was off to Dawson City on the Yukon River to exploit the fabulous new gold finds there. As usual Siringo was forgiving, saying, "We only hope that he has become rich for the world is full of worse men than Charlie Hubbard. Whiskey was the cause of his downfall." Schell, on the other hand, appears to have become a desperado in constant trouble with the law.[15]

While still in Alaska Siringo heard that his old manager at the LX Ranch in the Texas Panhandle, W. C. "Outlaw Bill" Moore, was now living in Alaska under an assumed name, having committed several crimes since his departure from the LX. Moore was, in effect, living in exile. When Moore read of Lee Davis's (Siringo's name in Alaska) success in capturing Hubbard and Schell, he recognized Siringo, and was terrified that Siringo might arrest him. But that did not happen.[16]

On his return to the states Siringo had the pleasure of meeting famous persons who were on his boat, among them the nephew of Prince Otto Von Bismarck of Germany, who appears to have been an arrogant, stupid fellow. But he also recorded with undisguised glee meeting attractive, socially prominent ladies on board. Then after convening with their fellow Pinkertons in Portland, Siringo and Sayles arrived in Denver to be congratulated on their Alaskan success by Superintendent McParland.[17]

KENTUCKY

Siringo liked to boast that he was a Texan and a Southerner who had always shouted a "hurrah" for Jefferson Davis. But he came to hold different views of the American South after his terrifying experiences with Kentucky and Virginia moonshiners; in fact he devoted two chapters in his *A Cowboy Detective* to this case. Because it is one of the bluntest, most cynical and critical of all his accounts of cases, it is quite revealing of his personality and his basic beliefs. Indeed, he introduces us to his narrative by saying, "My next operation was an education, as I was thrown among a strange class of people who think nothing of taking human life."[18]

In November 1903, Siringo's boss, James McParland, called him into his "private office" to say that after reviewing the operations in all of its national branches, the Pinkerton Detective Agency had selected him to handle a very dangerous, difficult, and sensitive case located in the East. More specifically it involved a major client who had sought help from the Pinkertons' Philadelphia office. Highly flattered that the higher-ups in Chicago, New York, and Philadelphia offices had chosen him, he comments: "Of course I replied yes, as I was itching to have some new experiences and to see new country."[19]

The client was a millionaire businessman, a Dr. Wentz, whose young adult son, Edward Wentz, had "been kidnapped in the mountains of Virginia, but was probably being held in Kentucky where he may have been murdered for revenge."[20] That was but the tip of the iceberg. As Siringo was soon to learn, Wentz Sr. was the powerful head of the Virginia Coal and Iron Company whose ruthless treatment of its workers had made him a hated man. Indeed, high-ranking Pinkerton officials in Chicago, New York, and Philadelphia (including William Pinkerton in Chicago, and his brother Robert at the New York office) all told Siringo they suspected young Wentz had been kidnapped more for revenge against the father and the company than for ransom. Siringo later discovered that Edward Wentz and his brother, Dan, who ran the coal company's many operations in Wise, Virginia, and elsewhere, were themselves hated employers.[21]

While consulting with Robert Pinkerton in New York, Siringo was warned by Pinkerton yet again of the extreme danger of the operation and even told Siringo "that he didn't expect to see me come out of those mountains alive. He said I had no idea of what kind of people inhabited those mountains; that they are a different class from those of Texas and the west; that they think nothing of shooting a man in the back on the least provocation; that they are not the kind of men who will fight it out face to face with an opponent, that records of the Dickinson Agency [Siringo's alias for the Pinkerton Agency] since 1850 prove this."[22]

The fact that these small communities had so few visitors meant that strangers were immediately suspect. And when a guilty person came to trial, the families were all so interrelated, no jury would convict. So pessimistic was Pinkerton about Siringo's chances of survival, that "I was instructed to leave the number of my watch, a description of my pocket knife, key ring, pistol, and the prominent marks on my body, including the fillings in my teeth, so that my body in case of death could be identified."[23]

Siringo began his search for young Edward Wentz, not by going to Wise, Virginia, where Wentz had lived, but by going to Winchester, Kentucky, a few miles southeast of the major town of Lexington. In short, he approached the town of Jackson in Breathitt County, where Wentz, Jr. was kidnapped, from the west, not from Philadelphia. Storing his good "detective" clothes and his boots, he boarded a branch train for Jackson. He found Jackson not only to be "a drunken tough town, but one in which units of the state militia had been stationed to bring and end to a whole series of killings."[24]

Siringo's forebodings about the different world he was entering seemed to be confirmed by an episode he witnessed on the streets of Jackson the day after he arrived there. We must let him tell it in his own words:

> An old man on a mule started out of town with two jugs of
> whiskey tied across the back part of his saddle. He hadn't
> gone but half a block when the string broke and the jugs fell
> to the ground and broke. The street was quite muddy and
> the whiskey lay in pools on the ground. The old man got
> down on his knees and began to drink from the fiery pools.
> Soon others came and followed suit. They put me in mind
> of a drove of human swine.[25]

Siringo himself bought a mule, whom he named "Donk," and an old spring wagon in order to travel to Letcher County, some 150 miles east of Jackson. Letcher County, which was on the border with Virginia, was where Wentz, Jr. was kidnapped. Siringo was late starting, however, because a drunken blacksmith had put horseshoes rather than mule shoes on his draft animal.[26]

Slowly making his way along abominable roads, full of deep mud and large rocks, he found that the road itself also served as a creek bed on occasion; but with the usual Siringo luck, Charlie met a man while traveling whose brother was a noted "bad" man in Wise County, Virginia, the neighboring county to Letcher, and its county seat, Whitesburg. It began to appear that the "bad" man, whom Siringo simply refers to as "Ash" or Ashord N___, may have had a hand in Wentz's kidnapping. It then turned out that "Ash," the brother of the man who was Siringo's traveling companion, had once lived in Texas. Seizing upon this fact, Siringo secured a letter of introduction to "Ash" using the excuse that he wanted to discuss Texas with him.

In addition to the nearly impossible roads from Hazard, Kentucky, to Whitesburg on the Virginia border, Siringo was driven nearly crazy by every person he met asking: "Say mister, wha'r you mought be goin?" Or "Say mister what mought your name be?"[27] When he responded that he was from Texas, that led to a hundred additional questions.

Later Siringo encountered an entire village drunk on moonshine and divided into two warring camps. He then learned to his dismay that the town of Craftsville, whose post office the Pinkertons had chosen for him to receive and send mail, was nothing but a house and a farm owned by Mrs. Craft, and that all mail for Craftsville was stored in a garret until someone called for it![28]

Having arrived in December, Siringo spent a bibulous Christmas with the Craft family, who greatly enjoyed their moonshine whiskey. The amount of drunkenness and near violence in an area already rendered doubly dangerous by a feud between the Potter and the Wright families made Siringo's own position even more untenable because everyone believed he was a revenue officer in disguise seeking to identify and arrest moonshiners.[29] But somehow Siringo managed to fill those determined to waylay and kill him so full of doubt that after confronting and accusing him, they let him alone.

Having befriended a very responsible citizen in Whitesburg, Sol Holcomb, Siringo arranged to board at the Holcomb house. He then sought out the "bad" man, Ashford N___, only to discover that he was spending six months in jail for selling liquor in the prohibition county of Letcher, Kentucky. Siringo visited Ash in jail and talked first of their memories of Texas, where Ash had lived for three years.[30] Prohibition county or not, Siringo realized that the only coin of the realm was moonshine whiskey, which he used to gain information. He discovered whiskey helped to befriend both men and women. He also continued to be amazed at the number of feuds and killings. Whiskey flowed so freely, Siringo himself was often drunk because moonshine was served day and night.

Eventually Siringo learned that young Wentz was dead, but in the process he found that Wentz, Jr., and his brother Dan had objected to state-line saloons being near their company coal mine at Stonaga, Virginia, saying they kept their workers drunk.[31] One of these saloons had been owned by no less than Ashford N___. One night the saloons were raided by the Stonaga town marshal, and in the fight between owners and lawmen, the marshal was fatally shot, as was the half-brother of one of the saloon owners. The liquor was destroyed, and the buildings on the state line were sawed in two. The half on the Virginia side was then demolished or burned and the womenfolk of the saloon owner put in jail at Wise, Virginia.

Inevitably, as Siringo notes, "And for their crime against blue-blooded Kentuckians, Ed and Dan Wentz were doomed to die, although after Ed was kidnapped, Dan kept out of the way, so that he couldn't be caught unaware." By befriending the women of the destroyed saloon, Siringo was able to discover why Wentz had been kidnapped and killed.

Siringo affability and flexibility even led the Whitesburg jailer to let Ashford N___ out of the jail to spend the night with Siringo in a small cabin on the Holcomb property. Finally, by constantly patronizing the illicit stills in Letcher County and by befriending Wentz haters, Siringo learned that Edward Wentz had been "taken from his horse alive by three men." In the early spring Wentz's body was found in a heavily wooded area in Virginia on the eastern slope of the Black Mountains near the head of the Cumberland River in Kentucky.[32] When Wentz's body was found, it was discovered that he had been shot through the heart and his right hand had been cut off. The assistant superintendent of the Philadelphia Pinkerton office came out to identify the body.

Siringo, calling himself Lloyd, justified his presence in these small mountain villages by going into the licensed still business himself. But his very efforts to be friendly almost led to his death. Having come to know an attractive mother and daughter, Lottie H. and Birdie, who had been in the saloon business, he often ate dinner at their house. Two men who were jealous of Siringo's making time with the mother and daughter decided to plot his death. A failed effort to trap him led Siringo's would-be assassin to threaten the women themselves, but at that moment a nephew of Lottie H., the mother, dropped in and tried to stop their harassment, for he was a deputy sheriff. A gun battle erupted in which the deputy sheriff was killed and the two assailants were wounded.[33]

Meanwhile other people kept sideling up to Siringo to say that "everyone thinks you are slated for death, leave the country." Fortunately the Philadelphia Pinkerton office had already decided that they could never get a conviction in the local Kentucky courts regarding Wentz's murder. Siringo himself had made many friends in Whitesburg, Kentucky, but he remained appalled at their "reckless regard for human life." He noted that during his short stay in the mountains at least twenty murders had been committed.[34]

> They also need education in their mode of living, especially
> in their home life, wherein one wife is not considered
> sufficient for one man. Also they need bath-tubs, I failed
> to see one bath-tub in the counties of Letcher, Perry and
> Knott. Possibly they are afraid of wearing out should they
> wash too much. . . . Another curse of this county is the
> marrying of first and second cousins.[35]

Siringo was also glad to leave Whitesburg because its inhabitants ate pork and chicken, but never beef. For a Texas cowboy this was a punishment that he found especially cruel. He also noted with relief that he would now "get away from the sound of banjos. Nearly every household had from one to half a dozen of these instruments, and nearly every child can pick the same tune. Some can pick as many as three or four tunes."[36]

After seeing Pinkerton officials in Washington and New York, Siringo took a train to St. Louis to see the 1904 World's Fair with his sister and her family, before turning north to Chicago to see William Pinkerton.[37] Once back in Denver after an absence of eight months, Charlie learned from his supervisor, V. S. Kaiser, that Pinkerton had sent a letter asking Siringo to make out a bill for his personal expenses while at the World's Fair. Siringo did so with great pride, saying "it pleased me, as this was something employers seldom do."

Siringo himself knew that he had had a unique experience in the Kentucky and Virginia mountains, for at the close of chapter XIX in *A Cowboy Detective*, he wrote: "Thus did the most interesting operation of my eighteen years' connection with the Pinkerton Agency end. I had been gone from Denver eight months."[38]

THE HAYWOOD TRIAL

When Charlie Siringo left Idaho after the Coeur d'Alene strike and the troubles of 1892–1893, the region was still full of bitterness, indeed, of hatred between labor and capital. The mood and actions of Frederick Worthen Bradley, manager of the Bunker Hill and Sullivan Mine, for example, were not only anti-union, but also anti-Irish and anti-Catholic. He proceeded to try to weed Irish and Catholics out of his company and employ only "regular Americans." Tensions remained so great that Idaho National Guard units were stationed in the Coeur d'Alene area in the 1890s. When they were called away to fight in the Spanish American War in 1898, the BH and S asked the governor to form national guard units out of their own non-union workers. Meanwhile the BH and S responded to a request for unionization by firing union men and raising the wages of non-union men.[39]

As has been noted in an earlier chapter, it was the decision of labor leaders in the West to found the Western Federation of Miners (WFM) at Butte, Montana, in 1893. It was successfully guided by Edward Boyce from 1890 to 1902 when two even more vigorous leaders succeeded him: Charles H. Moyer as president, and William D. Haywood as secretary. Although they concentrated their major activities on strikes at Colorado mines, they never stopped their crusade against the Bunker Hill and Sullivan Mine in the Coeur d'Alene area, which turned to violence in 1899 when the WFM blew up the company's concentrator at Wardner, Idaho. The aftermath seemed almost a repeat of the first strike, when U.S. troops were sent to restore order, and strikers were rounded up and placed in bull pens. The troops remained there for two more years.[40]

The Idaho governor who sent in troops was Frank Steunenberg, a likable, ambitious, able official who had been seen as a friend to labor. But after sending in troops, the WFM felt he had betrayed them, and he received death threats for several years thereafter. Steunenberg was caught in the middle: if he did not support labor, he must be for capital, and certainly the mine owners sought his allegiance. Having finished his governorship, Steunenberg returned to Caldwell, Idaho, where he ran a bank, and was engaged in many enterprises with his six brothers, all of whom wanted Caldwell to boom.

Frank Steunenberg had often felt he was marked for death, but by 1905 he began to relax and talk about reentering politics. As he walked home from his bank one December evening shortly after Christmas, however, he was killed by a bomb fastened to the front gate of his house, which was triggered when he opened the gate.[41]

Who had planted the bomb? Many thought it was the WFM's revenge for the governor's sending in troops to Wardner, Idaho. That belief was strengthened by the fact that violence and killings had been features of strikes in Colorado between 1902 and 1904 in which the WFM led the strikers. There was also the fact that in the January 1905 meeting in Chicago, the WFM, now dominated by Big Bill Haywood, had helped form a new, more radical union, the Industrial Workers of the World. Symbolically, "as Haywood would write much later: 'we met in a hall on Lake Street, often used as a meeting place by the Chicago anarchists, where Parsons and Spies had spoken to the workers.'"[42]

The Steunenberg murder attracted national attention and there was speculation that the guilty party was a member of the WFM. Local authorities in Caldwell soon noted that there was a stranger in town who called himself Hogan at first, and then said he was Harry Orchard (although his real name was Albert E. Horsley). Upon investigation of his boardinghouse room, the local police found "explosives, detonators and plaster of paris identical to the materials used in the deadly bomb." Orchard was quickly arrested and put in jail, but throughout maintained that he was innocent.[43]

It just so happened that because the WFM had been so active in Colorado strikes, the Pinkerton Agency chose James McParland of the Denver office to follow their activities. When McParland investigated the bombing of the Independence Depot at Cripple Creek, Colorado, in 1904, he was assisted by Siringo and other Pinkerton detectives. Both McParland and Idaho Governor Frank R. Gooding and most residents of Idaho believed Steunenberg's murder was an act of WFM revenge. Siringo himself said that because Steunenberg had "offended this Nobel Order of Dynamiters by putting them in the 'bull-pen,' . . . he was marked for a horrible death; this being done to intimidate other officials."[44]

McParland joined forces with Governor Frank R. Gooding by going to Boise, Idaho, where after conferring with other state officials they agreed to move Orchard from Caldwell to the Boise jail.[45] In what must have been a remarkable *tour de force*, McParland then met with Orchard and not only persuaded him to confess to killing Steunenberg, but got him to name Charles Moyer, Bill Haywood, and George Pettibone of the WFM as having ordered the murder.[46]

In the process of talking with Orchard, McParland identified himself as the detective who had broken up the Molly Maguires and then said many of them were decent men who had been manipulated by an "inner circle" of leaders. He went on to suggest Orchard had been manipulated by an inner circle of WFM leaders, namely Moyer, Haywood, and Pettibone. Orchard seemed to accept this argument, and what soon followed was what J. Anthony Lukas has described as "the most extraordinary confession in the history of American criminal justice."[47] Lukas's summary of that confession deserves quoting in full:

> Not only did Harry Orchard confess to setting the bomb that killed Frank Steunenberg, he accepted responsibility for killing seventeen other men—two supervisors in a mine explosion, thirteen men in the bombing of a railroad depot, a detective gunned down on a Denver street, and an innocent passerby who picked up a booby-trapped purse intended for somebody else—and attempting to assassinate the governor of Colorado, two Colorado Supreme Court Justices, an adjutant general of Colorado, and Frederick Worthen Bradley, president of the Bunker Hill and Sullivan Mining Concentrating Company, all on behalf of the inner circle of the Western Federation of Miners, particularly Charles H. Moyer, the federation president, William D. Haywood, its secretary-treasurer, and George A Pettibone, the former Coeur d'Alene miner... now an honorary member of the organization (WFM) and close adviser.

Orchard also identified two other men as guilty: Steve Adams and Vincent St. John, "both miners and longtime members of the WFM." When asked, Orchard later denied that McParland had coerced him, or had made any promises of immunity. Apparently Orchard did come to believe he had been manipulated by the Executive Board of the Western Federation of Miners. Orchard reportedly cried seven times while making the above statements.[48]

As sensational as Orchard's confession was, a second person was needed to confirm his testimony, for by Idaho law, one accused of murder required a second witness to corroborate the act before an Idaho court could try Moyer, Haywood, and Pettibone. A second, more daunting problem was: because these three men were legal residents of Colorado, how could Idaho officials gain access to them? The first issue seemed to be resolved when one Steve Adams, who had worked with Orchard, was brought to Boise and at first corroborated Orchard's story but later recanted and said his confession had been a lie.[49]

The response to the second was the virtual kidnapping of Moyer, Haywood, and Pettibone from their Colorado homes and bringing them to Boise by special train. This amounted to the most egregious flaunting of legal procedure by the governors of Colorado and Idaho the public had ever seen. As Michael Boudett has written: "They were arrested without warrant and without being permitted to call their lawyers. . . . Early the next morning they were put on a train for Idaho. It did not stop at any of the towns along the way . . . where a unit could catch up with it . . . but refueled at deserted points in between. They arrived in Idaho the next day and were put in cells in the death row block." Haywood later wrote "Here we were in murderers row, in the penitentiary, arrested without warrant, extradited without warrant, and under the death watch." McParland reportedly boasted, "They will never leave Idaho alive."[50] Although always loyal to McParland, Siringo felt that this action was illegal.

Of course the WFM made every effort to free them on a writ of habeas corpus, but courts in Colorado and Idaho evaded taking action, and upon appeal to the U.S. Supreme Court that court declined to take the case. Thus the three WFM leaders remained in prison for over a year awaiting trial. Meanwhile, Edmund Richardson, their Colorado attorney, did raise a large defense fund with which they decided to hire Clarence Darrow as the defense attorney.

Clarence Darrow, of Chicago, was already nationally known for his courtroom defense of labor. In 1894 he had defended Eugene V. Debs, who had been arrested for his role in the Pullman Company strike of 1894. A brilliant orator and a trusted supporter of progressive causes, he was undoubtedly the best lawyer for Haywood, Moyer, and Pettibone in the nation. What the WFM also knew was that as a young aspiring lawyer Darrow was shocked by the Haymarket trial, and had campaigned for John Peter Altgeld for the governorship of Illinois. Once elected governor, Altgeld was persuaded by Darrow and others to pardon the three Haymarket defendants, Samuel Fielden, Oscar Neebe, and Michael Schwab, still in prison. Altgeld later did so but it ruined his political career. J. Anthony Lukas has concluded, in fact, that Darrow, having moved to Chicago immediately after the Haymarket trial, considered the injustice of it the turning point of his life.[51] It is interesting that Siringo himself had always been convinced that Neebe had been unjustly treated.

All the legal talent and oratorical glitter was not confined to Darrow, however. The two prosecutors for the State of Idaho happened to be Idaho's most renowned attorneys who had long been in the public eye. The first, James Hawley, was a sixty-one-year-old attorney who was the epitome of the "old time western lawyer." In the words of Anthony Lukas, Hawley "liked to slouch in a chair, chewing on a toothpick, his boots on the table top. . . . He wasn't suave, but few lawyers could move an Idaho jury as Hawley could."[52] A pro-corporation lawyer, Hawley actually solicited funds from the mining companies to use to drive the WFM out of the West.

The second lawyer for the prosecution was William E. Borah, who had often been in opposition to Hawley in Idaho trials. Indeed, the fierce debates between the two sometimes resulted in their insulting one another. This image of two titans, now on the same side—that of the prosecution— led the Idaho public to follow this case with great interest.[53]

Borah could not have been more different in character and personality than Hawley, yet he, too, was a lawyer for big business, and he benefited accordingly, for his salary averaged about $30,000 a year. A natural orator, he had once joined a theatrical troop, before deciding to attend the University of Kansas. Later he read law in the office of his Kansas brother-in-law. In personality he seemed a set of contradictions. He neither smoked nor drank but he was a notorious womanizer while being an eloquent orator. Perhaps the second talent assisted him in successful pursuit of the ladies.

As a young man Borah was attracted to the booming town of Boise, Idaho, where he soon made his reputation as a lawyer for "the state's mine operators, timber barons and shop and cattle kings." Politically ambitious, he was active in the Republican Party and became a close friend of Governor Frank Steuncnberg. After many frustrations in his own search for political office, in 1906, he was finally elected to the United States Senate. He was yet to take his seat when he was asked to join Hawley in prosecuting Haywood, Moyer, and Pettibone.[54]

Beginning with the trial of Big Bill Haywood in May 1907, Hawley and Borah, using Harry Orchard's detailed confession about the role of the WFM leaders in bombings and assassinations, called for the death penalty. Orchard's cool, factual, and, indeed, unbreakable testimony on the witness stand seemed to indicate that the prosecutors had a winning case. But Clarence Darrow argued that the only piece of evidence against Haywood was that of Orchard's confession. To get a conviction there had to be another, or second witness, to verify that Haywood had ordered the Steunenberg bombing and other murders. In a trial that lasted for two and a half months, Darrow managed to convince the jury that Orchard had made a false confession "in order to save his own neck."[55] Then the defense turned to attack McParland's methods of exacting Orchard's confession: flattery, religious conversion, and using the examples of other men who had turned state's evidence and thereby had avoided execution. McParland was given a truly rough time on the stand, and ironically the public and the press began to show sympathy for Orchard despite his monstrous crimes because he was seen as having been duped by McParland!

This extraordinary trial finally came to its climax on July 24th and 25th. In Darrow's final summation, which lasted eleven hours over two days, he brilliantly twisted the image of Orchard to show him as such a monster that his word could not be used to convict anyone.[56] Darrow then denounced McParland's methods of extracting Orchard's confession. Sarcastically calling him "Father McParland" for having "convicted" Orchard to "religion," Darrow said: "If he could convert a man like Orchard in the twinkling of an eye, I submit he is too valuable a man to waste his time in a Pinkerton Detective office trying to catch men. He had better go out in the vineyard and go to work and bring in souls."[57]

Darrow, a progressive and a liberal in his views, turned to the theme of class in American society. As Michael Boudett has reported, "He told the jury that Haywood was being tried at the behest of the Mine Owners Association, not because he is Haywood, but because he represents a class."[58] Then he gave a tribute to the working men of America that is one of the most famous defense of working men we shall ever have.

> Gentlemen, it is not for him alone that I speak. I speak for the poor, for the weak, for the weary, for that long line of men, who, in darkness and despair, have borne the labors of the human race. The eyes of the world are upon you— upon you twelve men of Idaho tonight. . . . If you kill him, your act will be applauded by many. If you should decree Bill Haywood's death, in the railroad offices of our great cities, men will applaud your names. If you decree his death, among the spiders of Wall Street will go up paeans of praise for these twelve men good and true. In every bank in the world, where men hate Haywood because he fights for the poor and against that accursed system upon which the favored grow rich and fat—from all these you will receive blessings and unstinted praise.
>
> But if your verdict should be not guilty in this case, there are still those who will reverently bow their heads and thank these twelve men for the life and reputation you have saved. Out on the broad prairies, where men toil with their hands, out on the wide oceans where men are tossed and buffeted on the waves, through our mills and factories and down deep under the earth, thousands of men, and of women and children—men who labor, men who suffer, women and children will kneel tonight and ask their God to guide your hearts. These men and these women and these children— the poor, the weak and the suffering of this world—are stretching out their helpless hand to this jury in a mute appeal for Bill Haywood's life.[59]

Darrow had won. The jury refused to convict Haywood. Pettibone's trial also resulted in acquittal and Moyer was later freed without trial.[60] Scholars still disagree as to whether Orchard's testimony was true or false. But all agree that unlike the famous Haymarket case in Chicago, the jury reached the correct verdict: that guilt had not been proven. Thus ended the latest episode in Coeur d'Alene where Charlie Siringo had been involved in 1892–1893.

❧ ❧

It is not too much to say that dramatic episodes in Boise in 1907, almost equal to those of 1892–1893, were not confined to the courtroom. Charlie Siringo, although theoretically a mere observer and bodyguard, had his own story to tell about the intrigues surrounding his boss, James McParland, Harry Orchard, would-be vigilantes who tried to kill Haywood, and famous figures, passing through the town of Boise.

Let us begin in the fall of 1906 when Siringo, while working on a case in Spokane, Washington, received a telegram from James McParland in Denver, asking him to meet him in Boise, Idaho, as soon as possible. The next day Siringo met McParland in his quarters at the Idanha Hotel (which has survived into the twenty-first century). McParland, now an elderly, portly, slow-moving man, whose eyesight had almost failed him, informed Siringo that the central Pinkerton office said "Siringo and his Colt 45 were to accompany him in his trips to Idaho in the future, for it had been learned through secret sources that an attempt would be made on his life [in Siringo's words] by the Western Federation of Dynamiters."[61]

Charlie thus became McParland's bodyguard for the duration of the famous Haywood trial in 1906 and 1907. Initially he was in the curious situation of being a part of the famous Haywood trial as more a bodyguard and observer than a participant. But that proved to be far from true. After Orchard had confessed, every time McParland saw the latter in prison, Siringo was present. Fascinated as always by the presence of celebrities, whether felons or upright citizens, Siringo, contrary to orders, got Gifford Pinchot and the young actress Ethel Barrymore into the prison to see Orchard.[62] And, as in the case of the Haymarket trials in Chicago over two decades earlier, Siringo was in the courtroom when McParland was there. On another occasion, Siringo learned of vigilante plots to kill the three accused and Darrow, and appears to have alerted authorities so efficiently, this conspiracy was nipped in the bud.

The events that had the most profound effect on Siringo, however, were not physical threats to McParland, Orchard, or the accused, but McParland's and the Idaho officials' disregard of legal process. Siringo himself in his later anti-Pinkerton book, *Two Evil Isms*, states that "The kidnapping of Haywood, Pettibone and Moyer out of the state of Colorado into Idaho, was a boomerang which flew back and hit the prosecution in a tender spot. The Pinkerton Detective Agency was the cause of the kidnapping of these three citizens without due process of law."[63]

The second event that hit Siringo even more profoundly was Clarence Darrow's persuasive eloquence. Darrow not only attacked McParland and his methods to extract a confession from Orchard, he make a savage attack on the entire detective profession, and, incidentally on the methods Siringo had used in the Coeur d'Alene strike. Darrow's words were truly stinging. After describing how McParland infiltrated the Molly Maguires, pretending to be one of them, Darrow said, "And every moment, he was a traitor, a liar, and he was there to bring them to the gallows. . . . It is better a thousand crimes should go unpunished, better a thousand desultory acts of men should go without punishment than that State should lend itself to these practices of fraud and treachery and make liars of men."[64] Darrow did not trouble to mention that the Molly Maguires were nineteenth-century terrorists who killed at will.

Siringo then heard Darrow declaim that McParland's entire career was a living lie: "that is his business; he lives one from the time he gets up in the morning to the time he goes to bed; he is deceiving people, and trapping people and lying to people, and imposing on people; that is his trade."[65]

Siringo resigned from the Pinkertons after the Haywood trial, although the agency liked him and tried to give him a promotion. But Siringo, who had always decried the agency's more extreme methods of coercion and deception, and who always felt sorry for the nice "bad guys," must have been profoundly affected by Darrow's words.

Darrow had not only attacked his surrogate father, McParland, by implication he had condemned Siringo's role in the Coeur d'Alene strike. Moreover, he described the prosecution at the current Haywood trial as being supported by the MOA. Ironically both Darrow and Siringo had agreed that the last surviving Haymarket defendants deserved pardoning, and Darrow had done something about it. Curiously what further bound all three to the Haymarket case was that Siringo, Darrow, and Bill Haywood himself, as a youth, had been deeply affected by the unjust treatment of labor in the 1886 Chicago trial.[66]

In a poignant parting with McParland, in effect, his surrogate father and mentor for twenty-two years, after working on a few more cases, he decided to retire to his ranch in Santa Fe.[67] It was not a retreat, but a sober decision to change his lifestyle. Back among his favorite horses and dogs, raising vegetables and collecting eggs from his chickens, it seemed premature that he would retire at fifty-two. But of course Siringo had his "other" career in mind. He would write a bestselling account of his twenty-two years as a cowboy detective.

⊹ ⊹

After winning his second Pulitzer prize for *Common Ground: A Turbulent Decade in Two Lives of Three American Families*, *New York Times* reporter J. Anthony Lukas became fascinated with the story of the murder of ex-governor Frank Steunenberg and the famous trials of Big Bill Haywood, Charles H. Moyer, George Pettibone, and Harry Orchard in Boise, Idaho, after detective James McParland had spirited the first three out of Colorado into Idaho penitentiary cells. Lukas himself went to Boise over a period of many years to do research and stayed at the still extant Idanha Hotel where McParland and Charlie Siringo had stayed. The result was that Lukas wrote a most thorough, probing, and brilliant book about one of the most famous labor-versus-capital courtroom trials in American history. To Lukas it was a symbolic fight about the road Americans would choose to take in the new twentieth century. Would it be one that honored the rights of labor, or would it accept the rule of the powerful new corporate business elite, which Theodore Roosevelt himself came to oppose? For that reason Lukas gave his book the title *Big Trouble* and added the ominous subtitle: *Murder in a Small Western Town Sets Off a Struggle for the Soul of America*. In his version, Clarence Darrow and the aims of the WFM are justified, but what he could not in all honesty do, however, was to condone the methods of either the WFM or that of the mining corporation. As he himself wrote in his final chapter:

> Finally, the opposing camps in this nasty class war sputtering along the icy ridges of the Rocky Mountains had just about cancelled each other out. Operative for operative, hired gun for hired gun, bought jurors for bought jurors, perjured witness for perjured witness, conniving lawyer for conniving lawyer, partisan reporter for partisan reporter, these cockeyed armies had fought each other to an exhausted standoff.[68]

It was this phenomenal ruthless struggle that finally got to Siringo. Only seven years later he would himself attack the Pinkerton Agency in his book *Two Evil Isms: Pinkertonism and Anarchism* (1915). Finding himself threatened with libel by the Pinkerton lawyers, Siringo even showed the manuscript to Clarence Darrow, who told him that if he were convicted, the "worst penalty in Illinois for criminal libel would be a $500 fine and a year in jail." Charlie replied, "That wouldn't kill me."[69] One can only assume that Darrow must have smiled when he read *Two Evil Isms*.

44. *Photo of Siringo taken while trailing train robbers, most likely the "Wild Bunch." From Charles A. Siringo,* A Cowboy Detective *(1912).*

45. *Siringo and W. O. Sayles were both assigned to track down Butch Cassidy's gang. Their efforts proved unsuccessful. From Charles A. Siringo,* A Cowboy Detective *(1912).*

46. *The Hole-in-the-Wall area, Johnson County, Wyoming, where Butch Cassidy had a ranch. From the Caroline Lockhart Collection, no. 177, American Heritage Center, University of Wyoming.*

47. *Upper Horseshoe Canyon, Wayne County, Utah, used by Butch Cassidy and the Wild Bunch as a hideout. From Kelsey Publishing, Provo, Utah.*

48. *In their Tipton, Wyoming, robbery of a Union Pacific express car, the Wild Bunch dynamited the car, a photo of which is above. Union Pacific Historical Collection.*

49. *"Fort Worth Five." From left to right: Harry Longabaugh (the "Sundance Kid"), Will Carver, Ben Kilpatrick, Harvey Logan ("Kid Curry"), and Butch Cassidy. Union Pacific Historical Collection.*

50. Harry Longabaugh and Etta Place, 1901. From the Rocky Mountain House Books, Hamilton, Montana.

51. The dust jacket from Siringo's Two Evil Isms: Pinkertonism and Anarchism *(1915), in which he attacked his former employer, the Pinkerton Agency, for forcing him to use pseudonyms in his book,* A Cowboy Detective.

52.

Frank Steunenberg, ex-governor of Idaho, who was assassinated by a bomb in 1905 in Caldwell, Idaho, where he resided. Courtesy of Idaho State Historical Society, Boise, Idaho.

53.

Harry Orchard. Authorities determined that Harry Orchard, a professional bomber, had planted the bomb killing Frank Steunenberg. Thought to be an act of revenge by the leaders of the Western Federation of Miners (WFM), Orchard and three other WFM officials, Charles H. Moyer, William D. "Big Bill" Haywood, and George A. Pettibone, were brought to trial in Boise, Idaho, in 1907. Courtesy of Idaho State Historical Society, Boise, Idaho.

54. *Charles A. Moyer, William D. Haywood, and George A. Pettibone
of the Western Federation of Miners. Photo taken in 1907 when
they were being held in jail pending the Orchard trial. Courtesy of
Idaho State Historical Society, Boise, Idaho.*

55a and b.
William E. Borah (left), a leading trial lawyer in Idaho, who had just been elected to the U.S. Senate, served as a major lawyer, along with James H. Hawley (right), also an outstanding Idaho trial lawyer who was the chief special prosecutor, in the prosecution of Orchard, Moyer, Haywood, and Pettibone. Courtesy of Idaho State Historical Society, Boise, Idaho.

56. Clarence S. Darrow, a prominent Chicago trial lawyer, who defended William D. Haywood during the trial. Courtesy of Idaho State Historical Society, Boise, Idaho.

*57. Orchard and guards, of whom one was Charlie Siringo.
Because James McParland persuaded Harry Orchard to
confess to killing ex-governor Steunenberg and other crimes
in Colorado, McParland, now an old man, asked Siringo to
serve as his bodyguard during the Orchard-WFM trials. Thus
Charlie came to know Orchard and other law officers and
lawyers during the 1907 trials. From Charles A. Siringo,*
A Cowboy Detective *(1912).*

58. *"Jas. McCartney and the Author [Siringo]." Here Siringo uses the
pseudonym required by the Pinkerton Agency, calling [James]
McParland "McCartney." From Charles A. Siringo,* A Cowboy
Detective *(1912).*

59. *Charles A. Siringo. Photo taken during the trial of Harry Orchard,*
whom he came to know. The inscription on the original photo reads,
"To Harry Orchard, compliments yours Truly, Chas. A. Siringo."
Courtesy of Idaho State Historical Society, Boise, Idaho.

60. *The Idanha Hotel in Boise, Idaho, where many of the principal figures in the trial, among them James McParland and Charles Siringo, stayed. Courtesy of Idaho State Historical Society, Boise, Idaho.*

THE SUCCESS OF *A Texas Cowboy* CONVINCED SIRINGO,
WHO WAS EASILY CONVINCED, THAT HE COULD WRITE OTHER
SUCCESSFUL BOOKS. THE OPPOSITION OF THE POWERFUL
PINKERTON NATIONAL DETECTIVE AGENCY DID NOT DISSUADE HIM.
HE BELIEVED THAT WHAT HE HAD DONE AND WAS DOING WAS
INTERESTING AND SIGNIFICANT, AND HE WAS RIGHT. HIS BOOKS . . .
DO ADD MUCH TO THE HISTORY OF THE DEVELOPMENT OF
THE AMERICAN WEST FROM 1865 TO 1920.

—*Orlan Sawey,* Charles A. Siringo, *133*

DOWN IN THE STATE UNIVERSITY AT AUSTIN, TEXAS, THEY HAVE
DEDICATED SIX BRONZE TABLETS TO MEN REPRESENTING FORCES
THAT WENT INTO THE BUILDING OF THAT STATE: ON ONE OF THE
SIX IS INSCRIBED SIMPLY "CHARLIE COWBOY."

—*Neil M. Clark, "Close Calls:*
An Interview With Charles A. Siringo," 38

. . . NO OTHER COWBOY EVER TALKED ABOUT HIMSELF SO
MUCH IN PRINT; FEW HAD MORE TO TALK ABOUT.

—*J. Frank Dobie,* Guide to Life and
Literature of the Southwest, *119*

CHAPTER TWELVE

The Trials of an Author, 1912–1922

SIRINGO'S "A COWBOY DETECTIVE" AND "TWO EVIL ISMS" VERSUS THE PINKERTONS, AND A RETREAT DOWN MEMORY LANE—"BILLY THE KID" AND "LONE STAR COWBOY"

WHEN SIRINGO RESIGNED FROM THE PINKERTON AGENCY IN 1907, he looked forward to living on his Sunny Slope Ranch and to being with his animals: Rowdy and Patsy, his favorite horses; "Eat-Em-Up Jake," his Russian Wolfhound; and a lively feline, "Miss Pussy Cat." But he also had in mind marrying again, and writing an autobiographical account of his twenty-two years as a Pinkerton detective.

While on a case in Oregon, Siringo had met an attractive young woman whom he identified only as Grace in his writings, never disclosing her last name. They corresponded when he was in Boise at the Haywood trial and afterward. He proposed marriage; she accepted; and Grace came to live at Sunny Slope. But just as had been the case with Lillie Thomas, Siringo left Santa Fe to work on two cases: one in South Dakota for the

Pinkerton Agency, and a second in Nevada for its rival, the William J. Burns Detective Agency. These absences led Grace to visit her parents in the Pacific Northwest, but when Siringo returned to Santa Fe, she did not. After more than a year and a half of debate, Siringo filed a petition in the New Mexico courts to divorce her. The divorce was granted in April 1909.[1]

Meanwhile Siringo continued to work on occasional cases for both the Pinkerton and Burns agencies, and began to write his book, soon to be entitled, *A Cowboy Detective: A True Story of Twenty-Two Years with a World-Famous Detective Agency.* The fact was, however, Siringo no longer had a regular income, and he began to seek help from friends, but particularly from a brilliant Santa Fe lawyer, Alois B. Renehan, who in his younger years had lived in New York and Washington working a variety of jobs, until he decided to become a lawyer and go west to pursue that career. Siringo needed legal advice about a book contract, but he also sought Renehan's financial help. Renehan, though thirteen years younger than Siringo, soon became the latter's newest surrogate father—replacing James McParland.[2]

Backed by money borrowed from Renehan, in return for a share of his royalties, by 1910 Siringo had signed a contract for the publication of the book with W. B. Conkey Company of Hammond, Indiana. He sent the firm his manuscript early that year. Urged on by Siringo, who knew he had written a potential bestseller, the Conkey Company advertised the forthcoming book in lively posters in the Chicago newsstands and bookstores. Naturally the Pinkerton Agency soon noticed these posters, acquired galley sheets of the book, and immediately got an Illinois court injunction enjoining both Siringo and the Conkey Company from using the name Pinkerton in the publication. In effect the book could not be marketed in its present form.[3]

As Ben Pingenot, who has consulted Alois Renehan's papers in Santa Fe, tells us, Charlie was advised by Renehan, who did not feel the book was hostile to the Pinkertons, to write a diplomatic letter to William Pinkerton that might smooth over matters. Instead, Siringo fired off a furious letter to Pinkerton threatening to add chapters about cases that would indeed reveal dirty secrets about the agency.

As it turned out Charlie had actually "signed a contract when he went to work for the agency stipulating that all information he received during the course of his work 'should forever be kept secret...and never directly nor indirectly reveal except to the [agency] or a person authorized by the [agency] to receive the same.'" With a commendable patience Renehan negotiated with the Pinkerton lawyer for over a year, until finally William A. Pinkerton agreed to allow publication if both the agency's name and that of important individuals in the book "be fictionalized."[4] Actually the agency succeeded in holding up its publication for two years. Finally, in January 1912, two thousand copies of *A Cowboy Detective* appeared in print. In the amended version, the Pinkerton Agency became the Dickinson Agency, James McParland became McCarthy, and other persons were even more thinly disguised.[5]

A word about *A Cowboy Detective* as a book: it is actually a fascinating, logical, clearly written narrative of the many hundreds of cases on which Siringo worked. Vivid descriptions of the criminals, their acts and personalities, episodes in which his own life was in danger, plus revealing clues of his own brilliance, as a sleuth and as a fearless person, all come through in a chronicle that runs from the Haymarket Riot in 1886 to the Haywood trial in Boise in 1907.

While still nursing his anger against Pinkerton, Siringo's *A Cowboy Detective* did sell, and fan letters from readers all over the West began to come in, and were to continue for many years. Siringo himself enjoyed his ranch, horse riding, and frequent hunting. He was especially delighted to play host to his daughter Viola, who was just finishing her college program at a New Mexico normal school.

Siringo now wanted to show off as a successful author. Using the excuse of solving a case on the Texas Gulf Coast, he revisited the scenes of his youth in the Matagorda Bay area. He even came, one might way, with an entourage, for he had shipped his two horses, Rowdy and Patsy, and "Eat-Em-Up" Jake along with copies of his *A Cowboy Detective* to the Bay City area. Once there he assiduously promoted his book.[6]

Always nostalgic for the old days, he "harked back" with older friends of his mother's generation like Fred Cornelius and Christian Zipprian, while holding reunions with his childhood chums, Billy Williams and Horace Yeamans. He also visited one of his earliest mentors, Jonathan E. Pierce, Shanghai's quieter brother who had helped him so many times. Jonathan had just built a new hotel at Blessing and invited Siringo to stay there. Here memories of his life as a cowboy were so strong he visited the old Rancho Grande and the huge statue of Shanghai Pierce in nearby Hawley Cemetery.[7] But what Siringo must have enjoyed most were newspaper write-ups of himself as a prominent author from the Matagorda area. He would be even more pleased to know that the local historical society has kept records of him on file and old-time residents still consider him their best-known author.[8]

During this very sentimental visit to the Matagorda Bay area, Siringo met Ellen Partain, the wealthy widow of a cowboy whom he had known and liked while working for Shanghai Pierce at the Rancho Grande. Mrs. Partain and Charlie were attracted to one another and after a brief courtship were married at the Majestic Hotel in Hot Springs, Arkansas. The marriage was headlined in the local papers as "Old Couple is Married Here," finding romance and getting hitched late in life. Charlie was undoubtedly pleased to be described as "cowboy, author and famed detective." At the wedding were Siringo's former favorite boss on the Shanghai Pierce ranch, Wylie Kuykendall, and his wife.[9]

Once she had come to Sunny Slope, however, Ellen was not only lonely for Texas, she and Siringo were soon in conflict. He was obsessed with his writing and probably neglected her. Using the excuse that she had business in Texas and wanted to visit her relatives, she returned to Texas after only a few months. Siringo then filed for divorce once again in the New Mexico courts. The decree was made final in 1913. Ellen not only remained in Texas, she married again but this time tragically. Her new husband, a Mr. Sapp, took her on a hunting trip, killed her, and after a long trial, was convicted and sent to prison.[10]

Delighted with the success of the hardbound copies of *A Cowboy Detective*, Siringo decided to publish a paperbound edition with a Chicago publisher, but because he had mortgaged his ranch to pay for the costs of the new edition, the book stated that it had been published in Santa Fe, probably to escape a new threat from the Pinkertons. As Pingenot and others have noted, he added a more specific subtitle, which read "Twenty-Two Years with Pinkerton's National Detective Agency."[11] Luckily for Siringo the Pinkerton Agency chose to ignore this newest violation of the court injunction not to use its name.

Even so, Charlie was still seeking revenge, which soon took the form of a 109-page diatribe against the Pinkertons entitled *Two Evil Isms: Pinkertonism and Anarchism*. Alois Renehan was shocked when he read it and "told a friend that he thought Charlie was 'going wild.'"[12] Certainly the book was dramatic. Once it was printed, on its cover was an Uncle Sam being attacked by two snakes, one labeled "Pinkertonism" and the other "Anarchism." Charlie himself had gone to Chicago to get it printed under his own name as "Publisher" (Chicago, Illinois: Copyright 1915). The book was illustrated with photographs of the eight Haymarket anarchists on the front page, and then photos of one "Doc" Williams who falsely testified as to the guilt of some of the anarchists; also included were photos of Harry Orchard the bomber, and the renegade ex-Pinkerton Tom Horn, who was believed to have killed seventeen men, but was finally hanged in Wyoming for wantonly killing an innocent boy. Photos of Siringo and McParland were also included.[13]

During his stay in Chicago, Siringo corresponded with William E. Hawks, a former Idaho rancher who had now moved to Vermont, where he had become an avid collector of Western lore and cowboy songs. Charlie had occasionally supplied him with copies of cowboy songs and by 1914 they had become such pen pals that he told Hawks about his activities in Chicago as he prepared *Two Evil Isms* for publication. Writing in late November 1914, he told Hawks that when *Two Evil Isms* comes out "it will be a sensation without any doubt." He then invited Hawks to invest in the book.[14] Continuing to practice his lifelong habit of using aliases, he wrote signing his letter "Dull Knife," a false name he had employed in Denver while seeking to participate in a rodeo years before.[15] In mid-December, he asked Hawks for a loan of $200, which the latter sent immediately. In acknowledging the receipt of the check a week later, he said that he had allowed the head of the Burns Detective Agency to read the manuscript, who told him it would "sell a million copies."[16] In late January 1915, Siringo sent Hawks proofs of the outside cover of *Two Evil Isms* with some photos. Meanwhile, as noted earlier, Charlie had persuaded Clarence Darrow to read the book, not once but twice, and was reassured by his saying that a $500 fine and a year in jail would be all he would get.[17]

By March, however, Siringo was less confident, for he thought the Pinkertons might be holding up his book and that he had to leave town because he had no money to live in Chicago or pay for lawyers. As he wrote Hawks:

> It looks very much like I am up against the real thing. I expected to sell a lot of new books to Socialists—but find that it grates on their nerves. Headmen of [the] National Socialist party said they would buy 100,000 copies if I "would cut out the word *Anarchism* on the small snake on the front cover and put in the word *Capitalism*."

And also cut out all I say against Geo. A. Pettibone,
their idol, and the Western Federation. They agreed I
told the truth—but said if they helped push the book
as it is, they would be playing into the hands of the
capitalist class. I refused to make the changes.[18]

Siringo also reported "that the railroad news companies are afraid
to handle it on the trains owing to the influence of the Pinkertons with
Ry. officials. So it looks as if I am between the Devil and the deep sea."[19]

Then switching to a project Siringo had had in mind for some
years he told Hawks that he still planned to work on the old Chisholm
cattle trail to the Gulf of Mexico and write a book on it. "It seems I
cannot get this idea out of my system."[20] Siringo envisaged the trail as
running from Abilene to Gonzales, Texas. On his hasty retreat from
Chicago and escape from possible new libel charges by the Pinkertons,
Siringo actually stopped in Kansas City and Garden City, Kansas, to
confer with old ranching friends about erecting Chisholm Trail markers. His friends naturally urged him to post the markers and to write
the trail's history.[21]

Once back in Santa Fe, Siringo wrote Hawks about the efforts of
the Pinkertons to extradite him to Chicago, but gleefully reported that
the incumbent governor of New Mexico, William C. McDonald, said he
would not honor the request. News clippings from the *Santa Fe New
Mexican*, April 22, 1915, about the case, saved by Hawks, indicated,
however, that McDonald had sought the advice of his attorney general
and of Renehan, before making a decision. Meanwhile, a Chicago
policeman named Donnelly had already arrived in Santa Fe to arrest
Siringo and return him to Chicago for trial. The *Santa Fe Record*
reported that Donnelly's arrival "created a furor."[22] The irrepressible
Siringo ended his letter to Hawks on a high note by saying "'The
Cowboy Detective' is having a tremendous sale on every train that pulls
out of Chicago, and the train butchers are reaping a harvest."[23]

Once he felt safe in New Mexico, Siringo announced to Hawks that
he was now writing a new book, "Reminiscence of a Lone Star
Cowboy," which he hoped Rand McNally might publish. On a more
somber note, he told Hawks that he had learned that the Pinkertons had
seized and destroyed the plates of *Two Evil Isms*. Some but not many
copies of *Two Evil Isms* did get sold, however.[24]

In his analysis of Siringo's extreme actions, his biographer, Ben Pingenot, suspects that Charlie never really intended to publish *Two Evil Isms*, but wanted to use it as a threat to make them pay for his not publishing it. He even sent the New York Pinkerton office a copy of the manuscript, hoping that might produce action. Nothing could have been more foolish. The Pinkertons saw at once what the game was—one of blackmail—and refused to cooperate. The end result was tragic. Siringo went so deeply in debt that he had three mortgages on his property.

The book itself was such a financial disaster he had to ask his daughter, Viola, for a loan. The supreme irony was that while *Two Evil Isms* was a diatribe against the Pinkertons, much of the material was already in his *A Cowboy Detective*, and on occasion when he had solved a case described in his *Two Evil Isms*, he could not refrain from boasting about it.[25] If there is a good side to this sad episode, it was that Siringo was never cowed. Eugene Manlove Rhodes later recalled that Siringo once told him he had never had a sense of fear.[26]

After the debacle with *Two Evil Isms*, Charlie turned to three other projects he had in mind: to mark the Chisholm Trail with aluminum steer horns and to complete a history of the Long Drive. This proved to be more of a challenge than he at first realized, for although he had traveled the trail at least three times, initially he did not even know who Jesse Chisholm was, the Cherokee half-breed trader for whom it was named. Siringo solicited information from friends and tried to get sponsors, including the legislatures of states through which the trail had passed. But the project was put on hold with America's entry into the First World War in 1917, for aluminum to be used for steer horns on the guideposts became a valued mineral resource for the military.

Meanwhile he had already begun to revisit the areas of New Mexico where he had lived or traveled when Pat Garrett, Jim East, and others were chasing Billy the Kid, and while he was himself tracking down stolen LX cattle and hanging about to testify in court against Pat Coghlan, who had bought the stolen cattle. By 1915 he had already visited the area around White Oaks and Tularosa to interview old acquaintances about their recollections of Billy the Kid.

Then in 1916 the legendary serendipitous Siringo luck, absent for so long, seemed to return again when Governor McDonald offered him a job as a ranger for New Mexico's Cattle Sanitary Board, and assigned him and Bill Owens, a fellow ranger, to break up cattle stealing groups in central-southern New Mexico with headquarters in Carrizozo.[27] This location put him smack in the middle of the place he had known in the early 1880s—Lincoln, White Oaks, and Encinoso.

Governor McDonald had a strong personal interest in controlling stealing and outlawry in the area because he and several partners owned the Block Ranch, a large spread near the Capitan Mountains. The governor himself had built his own ranch house on the property. When Siringo took the assignment, McDonald warned him that cattle thieves were in league with the local law and court officials, so that he could expect little cooperation from them.[28] What no one said publicly, however, was that as in Las Vegas, decades earlier, large Anglo ranchers were competing for lands long occupied by poorer Hispanic New Mexicans.

Charlie soon learned what the governor was talking about. Mexican-American residents would seize Block cattle, slaughter them for food, and secret their branded hides in wells to prevent them from being found. Meanwhile an outlaw named Romero and his gang were busy stealing ranch horses. Siringo recovered the horses, but when he arrested cattle thieves who appeared to be working with Romero and brought them into the local court at Arabella, a village on the eastern slope of the Capitan Mountains, the judge not only freed them but charged the court costs of $25 to Siringo! Moreover, he told the constable to hold Siringo until the fees were paid!

This is when the old Siringo came alive again. Getting the drop on the constable with his trusty Colt 45, Siringo left the courtroom, jumped on his horse, which a Block cowboy had ready for him, and headed over the mountains for Governor McDonald's ranch house, where he had left the nine horses recovered from Romero and his allies.[29]

Within minutes after Siringo had left with the horses, a furious Arabella constable and deputy arrived at McDonald's ranch house in search of Siringo, but a quick-witted ranch manager told him that Siringo had left for Carrizozo by automobile and pointed to some fresh tire tracks to make his point. In the end, Siringo not only got the stolen horses to the main ranch, but went to Carrizozo and swore out warrants for the arrests of the men freed by the Arabella judge. Accompanied by a deputy sheriff, he arrested them and arranged for them to be tried in Carrizozo when the next district courts convened there.[30]

There were other harrowing confrontations as well. Once in Encinoso he was tracking down stolen butchered beef, and with the help of his dog, "Eat-Em-Up-Jake," Siringo spotted a newly cooked beef head in a Mexican-American kitchen and soon after discovered fresh-killed beef "high up in the rafters of a chicken house, already quartered and ready for barbequeing." When he arrested the householder and took him as a prisoner to the local court, he found that a crowd of citizens had gathered with a rope; but it soon became clear that they intended to hang Siringo and free his prisoner! Again the old Colt 45 came out. Holding it on the judge and the crowd, he made them stand back until, in his own words, he "got the hell out of there."[31]

But of course Siringo only temporarily retreated. Some days later, backed by the county sheriff and some deputies, he boasted: "We got the *hombre* I first caught and got in a few more [cattle thieves] besides." As usual Siringo later became sentimental about the event, saying "In a way, though, I couldn't blame those fellows. After all, that Block beef was pretty good stuff. I guess I'd a-done the same thing if I'd been in their place."[32]

Siringo and his partner Owens appear to have gained enough control over the thieving and butchery in the area to allow him to be reassigned to another locality: Glencoe, northeast of Ruidoso, where Siringo found that he was among old friends whose company and free meals he greatly enjoyed. This idyllic lifestyle ended in 1918, however, when his job as ranger was terminated. Although he had collected much material on Billy the Kid, he went back to writing his *A Lone Star Cowboy*, which was published in 1919.

As Orlan Sawey has noted, "The first 214 pages of *A Lone Star Cowboy* were a rewriting of *A Texas Cowboy*, with the style toned down somewhat, but the violent incidents played up."[33] The remainder of the book, as Sawey has pointed out, "deals with his life as a merchant in Caldwell, Kansas, the opening of Oklahoma to settlement, a brief mention of his twenty-two years of service to the Pinkerton's, his pursuit of a man whom he thought was 'Kid Curry' . . . a visit to the Gulf Coast County of his youth, a fairly accurate account of the establishment and use of the Chisholm Trail, and an account of his two years' service as a New Mexican Ranger."[34]

A Lone Star Cowboy was, in essence, a semi-rehash of his other publications and was probably most appreciated either by readers who did not know his *A Texas Cowboy*, or by his followers who saw it as a sort of reunion with Charlie. It was not nearly as good as *A Cowboy Detective*, nor was his accompanying forty-two-page publication *A Song*

Companion of a Lone Star Cowboy: Old Favorite Cow Camp Songs (1919). The song collection was neither original nor extensive. Indeed, J. Frank Dobie dismissed it as "shoddy!" In short, Siringo was trying to sell as much as to tell. Neither of these publications provided him with an income of any size. The real story was that Siringo was determined to print everything he had experienced. In 1920 he published a short *History of "Billy the Kid,"* which critics have justly said was merely a rehash of "what had already been recorded." In a new edition of a history of Billy the Kid in 2000, Frederick Nolan states that not only did Siringo copy Garrett, but invented some tales of his own.35

On the other hand, Charlie had consulted old-timers in New Mexico, and his friend Jim East, who had been with Garrett in the first capture of Billy the Kid. East sent Siringo a remarkable firsthand account on May 1, 1920, of his role in the capture and death of Tom O'Phalliard [O'Folliard] and Charlie Bowdre and the activities of Pat Garrett and the other members of his posse. Siringo did establish, however, that the Kid was armed when he was killed, and worked to have the Kid's grave in Fort Sumner marked, where it is now a major tourist attraction.36

Even so, Siringo did interview scores of persons who had known the Kid, some of whom were figures involved in his arrest and death. These interviews occurred eight years after the original author, Pat Garrett, had been killed in 1908. Despite its romantic bias and inaccuracies, Siringo's *History of "Billy the Kid"* should be consulted as a historical source.37

Meanwhile Siringo continued to pursue other writing projects. He thought that he could write a romantic western novel, a dream he kept alive almost every time he met a charming, beautiful girl. Indeed, he was still trying to write the novel when he died in Hollywood.38 He kept writing about the Chisholm Trail, and also completed a history of the most famous "bad men" in the West. None of these projects had resulted in publication although in March 1920 he renewed a long-lapsed correspondence with his Vermont friend Hawks to report on the Chisholm Trail project and to speculate on who had murdered Pat Garrett in 1908. He also boasted that his *Lone Star Cowboy* was selling.39 On April 2 he wrote Hawks to announce that he was going south by buggy to "drift." He had purchased a "dandy little tent with two screen windows" and enclosed a picture of himself and Rowdy.40

While Charlie's latest book, *Lone Star Cowboy*, never made him any money, it brought him fan letters from all over the West. They came

from old cowhands who had known him, as well as some highly successful businessmen who were anxious to share their own western memories with him. In all their letters they praised Siringo's writings, sought
his help in composing their own memoirs, or asked for information.

One of the most persistent correspondents was Orrie S. Clark, a
bank executive in Indiana, who had grown up in Texas, where he had
come to know and admire the famous gunman Clay Allison, saying he
"was a good looker and had an air about him that attracted almost
everyone." Clark wanted to write a biography of him. Clay Allison's life
is actually one of the most violent, contradictory, and yet heroic careers
of any western gunmen. He was the quintessential "good" bad man.[41]

Robert Clay Allison was born in Tennessee in 1840, the son of a
Presbyterian minister. His father died when Clay was only five, but he
appears to have been inbred with strong ideals of justice from the word go.
He fought in the Civil War on the Confederate side and by the end of the
conflict he was serving as a scout for General Nathan Bedford Forrest. Like
so many other Southerners he went to Texas after the war to the Brazos
River region. Allison had a violent temper, and at one point had a fight
with a ferryman named Colbert at a Red River crossing. This led the
Allison and Colbert families to hate one another, and a year later in 1874,
in New Mexico, Allison killed a nephew of the ferryman, "Chunk"
Colbert, who was a desperado. This was to be a feature of Allison's life: a
"justified killing."[42]

Allison became a cowhand for Oliver Loving and Charlie Goodnight and appears to have driven cattle for them when they took herds
west on the Goodnight-Loving Trail. In 1870 he joined his brother-
in-law L. G. Coleman in driving cattle to Colfax County, New Mexico,
where both started ranches. Allison's own was near the village of
Cimarron, which was near a mining boomtown—Elizabethtown. Colfax County was an unbelievably chaotic area. The mining rush was on
the famous Maxwell Land Grant where Apache Indians, Hispanic sheep
farmers, Anglo-squatters, and high-level land speculators vied for survival and/or domination. In this turbulent world, squatters and land
grant people were so violent they engaged in killings. Allison, who sided
with and was admired by the squatters, helped lynch a Hispanic man
named Cruz Vega, then killed his kinsman, "Pancho" Griego, and
attacked and destroyed the local newspaper office for writing critical
editorials about his actions.

In 1878 Allison left Colfax County to become a cattle broker in Hays City, Kansas. While in Kansas he heard that a friend named Hoy had been murdered in Dodge City. He went to Dodge to exact revenge. The story is hazy but he appears to have confronted both Bat Masterson and Wyatt Earp while there. No one was killed, the reason, say some accounts, being that Masterson and Earp made themselves scarce. Other historians of Dodge City disagree, saying that Earp persuaded Allison to leave town peacefully.[43]

By 1880 Clay and John Allison had settled on a ranch near the Washita River in Hemphill County in the Panhandle area of Texas. There Allison's activities, especially when drunk, earned him the name "Wolf of the Washita." As he grew older, however, he became quieter and after moving once more to Pecos, Texas, "became involved in politics." In July 1887, however, he was accidentally thrown from a heavily loaded wagon and crushed to death when he was "run over by its rear wheels."[44]

When Siringo told Clark he had known Clay Allison in Dodge City, Clark was so delighted that in 1923 he paid Siringo a visit in Los Angeles, where Charlie had moved. Having learned Siringo was writing a book on the "bad men of the West," in 1924 Clark sent his own biographical account of Allison to Siringo to use, and having learned Jim East also knew Allison, sent him a copy as well.[45] Eventually Siringo did include Allison in his "Bad Men of the West" manuscript.

Clay Allison's colorful, violent life not only captured the imagination of O. S. Clark, who did get information from Siringo about him and wrote a history of Allison, he also captured the imagination of J. Frank Dobie and other western journalists and writers. Without having been a Texas Ranger, Allison behaved like one, exacting justice through violence. He was, reported Clark admiringly, "A Self Constituted Executioner." One wonders if one of Charlie Siringo's favorite aliases, "Charles Leon Allison," was inspired by Allison's career in the 1880s. Others, fascinated with Billy the Kid, badgered Siringo for Jim East's address, or wrote to boast of knowing Pat Garrett and other pursuers of Billy.

The most rewarding renewal of friendships, however, came in June 1921 when Dr. Henry F. Hoyt, who had been at the LX Ranch where Siringo had taught him how to ride and lasso, contacted Siringo. Hoyt was now a successful physician in Long Beach, California. After having read *A Lone Star Cowboy*, Hoyt wrote Siringo to urge that they renew their acquaintance. Hoyt even suggested that Siringo come to California to live. While on the LX Ranch Hoyt had bought a horse from Billy the Kid in Tascosa, and he had never gotten over his fascination with the young outlaw. Moreover, Hoyt was planning to write his own memories about being a frontier doctor in Texas, New Mexico, and Minnesota.[46]

Just as thousands of other old cowboys in the West were fascinated with the rise of Hollywood's western films, so was Siringo. He liked the early ones, but after 1914 he became an ardent admirer of the actor William S. Hart, whose serious, if romantic films featuring himself as the "good bad man" in the starring role, made such an impression that Siringo wrote him a fan letter. Perhaps unknown to Charlie, Hart maintained an efficient and widespread correspondence with his fans. In his response, "Hart said he knew of Siringo from his writings and was himself an admirer of the old cowboy detective."[47] Absolutely elated by Hart's letter, he used parts of it on his business cards, one of which he sent to Dr. Hoyt. Hoyt replied at once to say that Hart was also a great favorite of his and was often seen in Long Beach. Hoyt then confided, "I never miss one of his shows." Hoyt also suggested that Charlie come out to Hollywood and "get in the game with your expert horsemanship, quick gun work, etc. etc." One can easily assume that Hoyt's dangling a Hollywood career before Siringo eventually helped persuade him to move to California.[48]

Already faced with many debts, foreclosures on his Santa Fe ranch, and continuing disappointment with the sales of his books, Charlie Siringo was unexpectedly hit by ill health. In November 1921, he had gone on a hunting trip where he had to sleep in the snow without adequate cover. As Ben Pingenot has told us, he returned to Sunny Slope with a bad case of bronchitis, which turned into a permanent debilitating cough. Keenly aware of how frail he had become, his daughter Viola, now living in San Diego, California, had urged him to join her, even before he became ill.[49] After consulting Renehan about whether the Pinkertons could extradite him from California for a Chicago trial, and having been assured that all the Chicago charges had been put aside by the courts, Charlie decided to move.

To break his train trip to San Diego, Charlie dropped off at Douglas, Arizona, to spend Christmas and New Year's with his dear friend of LX Ranch days, James H. East, and his wife. As ill and fragile as he was, he and East appear to have had a glorious time "harking back" to their years in the Texas Panhandle. Undoubtedly East filled Charlie in on his own life there after Siringo had moved to Caldwell. In 1882, after leaving the LX himself, East was elected sheriff of Oldham County, of which Tascosa was the county seat. In Tascosa he also acquired the Equity Bar and later a second one, the Cattle Exchange Saloon.[50] Even so, Jim East's presence alone did not deter rustlers from continuing to seize the cattle of large ranchers. Indeed, the thieving was so prevalent, Pat Garrett was hired by the large ranchers, such as George Littlefield and Charles Goodnight, to form a Home Ranger outfit to track them down. East cooperated with the group. The confrontation became more and more violent until in 1886 in a "Big Fight" at Tascosa, four men were killed.[51] It looks as if East was always on the side of the ranchers.

Meanwhile East was hired by the W. M. Lee–Lucien B. Scott or LS Ranch near Tascosa as range foreman while continuing to be a deputy sheriff. The LS rangeland was nearly the size of Connecticut. Things never seemed to be quiet in the Panhandle, for in addition to rustlers, in 1883 Tom Harris, the wagon boss at the LS, led a cowboy strike for better wages and treatment, which of course failed. Nettie Boulding East, Jim's wife, became so nervous that one night she shot at what she thought was an outlaw "wanting to kill her husband, only to discover she had killed the LS's prize bull."[52]

In 1903 East and his wife moved to Douglas, Arizona, the copper-mining town almost on the Mexican border. There he served as city marshal, chief of police, and police judge until he retired in the late 1920s. O. S. Clark not only corresponded with East about Allison, but visited him in September 1929 about nine months before East died in 1930. East had also become a Clark hero, for when the latter turned all his western notes over to J. Evetts Haley in 1931, he confessed that he couldn't seem to write them up. In his correspondence with Haley, Clark referred to East as "this wonderful man."[53]

East seemed to inspire everyone he met with his intelligence and his spellbinding but accurate accounts of his experiences. J. Evetts Haley himself recalled that "Upon more than one occasion I drove over a thousand miles to see him and to listen to the tales of Old Tascosa and unfenced ranges." Haley had visited East in September 1927 and February 1928, and after East died, wrote a moving account of his life in the *Panhandle-Plains Historical Review* in 1931.[54]

As Jim East and Charlie Siringo talked over Christmas, they knew they had become part of the "good cowboy and bad men" (Billy the Kid) mystique that had fascinated American readers from the 1900s onward. They not only knew the old-timers, but had read the works of Western novelists and writers such as Andy Adams, Emerson Hough, and Zane Grey and followed them and scores of other western writers whose stories were serialized in the *Saturday Evening Post* from the turn of the century through the 1930s, among them Emerson Hough, Eugene Manlove Rhodes, and Henry H. Knibbs. Siringo himself dreamed of placing a story in the *Post*, as did O. S. Clark, the Clay Allison admirer, after Emerson Hough advised him to do so.[55] Sometime during the 1920s Walter Noble Burns wrote a fictionalized, sensational, and totally inaccurate but successful biography of Billy the Kid. Burns came to Douglas to interview East for information, but seems not to have used it. East, normally a believer in straight accounts, was himself persuaded by Viola Vivian in 1928 to collaborate in writing a play entitled *Billy the Kid*, which was performed at Tucson, Arizona.[56]

Siringo undoubtedly rehashed not only Panhandle stories with East, but told him of his own Pinkerton and publication troubles. Indeed, he had borrowed money from East to assist in one of his publications.[57] Certainly they must have talked about Nathan Howard "Jack" Thorp, who published a booklet, *Songs of the Cowboys*, in 1908, and a larger book bearing the same name with Houghton Mifflin in 1921.[58] Undoubtedly Thorp's original 1908 booklet must have inspired Siringo to publish his own *A Song Companion of a Lone Star Cowboy* in 1919. Thorp himself also knew the Texas Panhandle, the story of outlaw Bill Moore, and the area of New Mexico where Billy the Kid hung out, and was to write about both, depending heavily on Siringo's writings, when he published his final book, *Pardner in the Wind*, in 1941.[59] Indeed, Thorp paid tribute to Siringo by including a full-page photograph of him in his book.[60]

East and Siringo must also have chatted about how letters of recommendation from Sheriff Pat Garrett and Sheriff James East to William A. Pinkerton helped land Siringo his job as a detective with the Pinkerton Agency. They must have laughed at how young Dr. Hoyt innocently bought a stolen horse from Billy the Kid in Tascosa as Siringo told of Hoyt's letters urging him to move to California. If they talked about famous older Panhandle ranchers, they would have noted that Charles Goodnight had recently joined other ranchers like C. J. "Buffalo" Jones to save the buffalo from extinction by raising them on their own ranches.[61]

By 1922, Charlie Siringo, Jim East, and Dr. Henry Hoyt, who had only been a cowboy for a few years, all realized that as cowboys they had now become shapers of the western myth of the cowboy, and were seen as almost legends themselves. Unlike Siringo or Hoyt, however, Jim East did not choose to tell his experiences in print. As a pastime he wrote his stories down "and then filed them in his desk. No one except Mrs. East ever saw them. Just two or three days before his death, he piled them in his back yard and burned them all. He wrote well but his diffidence kept others from knowing the fact."[62]

In the end it was J. Evetts Haley, the indefatigable Texas collector and writer, who interviewed East several times, who best described Jim East's important role in the history of the Texas Panhandle and the capture of Billy the Kid. But acknowledging his debt to Siringo he graciously wrote: "Among those who ranged the Western Panhandle and pulled bog along the treacherous Canadian were Charlie Siringo, Henry Hoyt and Jim East. They, in particular, have enriched the tradition of the Texas Plains."[63]

WHAT MAKES THE IDEA OF THE JOURNEY COMPELLING IS THAT
LIFE IS A JOURNEY UNDERTAKEN BY EVERYONE.

— *William Ferris*

COWBOYS COULD PERFORM TERRIBLE LABORS AND ENDURE
BONE-GRINDING HARDSHIPS AND YET CONSIDER THEMSELVES THE
CHOSEN OF THE EARTH; AND THE GRACE THAT REDEEMED IT ALL
IN THEIR OWN ESTIMATION WAS THE FACT THAT THEY HAD GONE
A-HORSEBACK. THEY WERE RIDERS, FIRST AND LAST. I HAVE KNOWN
COWBOYS BROKEN IN BODY AND TWISTED IN SPIRIT, BRUISED BY
DEBT, FAILURE, LONELINESS, DISEASE AND MOST OF THE OTHER
AFFLICTIONS OF MAN, BUT I HAVE SELDOM KNOWN ONE WHO
DID NOT CONSIDER HIMSELF PHENOMENALLY BLESSED TO HAVE
BEEN A COWBOY, OR ONE WHO COULD NOT CANCEL HALF THE
MISERIES OF EXISTENCE BY DWELLING ON THE HORSES HE HAD
RIDDEN, THE COMRADES HE HAD RIDDEN THEM WITH,
AND THE MANLY TIMES HE HAD HAD.

— *Larry McMurtry, quoted in* No Traveler Remains Untouched:
Journey and Transformation in the American Southwest
(San Marcos: Southwest Texas State University, 1995), 47

WILLIAM S. HART "PLAYED A CRUCIAL ROLE IN THE
DEVELOPMENT OF THE WESTERN FILM, THE ONLY UNIQUELY
AMERICAN CATEGORY. HE MADE THE WESTERN INTO A
SERIOUS NARRATIVE RATHER THAN A TRIVIALITY."

— *Martin Ridge, editor,* My Life East and West,
by William S. Hart, 401

CHAPTER THIRTEEN

Recognition at Last!

CHARLIE SIRINGO IN

HOLLYWOOD, 1923–1928

DURING THE THREE MONTHS SIRINGO WAS IN SAN DIEGO WITH HIS daughter, Viola, and granddaughter, Margaret May, he did recover his health to a remarkable degree. He now felt that he could pursue his initial goal of moving to Los Angeles to see his old friend, Dr. Henry F. Hoyt, now an extremely successful physician in Long Beach, California, and to meet his cowboy actor hero, William S. Hart, in Hollywood.

Siringo counted on other connections as well. Some years earlier, George T. Cole, an artist-attorney and writer from Los Angeles, had visited Santa Fe in search of the "ancient city's fabulous Indian and Hispanic past," and also because of its attraction as a mecca for artists and/or writers. The Taos and Santa Fe colonies of artists were already nationally known, as were many literary figures such as Mabel Dodge Luhan and Mary Austin. While in Santa Fe Cole met Siringo and the two became good friends.

In addition to being an artist and a lawyer, "Jack" Cole, as he liked to be called, was also very successful in real estate, perhaps in part because his father, Captain Cornelius Cole, had been a United States Senator from California, and although now 101 years old was still active in the area; but a main reason was because Jack was a kindly, outgoing man who liked to help people. Indeed, soon after Siringo moved to Los Angeles, Cole loaned him money to pay off a publication debt to the

Santa Fe New Mexican newspaper. When Siringo first moved to Los Angeles, he engaged in what must have been a desperate search for the cheapest living accommodations, so short was he of cash.[1] After having moved three times over several months, Siringo was persuaded by Jack Cole to rent a cabin behind a large house he owned on Eleanor Avenue in Hollywood. Not only did Jack Cole live nearby, the cabin was, as Ben Pingenot tells us, near "the Water Hole Saloon, . . . at the corner of Cahuenga Avenue and Hollywood Boulevard." Soon Siringo was hanging out there watching the young cowboy and cowgirl actors. As he wrote his friend Alois Renehan, "I feel better since moving to the heart of Hollywood, where I can see the Flappers as they pass by." He named his cabin "Siringo's Den," with a sign over the door to that effect.[2]

The Hollywood in which Charlie found himself had had a meteoric rise in just twenty-five years. As Kevin Starr has noted, Hollywood was unknown to the film world in 1900, but "by 1915 . . . was a film center, and by 1926 it was the United States' fifth largest industry, grossing $1.5 billion a year and accounting for 90 percent of the world's films." An important portion of that fabulous income came from the western films made first as action-packed two-reelers and later as full-fledged movies using the magnificent outdoor scenery of southern California. When he arrived in 1923, in a letter to Alois Renehan, Charlie exclaimed, "Gee, but this city has grown since I was last here in '98."[3]

So-called "Westerns" were made first in the East, then later in locations as different as Colorado and San Francisco, and only after 1910 in Los Angeles and Hollywood. In the early days three actors reached stardom. The first was G. M. ("Broncho Billy") Anderson, who had several bit parts in *The Great Train Robbery* in 1903, often called the first western. "Broncho Billy" then went on to produce and act in his own westerns and by 1915 had made 375 short films that historian Charles Musser describes as rarely rising "above the dime-novel level." Nevertheless they were incredible successes. Anderson usually played the role of "a virtuous, self-sacrificing man" who ended up as the hero.[4]

The second western star and first superstar was William S. Hart, a fine Shakespearean actor who had already made his reputation on the New York stage in plays as diverse as *Romeo and Juliet* and *Ben Hur*. Even so he scored even greater successes in plays with a western setting such as *The Squaw Man* and the stage adaptation of Owen Wister's *The Virginian*. Moreover, Hart loved these plays because he had lived in various parts of the frontier Midwest as a boy, was a splendid horseman, and had actually learned to speak the Sioux language at a basic level. When he came west in 1914 to make western films, his knowledge of the West and his seriousness of purpose immediately raised his films to a much higher level of cinematic art—whether it was the story, the setting and costumes, or moral themes. As historian Martin Ridge had noted: Hart "played a crucial role in the development of the western film, the only uniquely American category. He made the western into a serious narrative rather than a triviality."[5]

By 1916 his reputation as a cowboy actor was national, in part because this tall, thin, athletic man with an angular face was so striking, and in part because he became a true cowboy, living the part offstage as fully as onstage. He was a superb horseman whose favorite horses became almost as well known as he was. It seems likely that Siringo saw his early films, *The Bargain* (1914) and *Hell's Hinges* (1916) in Santa Fe, in which Hart played what was to become his classic role: "a kind of antihero or good bad man." After seeing Hart's films, Siringo was prompted to write him a fan letter. To his delight Hart responded, praised Siringo's writings, and they became, in effect, pen pals.[6]

The third major western star in the decades of the silent movies was Tom Mix, who in the 1920s emerged as the king of the western stunt men in Hollywood. Mix, a handsome, truly dashing athletic performer who made films that were all action, had risen to prominence honestly. Born in 1880 in Pennsylvania, he could boast of having as varied a career as anyone in Hollywood. Because his father was a stable-master for a rich lumber baron, Tom was early interested in horses and dreamed of becoming a cowboy. Just as Charlie Siringo had tried to lasso crabs on Matagorda Bay, Mix's biographer, Robert S. Birchard, tells us Tom made a lasso from his mother's clothesline and practiced roping local farm animals. Indeed, at age twelve "he made his own cowboy suit."[7] He served in the Spanish American War, was in the Philippines, later visited China, and then "trained horses for the British during the Boer War."[8]

In 1906, however, he began working with the Miller Brothers 101 Ranch and Wild West show in Oklahoma. The Miller Brothers specialized in western shows featuring rodeo skills and the like that toured the country. Besides Tom Mix, among their other famous performers were Bill Pickett, a Black cowboy from Texas who made "bull dogging" (or steer wrestling) famous, and Will Rogers, whose horse and rope tricks plus a brilliant wry folksy stage humor eventually took him to Broadway. There, as a performer with the Ziegfeld Follies, he became one of the highest paid actors on the American stage.[9] Rogers not only knew Mix, while in New York he also became a fast friend of Hart, who was still performing on the New York stage. After show time the two would frequently have a bite to eat at Dinty Moore's. Hart preceded Rogers to Hollywood, but their close friendship continued there.[10]

After an off-and-on relation with the Miller Brothers and other western Wild West shows, Tom Mix made his first movie appearance in *Ranch Life in the Great Southwest*, for the Selig Polyscope Company. By 1921 he had become so popular it was estimated that his fan club numbered over two million members. By 1925 he had replaced Hart as the top cowboy star. Mix himself survived the transition from silents to the talkies with difficulty in the 1930s, and was still active in 1940 when he was tragically killed in a car crash in Arizona.[11]

So great was the demand for stunt cowboys, at the invitation of Thomas Ince, Hart's major film director, the Miller Brothers 101 Ranch group moved, in effect, to Hollywood. After booming in the 1920s, however, their own Wild West show went bankrupt during the Great Depression.[12]

Meanwhile a galaxy of other cowboy stars with long-term careers lived and performed in Hollywood westerns: Hoot Gibson, Buck Jones, Ken Maynard, and Will Rogers, among others. Certainly one of the most impressive western stars was Harry Carey who had been in films since 1901, but having become fascinated with the West, he acted in some twenty-five films directed by John Ford, who was himself already making western movies as early as 1917, and was to be the director of classic outstanding western films in later decades.[13]

The Hollywood scene between 1910 and the 1930s would not have been complete without real bad men, ex-sheriffs, and genuine cowboys. Emmett Dalton of the infamous Dalton gang, who terrorized the Oklahoma-Kansas area between 1890 and 1892 in bank and other robberies, had reformed after prison and lived in the Los Angeles area.[14]

Wyatt Earp, veteran of the fight at the OK Corral in Tombstone, Arizona, where two of his brothers were wounded, and a former assistant marshal in Dodge City, later moved all over the West, usually in search of gold. In 1884 he joined the early gold rush to the Coeur d'Alene region where he ran a saloon. He then joined the Alaskan gold rush, but in the early twentieth century returned to the States to participate in the Nevada rushes at Tonopah and Goldfield. Now old and ailing, he and his wife moved to Los Angeles, where he tried to interest Bill Hart in his life story. Instead he was exploited for information by other directors and scriptwriters. Hart did play a role in persuading journalist Stuart Lake to write Earp's biography but it was not published until after Earp's death in 1929. Earp was probably fortunate that he never saw it, for although it brought Earp national visibility and was very popular, the account was so outrageously imaginative, it was not until Casey Tefertiller's excellent biography, *Wyatt Earp: The Life Behind the Legend*, appeared in 1997, that he was finally treated accurately and intelligently.[15]

This then, was the Hollywood into which Charlie Siringo moved in 1923–1924. As noted earlier his "Den" was close to Cahuenga Avenue and Hollywood Boulevard where young actors and actresses hung out at restaurants and cafes. He did not hesitate to join them.[16]

At the top of the professional westerners, however, were poets, actors, able scriptwriters, and outstanding novelists whose works survive today as serious American literature. It tells us something about Siringo's reputation and storytelling charm that he became a respected and beloved member of one of these inner circles of able professionals. Because the story of this remarkable group and their relation to Siringo is largely untold, we should take note of them and their careers and explain why they were so attracted to Siringo, and he to them, and what they did for him.

Certainly one of the most delightful, intelligent, and sensitive of this literary circle was Henry Herbert Knibbs (1874–1945), a Canadian-born American who "became famous for western stories, novels, screen plays and poems." Ronna Lee Sharpe and Tom Sharpe have observed, "Although he never earned a dime as a cowboy...his ballads and poems were so on target and lyrical, cowboys sang them." Like Jack Cole, Knibbs had visited Santa Fe where he knew Siringo's friend and lawyer, Alois Renehan, who in turn introduced Knibbs to Siringo. As an avid horse lover, and a writer of poems about horses and cowboys, as well as a collector of cowboy songs, he and Siringo got along famously. Thus shortly after Siringo moved into his "Den" on Eleanor Avenue, Knibbs paid him a call, and invited him to a social gathering at his home. Later, Siringo was invited to join Knibbs and others to lunch at the University Club.[17]

There western novelist W. C. Tuttle, from Montana, introduced Siringo to Eugene Manlove Rhodes, a respected novelist whose short stories for the *Saturday Evening Post* had made him one of the most popular yet serious western writers of his time.[18] Years before, Harry Knibbs had met Rhodes while both were living in the East and came to admire him so much that Rhodes became a literary mentor to Knibbs. When Rhodes left the East and moved to his own ranch in the San Andres Mountains in New Mexico, Knibbs visited him there and fell in love with the New Mexican ranching life. In his later years, Rhodes, troubled by ill health, moved to San Diego but was often in Los Angeles, where he and Knibbs saw one another all the time. The two also shared the Boston firm of Houghton Mifflin as their publisher. Indeed, Knibbs eventually published twelve of his novels and five of his six books of poetry with Houghton Mifflin, whereas nearly all of Rhodes's writings bore their imprint.[19]

Through Knibbs, Siringo also got to know Charles F. Lummis, who had not only lived in the Southwest, but through his writings had introduced the story of Hispanics and Indians living there to the nation at large. After many years of wandering and adventures, Lummis settled in Los Angeles, where he became a crusader devoted to preserving Hispanic and Indian cultures, maintained a literary salon of budding writers, among them Mary Austin, and became the editor of *Out West* and *Sunset Magazine*.[20]

Henry Knibbs admired Lummis almost to the point of idol worship. Indeed, he eventually divorced his first wife after many years of marriage, in order to marry Lummis's daughter, Turbese. The boundless affection he had for his father-in-law, whom he called Don Carlos, is expressed in a note to Lummis on September 12, 1922, when the latter was ill. "We want you to get on your feet again. We need you. And we need many more similar institutions. There are so few survivals of native hospitality and entertainment in this god-awful time of high speed and low mentality."[21]

Knibbs then told Lummis he had written a verse to him "printed in my new book, *Saddle Songs*," and had printed upon the same page— "'To Dr. Charles F. Lummis.' The book itself is dedicated to Gene Rhodes. Through Rhodes I met you. Through you I met *you*. And the Saddle is cinched with a double-rig to the Pegasus of the sage brush."[22]

Although Siringo was taken to visit Lummis at his famous South Pasadena home, he never knew him well. Through Knibbs, however, he did get to meet and befriend E. A. Brininstool, the incredibly vigorous reporter who, in addition to working for three Los Angeles newspapers, wrote more than five thousand poems about cowboys and ranch life.[23] Brininstool became such a good friend of Charlie's that he attended Siringo's funeral, served as a pallbearer, and wrote a moving obituary of Siringo for the *Los Angeles Times* on October 21, 1928.[24] Siringo so enjoyed Brininstool we learn that Charlie invited him to lunch on occasion, although Brininstool must have picked up the tab, because Charlie had no money. Brininstool was also a good photographer who took pictures of Siringo when his last book, *Riata and Spurs*, was published.[25]

Meanwhile Knibbs was making his own reputation as a screenwriter. Three of his screenplays were made into films and two had remakes later, all while he was writing novels and stories for magazines. It is possible that Knibbs helped get Siringo a bit part in a western film. As Charlie reported to Renehan in July 1924, "for the past three days I have acted cowboy in a picture play called 'Nine Scars Make a Man.' I went into it as an extra to earn some 'Eatin' Money.'"[26]

The two most famous members of Knibbs's circle, however, were William S. Hart and Will Rogers. The former called on Siringo in his Den, and gave him a bit part in one of his films. They continued to see one another and eventually Hart hired Siringo to advise him on his last and greatest film, *Tumbleweeds*, about which we shall hear more later.

Will Rogers (1879–1935) was nationally known during the 1920s and 1930s as the "cowboy philosopher" who, in addition to being a stage performer and western movie actor, wrote a column for national newspapers in which he commented on the Roaring Twenties, the foibles of politicians, and the Depression of 1929. As a young man he was as adventurous as Siringo, Tom Mix, and Jack Thorp. He ran away from his father's Oklahoma ranch to be a cowboy in the Texas Panhandle. Then in 1902 he went to Argentina, and later to South Africa where, as Don Cusic tells us, "he began to appear in Texas Jack's Wild West Circus as 'The Cherokee Kid' rope artist and bronco buster." Rogers was part Cherokee and was proud of his Indian forebears.

After visiting Australia he later performed at the St. Louis World's Fair in 1904, which Siringo attended. Rogers began his career in New York doing horse and rope tricks accompanied by such humorous monologues that some critics claimed he was the true successor to Mark Twain. So successful was he in New York, and especially in the Ziegfeld

Follies, he did not move to Hollywood until 1925, where he became a folksy star in both western and non-western films—altogether in some fifteen movies. Just as he was at the height of his career as performer, actor, and national columnist, he was tragically killed in an airplane crash while touring Alaska in 1935.[27]

Besides old friends like Jack Cole, still other well-known artists and writers often joined the Knibbs social gatherings or University Club lunches, among them Will James (1892–1942), who had been a cowboy on "ranches in the United States and Canada, had captured wild horses in Nevada, entered rodeo competitions, and was a stunt rider for a number of Hollywood westerns."[28] Even so, James could boast, which he never did, of two other careers. In 1926 he wrote *Smoky*, "one of the all time favorite animal stories for children." While his reputation is that of an author writing for juveniles, three years before *Smoky* appeared, James wrote a heavily autobiographical novel, *Cowboys, North and South*, which demonstrated his talent for colloquial western prose, which as James K. Folsom has observed, was "closer to spoken than to written English."[29] Yet that book appeared only after he had begun another career: that of a painter and illustrator. Sometime after 1920 he studied art in San Francisco, and was soon hired by *Sunset Magazine*, which meant that he knew Charles Lummis, to produce illustrations. Both James's stories and his drawings appeared in other magazines, such as *Scribner's Monthly* and the *Saturday Evening Post*. Meanwhile he wrote two nonfiction books, *The Drifting Cowboy* (1925) and *Cow Country* (1927). When James died in 1942 he had become one of the most respected "chroniclers of cowboy life" in America.[30]

As if two good artists, Cole and James, in the circle were not enough, who should appear on the Los Angeles scene in the mid-1920s but the famed Montana painter, Charles Marion Russell (1864–1926), and his loving but tough and practical-minded wife, Nancy? Russell's superb western paintings rivaled those of Frederic Remington. Charlie and Nancy Russell, obviously attracted to the glamour of Hollywood and western films, moved to Pasadena, where he maintained a studio for a brief time. Siringo soon befriended the Russells, who sometimes volunteered to take him to parties in their car.[31]

Russell must have felt comfortable in Los Angeles in that he had met Bill Hart in 1902 when the latter was touring Montana in a play. Not only did they become good friends, Hart boasts that "I was one of those who induced him to come to New York and meet all the artists. It was the opening of his splendid career."[32] A few years later Russell painted a portrait of Hart, "riding a bronco through the sagebrush." Hart's admiration for Russell was so great, the actor's ranch house in Newhallville, California, "was essentially a museum with paintings by Charlie Russell and James Montgomery Flagg."[33] Will Rogers was also such an admirer of Russell that in 1929, when a volume of Russell's illustrated letters appeared under the title *Good Medicine*, Rogers wrote the introduction to the book.[34]

As noted earlier, because Henry Knibbs was a friend of Charlie's lawyer and dear friend, Alois Renehan, Siringo soon began receiving invitations to the Knibbses' gatherings. One can only imagine his joy as he talked to Hart and Rogers, discussed horses with Knibbs, some of whose best poems were about horses, and Will James, whose understanding of horses was incredible. E. A. Brininstool was a storehouse of knowledge about cowboy history and poetry, and Eugene Manlove Rhodes swapped stories with Siringo about their New Mexico ranching experiences. Indeed, Rhodes developed a special bond with Siringo because he felt his and Siringo's early cowboy experiences were practically identical.

In particular Hart and Siringo's friendship got off to a great start in late April 1925 when Hart visited Siringo at his Den twice. As Charlie reported to Renehan,

> the first time to ask if I needed money to live on, and the last time, just before he started for New York, to bring me a full set of eight of the books he has written—all autographed. With the books came a great bottle of imported wine—that is imported from his ranch at Newhall in Calif., where it has been (resting?) since 1918. I told the big hearted six-footer that I didn't need money bad enough to accept it now, but that the day might come when I would call on him. That the fact of his offering it to me, was worth more than the money would be.[35]

Meanwhile Hart had decided to produce a movie called *Tumbleweeds*, based on a story of the same name written by Hal G. Evarts for *The Saturday Evening Post*.[36] The film was based on the Oklahoma Land Rush of 1893, which Siringo had actually witnessed while in

Caldwell, Kansas, on a Pinkerton case. Knowing of Siringo's familiarity with Caldwell and the Rush, he asked Charlie to serve as a consultant.

Charlie was close to ecstatic with joy, writing Renehan he said he had to get dental work done so that he could eat "when I go out in the woods with Bill Hart to help put on a new play—'The Tumble Weed,' a story on the opening of Oklahoma. Bill Hart wants me with him to give his director some pointers, and to work as an extra." The film was so faithful to the story, which included scenes of Caldwell, Kansas, it is said an entire Caldwell set was built on Siringo's advice.[37]

On October 3, 1925, Siringo wrote Renehan, "Have just finished seven weeks work in Wm. S. Hart's picture 'Tumble-Weeds,' which is the opening of the Cherokee strip of Oklahoma to settlement in 1893. The scene is laid at Caldwell, Kansas, my old stamping ground. My work in the play was easy and the money earned proved a God-send."[38] Released by United Artists, this was Hart's last and probably greatest film, and yet it was one in which, as in his earlier films, he defeats the villain's attempt to steal both the land and Hart's girl.[39]

Nearly five months later, Siringo, accompanied by William E. Hawks, his old friend from Vermont, saw *Tumbleweeds*. He wrote to Hart at once to offer his congratulations. "I have been boiling over with enthusiasm. You and King Baggott [the Director] deserve congratulations."

Siringo then said that he had attended many western movies in Hollywood before he saw *Tumbleweeds*, "But for a thriller which penetrates through to the heart, the Tumbleweeds has got it skinned a mile, each way from the center." Siringo added that he had a right to say this "as I have been in the Saddle, and on the scene of action, since 1867, from the Gulf of Mexico to the British possessions on the North."

Siringo also described his friend William Hawks's reaction to the movie. "By nature Mr. Hawks is a little cold-blooded, and it takes a lot to get him stirred up to a high pitch, but the Tumbleweeds did it to the Queen's taste. The people around us seemed equally enthused. One little girl, the daughter of our friend, Ben N. Powers, got worked up to a high pitch, and insisted on seeing the play again at night. This shows that the young as well as the old get a kick out of the play."[40]

Meanwhile Siringo had already met with Dr. Henry Hoyt, who soon became his personal physician, for Siringo was still troubled by a debilitating cough. Other Santa Feans who had moved to Los Angeles held "reunion" picnics to which they invited Charlie. Equally pleasing were Jack Cole's invitations and that of other prominent residents who had known Siringo many years before and wanted to "hark back" to old times with him.⁴¹

Perhaps the most extraordinary reunion occurred in 1925 when it was discovered that Dr. A. M. Pelton, who had treated Siringo when he was shot in the knee while a cowboy in South Texas in 1875, was now living in the Los Angeles area. Pelton was so delighted to meet his old patient after a half a century that he gave his story to the newspapers, and some years after Siringo's death it was also published in *True West*, a Texas magazine devoted to western stories.⁴²

Siringo's social success was more than countered by the fact that he was desperately short of cash. Although he had earned a bit working with Hart, he was, in effect, virtually destitute. Even so, he had not stopped writing. He had already written the draft of a book entitled "Bad Man Cowboys of the Early West," which he submitted to the Yale University Press, which rejected it. The *Saturday Evening Post* also rejected one of his articles.

Then came a breakthrough. Undoubtedly at the suggestion of Harry Knibbs, Houghton Mifflin was reviewing Siringo's books to see if any could be republished. As early as 1926, Harry Knibbs himself suggested that Siringo write the full story of his life and submit it to the Houghton Mifflin Press in Boston. Instead Charlie wrote Ferris Greenslet, Houghton Mifflin's editor-in-chief, about his "Bad Men of the West." In turn Greenslet asked his assistant editor, Ira Rich Kent, to read all of Siringo's books, which they asked Charlie to send them.⁴³

Then in March 1926, Greenslet wrote Siringo acknowledging receipt of the books, leaving Charlie with the mistaken impression that they might publish all of them. A week later, however, Greenslet wrote to Siringo to propose a single book of a hundred thousand words, saying that as an autobiography it could bring more and be illustrated by a very good western artist such as Will James or Russell, and be sold at four or five dollars. On March 31st, Siringo shared this information with Renehan, saying that Houghton Mifflin wanted him to do a new book for them called *Riata and Spurs*, the firm explaining that they "couldn't publish a Cowboy Detective owing to the fight we had with the Pinkertons, and the fact that J. S. Ogilvie and Co. are getting it out in two volumes to sell cheaply on trains." Siringo was so excited he told Renehan he had gotten nine chapters of the *Riata and Spurs* book completed and hoped to do more soon. He had done this by combining pages taken from his *Lone Star Cowboy* and *A Cowboy Detective*.[44]

Knowing that it would be his last big hurrah, Siringo wanted John Hays Hammond, the world-famous mining engineer whom Charlie had met in the Coeur d'Alene strike, to write an introduction, and he much preferred Charlie Russell be the illustrator for it. As he wrote Greenslet, he felt that Charlie Russell "is the one artist who punched long horn cattle and saw wild buffalos in the early days. Hence he could draw them true to life, and not from imagination, as Will James would have to do."[45] In the end neither Hammond nor Russell agreed to help Siringo. Charlie then invited Governor Gifford Pinchot of Pennsylvania to write a foreword, for not only had the two met in Boise, Idaho, during the Haywood trial, they continued to correspond and Pinchot himself paid a call on Siringo in 1925 when he was visiting Los Angeles.[46]

Writing *Riata and Spurs* proceeded at such a fast pace that in early May he had mailed nine chapters to Houghton Mifflin and continued writing the last chapters. In Boston Ira Rich Kent realized that it needed much editing and was concerned that many episodes were reported without any context. However, he was able to persuade Charlie to add background and detail to some of the famous detective cases. The firm was also not especially pleased with the choice of Pinchot to write the foreword and they decided to cut costs by opting for photographs rather than illustrations.[47]

It is unclear whether Charlie was aware of it or not, but from the start of his relationship with Houghton Mifflin, no one was a more ardent and eloquent supporter than Eugene Manlove Rhodes. In a February 15, 1926, letter while he was visiting in New York state, Rhodes wrote Ferris Greenslet to say:

> It warms the cockles of my heart to think that you
> may take on Charlie Siringo. You couldn't do better...
> *The Yale Review* has reprinted Capt. Gillett's "SIX YEARS
> AS A TEXAS RANGER," and Cook's "FIFTY YEARS
> ON THE FRONTIER," with gratifying results. . . .
> Did you read Siringo's "A TEXAS COWBOY"? There
> is a human document, if there ever was one. No posing;
> the truth, the whole truth, and nothing but the truth. . . .

Ask Andy Adams. And you would never believe how
many people had read that book.... A curious sub-public,
for a large part that is hard to reach.... All I fear is that
in later editions, he may have edited, in light of experience,
and destroyed the naivete of his sprightly youth....
Greenslet, that was my youth, or rather my boyhood,
the place and time of which he writes; those were the
companions of my wild noon.[48]

Rhodes went on to explain that "I have lived *two* separate and dis-
tinct lives." Referring to his friend and fellow rancher Howard (Jack)
Thorp's book, *Tales of the Chuck Wagon*, which came out in 1926, he
said, "Thorp's book, too, left me wild with delight and with grief. I knew
nineteen of every twenty men he mentions. Len Brennan (page 11 or 13)
was in the first story I ever wrote. Knew them! I worked, ate, slept,
fought and sinned with them.... And there is no bond so close as this
last.... If you reprint 'A Texas Cowboy' I do here and eagerly put in my
order for the first copy."[49]

Only nine days later Rhodes wrote Greenslet again, this time
enclosing three accounts that he called

three bits of simon-pure westernism, the which I make bold
to hope you will enjoy. *Please return....* Self evidently
these go to you largely to see how Adams and Siringo
stand in the minds of men who know, with the bit about
Gillett's book to emphasize what a hit had been made of
an unknown book, time and chance favoring; whereas,
if you were told how many copies of Siringo's first (and
best) book had been sold, you probably would have your
doubts. Paper bound, you know, poor type, poor paper,
and all the faults known, with some fine new ones—but
with it, the first fine careless rapture, and the very voice
of youth.[50]

Based on clues in his note, the accounts Rhodes sent Greenslet
appear to have been by J. Frank Dobie, William McLeod Raine, and
Andy Adams. Worried that he had pressed Greenslet too much about
publishing a Siringo book, he signed the letter "Buttinsky."[51]

As Siringo's book neared publication a year later, unknown to him, Gene Rhodes also wrote Mr. Dale Warren of the Houghton Mifflin Company explaining that

> Because I know local conditions in the Southwest as you can hardly know them, let me suggest that you get Mr. Dobie to review Siringo's book in Dallas, [the] Galveston News or elsewhere; and also to get his ideas as to San Antonio Express, the Pioneer, and The Frontier Times as publicity for Siringo. The last two reach *all old timers*—the many men who would buy a copy if they had to borrow the money to buy it. For myself, I am taking it upon that same person to try to get Will Rogers to review Siringo's book for the N.Y. Times. He is busy night and day, so I judge he will find a time. I figure that a review by Rogers would carry more authority than one by any other, living or dead: and, Mrs. Rogers helping me, I do believe that we can coax Will to lose a little sleep for the credit of the High Country, where he and Siringo were young together—only that Siringo is about 25 years older of the two.[52]

In March, Rhodes wrote Ira Kent, the editor who had overseen the publication of Siringo's *Riata and Spurs*, in which he reported: "Am doing sketch of Charlie Siringo for Greenslet: Never more interested in my life than in seeing his book go over the top. Siringo steps out of Plutarch's pages to us. No man alive—and few dead—with such wealth of experience."[53]

Meanwhile in Los Angeles everyone was already celebrating Charlie's achievement. Harry Knibbs gave a party honoring Charlie, which both the Russells and the Jameses attended. But delays of many kinds interfered before the book finally appeared. Charlie himself became so ill with his cough in September 1926, his son, Lee Roy, persuaded him to move to Altadena, where he lived, so that he and his wife could take care of him, and where the climate was drier. Charlie finally moved to a small bungalow in Altadena in November. During the late fall, Ira Kent continued to press Charlie for more personal details of his marriages and family. Kent was also worried that the Pinkertons' earlier refusal to allow their names to be used in Siringo's previous books might cause trouble regarding *Riata and Spurs*. Indeed, Charlie had reminded Greenslet at the outset of his troubles with the Pinkertons. Later Kent twice reminded his own boss about this issue, but the latter seems to have ignored the warning.[54]

Once the manuscript was submitted, it was time for a second celebration, and so in January 1927, a party of old-timers gathered at Siringo's Altadena Den to raise their glasses. Present were Jack Cole, Will James and his wife, Emmett Dalton, Major Gordon W. Lillie (Pawnee Bill), and about a half-dozen others.[55]

Determined to gain as much publicity as possible for his new book, he wrote his friend, Neeta Marquis (1862–1957), a California poet and author who published articles about famous people from all over the nation, often in the *Los Angeles Times*. As early as 1924 she had invited Siringo to speak to her writers' group but he was not free. In the fall of 1926, however, he finally accepted, flattering her with the comment: "Thanks for putting me down as an honored guest, I am liable to get the Swell-head over such honor being showered onto my old head." At the same time he urged her to plug his forthcoming book, *Riata and Spurs*, in a *Times* article.[56]

In a later note promising to attend her writers' meeting, he urged her to invite Will James and his "interesting wife," and Jack Cole, the artist, even to giving Marquis the latter's address and telephone number. To stimulate her interest, he enclosed a copy of Governor Gifford Pinchot's foreword to the book. In the following weeks he deluged her with an account of the party he had given at his Altadena Den and information about securing photographs of the persons who were there.[57]

On March 23rd he wrote Marquis a hasty note saying, "Have been too sick to write you. Have been down for over a week. Am straining every nerve to be able to attend the Houghton Mifflin Co. dinner at the Alexander on the eve of March 25. Will have the rifle that wounded Billy the Kid. . . . Bill Hart will be there with the pistol that shot Billy the Kid into fame. Tom Power of El Paso may be there with the Pat Garrett pistol which killed the kid."[58]

Shortly before *Riata and Spurs* was to appear, Harrison Leussler, the energetic Houghton Mifflin representative in California, hosted a banquet at the Alexandria Hotel in Los Angeles. As the local papers of March 26, 1927, reported, joining Siringo at the head table were

Leussler; William S. Hart; Harry Knibbs; the writer James Schultz; W. C. Tuttle, the western writer from Montana; and the well-known Sioux Indian Chief, Luther Standing Bear, who was about to publish a book, *My People the Sioux*, with Houghton Mifflin. Bill Hart, who in his peripatetic youth had learned Sioux, gave a speech in the Sioux language, which Luther Standing Bear then translated into English! Standing Bear had actually co-starred with Hart in films, so they were old friends, but the scene, by itself, must have been electric.⁵⁹

Following that performance, Siringo and Jim Schultz used sign language to engage in a conversation. Then finally Siringo rose to tell the audience of his experiences with Billy the Kid. As he did so he held in one hand the actual Winchester rifle that had wounded the Kid in one of the latter's many confrontations. The climax came when Siringo, using one of Billy's own guns—now owned by Bill Hart—whipped it out with lightning speed, startling the audience. Although ill, gaunt-eyed, and hollowed-cheeked, Siringo was dressed as a cowboy with a gun; and according to the papers made a tremendous impression.⁶⁰ It was truly ironic that Siringo, who knew but never chased Billy the Kid, and who had spent twenty-two years as a detective reputedly without ever having killed a man, should have succumbed to both Hollywood's Billy the Kid cult and the gun cult.

In the days after the banquet, Siringo must have thought he was in heaven. Mrs. Betty Rogers, Will's wife, called on him, and then he received a letter from Rogers himself—who was camping in Montana—praising *Riata and Spurs*. Unknown to Siringo, Houghton Mifflin had followed up Rhodes's suggestion to ask Rogers to write a tribute to the book. The letter was so moving it deserves a quotation in full.

Dear Charlie,
Somebody in some town gave me the proof sheets of your book and wanted to know what I think of it. I think the same of it as I do the first Cowboy Book I ever read: "Fifteen Years on the Hurricane Deck of a Spanish Pony." Why, that was the Cowboy's Bible when I was growing up.

I camped with a herd one night at the old L.X. Ranch, just north of Amarillo in '98 and they showed us an old forked tree where some Bronk had bucked you into. Why, that to us was like looking at the shrine of Shakespeare is to some of

these "deep foreheads." Well, this one you have written now is
just what that was then. Why, if you live to be a thousand
years old, you couldn't write a bad book about the Cowboys.
The stuff they did might be bad, but you could tell it so well it
would almost sound respectable. My Lord! With Western stuff
being written by Soda Jerkers and Manicure Girls, there must
be millions who would like to read the straight facts if they
could find the book that had them.

This is to tell the world that your Riata and Spurs *is IT.*
I hope to see you this summer. Will be home all summer.
Where is Gene Rhoades [sic]—and Dane Coolidge? I am
heading across Montana next week, but I make towns
every night to camp in.

I got your picture of you and Pawnee Bill. Use this
about the book any way you want if it is any good to you,
for I sure mean it.

Visited the old L.X. Ranch when in Amarillo lately.
The corral is full of oil wells.

(signed) *Will Rogers*[61]

Given Houghton Mifflin's careful editing and vigorous promotion, the initial issue of *Riata and Spurs* sold 3500 copies and received favorable reviews from East Coast newspapers, and the two distinguished Texans, Walter Prescott Webb and J. Frank Dobie. Then in May his old nemesis, the Pinkerton Agency, told Houghton Mifflin that given the fact they had used the firm's name without permission in the detective chapters, the book had to be suppressed. Despite diplomatic overtures and explanations by Ferris Greenslet, the Pinkerton lawyers were unrelenting. As a result Houghton Mifflin was forced to delete over one hundred pages after page 120 of *Riata and Spurs*, but in a heroic effort substituted Siringo's manuscript of "Bad Man Cowboys of the Early West" in the yawning gap. They brought out the revised edition mid-October 1927. Ironically, the book continued to sell and Charlie himself appears to have been pleased with the new version.[62] Even so the irony of substituting "bad men of the West" for his twenty-two-year-old career as a detective and law man must have depressed him.[63]

What is most impressive is that Houghton Mifflin proved to be so understanding about the whole imbroglio. They knew Charlie was an ill old man, but they were determined to help him. They sent him small advance checks on his royalties to keep him going. And despite very threatening bouts of ill health, he began writing again. This time it was short stories that he hoped *The Saturday Evening Post* or Houghton Mifflin might accept, but that did not happen.

Siringo's persistent optimism led him to return to a project he had had in mind even before he left New Mexico for Hollywood. It was a novel called "Prairie Flower," whose female heroine was named Bronco Chiquita. He actually hoped it could become the basis for a Hollywood screenplay. After *Riata and Spurs* was published, through his friend E. A. Brininstool, he met an ex-Pinkerton detective, Charles Smith, with whom he had worked on several dynamiting cases in Colorado, especially the destruction of the Independence Depot in Cripple Creek, Colorado, in 1904.[64]

With Charlie on that occasion was a pretty, twenty-one-year-old woman, Miss Evelyn Ramey, whom Charlie called "his bodyguard" in a letter to Bill Hart. In the same note he reassured Hart that the yellow cat he had given Charlie was being cared for by Bronco Chiquita after Charlie had to move to Long Beach to be nearer his physician, Dr. Hoyt. In this case Bronco Chiquita was actually Miss Ramey.[65]

Determined to publish his novel, he sent it to Ferris Greenslet at Houghton Mifflin, who through his diplomatic assistant editor, Ira Kent, declined to publish it.

Never one to limit himself to a single project, Siringo tried his hand at writing a series of short stories based on his own past experiences, called "Flashes from a Cowboy's Pen." In the end he failed to find a western magazine that would serialize them, but ever the optimist, he decided to turn them into a book. Meanwhile Charlie's health steadily got worse. Even so, he still dreamed of building a "Cabin on Wheels" to follow and mark the Chisholm Trail. Because the cabin was to be a small truck, Bill Hart humorously referred to it as his "smoke wagon on wheels."[66]

Then in a flash everything changed. On April 20, 1928, his closest friend and advisor, Alois B. Renehan, died suddenly while on a trip east. After Charlie moved to California the two men had become even closer. Charlie sent him frequent news of his life in Hollywood, and sought his legal advice constantly. When he became convinced that the writer Walter Noble Burns, who had published a popular biography of Billy the Kid in 1926, was guilty of stealing passages and sentences from his own biography of the Kid, Renehan patiently pursued the issue with Burns's publisher but to no avail.[67]

Not only was Charlie's spirit broken by the news of Renehan's death, Dr. Hoyt found that Siringo's severe bronchitis had worn him out, and that he was so frail he warned Charlie's son, Lee Roy, that there was nothing more he could do—the end was near. Lee Roy, a successful businessman, responded by offering Siringo two rooms in his own Altadena house. However, Siringo was now in a centrally located new apartment house owned by George Cole that allowed him to entertain his friends, so he only reluctantly accepted his son's offer in late August.[68]

On October 8, 1928, Siringo died of a heart attack at the age of seventy-three. When the funeral was held, his faithful friends, Harry Knibbs, Jack Cole, and E. A. Brininstool attended. Unable to be there, Will Rogers and Bill Hart sent a moving telegram from New York: "Another American plainsman has taken the long trail. May flowers always grow over his grave."[69]

✦   ✦

What seemed so remarkable is that Charlie Siringo had only come to Hollywood in 1923–1924, but by 1927 he had befriended a truly exceptional set of talented and able people who knew and loved the cowboy West and thus respected his career and writings. They did so in part because the whole of America was in love with Hollywood's production of westerns and with such colorful figures as Billy the Kid. Meanwhile, Hollywood's obsession with cowboys, outlaws, and the West grew over the next forty years, beginning in the case of Billy the Kid, with Johnny Mack Brown, who played the lead in the first Billy the Kid film in 1930, to be followed by others right into the 1940s and 1950s. Siringo's surrender to the story of outlaws, and Billy the Kid, after a life of chasing criminals is very troubling. Was he cynically writing to sell? Was he overwhelmed with Hollywood's obsession with guns and violence? Was he naive and gullible—seeking approbation by pleasing?

Despite having written seven books about himself, Charlie Siringo remains a hard man to explain or categorize. He was a crack shot with the Colt 45 but never used it to kill as a detective. He was a superb cowboy but never succeeded at ranching; he was a brilliant, clever detective, a master of disguise, but in a fit of anger as expressed in *Two Evil Isms*, he foolishly made a lifelong enemy of his former employer, the Pinkerton Agency. J. Frank Dobie said of him that he was not thought but action, and certainly his naiveté about money and his unhappy marriages make him seem more simple than he was. His biographer, Charles D. Peavy, tried to explain Charlie's adventurous nature by calling him "A Texas Pícaro." Ben Pingenot, who best understood Siringo, was certainly on target when he concluded that Siringo and Bill Hart were hopelessly romantic and sentimental.

J. Evetts Haley and Jack Thorp, on the other hand, found him an invaluable source for the cowboy West, which another biographer, Orlan Sawey, confirmed when he found that Siringo had been constantly cited in other books about his era in the West. He also thought that this unlettered Texas wrote prose that told us how regular Texas-Americans talked. Sawey's impression of a primitive Texan misses the point. Over a span of forty-two years Siringo had published seven books, four of which were successes: *A Texas Cowboy*, *A Cowboy Detective*, *Lone Star Cowboy*, and *Riata and Spurs*. In the process he became not only a historian of the cowboy and bad men, but an articulate writer.

His letters to Alois Renehan and William S. Hart are extraordinarily succinct, largely grammatically correct (with an occasional misspelling), and exhibit a compelling logic. Echoing his remarkable Pinkerton Reports he was exceptionally accurate and factual. Yet his real forte was that of a professional storyteller, both in his books and to his friends in Hollywood and elsewhere. That careful timing of the punch line and his confidence in what he was saying tells us that he was an effective author-historian.[70]

Even so, none of these comments really explain Siringo himself. After more than a quarter century of studying Siringo and trying to understand him, I have come to some firm conclusions about this curious, mesmeric man. The first is that he was incredibly ambitious. His dream was to be successful at whatever he did: through remarkable physical feats of horsemanship, roping, bronco-busting, driving cattle, or sharp-shooting. He could have been a rodeo star. That athletic side of his personality never left him.

A second aspect of his ambition was to move on once he had mastered one skill or career. As modest as they may seem to us in retrospect, in addition to being a cowboy in two very different areas of Texas, he tried to be a fur trapper, became a successful merchant, and was a brilliant

Pinkerton detective. The latter was his most satisfying career, for Siringo was a born actor, and as a detective he could playact to his heart's content.

Ironically his playacting probably prevented him from ever settling into marriage after his first wife, Mamie, whom he adored, died while very young. He was most at home in the male world, and in that world he found his father-image heroes: Shanghai and Jonathan Pierce, David Beals, James McParland, Jim East, Alois Renehan, and in the end, William S. Hart and Will Rogers, although Harry Knibbs and Eugene Rhodes were far more true father figures than he fully realized, for he thought he was using them.

Just how much the Hollywood literati admired and respected him as a remarkable man and an original resource is demonstrated by Eugene Rhodes in an article he wrote about Siringo for Charles F. Lummis for *Sunset Magazine* in June 1927.[71] Entitled "He'll Make a Hand," it read:

> Faded brown eyes, but sharp eyes that never miss the
> slightest movement of any person or anything. Not
> nervous, but always alert. A thin face, brown like
> saddle leather; wind and sun have tanned that face
> beyond all changing. Most expressive hands; thumbs
> which fill out and picture forth the story as he talks;
> a trigger finger that sticks out with every gesture.
> Fascinating forefinger. You can't take your eyes
> from it. Thin lipped; a mouth that would be hard
> if it were not for an occasional quirk of humor.
> Quite a frank smile, and often a chuckle. Not a tall
> man; slender—yes frail. You note this with a shock;
> listening, not once had you thought of him as a small
> man or as an old man. A small head, a boy's head.
> And he is a boy, full of mischief and keen fun. Looks
> right at you when you talk, but always notices what
> anyone else happens to be doing. . . . Small feet.
> Corded throat. . . . Carries a loaded cane; polished
> steer-horn tips on a steel rod, probably made for
> him in a penitentiary. Wears a small red silk handkerchief,
> a low-crowned Stetson, neat clothing and shoes; not boots.
> Straight back; does not stoop; head carried like Chanticleer.

How he befriended these remarkable people in Hollywood in only four years and how they saw to it that his last book was published is the exciting untold story of Siringo's last days. It was not only the climax of his career, it tells us of a ruthless Siringo we had not fully seen before: in the best tradition of the western hero-protagonist who won over all odds to die recognized and in peace. At the end he had respectful supporters elsewhere in the nation: Alois Renehan, J. Frank Dobie, J. Evetts Haley, Gifford Pinchot, and Jack Thorp. Thus the older image of the old cowboy dying unappreciated must give way to a Siringo who was "with it" to the end.

Charlie Siringo died seventy-six years ago, but the West he knew and loved lives on. Ranching and cattle raising remain a major feature of the American West and its economy.[72] But they flourish even more vigorously in the West of our imagination, in Hollywood, in thousands of novels, and at the annual cowboy poetry convention in Elko, Nevada. There, for decades, as William Kittredge writes, "All over the American West, cowboys and ranch owners and farmhands and sheep herders have been gathering to declaim verse to one another. Such gatherings are heartbreaking in their openness, celebrations of things ranchland people respect and care about most deeply—the land they have chosen to live on, their work, and right at the center, one another, this companionship. We can all take heart from their willingness to name those things they take to be sacred. Their story telling is as useful as anything we have."[73]

Among the enduring western master storytellers is Charlie Siringo, cowboy, detective, author, whose career and writings still live in the psyche of millions of westerners today.

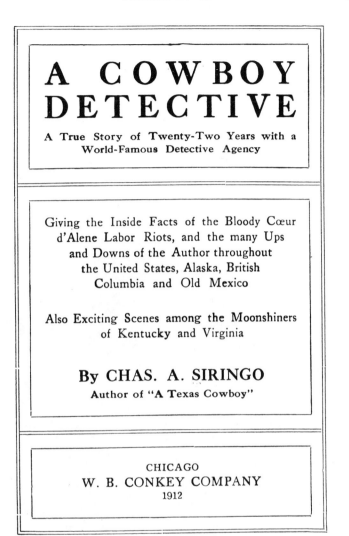

61. Title page of Charles A. Siringo,
A Cowboy Detective *(1912).*

62. *"[Siringo] on his horse Patsy. Roswell, N.Mex., February 15, 1921." Charles A. Siringo*, Riata and Spurs *(1927)*.

63. Will Rogers and Charlie Russell. Courtesy of the Britzman Collection, Taylor Museum, Colorado Springs Fine Arts Center.

64. *William Roderick "Will" James, cowboy, author, and illustrator, whom Siringo befriended in Los Angeles in the mid-1920s. Photograph taken in Canada in 1911. Courtesy of the Glenbow Archives, Calgary, Alberta.*

65. *William S. Hart and Charlie Siringo on the set of* Tumbleweeeds, *possibly Hart's best film. Hart had asked Siringo to advise him on sets that represented Caldwell, Kansas, where Siringo had lived from 1882 to 1885 and which he had visited during the famous Oklahoma Land Rush of 1893. Courtesy of the Seaver Center for Western History Research, Natural History Museum of Los Angeles County.*

STIRRING DAYS WHEN SIX-SHOOTERS RULED WEST RECALLED

Once a part of the old West and now writing books and stories of that rapidly vanishing phase of American life, a group of western authors met last night at a dinner given at the Alexandria under the auspices of Houghton Mifflin Company, Boston book publishers.

More than 100 book sellers and authors were present and a novel program was presented. Big Bill Hart, western screen actor, gave a talk in the Sioux tongue that was interpreted by Chief Standing Bear, while James W. Shultz and Charley Sirengo, former New Mexico Sheriff and now a western story writer, conversed in sign language. Citizens of Santa Fe, N. M., wired congratulations to Sirengo on the occasion and Eugene Manlove Rhodes, well-known author, telegraphed regrets that he was unable to attend. The dinner was presided over by Harrison Leussler, western representative of the Houghton Mifflin Company.

Photograph below, reading from left to right, shows: Dr. W. A. Hoyt, W. C. Tuttle, James W. Shultz, Harrison Leussler, Charles A. Sirengo, William S. Hart, Henry H. Knibbs and Chief Standing Bear.

66. *When Siringo's last book*, Riata and Spurs, *was published in 1927 by Houghton-Mifflin, the publisher sponsored a banquet in his honor at the Alexandria Hotel.* The Los Angeles Times, *March 26, 1927, [pt II, p. 9] recorded the event in the headline "Stirring Days When Six-Shooters Ruled West Recalled" and the above photograph accompanied a brief article. His guests at the head table were (from left): Dr. H. F. Hoyt, W. C. Tuttle, James W. Shultz, Harrison Leussler (Houghton-Mifflin California representative), Charlie Siringo, William S. Hart, Henry H. Knibbs, and Chief Standing Bear. The newspaper article noted "a novel program was presented. Big Bill Hart, western screen actor, gave a talk in the Sioux tongue that was interpreted by Chief Standing Bear, while James W. Shultz and Charley Sirengo [sic], former New Mexico Sheriff and now a western story writer, conversed in sign language." Clipping in Charles A. Siringo Papers, 1896–1928 (AC212), Museum of New Mexico, Fray Angelico Chavez History Library.*

67. *Eugene Manlove Rhodes. Huntington Library,*
   San Marino, California.

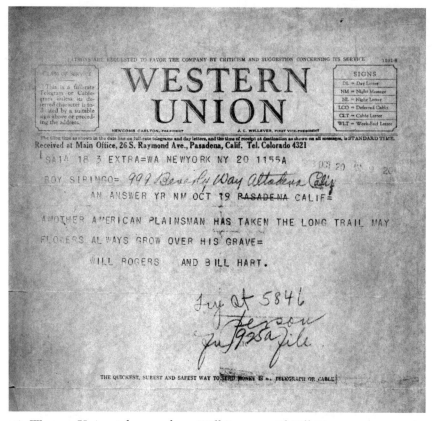

68. *Western Union telegram from Will Rogers and Bill Hart on the occasion of Charlie Siringo's death on October 18, 1928. Courtesy Mrs. William J. McFarland, Siringo's granddaughter, sent to author as a gift in July 1976.*

Notes

CHAPTER ONE

1. Charles Siringo, *A Texas Cowboy, or Fifteen Years on the Hurricane Deck of a Spanish Pony, Taken from Real Life by Charles Siringo, an Old Stove Up "Cow Puncher" Who Has Spent Nearly Twenty Years on the Great Western Cattle Ranches* (Chicago: M. Umbdenstock & Company, Publishers, 1885). Siringo's original volume has been reprinted many times, but the most informative and inclusive edition was published by the University of Nebraska Press in 1966 and as a Bison Book reprinted in paperback in 1979. It contains a valuable and critical introduction by J. Frank Dobie as well as an "Addenda" Siringo wrote on the stock business taken from the 1886 edition. The 1979 Nebraska reprint is the most accessible to the public, and has been used throughout as a reference in this volume. See *A Texas Cowboy* (1979), 7–8.

2. Siringo, *A Texas Cowboy*, 10; Mary B. Ingram, chief compiler, "The County," in Matagorda County Historical Commission, *Historic Matagorda County* (Houston: D. Armstrong Company, Inc,. 1986–88), I: 1–4; "Matagorda County," in *The New Handbook of Texas* (Austin: The State Historical Association, 1966) 4, 556; "Matagorda Peninsula," 560; "Caney Creek," idem, 1, 959–60.

3. *A Texas Cowboy*, 8, 16–17; Rockette L. Woolridge, "Here Come the Herds to Matagorda," *Texas Historian*, January 1975; Matagorda County Historical Commission, *Historic Matagorda County*, I: 241.

4. Matagorda County Historical Commission, *Historic Matagorda County*, I: 175–78.

5. Charles A. Siringo, *The Song Companion of A Lone Star Cowboy* (Santa Fe, 1919).

6. See note 1 for full citation.

7. Rogers to Siringo, March 27, 1927, quoted in full in Ben E. Pingenot, *Siringo* (College Station: Texas A&M University Press, 1989), 121. The original letter is in Houghton Mifflin Company Records in the Houghton Library, Harvard University, Cambridge, Massachusetts.

8. J. Frank Dobie, "Introduction," in *A Texas Cowboy*, xxxv.

9. Siringo's incredible career as a master detective for the Pinkerton Agency is detailed in his *A Cowboy Detective: A True Story of Twenty-Two Years with a World-Famous Detective Agency* (Chicago: W. B. Conkey Company, 1912).

10. Ibid., 7; Pingenot, *Siringo*, xvii–xviii.

11. Matagorda County, Texas Brand Book, vol. 1, Antonio Siringo Brand, AS, recorded December, 1850; Catherine Seringo [sic] and her children's brand, CS, recorded October 4, 1855. Record of land sale in Matagorda County Records, sale by George W. H. Smith of Lot 5, Block A, Tier 4, October 2, 1854. Xerox of records in Matagorda county clerk's office now in Matagorda County Museum and Historical Society.

12. *A Texas Cowboy*, 7.

13. Ibid., 9.

14. Ibid.

15. Ibid., 10

16. "Zipprian," in Matagorda County Historical Commission, *Historic Matagorda County*, 1, 106–7.

17. *A Texas Cowboy*, 44.

18. "Karankawa Indians," in *New Handbook of Texas*, 3: 1031–33; William Newcomb, *The Indians of Texas* (Austin: University of Texas Press, 1961); Robert A. Rickles, *The Karankawa Indians of Texas: An Ecological Study of Cultural Tradition and Change* (Austin: University of Texas Press, 1996).
   For a general view of Indians in the Southwest see Howard R. Lamar and Sam Truett, "The Greater Southwest and California from the Beginnings of European Settlement to the 1880s," in *The Cambridge History of the Native Peoples of the Americas*, ed. Bruce G. Trigger and Wilcomb E. Washburn (Cambridge: Cambridge University Press, 1996), vol. 1, Part 2, 62.

19. The truly incredible story of Cabeza de Vaca's experiences among the Texas Indians has now been exhaustively recounted in Rolena Adorno and Patrick Charles Pautz, *Alvar Núñez Cabeza de Vaca: His Account, His Life, and the Expedition of Pánfilo de Narváez* (Lincoln and London: University of Nebraska Press, 1999), in three volumes. See 1: 372–78; 2: 97–351, but especially 172–73, 218–19, 235, 237ff. See also *Cabeza de Vaca's Adventures in the Unknown Interior of America*, translated and annotated by Cyclone Covey (Albuquerque: University of New Mexico Press, 1990), 99–100.

20. "Karankawa Indians," *New Handbook of Texas*, 3: 1031–33.

21. Although the story of La Salle is superbly narrated in Francis Parkman, *La Salle and the Discovery of the Great West* (1910), a modern biography is badly needed. See W. J. Eccles, *The Canadian Frontier, 1534–1760* (New York: Holt, Rinehart, 1969; repr. 1974). A useful summary of La Salle in Texas is in David J. Weber, *The Spanish Frontier in North America* (New Haven: Yale University Press, 1992), 148–52; Robert S.

Weddle, ed., *Wilderness Manhunt: The Spanish Search for La Salle* (Austin: University of Texas Press, 1971); "La Salle Expedition," in *New Handbook of Texas*, 4: 86–87.

22. "La Salle," in *New Encyclopedia of the American West*, ed. Howard R. Lamar (New Haven: Yale University Press, 1998), 619. (Hereafter Lamar, *NEAW*.)

23. Ibid., 619.

24. "La Salle Expedition," in *New Handbook of Texas*, 4: 86; "Talon Children," in idem, 6, 197–98.

25. "Alonzo de Leon," in *New Handbook of Texas*, 2: 570; Weber, *Spanish Frontier*, 151–54, 161.

26. See "Nuestra Señora del Espiritu Santo de Zuñiga Mission," in *New Handbook of Texas*, 4: 1062–64, which contains an extensive bibliography.

27. Ibid., 4: 1072–73; "Karankawa Indians," in idem, 3: 1032–33.

28. The material on Moses and Stephen F. Austin is truly immense, but see the following: Eugene C. Barker, ed., *The Austin Papers* (Washington, D.C.: Government Printing Office, 24–28), 3 vols. David B. Gracey II, *Moses Austin: His Life* (San Antonio: Trinity University Press, 1987); Eugene C. Barker, *The Life of Stephen F. Austin* (Nashville: The Cokesbury Press, 1925, reprinted in 1949 and 1970); an excellent new biography is Gregg Cantrell, *Stephen F. Austin: Empresario of Texas* (New Haven: Yale University Press, 1999). For the location of the Austin Colony, see Cantrell, 8, 93–98, and A. Ray Stephens and William M. Holmes, *Historical Atlas of Texas* (Norman: University of Oklahoma Press, 1989), 22.

29. Cantrell, *Austin*, 87–91.

30. Ibid., 92–94.

31. Lamar and Truett, "The Greater Southwest and California from the Beginning of the European Settlement to the 1880s," 1, Part 2, 81–86.

32. See "Mexican Colonization Laws," in *New Texas Handbook*, 4: 684–85; Cantrell, *Austin*, 174–75, 198–99, 223–24, as well as her discussion of "Colonization Laws," 121–26, 162, 174, 181, and "Land Fees," 99, 152–22, 163, 165, 179, also in *Austin*.

33. Cantrell, *Austin*, 99, 132–33, 175–77, 195–96, 220–21, 89–90, 92, 93, 100, 175, 223–24. "Old Three Hundred," in *New Handbook of Texas*, 4: 1141–42. "S. F. Austin," in idem, 1: 294.

34. "Elias R. Wightman," in *New Handbook of Texas*, 6: 964–95.

35. "Elias R. Wightman," in *Historic Matagorda County*, I: 101–2. "Elias R. Wightman," *New Handbook of Texas*, 6: 964–65.

36. "Hosea H. League," in *New Handbook of Texas*, 4: 128–29.

37. "William Selkirk," in *New Handbook of Texas*, 5: 968.

38. "Thomas J. Tone," in *New Handbook of Texas*, 6: 524–25; "Horace Yeamans Family," in *Historic Matagorda County*, I: 105–6.

39. "John Duncan," in *Historic Matagorda County*, I: 109–13, 129; see also chapters VII, VIII, IX.

40. "Matagorda County," in *New Handbook of Texas*, 4: 557.

41. "Martin de Leon," in *New Handbook of Texas*, 2: 571; also A. B. J. Hammett, *The Empresario Don Martin de Leon* (Waco: Texas Press, 1973).

42. "Matagorda County," in *New Handbook of Texas*, 4: 557.

43. David Dary, *Cowboy Culture: A Saga of Five Centuries* (New York: Alfred A. Knopf, 1981), 138–39.

44. Rena Maverick Green, ed., *Samuel Maverick, Texan, 1803–1870: A Collection of Letters, Journals and Memoirs* (San Antonio: privately printed, 1952), 60–62; Paula Mitchell Marks, *Turn Your Eyes Toward Texas: Pioneers Sam and Mary Maverick* (College Station: Texas A&M University Press, 1989), 62.

45. Rena Maverick Green, *Memoirs of Mary A. Maverick* (San Antonio: Alamo Printing, 1921); Marks, *Turn Your Eyes Toward Texas*; and "Mary Ann Adams Maverick," in *New Handbook of Texas*, 4: 573–74.

46. Green, *Mary Maverick*, 281.

47. Ibid., 326.

48. Ibid., 295 ff., 301.

49. Ibid., 321–26.

50. Ibid., 413.

51. Dary, *Cowboy Culture*, 139.

52. See chapter XI in *Historic Matagorda County*, I: 175–87. Siringo first worked for a Mr. Faldien, whose ranch was on Big Boggy Creek at Lake Austin, when he was only twelve, but he remembered putting Faldien's brand on "one to four-year old 'mavericks,'" 176–77.

CHAPTER TWO

1. "Rafael Vasquez," in *New Handbook of Texas*, 6: 713.

2. "Adrian Woll," in *New Handbook of Texas*, 6: 1035–36; "Battle of Salado Creek," idem, 5: 772–73.

3. "Alexander Somervell," in *New Handbook of Texas*, 5: 1144; and "Somervell Expedition," idem, 1145; "Mier Expedition," idem, 4: 715–16.

4. "Matagorda," in *New Handbook of Texas*, 4: 555; also "Matagorda Bulletin," idem, 556.

5. "James Boyd Hawkins," in *New Handbook of Texas*, 3: 510. On his Caney Creek site Hawkins built "a two-story colonial-style plantation house, the remains of which stood as late as the 1970s." See also "Hawkinsville, Texas," idem, 3: 512. For a larger perspective, see Randolph B. Campbell, *An Empire for Slavery: The Peculiar Institution in Texas, 1821–1865*

(Baton Rouge: Louisiana State University Press, 1989). Ralph H. Wooster, "Notes on Texas' Largest Slaveholders, 1860," *The Southwestern Historical Journal Quarterly* vol. LXV, no. 1 (July 1961): 79.

6. "John Rugeley," in *New Handbook of Texas*, 5: 710.

7. "DeCrows Point, Texas," in *New Handbook of Texas*, 2: 558.

8. "Tres Palacios, Texas," in *New Handbook of Texas*, 6: 562.

9. Claude A. Talley, Jr., "Geographic Factors in the Indianola–Matagorda Bay Area of Texas that Influenced the Development of the Southwest from 1840–1875" (Victoria, Texas, March, 1970), brochure in Matagorda County Museum and Historical Society.

10. "Port Lavaca, Texas," in *New Handbook of Texas*, 5: 281–82.

11. Talley, "Geographic Factors," 4; "Indianola," in *New Handbook of Texas*, 3: 830–31.

12. "Indianola," in *New Handbook of Texas*, 3: 831.

13. "Charles Morgan" and "Morgan Lines," both in *New Handbook of Texas* 4: 834, 838–39.

14. "A History of Indianola," compiled by Mrs. Lelia Seeligson for the Indianola Historical Association in 1930. Xerox of printed copy (n.d.) in Matagorda County Historical Society, courtesy of Paul C. Stone, July 2001.

15. "John Russell Bartlett, in *NEAW*, 82.

16. Seeligson, "Indianola" (article not paginated).

17. "Morgan," in *New Handbook of Texas*, 4: 83.

18. "Civil War," in *New Handbook of Texas*, 2: 121–26.

19. The major source for this and succeeding paragraphs about the Civil War in Texas are: T. R. Fehrenbach, *Lone Star*, Part IV, "The Confederacy and the Conquered," 327–442; Ralph Wooster, "Civil War," in *New Handbook of Texas*, 2: 121–26; Alwyn Barr, "Texas Coastal Defense, 1861–1865," *Southwestern Historical Quarterly* XLV, no. 1 (July 1961): 1–31; Matagorda County Historical Commission, *Historic Matagorda County*, I: throughout.

20. Wooster, "Civil War," in *New Handbook of Texas*, 2: 121.

21. Barr, "Texas Coastal Defense," 5–6.

22. Matagorda County Historical Commission, *Historic Matagorda County*, I: 163.

23. Ibid., 163–64; Barr, "Texas Coastal Defense," 8.

24. Siringo, *A Texas Cowboy*, 11–12.

25. Ibid., 13; Matagorda County Historical Commission, *Historic Matagorda County*, I: 163.

26. "Fort Esperanza," in *New Handbook of Texas*, 2: 1100.

27. "John Bankhead Magruder," in *New Handbook of Texas*, 4: 464–65.

28. Ibid., 465; Fehrenbach, *Lone Star*, 360.

29. Ibid., p. 369.

30. "Battle of Galveston," in *New Handbook of Texas*, 3: 51; and Fehrenbach, *Lone Star*, 369.

31. Ibid., 3, 51; Barr, "Texas Coastal Defense," 1–31. An excellent overall account of the conflict is Alvin M. Josephy, Jr., *The Civil War in the American West* (New York: Alfred Knopf, 1991); see Lamar, *NEAW*, 214–18 for a brief summary.

32. Siringo, *A Texas Cowboy*, 14, 16; B. P. Galloway, ed., *The Dark Corner of the Confederacy* (Dubuque, Iowa: Kendall/Hunt Publishing Company, 1964–1972), 168–73, 181–85.

33. Siringo, *A Texas Cowboy*, 16.

34. Matagorda County Historical Commission, *Historic Matagorda County*, I: 150, 166–67.

35. Ibid., I: 165.

36. Lubbock, in Galloway, *The Dark Corner of the Confederacy*, 171.

37. Matagorda County Historical Commission, *Historic Matagorda County*, I: 168. Magruder himself visited the region and met with local commanders.

38. Siringo, *A Texas Cowboy*, 14.

39. Matagorda County Historical Commission, *Historic Matagorda County*, I: 172.

40. Siringo, *A Texas Cowboy*, 14–16.

41. Barr, "Texas Coastal Defense," 28–29; *New Handbook of Texas*, 5: 281–82. One major reason Lavaca was a target for Union troops and gunboats was that the town had a large Confederate arsenal and a small arms manufactory. See also Matagorda County Historical Commission, *Historic Matagorda County*, I: 168.

42. Fehrenbach, *Lone Star*, 372.

43. Shelby Foote, *The Civil War: A Narrative* (Alexandria, Va.: Shelby Foote and the Editors of Time-Life Books, 1963), vol. 9. "Mine Run to Meridian," 46, 49.

44. This decline in morale toward the end of the war is expressed by various observers in Galloway, *The Dark Corner of the Confederacy*, 168–73, 181–85.

45. Excerpts from Ralph J. Smith, "Reminiscences of Life of the Gulf Coast with the Second Texas Infantry," in Galloway, *The Dark Corner of the Confederacy*, 182–84.

46. "John Salmon Ford," in *New Handbook of Texas*, 2: 1072–73.

47. "Hamilton P. Bee," in *New Handbook of Texas*, 1: 458.

48. "Battle of Palmito Ranch," in *New Handbook of Texas*, 5: 25–26. Ford's incredible career is detailed in R. J. Hughes, *Rebellious Rangers: Rip Ford and the Old Southwest* (Norman: University of Oklahoma Press, 1964); Stephen B. Oates, ed., *Rip Ford's Texas* (Austin: University of Texas Press, 1963). His career as a Texas Ranger is covered in Robert M. Utley, *Lone Star Justice: The First Century of the Texas Rangers* (New York: Oxford

Press, 2002); Fehrenbach, *Lone Star*, devotes an entire chapter to Ford, 373–93. For the record, some authors spell it Palmetto Ranch.

49. "Edmund Kirby Smith," in *New Handbook of Texas*, 5: 1093–94.

50. Siringo, *A Texas Cowboy*, 16.

51. "Hawkins," in *New Handbook of Texas*, 3: 510.

52. Fehrenbach, *Lone Star*, 395–96.

53. Sara R. Massey, *Black Cowboys of Texas* (College Station, Tex.: Texas A&M University Press, 2000). See especially part 2, "Cowboys of the Cattle Drives," 93–214, and Alwyn Barr's excellent "Introduction," which reviews the scholarly studies of Black cowboys.

54. Siringo, *A Texas Cowboy*, 16–17.

55. Ibid., 16–17.

56. Ibid., 17.

57. Ibid.

CHAPTER THREE

1. Siringo, *A Texas Cowboy*, 18.

2. Matagorda County Historical Commission, *Historic Matagorda County*, I: 176–77.

3. Ibid., 177.

4. See Joseph G. McCoy, *Historic Sketches of the Cattle Trade of the West and Southwest* (Kansas City, Mo.: Ramsey, Millet, and Hudson, 1874) for his own account of his accomplishments. McCoy and the Chisholm Trail will be treated in a later chapter.

5. "Chisholm Trail," in *New Handbook of Texas*, 2: 85 is an excellent thumbnail sketch, but for a full treatment see Wayne Gard, *The Chisholm Trail* (Norman: University of Oklahoma Press, 1954).

6. Siringo, *A Texas Cowboy*, 18–20.

7. Ibid., 20–21.

8. Ibid., 23.

9. Ibid., 22–23.

10. Ibid., 24–25.

11. Ibid., 26–30.

12. Ibid., 30–31.

13. Ibid., 31–33.

14. Ibid., 34–36.

15. Ibid., 42.

16. Ibid., 37–42. As early as 1860, 21,685 head of cattle and 42,559 hides were shipped from the port of Indianola alone. By 1872 the number of hides shipped that year had increased to 330,875. See Matagorda County Historical Commission, *Historic Matagorda County*, I: 176, 178. The town boasted three turtle packeries and three hide and tallow firms,

the most prominent of which was owned by H. Selickson. Naturally that was the firm that hired Siringo. See idem, 177, and Seeligson, "History of Indianola," 4–5 of Xerox copy.

17. Mark Twain, *The Adventures of Huckleberry Finn.* "Afterword" by Alfred Kazin (New York: Bantam Books, 1981). The original novel was first published in 1884.

18. Twain, *The Adventures of Huckleberry Finn*, chapter 1, pp. 3–6, and Kazin, "Afterword," 283.

19. Kazin, "Afterword," 290.

20. Twain, *The Adventures of Huckleberry Finn*, chapters 25–40, pp. 229–64.

21. Ibid., 281.

22. Siringo, *A Texas Cowboy*, 41.

23. "David Crockett," in Lamar, *NEAW*, 274.

24. "Kit Carson," in Lamar, *NEAW*, 274.

25. "Buffalo Bill (William Frederick) Cody," in Lamar, *NEAW*, 228–29.

26. Robert M. Utley, *Billy the Kid: A Short and Violent Life* (Lincoln: University of Nebraska Press, 1989); "Billy the Kid," in Lamar, *NEAW*, 100–101.

27. "Charles Morgan," in *New Handbook of Texas*, 4: 834.

28. "Wylie Martin Kuykendall," in *New Handbook of Texas*, 3: 1171.

29. Elliott West, *Growing Up with the Country: Childhood on the Far Western Frontier* (Albuquerque: University of New Mexico Press, 1989); Howard R. Lamar, "Rites of Passage: Young Men and Their Families in the Overland Trails Experience, 1843–1869," *Charles Redd Monographs in Western History*, no. 8, ed. Thomas G. Alexander (Provo, Utah: Brigham Young University Press, 1978), 33–67; Ruth Barnes Moynihan, "Children and Young People on the Overland Trail," *Western Historical Quarterly* IV (July 1975): 279–94.

30. Siringo, *A Texas Cowboy*, 44.

31. Shanghai Pierce is treated at length in chapter 4, but for a quick summary of his life, see "Abel Head Pierce," in *New Handbook of Texas*, 5: 194.

CHAPTER FOUR

1. *The Trail Drivers of Texas* (Austin: University of Texas, rev. ed., 1986). Originally compiled and edited by J. Marvin Hunter and published under the direction of George W. Saunders. Introduction by B. Byron Price. Pp. 923–24.

2. Chris Emmett, *Shanghai Pierce: A Fair Likeness* (Norman: University of Oklahoma Press, 1953), 13–14, 15–16. Emmett's biography of Pierce is the most extensive and carefully documented yet published. I have relied on the volume in my narrative of Pierce's career for information and an accurate chronology of events. Pierce's career is briefly summarized in

"Abel Head Pierce," in *New Handbook of Texas*, 5: 194. Pierce's papers are housed at the Barker Texas History Center, University of Texas at Austin. See also Siringo, *A Texas Cowboy*, 44–45; Bill O'Neal, *Historic Ranches of the Old West* (Austin: Eakin Press, 1997), 17–22.

3. Emmett, *Pierce*, 16–19.

4. Ibid., 19–21.

5. Ibid., 21.

6. "Jonathan Edwards Pierce," in *New Handbook of Texas*, 5: 195. See also references to Pierce in Siringo, *A Texas Cowboy*, throughout; O'Neal, *Historic Ranches*, 18–19.

7. Emmett, *Pierce*, 34–35, 37.

8. Ibid., 38.

9. Ibid., 56, 120–21; O'Neal, *Historic Ranches*, 17–22.

10. "Samuel William Allen," in *New Handbook of Texas*, 1: 115.

11. Emmett, *Pierce*, 120–21.

12. "William Demetris Lacy," in *New Handbook of Texas*, 3: 1186.

13. Emmett, *Pierce*, 57–58.

14. "Sutton-Taylor Feud," in *New Handbook of Texas*, 6: 162–63; Emmett, *Pierce*, 49–50, 58–59, 79–90; *Trail Drivers of Texas*, 762, 826–27. See also Jack Hays Day, *The Sutton-Taylor Feud* (San Antonio: Murray, 1937), and Robert M. Utley, *Lone Star Justice: The First Century of The Texas Rangers* (New York: Oxford University Press, 2002), 158–59, 171–72.

15. Emmett, *Pierce*, 58–59.

16. Ibid., 60–65.

17. "John Wesley Hardin," in *New Handbook of Texas*, 3: 454–55. Hardin's relation to the Sutton-Taylor feud is succinctly summarized in Utley, *Lone Star Justice*, 172–75; "Ben Thompson," in *New Handbook of Texas*, 6: 468–69; "Philip Houston Coe," in idem, 2: 188; Chuck Parsons, *Phil Coe, Texas Gambler* (Wolf City, Tex.: Hemington, 1984). Coe is treated in detail in Floyd B. Streeter's *Ben Thompson* (New York: Fell, 1957).

18. Emmett, *Pierce*, 58–59.

19. Ibid., 69, 99, 104, 154, 196. Also "Kountze, Texas," in *New Handbook of Texas*, 3: 1159; Howard R. Lamar, *The Far Southwest, 1846–1912: A Territorial History* (Albuquerque, University of New Mexico Press, 2000), 240 for activities of the Kountze Brothers in Denver.

20. Thomas C. Nye is mentioned in Siringo, *A Texas Cowboy*, 44, 46, and in Emmett, *Pierce*, 50, 52, 54, 56, 160–61, 184.

21. Asa Dawdy is treated in Emmett, *Pierce*, 52–53, 123, 140, 267. He is mentioned in Siringo, *A Texas Cowboy*, 62, 76–79.

22. Emmett, *Pierce*, 91.

23. Ibid., 129.

24. "Robert H. Kuykendall, Sr.," in *New Handbook of Texas*, 3: 1170.

25. "Abner Kuykendall," in *New Handbook of Texas*, 3: 1168, and "Joseph Kuykendall," idem, 1169–70.

26. "Jonathan Hampton Kuykendall" and "Gibson Kuykendall," in *New Handbook of Texas*, 1168–69.

27. "Wiley Martin Kuykendall," in *New Handbook of Texas*, 1171.

28. Ibid.; Emmett, *Pierce*, 45, 55–56, 82, 139.

29. Emmett, *Pierce*, 45; *New Handbook of Texas*, 3: 1171.

30. *Trail Drivers of Texas*, 31.

31. "Wiley Kuykendall," in *New Handbook of Texas*, 3: 1171.

32. Emmett, *Pierce*, viii, 5–6, 122, 310.

33. "Brahman Cattle," in *New Handbook of Texas*, 1: 697–98, corrects the popular image that only Pierce and Borden promoted the introduction of Brahma cattle to Texas.

34. Emmett, *Pierce*, viii, 5, 7, 101, 123, 167, 171.

35. Frederick C. Proctor in Emmett, *Pierce*, 3–8, 183.

36. Kitty Henderson and Charlie Woodson, "Neptune Holmes: A Lifetime of Loyalty," in *Black Cowboys of Texas*, ed. Sara R. Massey (College Station: Texas A&M University Press, 2000), 117–21. See also Emmett, *Pierce*, 4, 10, 47, 51, 101, 123, 133, 191.

37. "Black Cowboys," in *New Handbook of Texas*, 1: 565–66. Also Emmett, *Pierce*, 123.

38. Emmett, *Pierce*, 205.

39. "Samuel W. Allen," in *New Handbook of Texas*, 1: 115; "Dillard Rucker Fant," idem, 2: 948; "George W. Littlefield," idem, 4: 230–31; "George W. Saunders," idem, 5: 902–3. For the railroad story, see Emmett, *Pierce*, 115–18, but also "New York, Texas and Mexican Railway," in *New Handbook of Texas*, 4: 1008.

40. Jimmy M. Skaggs, *The Cattle-Trailing Industry* (Lawrence: University Press of Kansas, 1973), discusses yet another professional group, "cattle trail contractors"; Captain John T. Lytte, Tom M. McDaniel, Captain Schreiner, John W. Light, Captain E. B. (Eugene) Millett, the Blocker Brothers, the Pryor Brothers, J. Monroe Choate, Col. James F. Ellison, Colonel John O. Denver, Colonel J. J. Meyers, and George W. Saunders, all of whom are cited in Hunter, *Trail Drivers of Texas* (see index).

41. Siringo, *A Texas Cowboy*, 44.

42. Ibid.

43. Ibid., 44–45.

44. Ibid., 46.

45. Ibid., 49.

46. Ibid., 48–49.

47. Ibid., 50.

48. Ibid., 51.

49. Ibid., 52.

50. Ibid., 55–56.

51. Ibid., 56.

52. Ibid.

53. Ibid., 58.

54. Ibid., 63–69.

55. Ibid., 70.

56. Ibid., 71–72. Siringo gives more details about the shooting in his *A Lone Star Cowboy*, 31–32.

57. Siringo, *A Texas Cowboy*, 75.

58. Ibid.

59. Ibid., 78–79.

60. Ibid., 82.

61. Ibid., 88–92.

62. Ibid., 90–93. See also "George W. Littlefield," in *New Handbook of Texas*, 4: 230–31 for an excellent summary of his career. The classic biography is J. Evetts Haley, *George W. Littlefield, Texan* (Norman: University of Oklahoma Press, 1943), generally thought to be the best biography of a rancher yet written.

CHAPTER FIVE

1. Frederick W. Rathjen, *The Texas Panhandle Frontier* (Lubbock, Tex.: Texas Tech University Press, 1988, rev. ed.), provides an excellent overview.

2. "William C. Moore," in *New Handbook of Texas*, 4: 824–25, summarizes fuller descriptions of Moore in Pauline D. and R. L. Robertson, *Cowman's Country: Fifty Frontier Ranches in the Texas Panhandle, 1876–1887* (Amarillo, Tex.: Paramount, 1981), in Margaret Sheers, "The LX Ranch of Texas," *Panhandle-Plains Historical Review* 6 (1933), and Siringo's *A Texas Cowboy* and his *A Lone Star Cowboy* (Santa Fe, 1919).

3. Walter Prescott Webb, *The Great Plains* (New York: Ginn and Company, 1931); J. Frank Dobie, *A Vaquero of the Brush Country* (New York: Grossett & Dunlap, 1929); J. Evetts Haley, Sr., *Charles Goodnight: Cowman and Plainsman* (Boston: Houghton Mifflin, 1936). See also "Haley," in Lamar, *NEAW*, 465–66. For a splendid overview, see Terry G. Jordan, *North American Cattle-Ranching Frontiers* (Albuquerque: University of New Mexico Press, 1993), esp. chapter 7, "The Anglo-Texas Ranching System," 208–40.

4. Dobie, *A Vaquero of the Brush Country*, 133, but also extensive coverage in Sallie Reynolds Matthews, *Interwoven: A Pioneer Chronicle* (College Station: Texas A&M University Press, 1936; new ed. 1999), especially 105–50, passim.

5. See John L. McCarty, *Maverick Town: The Story of Old Tascosa* (Norman: University of Oklahoma Press, 1946; enlarged ed. 1968); also "Casimero Romero," in *New Handbook of Texas*, 5: 671–72. See also John Arnot, "My Recollections of Tascosa Before and After the Coming of the Law," *Panhandle-Plains Historical Review* 6 (1933): 58–79.

6. "Tascosa-Dodge City Trail," in *New Handbook of Texas*, 5: 210.

7. "Casimero Romero," in *New Handbook of Texas*, 5: 671–72.

8. José Ymocencio Romero and Ernest L. Archambeau, "Spanish Sheepmen on the Canadian at Old Tascosa," *Panhandle-Plains Historical Review* 19 (1946).

9. Ibid.

10. Haley, *Goodnight*, ix.

11. "Oliver Loving," in *New Handbook of Texas*, 4: 309–10.

12. "Goodnight-Loving Trail," in *New Handbook of Texas*, 3: 244–45.

13. "John Chisum," in Lamar, *NEAW*, 209.

14. "Loving," in *New Handbook of Texas*, 4: 310. Loving family tradition says Loving's son and a cavalcade of cowboys, rather than Goodnight, brought Loving's body back to Texas.

15. Haley's remarkable biography, *Charles Goodnight: Cowman and Plainsman*, remains the key source for information on the great rancher, but see H. Allen Anderson's fine summary of his life in "Charles Goodnight," in *New Handbook of Texas*, 3: 240–43. See also the sketch of his wife: "Mary Ann Dyer Goodnight," idem, 243–44.

16. "JA Ranch," in *New Handbook of Texas*, 3: 885–86; Harley True Burton, *A History of the LX Ranch* (Austin: Von Boeckmann Jones, 1928; reprint New York: Argonaut, 1966).

17. Siringo, *A Texas Cowboy*, 93. Virtually all of the great ranchers from South Texas and the Panhandle are treated in a remarkable book by James Cox, *Historical and Biographical Record of the Cattle Industry and the Cattlemen of Texas* (St. Louis: Woodward and Tiernan Printing Company, 1895).

18. Siringo, *A Texas Cowboy*, 98. Siringo, excited by the presence of buffalo, tried to rope and skin a buffalo calf, foolishly forgetting both his gun and his Bowie knife. In a comical set of mishaps, Siringo finally roped a calf only to realize he had no way of killing it. He finally killed by using his red sash to tie the legs of the animal, and then cutting its throat with his pocket knife.

19. "David T. Beals," in *New Handbook of Texas*, 1: 436–37.

20. Sheers, "The LX Ranch of Texas," 47; "David Thomas Beals," in *New Handbook of Texas*, 1: 437.

21. "David Thomas Beals," in *New Handbook of Texas*, 1: 437.

22. "Rodeo," in Lamar, *NEAW*, 970–74; "Buffalo Bill Cody," 228–29; and "Wild West show," 1215–17.

23. Siringo, *A Texas Cowboy*, 101.

24. Ibid., 100–101.

25. Ibid., 103–5.

26. Sheers, "The LX Ranch of Texas," 24; Siringo, *A Texas Cowboy*, 105.

27. Siringo, *A Texas Cowboy*, 105.

28. Ibid., 106–9.

29. Ibid., 110.

30. Ibid. Perhaps more than a thousand books and articles have been written about Henry McCarty, who changed his name to William Antrim and then to Bill Bonney, who was then known as Billy the Kid. The best biographies are: Robert M. Utley, *Billy the Kid: A Short and Violent Life* (Lincoln: University of Nebraska Press, 1989); John Tuska, *Billy the Kid: His Life and Legend* (Westport, Conn.: Greenwood Press, 1994). A superb broader coverage of his role is in Frederick Nolan, *The Lincoln County War: A Documentary History* (Norman: University of Oklahoma Press, 1992).

31. Henry F. Hoyt, *A Frontier Doctor* (Chicago: The Lakeside Press: R. R. Donnelley and Sons Company, 1979), 147–55; see also Utley, *Billy the Kid*, 109.

32. Charles D. Peavy, "Introduction," in Siringo's *History of "Billy the Kid"* (Facsimile ed., Austin: Steck-Vaughn, 1967), vi.

33. Siringo, *A Texas Cowboy*, 112–13.

34. Ibid., 116.

35. Ibid., 119–24.

36. Ibid., 124–25.

37. Nolan, *The Lincoln County War*, 402.

38. Ibid., 403.

39. Ibid., 402–26, passim, esp. 423–26. See also Leon C. Metz, *Pat Garrett; The Story of a Western Lawman* (Norman: University of Oklahoma Press, 1974).

40. Siringo, *A Texas Cowboy*, 126–37, 138–40.

41. Ibid., 143–50.

42. Ibid., 151–54.

43. Ibid., 155–59.

44. Ibid., 161–66.

45. See his "A True Sketch of 'Billy the Kid's' Life," in *A Texas Cowboy*, 168–77; his *History of "Billy the Kid"* (Santa Fe: Chas A. Siringo, 1920). See also a later edition by the University of New Mexico Press, and a facsimile edition with an introduction by Charles D. Peavy (Austin: Steck-Vaughan Company, 1967).

46. Siringo, *A Texas Cowboy*, 177.

47. Utley, *Billy the Kid*, 207.

48. Siringo, *A Texas Cowboy*, pp. 178–92, passim, especially 191–92 for outcome of the Coghlan trial.

49. Ibid., 193.

CHAPTER SIX

1. John Dunkel and John M. Faragher, "Westerns on Radio and Television," in Lamar, *NEAW*, 936.

2. See "Joseph McCoy," in Lamar, *NEAW*, 668 for a brief summary of his life, but most important is McCoy's own account of his career in his 1874 publication: *Historic Sketches of the Cattle Trade of the West and Southwest*, which was edited and reprinted under its original title in Ralph P. Bieber, ed., *The Southwestern Historical Series*, no. 7 (1940). Bieber's own essay on McCoy is outstanding.

3. These early attempts by Texans to trail cattle to Kansas, Missouri, and Illinois are described in Wayne Gard, *The Chisholm Trail* (Norman: The University of Oklahoma Press, 1954), 20–36.

4. Ibid., 64–69.

5. Arrell M. Gibson, "Jesse Chisholm," in Lamar, *NEAW*, 208–9, summarizes Chisholm's life, but see also Gard, *Chisholm Trail*, 72–75; T. C. Richardson, "Jesse Chisholm," in *New Handbook of Texas*, 2: 88–89. See also Stan Hoig, *Jesse Chisholm: Ambassador of the Plains* (Niwot: University of Colorado Press, 1991), and Thomas Alvar Taylor, *Jesse Chisholm* (Bandera, Tex.: *Frontier Times*, 1939).

6. Donald E. Worcester, *The Chisholm Trail* (Lincoln: University of Nebraska Press, 1980), and Gard, *Chisholm Trail*.

7. Wayne Gard, "Shawnee Trail," in *New Handbook of Texas*, 5: 1003–4.

8. Gard, *Chisholm Trail*, 76–79; Siringo, *A Texas Cowboy*, 77–79.

9. Worcester, "Chisholm Trail," in *New Handbook of Texas*, 2: 89; Jimmy M. Skaggs, "Isaac Thomas Pryor," in idem, 5: 365; also Skaggs, *The Cattle-Trailing Industry: Between Supply and Demand, 1866–1890* (Lawrence: University Press of Kansas, 1973).

10. Worcester, "Chisholm Trail," in *New Handbook of Texas*, 2: 89.

11. Joseph A. Stout, Jr., "Cattle Towns," in Lamar, *NEAW*, 183. See reference to Abilene in two enduring classic studies: Floyd B. Streeter's sympathetic *Prairie Trails and Cow Towns* (New York: The Devin Adair Company, 1963), and Robert R. Dykstra, *The Cattle Towns* (New York: Alfred A. Knopf, 1968), a social history of Abilene, Ellsworth, Wichita, Dodge City, and Caldwell 1867 to 1885.

12. Dykstra, *The Cattle Towns*, 30–41 and references throughout.

13. "Wichita," in Dykstra, *The Cattle Towns*, 41–47 and scores of references throughout.

14. See references to Wichita in Dykstra, *The Cattle Towns*, 56–62, ff. throughout.

15. Jimmy M. Skaggs, "Western Trail," in *New Handbook of Texas*, 6: 894.

16. Dykstra, *The Cattle Towns*, 144.

17. Ibid., 63.

18. Cherokee Strip in Dykstra, *The Cattle Towns*, 210–11, 342–54.

19. Ibid., 348.

20. Ibid., 116, 144.

21. Ibid., 154–59.

22. Ibid., 76–91, 181, 211–13.

23. Ibid., 214.

24. Ibid., 211–12, 285.

25. Ibid., 347, 349–52; Charles A. Siringo, *Riata and Spurs* (Boston: Houghton Mifflin, 1927), 116–17.

26. Siringo, *A Texas Cowboy*, 192.

27. Siringo, *Riata and Spurs*, 112.

28. Siringo, *A Texas Cowboy*, 193–98.

29. Siringo, *Riata and Spurs*, 113–14.

30. Ben E. Pingenot, *Siringo*, 12–13.

31. Siringo, *Riata and Spurs*, 114–15.

32. Ibid., 116.

33. Dykstra, *The Cattle Towns*, 346–54.

34. Siringo, *Riata and Spurs*, 117–18.

35. Ibid., 118.

36. Douglas Lober, "Caldwell, Kansas and the Cattletown Solution, 1879–1885" (unpublished manuscript, Senior Essay in History, written at Yale University, May 1982. Cited with author's permission, December 2, 2002).

37. Ibid., 2.

38. Ibid., 14.

39. Ibid.

40. Ibid., 23–24.

41. Ibid., 23–31.

42. Siringo, *A Cowboy Detective*, pp. 13–14.

43. Lober, "Caldwell," 30. See also "Henry Newton Brown," in Lamar, *NEAW*, 133–34, and Bill O'Neal, *Henry Brown, the Outlaw-Marshal* (College Station, Tex.: Creative Pub. Co., 1980).

44. Lober, "Caldwell," 31.

45. Ibid., 52.

46. Ibid., 36.

47. Ibid., 17–18.

48. Ibid., 16.

49. Ibid.

50. Ibid., 33.

51. Ibid., 53.

52. Siringo, *A Texas Cowboy*, 3.

53. Ibid., 3.

54. Ibid., 4–5.

55. Siringo, *Riata and Spurs*, 119.

56. Siringo, *A Cowboy Detective*, 15.

57. Ibid., 15–16.

58. Wilson M. Hudson, *Andy Adams: His Life and Writings* (Dallas: Southern Methodist University Press, 1964), 16. See also his *Andy Adams: Storyteller and Novelist of the Great Plains* (Austin: Steck-Vaughn, 1967). J. Frank Dobie, who greatly admired Adams, wrote his own account: *Andy Adams: Cow Chronicles* (Dallas: Southern Methodist University Press, 1926).

59. Hudson, *Adams his Life and Writings*, 22–23.

60. Ibid., 23.

61. Ibid., 190–95 ff. Adams was jealous that Emerson Hough, who knew less about cattle and cowboys than he did, had made so much money as a "Western" author. See especially Hudson's chapter, "The Writing Game," 190–211.

62. Ibid., traces the popularity of *Log of a Cowboy*, 3–11, 81–88, 104–7, 225–26.

63. Ibid., ix–x, 6–8.

64. Ibid., 59–60.

65. Ibid., 60–61.

66. Ibid., 61–62, 67, 75. In *A Cowboy Detective*, 159, Siringo describes Baughman's session with the blind phrenologist, who called him a boastful, even lying, man. Siringo diplomatically referred to Baughman as "Baufman," but there was no mistaking the real identity of the person. Always an egotistical man, Baughman published his own autobiography, *The Oklahoma Scout*, in 1886.

67. Hudson, *Adams*, 68.

68. Ibid., 45–46, 59, 147, 220.

69. Pingenot, *Siringo*, xxi.

CHAPTER SEVEN

1. These various labor groups and their beliefs are brilliantly presented in Paul Avrich's *The Haymarket Tragedy* (Princeton: Princeton University Press, 1984), in parts I and II, 3–160.

2. "The Cult of Dynamite," in Avrich, *The Haymarket Tragedy*, 160 ff.

3. Henry David, *The History of the Haymarket Affair: A Study in the American Social-Revolutionary and Labor Movements* (New York: Russell and Russell, 1964, but originally published in 1936), 120.

4. "Parsons," in Avrich, *The Haymarket Tragedy*, xii, 3–25, 42.

5. "Spies," in Avrich, *The Haymarket Tragedy*, 121–22, 128 and throughout the text.

6. Lingg, discussed in Avrich, *The Haymarket Tragedy*, 157 and throughout the text. Similarly Johann J. Most is covered on 50, 171, and throughout the text.

7. "Fielden," in Avrich, *The Haymarket Tragedy*, 103 ff.

8. "Schwab," in Avrich, *The Haymarket Tragedy*, 130 ff.

9. "Neebe," in Avrich, *The Haymarket Tragedy*, 107–9 ff.

10. Avrich, *The Haymarket Tragedy*, 175.

11. Ibid., 150–51.

12. "Fischer," in Avrich, *The Haymarket Tragedy*, 152–53 ff.

13. "Engel," in Avrich, *The Haymarket Tragedy*, 153–56 ff.

14. Ibid., 133, 156, 159, 228.

15. See coverage in Avrich, *The Haymarket Tragedy*: "The Trial," and chapter 18, "The Verdict," 260–93. The trial, verdict, and appeals are also covered in David, *The History of the Haymarket Affair*, 236–328.

16. David, *The History of the Haymarket Affair*, 211, 325, and 407 ff. See also Avrich, *The Haymarket Tragedy*, 220, 309–10, 348–50, and 429 and 432.

17. Avrich, *The Haymarket Tragedy*, 187–90.

18. Ibid., 194.

19. Ibid.

20. Charles A. Siringo, *A Cowboy Detective, a True Story of Twenty-Two Years with a World-Famous Detective Agency* (Chicago: W. B. Conkey Company, 1912), 12.

21. Ibid., 16–17.

22. Ibid., 17.

23. Avrich, *The Haymarket Tragedy*, 235, 239, 269–70, 439–41. In *A Cowboy Detective*, 22, Siringo spells the name "Schnoebelt." It is difficult to tell if this is deliberate or if his spelling, always erratic, is off course again!

24. Siringo, *A Cowboy Detective*, 21–22.

25. Ibid., 22–23.

26. All of these "bomb" cases will be treated in subsequent chapters.

27. James D. Horan, *The Pinkertons: The Detective Dynasty That Made History* (New York: Crown Publishers, Inc., 1967; second printing in 1969).

28. Ibid., 3–21.

29. Ibid., 15–18.

30. Ibid., 39–42.

31. Ibid., 23–24.

32. Ibid., 24–29.

33. Siringo, *A Cowboy Detective*, 24.

34. Ibid., 23; Horan, *The Pinkertons*, 29–30.

35. Horan, *The Pinkertons*, 151.

36. Ibid., 31–33, 204–37.

37. Ibid., 52–61.

38. See Ibid., 81–91 for an account of the Confederate spy ring in Washington, and 98–114 for the capture and hanging of Timothy Webster, Pinkerton's chief spy in Richmond.

39. Ibid., 158, 189–202.

40. Siringo, *A Cowboy Detective*, 24.

41. Ibid., 25–26.

42. Ibid., 26.

43. Ibid., 27.

44. Ibid., 28–31.

45. Ibid., 32.

46. Ibid., 32–33.

47. Ibid., 33–35.

48. Ibid., 38.

49. Ibid., 38–43. To cover his tracks Siringo often disguised the names of persons, whether law abiding or criminals, in his *A Cowboy Detective*. It is next to impossible to identify the correct name in most instances.

50. Ibid., 51–65.

51. Ibid., 66–69.

52. Ibid., 69.

53. Siringo, *Two Evil Isms*, 9–11.

54. Ibid., 10; Ben Pingenot, *Siringo*, 17–18.

55. Pingenot, *Siringo*, 18; Siringo, *A Cowboy Detective*, 67.

56. Pingenot, *Siringo*, 18–19. McParland's career is summarized in Horan, *The Pinkertons*, 204–37, 461–79, and in Wayne G. Broehl, Jr., *The Molly Maguires* (Cambridge, Mass: Harvard University Press, 1964).

57. Siringo, *A Cowboy Detective*, 70–74.

58. Ibid., 75–77. Here Siringo disguised the contractors' names, using Parsons and Ayllmers for the well-known firm Frazier and Chalmers.

59. Ibid., 77–78.

60. Ibid., 79.

61. Ibid., 80, 82–83.

62. Ibid., 83–84.

63. Ibid., 91.

64. Ibid., 92–93.

65. Ibid., 94–95.

66. Ibid., 98–111 passim.

67. Ibid., 110–13.

68. Ibid., 99.

CHAPTER EIGHT

1. Pingenot, *Siringo*, 22; Siringo, *A Cowboy Detective*, 116.

2. Pingenot, *Siringo*, 25–26; Siringo, *A Cowboy Detective*, 116–17.

3. Robert W. Larson, *New Mexico Populism: A Study of Radical Protest in a Western Territory* (Boulder: Colorado Associated University Press, 1974), 60–61.

4. Catron's career and the Santa Fe Ring are treated in detail in "The Santa Fe Ring, 1865–1885," in Howard R. Lamar, *The Far Southwest, 1846–1912: A Territorial History* (Albuquerque, University of New Mexico Press, 2000), 121–47. See also Victor Westphall, *Thomas Benton Catron and His Era* (Tucson: University of Arizona Press, 1973).

5. Lamar, *The Far Southwest*, 164-65.

6. Siringo, *A Cowboy Detective*, 117.

7. Ibid.

8. Ibid.; Larson, *New Mexico Populism*, 36.

9. Larson, *New Mexico Populism*, 36.

10. Siringo, *A Cowboy Detective*, 121.

11. Larson, *New Mexico Populism*, 36–39.

12. Ibid., 39.

13. Ibid., 44–45.

14. Ibid., 46–47; Siringo, *A Cowboy Detective*, 118; Pingenot, *Siringo*, 27.

15. Larson, *New Mexico Populism*, 45–46, 54, 61–63.

16. Ibid., 60.

17. Pingenot, *Siringo*, 30; Larson, *New Mexico Populism*, 61.

18. Siringo, *A Cowboy Detective*, 118.

19. Ibid.

20. Ibid., 120.

21. Larson, *New Mexico Populism*, 54.

22. Siringo, *A Cowboy Detective*, 28.

23. Pingenot, *Siringo*, 28.

24. Siringo, *A Cowboy Detective*, 131.

25. Ibid., 132–33.

26. Ibid., 122.

27. Lamar, *Far Southwest*, 166.

28. Ibid., 163–64.

29. Ibid., 164.

30. Ibid., 165.

31. Ibid., 166–67.

32. Ibid., 167.

33. Ibid.

34. Westphall, *Catron*, chs. 12 and 13, pp. 208–68, which covers the Borrego murder case.

35. Lamar, *Far Southwest*, 168.

36. Ibid.

37. Ibid., 169, and Larson, *New Mexico Populism*, 42–47, 80–96, 162–79.

38. Larson, *New Mexico Populism*, 137–52, 158, 160–62, 164–65.

39. Lamar, *Far Southwest*, 170–71, 424, 429, 430.

40. Siringo, *A Cowboy Detective*, 132–33.

41. Ibid., 133; Pingenot, *Siringo*, 31–32, states Siringo first filed a homestead claim for 160 acres for himself; then purchased more property and a second homestead claim for his mother. Eventually Sunny Slope Ranch consisted of 365 acres.

42. Siringo, *A Cowboy Detective*, 134.

43. This information is found in his *A Cowboy Detective*, and his final book, *Riata and Spurs*.

CHAPTER NINE

1. "Simeon G. Reed," in *Dictionary of American Biography* (hereafter *DAB*), Edited by Allen Johnson and Dumas Malone. Twenty vols. and index, (Charles Scribner and Sons, 1928-1937), vol. 15, 456; Dorothy O. Johansen and Charles M. Gates, *Empire of the Columbia: A History of the Pacific Northwest* (New York: Harper & Brothers, 1957), 339–40; E. Kimbark MacColl and Harry H. Stein, *Merchants, Money, and Power: The Portland Establishment, 1843–1913* (Portland, Ore: Georgian Press, 1988).

2. "Simeon G. Reed," in Lamar, *NEAW*, 954.

3. "Simeon G. Reed," *DAB*, 15: 456; John Fahey, "Coeur d'Alene Confederacy," *Idaho Yesterdays* 12 (spring 1968): 2–3.

4. Fahey, "Coeur d'Alene Confederacy," 5; Clark G. Spence, *Mining Engineers & The American West: The Lace-Boot Brigade, 1849–1933* (New Haven: Yale University Press, 1970), 159–60, 267, 273–74. John Hays Hammond, *The Autobiography of John Hays Hammond*, 2 vols. (New York: Farrar and Reinhart, 1935); also John Hays Hammond, "Strong Men of the Wild West," *Scribner's Magazine* 77 (February–March 1925): 215–25, 246–56.

5. Spence, *Mining Engineers*, 47, 163–64, 169, 180–81, 276–77; "Frederick Worthen Bradley," in *DAB*, vol. 21, Supplement One (1944), 107–8.

6. Spence, *Mining Engineers*, 276.

7. Ibid., 205.

8. Fahey, "Coeur d'Alene Confederacy," 3.

9. Ibid. The quotation by Fahey is from a letter, V. M. Clement to S. G. Reed, November 23, 1889, in the *Letters and Private Papers of Simeon Gannett Reed* (Portland: Reed College, 1940), 24–95.

10. Spence, *Mining Engineers*, 170–71.

11. Fahey, "Coeur d'Alene Confederacy," 3–4.

12. Ibid., 4.

13. Ibid.

14. Ibid., 5.

15. Siringo, *A Cowboy Detective*, 135–36.

16. Ibid., 136.

17. Ibid., 136–37.

18. Ibid., 140–41.

19. Ibid., 137.

20. Pingenot, *Siringo*, 38–39.

21. Siringo, *A Cowboy Detective*, 139.

22. Ibid., 140–41.

23. Ibid., 142–43.

24. Ibid., 137–38, 144.

25. Ibid., 144.

26. Ibid., 145.

27. Ibid., 145–47.

28. The following paragraphs are a summary of Siringo's account in *A Cowboy Detective*, 148–53.

29. Ibid., 154.

30. Ibid., 157–67; Siringo, *Riata and Spurs*, 171. The Frisco Mill was farther up the narrow valley in which Gem, the railroad, and a small stream were located. The Gem Mill was just across the stream from the town of Gem. One of the plans of the miners was to send a railroad car full of dynamite down the slope to the Gem Mill so that it would be blown up as well.

31. Siringo, *A Cowboy Detective*, 159–60.

32. Ibid., 160–64; Siringo, *Riata and Spurs*, 173.

33. Siringo, *A Cowboy Detective*, 165.

34. Siringo, *Riata and Spurs*, 175–76.

35. Ibid., 176 ff; Siringo, *A Cowboy Detective*, 169–71.

36. Pingenot, *Siringo*, has an excellent account of the Coeur d'Alene events, 33–46, but see especially 44–46 for Siringo's activities after the troops arrived; but see also Siringo, *Riata and Spurs*, 182.

37. Siringo, *A Cowboy Detective*, 181–82.

38. See a good account of the trial in Richard G. Magnusen, *Coeur d'Alene Diary* (Portland: Metropolitan Press, 1968), 226–27, 248, 256–59.

39. Pingenot, *Siringo*, 47–48.

40. Richard Maxwell Brown, "Labor Movement," in Lamar, *NEAW*, 604–5.

41. Richard Maxwell Brown, "Western Federation of Miners," in Lamar, *NEAW*, 1196–97. See also Vernon H. Jenson, *Heritage of Conflict: Labor Relations in the Nonferrous Metals Industry up to 1930* (New York: Greenwood Press, reprint, 1968); and Carlos A. Chants, "The History of Pacific Northwest Labor History," *Idaho Yesterdays* 28 (winter 1985): 23–35.

42. Brown, "Labor Movement," p. 1197.

43. Richard Maxwell Brown, "Industrial Workers of the World," in Lamar, *NEAW*, 546–47.

44. J. Anthony Lukas, *Big Trouble: A Murder in a Small Western Town Sets off a Struggle for the Soul of America* (New York: Simon & Schuster, 1997) is an 875-page definitive account of the Steunenberg case, the role of Harry Orchard and James McParland, and the trial of Moyer, Haywood, and Pettibone. It will be cited in chapter 11 when Siringo was present at the famous trial.

45. Siringo, *A Cowboy Detective*, 492–96.

CHAPTER TEN

1. Many films have been made about Billy the Kid. The first major *Billy the Kid* film, staring Johnny Mack Brown, appeared in 1930. In 1938 Roy Rogers appeared in *Billy the Kid Returns*. A major film, *The Left-Handed Gun*, released in 1958, featured Paul Newman. It was originally written as a play for television by Gore Vidal. Another television show, *The Tall Texan*, about Billy the Kid and Sheriff Pat Garrett, played on NBC from September 1960 to September 1962. The most ambitious and star-studded account, *Pat Garrett and Billy the Kid*, was directed by Sam Peckinpah and released by MGM in 1978. Its notable cast included James Coburn, Kris Kristofferson, Richard Jaeckel, Katy Jurado, Chill Wills, Jason Robards, Bob Dylan, and Slim Pickens.

   No other film involving Butch Cassidy has come up to the standards set by George Roy Hill's *Butch Cassidy and the Sundance Kid* (1969), which won three Academy Awards. In a novel written by John Byrne Cooke, called *South of the Border* (1989), however, he brings Butch Cassidy and Charlie Siringo together in Hollywood by imagining that Butch Cassidy returned from South America and fell in love with Siringo's beautiful daughter, Victoria (a fictional character), as the three go off to Mexico to make a film about Pancho Villa. Back in Hollywood Butch and Victoria marry, but he robs a bank and has to flee. Siringo, the narrator of the novel, in the end forgives Cassidy and allows his daughter to continue to see her fugitive husband when she can.

   Unlike Billy the Kid and Butch Cassidy, Siringo himself met the actor William S. Hart in Hollywood and advised him about authentic western costume, guns, and the proper gear for horses. He even played a bit part in Hart's last film, *Tumbleweeds*.

   In the 1970s, long after Siringo's death in 1928, the Yale Media Design Studio made a film about Siringo starring Stephen Railsback as Siringo and Jennifer Warren as Mrs. Shipley. Sponsored by the National Endowment for the Humanities, it was released for public television as *Siringo and the West* in 1978.

   See John A. Murray, *Cinema Southwest: An Illustrated Guide to the Movies and Their Locations* (Hong Kong: Midas Printing Company, 2000), 107, 116, 120, 121, and 89–92; Don Cusic, *Cowboys and the Wild West: An A–Z Guide from the Chisholm Trail to the Silver Screen* (New York: Facts on File, Inc., 1994), 169, 220, 264, 274, 276, 280; John Byrne Cooke, *South of the Border* (New York: Bantam Press, 1989).

2. Laurent Bouzereau, *Ultraviolent Movies: From Sam Peckinpah to Quentin Tarantino* (New York: Citadel Press, Kensington Publishing Company, 1996), 2–13.

3. John A. Murray, *Cinema Southwest*, 89–92.

4. Ibid., 91.

5. Hole-in-the-Wall in Wyoming is described in Richard Patterson, *Butch Cassidy: A Biography* (Lincoln: University of Nebraska Press, 1998), 50–52, 124, 174, 244, fn. 7, 273.

6. Murray, *Cinema Southwest*, 90.

7. Patterson, *Butch Cassidy*, 1–362.

8. Howard R. Lamar, "Review of Patterson, *Butch Cassidy*," *History Book Club* (May 1999), pp. H (9906)–B.

9. Ibid.

10. Ibid.

11. See coverage of Matt Warner and Tom McCarty in Patterson, *Butch Cassidy*, 21–31; also in Pearl Baker, *The Wild Bunch at Robbers Roost* (New York: Abelard-Schuman, 1969, 1971), 55–64. Tom, Billy, and Fred McCarty are also treated in Baker, idem, 149–57.

12. Murray E. King, *The Last of the Bandit Riders* (New York: Bonanza Books, 1938; Reprint, 1950). Patterson has summarized Warner's account in *Butch Cassidy*, 53–57, 86–87, 93–97, and elsewhere.

13. Patterson, *Butch Cassidy*, 37–38.

14. Ibid., 41.

15. Ibid.

16. Ibid., 54.

17. Preston is treated in some length in ibid., 64–69, 94–95, 144–45, 170–71, and more briefly in Baker, *The Wild Bunch*, 63, 188, 190.

18. George W. Hufsmith, *The Wyoming Lynching of Cattle Kate, 1889* (Glendo, Wyo.: High Plains Press, 1993) is a persuasive revisionist account.

19. T. A. Larson, "Johnson County War," Lamar, NEAW, 577–79.

20. Larson, "Johnson County War," 578; see also James D. Horan, *Desperate Men: Revelations from the Sealed Pinkerton Files* (New York: G. P. Putnam's Sons, 1949), 183, 189, 190.

21. Patterson, *Butch Cassidy*, 71–78.

22. Ibid., 80–83, 100–103. Lay is also treated in Baker, *The Wild Bunch*, 170–80.

23. Patterson, *Butch Cassidy*, 86.

24. Ibid., 101.

25. Ibid., 102–3.

26. Ibid., 103–4. The Castle Gate robbery is also well covered in Baker, *The Wild Bunch*, 201–12.

27. Baker, *The Wild Bunch*, 201–12; and Patterson, *Butch Cassidy*, 103–10, fn. 45, 290.

28. Patterson, *Butch Cassidy*, 106.

29. Ibid., 108. One can trace the routes the robbers took by consulting the end paper map in Baker, *The Wild Bunch*.

30. Ibid., 114–16, iii–12, 123–24, 224, 292, fn. 35, and many other references.

31. Ibid., 124–25. Members of the Wild Bunch, for example, had attempted to rob the Butte County Bank in Belle Fourche, South Dakota, without success.

32. Posses were also penetrating Robbers Roost and other hangouts more successfully, and in one raid, Joe Walker, a Cassidy ally, was killed with another man by a posse led by Sheriff C. W. Allred. For a few days the gleeful officers thought the unknown man was Cassidy. See Baker, *The Wild Bunch*, 55–64; Patterson, *Butch Cassidy*, 137–39.

33. Patterson, *Butch Cassidy*, 142.

34. Ibid., 143–44.

35. Ibid., 148.

36. Ibid., 141–43, 151–52, 152–54, 158; Baker, *The Wild Bunch*, 170–80.

37. Patterson, *Butch Cassidy*, 152–54, 158.

38. Siringo, *A Cowboy Detective*, 354–56.

39. Patterson, *Butch Cassidy*, 165, 166–72.

40. Ibid., 166–72, 173, 235; Baker, *The Wild Bunch*, 191–92; Siringo, *A Cowboy Detective*, 365.

41. Patterson, *Butch Cassidy*, 158–63.

42. Ibid., see reference, Index, 355.

43. Ibid., 177–78, 184–86, 192–94.

44. Ibid., 187–88.

45. Ibid., 214–26.

46. Ibid., 148.

47. Siringo, *A Cowboy Detective*, devotes two chapters to the Wild Bunch, see 305–80. See also Siringo's account in his last book, *Riata and Spurs*, 209–51. Also Patterson, *Butch Cassidy*, 148–50, 173–75, 309, fn. 2, 310, fn. 4.

48. Patterson, *Butch Cassidy*, 138–39. In *The Pinkertons*, 363–80, James D. Horan had noted that aiding the Pinkertons "was a network of reward-eager sheriffs the Pinkertons had established during the 1870s." "Doc" Shores was one of these.

49. Patterson, *Butch Cassidy*, 72–73.

50. Siringo, *Riata and Spurs*, 210.

51. Ibid., 210–12. See also Siringo, *A Cowboy Detective*, 310–12.

52. Siringo, *A Cowboy Detective*, 310; Siringo, *Riata and Spurs*, 213.

53. Siringo, *Riata and Spurs*, 214–15.

54. Siringo, *A Cowboy Detective*, 314, 319–24.

55. Siringo, *Riata and Spurs*, 217.

56. Ibid., 221.

57. Ibid., 222.

58. Ibid., 227–28; Patterson, *Butch Cassidy*, 249.

59. Siringo, *Riata and Spurs,* 232; Patterson, *Butch Cassidy*, 108–9, 136–38.

60. Baker, *The Wild Bunch*, 80–82.

61. Patterson, *Butch Cassidy*, 176–77; Siringo, *Riata and Spurs*, 238–45.

62. Siringo, *Riata and Spurs*, 251.

63. Western Literature Association, *A Literary History of the American West* (Fort Worth: Texas Christian University Press, 1987), 123.

64. Siringo, *A Cowboy Detective*, 339–80.

CHAPTER ELEVEN

1. Pingenot, *Siringo*, 48.

2. Ibid., 48, 55.

3. Siringo, *A Cowboy Detective*, 197–98.

4. Ibid., 199–200.

5. Ibid., 201.

6. *National Geographic Atlas of the World*, seventh edition (Washington, D.C.: National Geographic Society, 1999), 56–E1.

7. Siringo, *A Cowboy Detective*, 202.

8. Ibid., 206.

9. Ibid., 208.

10. Ibid., 209.

11. Ibid., 211.

12. Ibid., 212.

13. Ibid., 216.

14. Ibid., 222.

15. Ibid., 223–24.

16. Ibid., 225; also Siringo mentions meeting W. C. "Outlaw Bill" Moore in his *A Lone Star Cowboy*, but see H. Allen Anderson, "William C. Moore," *New Handbook of Texas*, 4: 824–25.

17. Siringo, *A Cowboy Detective*, 227–28.

18. Ibid., 305.

19. Ibid., 395.

20. Ibid. Wentz may well have been an alias for the real name of the owner and his sons.

21. Ibid., 402.

22. Ibid., 397.

23. Ibid., 398.

24. Ibid., 400.

25. Ibid.

26. Ibid., 400–401.

27. Ibid., 403.

28. Ibid., 406.

29. Ibid., 415.

30. Ibid., 418.

31. Ibid., 435.

32. Ibid., 437–40.

33. Ibid., 447–48. Siringo observed in passing that the brother of Lottie H. was an aggressive, feuding sheriff who had committed many murders, and may have been involved in the notorious Hatfield-McCoy feud. See Altina Waller, *Feud: Hatfields, McCoys, and Social Change in Appalachia, 1860–1900* (Chapel Hill: University of North Carolina Press, 1988); and Wilbur Miller, *Revenuers and Moonshiners: Enforcing Federal Liquor Law in the Mountain South, 1865–1900* (Chapel Hill: University of North Carolina Press, 1991).

34. Siringo, *A Cowboy Detective*, 449–50.

35. Ibid., 450.

36. Ibid., 451.

37. Ibid., 453.

38. Ibid.

39. J. Anthony Lukas, *Big Trouble: A Murder in a Small Western Town Sets Off a Struggle for the Soul of America* (New York: Simon & Shuster, 1997), 110–11.

40. Carlos A. Schwantes, *In Mountain Shadows: A History of Idaho* (Lincoln: University of Nebraska Press, 1991), 157–60.

41. Lukas, *Big Trouble*, 15–54.

42. William D. Haywood, *Bill Haywood's Book* (New York: International, 1929), 175, as quoted in Michael Boudett, "Charles Siringo and the Anarchists," Senior History Essay, Yale University, April 1988. By permission of the author.

43. Boudett, "Siringo and the Anarchists," 35.

44. Siringo, *A Cowboy Detective*, 493; Pingenot, *Siringo*, 129.

45. Lukas, *Big Trouble*, 158, 162–67, 170, 172–73.

46. Ibid., 174–75, 195–200. See also Joseph R. Conlin, *Big Bill Haywood and the Radical Union Movement* (Syracuse, N.Y.: Syracuse University Press, 1969), 65; and Horan, *The Pinkertons*, 475.

47. Lukas, *Big Trouble*, 199.

48. Ibid., 199–200.

49. Boudett, "Siringo and the Anarchists," 36.

50. Ibid., 36–37; Haywood, *Bill Haywood's Book*, 194; Peter Carlson, *Roughneck: The Life and Times of Bill Haywood* (New York: W. W. Norton, 1983), 87. The most vivid account of the kidnapping, however, is superbly narrated in great detail in Lukas, *Big Trouble*, 251–71.

51. Lukas, *Big Trouble*, 299–345; Siringo, *A Cowboy Detective*, 21–22.

52. Lukas, *Big Trouble*, 289–90. See also "James Henry Hawley," in Lamar, *NEAW*, 477, which cites sources for Hawley's career.

53. Lukas, *Big Trouble*, 289.

54. Ibid., 290–93. See also "William Edgar Borah," in Lamar, *NEAW*, 119, with bibliography.

55. Boudett, "Siringo and the Anarchists," 39.

56. Ibid., 41.

57. Arthur Weinberger, ed., *Attorney for the Damned* (New York: Simon & Schuster, 1957), 469.

58. Boudett, "Siringo and the Anarchists," 42.

59. Quoted in Weinberger, ed., *Attorney for the Damned*, 486–87.

60. Lukas, *Big Trouble*, 721–31, 735.

61. Siringo, *A Cowboy Detective*, 493.

62. Ibid., 513; see also Boudett, "Siringo and the Anarchists," 43.

63. Siringo, *Two Evil Isms: Pinkertonism and Anarchism* (Chicago: Charles A. Siringo, Publisher, 1915), 95.

64. Weinberger, *Attorney for the Damned*, 433–34.

65. Ibid., 469.

66. Lukas, *Big Trouble*, 206, 466.

67. Siringo, *A Cowboy Detective*, 516.

68. Lukas, *Big Trouble*, 748.

69. Siringo to Renehan, December 17, 1914, Chicago, Siringo Papers; Siringo, *Riata and Spurs*, 257–61.

CHAPTER TWELVE

1. Pingenot, *Siringo*, 64–69, n. 18–21; Siringo, *A Cowboy Detective*, 516–17.

2. Pingenot, *Siringo*, 69–70. The remarkable Renehan-Siringo friendship can be traced in many hundreds of letters between the two men from 1909 when Siringo sought Renehan's assistance in his fight with the Pinkertons, to April 20, 1928, when Renehan unexpectedly died. See Alois B. Renehan, Charles A. Siringo Correspondence, History Library, Museum of New Mexico, Santa Fe, New Mexico. Hereafter cited as Siringo Papers, Fray Angelico Chavez Library.

3. Pingenot, *Siringo*, 71, 183, n. 11–14; Siringo himself traces his controversy with the Pinkertons in his *Two Evil Isms*, ch. XVI, 106–7. See also Charles D. Peavy, *Charles A. Siringo: A Texas Pícaro* (Austin, Tex.; Steck-Vaughn Company, 1967), 21–22; and Orlan Sawey, *Charles A. Siringo* (Boston: Twayne, 1980), 91–97.

4. Siringo to W. A. Pinkerton, March 7, 1910, Siringo Papers, Fray Angelico Chavez Library, for his furious nine-page letter to Pinkerton. See also Pingenot, *Siringo*, 72–73; Peavy, *Siringo*, 12–13.

5. Siringo, *A Cowboy Detective: A True Story of Twenty-Two Years with a World-Famous Detective Agency* (Chicago: W. B. Conkey Company, 1912).

6. Siringo to Renehan, February 17, 1913, Siringo Papers, Fray Angelico Chavez Library.

7. Siringo, *Riata and Spurs*, 245–46, 248–50.

8. Interviews between Mrs. Mary Bell Ingram of the Matagorda County Museum and Historical Society, Bay City, Texas, and Dr. Paul C. Stone, my research assistant in July 2001. Mrs. Ingram not only provided valuable information about Siringo's parents, youth, and later visits, but introduced him to descendants of the Pierce and Cornelius families.

   Siringo's enduring prominence as a local author is demonstrated in "Charles A. Siringo. Matagorda County's most prolific writer penned seven books," Bay City *Daily Tribune*, Wednesday March 7, 1984.

9. "Old Couple is Married Here," *The Daily Tribune*, May 29, 1913, vol. 8, #151 (microfilm collection in Bay City Library). Courtesy of Matagorda County Museum and Historical Society.

10. See biography of Ellen (Partain, Rugeley), Siringo in Matagorda Historical Society File, p. 3, and account of Sapp's conviction in *Bay City News*, May 26, 1916. See also Pingenot, *Siringo*, 76, 165, and 184 n. 25.

11. Pingenot, *Siringo*, 77–78.

12. Ibid., 78.

13. Siringo, *Two Evil Isms, Pinkertonism and Anarchism, by a Cowboy Detective Who Knows, as He Spent Twenty-Two Years in the Inner Circle of Pinkerton's National Detective Agency* (Chicago: Charles A. Siringo, Publisher, 1915). Fortunately Charles D. Peavy has done a facsimile reprint of *Two Evil Isms* (Austin: Steck-Vaughn Company, 1967).

14. Siringo to William E. Hawks, Chicago, November 20, 1914. Hawks Letters in Beinecke Library, Yale University, New Haven, Connecticut.

15. Siringo to Hawks, Chicago, November 31, 1914.

16. Siringo to Hawks, Chicago, December 17, 1914, and December 22, 1914.

17. Siringo to Hawks, Chicago, January 23, 1915; Siringo to Renehan, December. 17, 1914, Chicago, Siringo Papers, Fray Angelico Chavez Library.

18. Siringo to Hawks, Chicago, March 2, 1915.

19. Ibid.

20. Ibid.

21. Siringo to Hawks, Santa Fe, March 27, 1915.

22. Siringo to Hawks, Santa Fe, April 25, 1915. The newspaper clippings Siringo sent Hawks are from *The New Mexican*, April 1915, and the *Record*, April 23, 1915.

23. Ibid.

24. Siringo to Hawks, Santa Fe, August 9, 1915.

25. Sawey, *Siringo*, 15; Pingenot, *Siringo*, 86–88.

26. Peavy, *Siringo*, 36.

27. Pingenot, *Siringo*, 89–90, and his excellent article, "Charlie Siringo: New Mexico's Lone Star Cowboy," *Cattlemen* 63 (November 1976): 56–57, 122–28. See also Siringo, *A Lone Star Cowboy*, 260–72.

28. Siringo, *A Lone Star Cowboy*, 273–78.

29. Ibid., 276–78.

30. Ibid., 278–79.

31. Clarence Siringo Adams, "Fair Trial at Encinoso," *True West* 13 (March–April 1966): 32–33, 50–51, which varies from other accounts of the incident. It is difficult to know which one is more accurate.

32. Ibid., 51.

33. Sawey, *Siringo*, 15–16.

34. Ibid., 16.

35. Ibid., 17; Charles A. Siringo, *History of "Billy the Kid"* (Albuquerque: University of New Mexico Press, 2000), vii–xx.

36. James H. East to Charlie Siringo, Douglas, Arizona, May 1, 1920. Typescript in Rasch Collection (O'Folliard File), Lincoln State Monument, Lincoln, N.Mex. (Xerox copy, courtesy of Robert M. Utley, November, 2002). Also Siringo, *History of "Billy the Kid"* (2000), xvii–xx.

37. Siringo, *History of "Billy the Kid," The True Life of the Most Daring Young Outlaw of the Age* (Santa Fe: Charles A. Siringo, 1920), has been reproduced in a facsimile edition, by Charles D. Peavy (Austin: Steck-Vaughn Company, 1967).

38. His favorite title was "Prairie Flower, or Bronco Chiquita." See Pingenot, *Siringo*, 94, 101, 143–45; 191 n. 7.

39. Siringo to Hawks, Sunny Slope, N.Mex., March 14, 1920.

40. Siringo to Hawks, Santa Fe, April 2, 1920.

41. "Clay Allison," in *New Handbook of Texas*, 1: 123–24.

42. Ibid.

43. The most recent and detailed account is Casey Tefertiller, *Wyatt Earp: The Life Behind the Legend* (New York: John Wiley & Sons, Inc., 1997), 24–26.

44. "Clay Allison," in *New Handbook of Texas*, 1: 124.

45. Papers and Letters of O. S. Clark, deposited in J. Evetts Haley Panhandle Plains Museum, June–July 1931. Xerox copies obtained from the Eugene G. Barker Texas History Center, University of Texas, Austin, via Dr. Paul C. Stone. See especially Clark's typescript, "Clay Allison of the Washita," 7 pages, in which the phrase "A Self Constituted Executioner" is used on p. 7.

46. See Henry F. Hoyt, *A Frontier Doctor*, Introduction by Frank B. Kellogg (Boston: Houghton Mifflin, 1929); see also a later printing by the Lakeside Press, Chicago, 1979, with a historical introduction by Doyce B. Nunis, Jr.

47. Pingenot, *Siringo*, 101.

48. Ibid.

49. Ibid., 102.

50. H. Allen Anderson, "James H. East," in *New Handbook of Texas*, 2: 757.

51. Bill O'Neal, *Historic Ranches of the Old West* (Austin: Eakin Press, 1997), 22–27.

52. Anderson, "James H. East," in *New Handbook of Texas*, 2: 757.

53. J. Evetts Haley, "Jim East—Trail Hand and Cowboy," *Panhandle Plains Historical Review* 4 (1931): 39–61, but especially 39.

54. Ibid.

55. See Clark file, Barker Texas History Center, 7-page memoir.

56. Anderson, "James H. East," in *New Handbook of Texas*, 2: 759.

57. Clark-Haley files, Siringo to East, Roswell, N.Mex., March 15, 1921. Siringo had borrowed $100 from East. This letter acknowledged receipt and promised to pay the sum back.

58. See "Introduction" by Neal M. Clark to N. Howard "Jack" Thorp, *Pardner of the Wind* (Lincoln: University of Nebraska Press, 1941), 13–20.

59. Ibid., 153–57, 169–93.

60. Ibid., 193. See also letter from Siringo to Thorp, September 22, 1927, 191–92.

61. "Charles Goodnight," in Lamar, *NEAW*, 439–40.

62. Haley, "Jim East—Trail Hand and Cowboy," 39. See also obituaries of East, who died May 13, 1930, in Douglas [AZ] *Daily Dispatch*, May 14, 1930, in Clark-Haley Collection, Xeroxes in Barker Texas History Center.

63. Haley, "Jim East—Trail Hand and Cowboy," 39.

CHAPTER THIRTEEN

1. Siringo to Renehan, October 21 and November 5, 1923, Siringo Papers, Fray Angelico Chavez Library, Santa Fe, New Mexico; Pingenot, *Siringo*, 104.

2. Pingenot, *Siringo*, 104. See also Siringo to Renehan, June 11, 1924, Siringo Papers, Fray Angelico Chavez Library.

3. Kevin Starr, *Inventing the Dream, California through the Progressive Era* (New York: Oxford University Press, 1985), 313. See also Siringo to Renehan, April 19, 1923, Renehan Papers, LMNM. Quoted in Pigenot, *Siringo*, 105.

4. Charles Musser, "Western Films," in Lamar, *NEAW*, 364. See also Jon Tuska, *The Filming of the West* (Garden City, N.Y.: Doubleday and Company, Inc., 1976), 45, 11–18, and throughout.

5. Martin Ridge, ed., *My Life East and West*, by William S. Hart (Chicago: The Lakeside Press, R. R. Donnelley & Sons Company, 1994), 401.

6. Musser, "Western Films," 364; and Pingenot, *Siringo*, 101, 108. Siringo actually used a favorable quote from Hart about one of his books to promote it.

7. Robert S. Birchard, *King Cowboy: Tom Mix and the Movies* (Burbank, Calif.: Riverwood Press, 1993), 3.

8. Don Cusic, *Cowboys and the Wild West: An A–Z Guide from the Chisholm Trail to the Silver Screen* (New York: Facts on File, Inc., 1994), 197–98; Lamar, *NEAW*, 329, 364, 700, 935, 1217. See also Tuska, *Filming of the West*, 51–59, 134–46, passim, 230–45, and throughout.

9. Guy Logsdon, "Rodeo," in Lamar, *NEAW*, 970–74, but especially 972.

10. Hart, *My Life East and West*, 331–36. The two showmen conspired to outwit one another with humorous stories when together in New York. See also Logsdon, "Will Rogers," in Lamar, *NEAW*, 975; and Ben Yagoda, *Will Rogers: A Biography* (New York: Knopf, 1993).

11. Birchard, *King Cowboy*, 5–8, 277–78; also Cusic, *Cowboys and the Wild West*, 198.

12. M. J. Van Deventer, "Miller Brothers," in Lamar, *NEAW*, 700. Among other Wild West showmen who came to Hollywood was Gordon William ("Pawnee Bill") Lillie, who headed his own Wild West show early in the century, and was a partner in Buffalo Bill Cody's show in its last few seasons. Lillie, who had met Siringo in Caldwell, Kansas, many years before, saw him on occasion in Los Angeles.

13. Cusic, *Cowboys and the Wild West*, 55–56, 110, 117, 187–88, 202–6, 248–49.

14. Ibid., 90.

15. Gary L. Roberts, "Earp Brothers," in Lamar, *NEAW*, 327–29; and Casey Tefertiller, *Wyatt Earp: The Life behind the Legend* (New York: John Wiley and Sons, 1997).

16. Pingenot, *Siringo*, 104.

17. Ronna Lee Sharpe and Tom Sharpe, "Some Folks Wouldn't Understand It: A Study of Henry Herbert Knibbs," in *Cowboy Poets and Poetry*, ed., David Stanley and Elaine Thatcher (Urbana and Chicago: University of Illinois Press, 2000), 175–85, especially 175–76. See also Siringo to Renehan, June 11, 1924, Siringo Papers, Fray Angelico Chavez Library.

18. W. H. Hutchinson, *A Bar Cross Liar: Biography of Eugene Manlove Rhodes Who Loved the West* (Stillwater, Okla.: Redlands Press, 1955), 3–22, 56–77.

19. Ibid. See also Frank V. Dearing, ed., *The Best Novels and Stories of Eugene Manlove Rhodes*, with an introduction by J. Frank Dobie (Boston: Houghton Mifflin Company, 1949), 183 ff.

20. Edwin R. Bingham, *Charles F. Lummis: Editor of the Southwest* (San Marino, Calif.: The Huntington Library, 1955); Turbese Lummis Fiske and Keith Lummis, *Charles F. Lummis: The Man and his West* (Norman: University of Oklahoma Press, 1975). For a quick summary of his career, see James K. Folsom, "Charles Fletcher Lummis," in Lamar, *NEAW*, 665; J. Golden Taylor, Editor-in-Chief, *A Literary History of the American West* (Fort Worth: Texas Christian University Press), 625–26; and Pingenot, *Siringo*, 200, n. 21.

21. Henry Knibbs to Charles F. Lummis, September 12, 1922. MS in Charles F. Lummis Papers, Henry Huntington Library, HM 44877.

22. Ibid.

23. Pingenot, *Siringo*, 204, n. 29.

24. Ibid., 204–5, n. 29.

25. Ibid., 147. The author, Howard Lamar, is the fortunate recipient of a Brininstool photo of Siringo.

26. Sharpe and Sharpe, "Some Folks Wouldn't Understand It," 183–85. See Siringo to Renehan, July 3, 1924, Siringo Papers, Fray Angelico Chavez Library.

27. Cusic, *Cowboys of the Wild West*, 248–49; Logsdon, "Rogers," in Lamar, *NEAW*, 975; Taylor, *A Literary History of the American West*, 1047–48. There are many biographies of Rogers, plus extensive editions of his writings. One of the best biographies is Yagoda, *Will Rogers: A Biography*.

28. David C. Hunt and James K. Folsom, "William Roderick James," in Lamar, *NEAW*, 565.

29. Ibid.

30. Ibid., but see Anthony Amaral, *Will James: The Gilt Edged Cowboy* (Los Angles: The Westernlore Press, 1967); also comments on James in Thorp, *Pardner of the Wind*, 287, n.9.

31. David C. Hunt, "Charles Marion Russell," in Lamar, *NEAW*, 991–92; excellent accounts by Brian W. Dippie, *Looking at Russell* (Fort Worth, Tex.: Amon Carter Museum, 1987); Peter Hassrick, *Charles M. Russell* (Norman: University of Oklahoma Press, 1999); and John Taliaferro, *Charles M. Russell: The Life and Legend of America's Cowboy Artist* (Boston: Little, Brown and Company, 1996). In *My Life East and West*, 383, William S. Hart wrote, "One could never see Charlie without seeing Nancy, too, for they were always together—a real man and a real woman."

32. Hart, *My Life East and West*, 156–59.

33. Ibid., 179–398.

34. Hunt, "Russell," in Lamar, *NEAW*, 991–92.

35. Siringo to Renehan, April 24, 1925, Siringo Papers, Fray Angelico Chavez Library.

36. Pingenot, *Siringo*, 109–10.

37. Siringo to Renehan, June 22, 1925, Siringo Papers, Fray Angelico Chavez Library.

38. Siringo to Renehan, October 3, 1925, Siringo Papers, Fray Angelico Chavez Library.

39. Cusic, *Cowboys and the Wild West*, 292, but see Hart, *My Life East and West*, 361–90 for a detailed account of how many controversies Hart and the studio officials engaged in during its making.

40. Siringo to William S. Hart, February 27, 1926, William S. Hart Papers, Seaver Center for Western History Research, Natural History Museum of Loa Angeles County, Los Angeles, California.

41. Pingenot, *Siringo*, 109.

42. Siringo to Renehan, April 24, 1925, Siringo Papers, Fray Angelico Chavez Library, in which he took a dislike to Dr. Pelton's showing off his fine house and asking him to be a pallbearer if he died before Siringo. See also Stony Nagel, "When Siringo was Marked for Death," *True West* 18 (November–December 1970): 31, 68–69.

43. Siringo to Renehan, March 8, 1926, Siringo Papers, Fray Angelico Chavez Library.

44. Siringo to Renehan, March 31, 1926, Siringo Papers, Fray Angelico Chavez Library, in which he spelled out Greenslet's proposal in a letter dated March 17, 1926.

45. Siringo to Greenslet, April n.d., 1926, Siringo Papers, Fray Angelico Chavez Library.

46. Pingenot, *Siringo*, 111–14.

47. An extensive correspondence of 165 letters between Siringo, Ferris Greenslet, editor-in-chief of Houghton Mifflin, and Ira Rich Kent, are deposited in the Charles A. Siringo File, Houghton Mifflin Company Records, Houghton Library, Harvard University, Cambridge, Massachusetts. These letters cover the years 1926–1928, and reveal a happy working relationship between these three men. I have used the Siringo file, but the letters are far too numerous to cite individually. However, see especially the Houghton Mifflin original proposal for a book in Greenslet to Siringo, February 26, 1926, Siringo File, Houghton Mifflin Company Records, Houghton Library. See also Pingenot, *Siringo*, 114.

48. Eugene Manlove Rhodes to Ferris Greenslet, Apalachin, N.Y., February 15, 1926. MS in Rhodes Collection, Box 2, Huntington Library.

49. Ibid. Rhodes ended his letter to Greenslet asking for Charlie's present address, saying, "He was suffering from bronchitis—I sent to his former address, Lynnwood, Calif., particulars of the treatment which had brought relief to me, and letter has just returned as unclaimed. Yours joyously, E. M. Rhodes."

50. Rhodes to Greenslet, Apalachin, New York, February 24, 1926. Rhodes Collection, Box 2. MS in Huntington Library.

51. Ibid.

52. Rhodes to Dale Warren, Houghton Mifflin Co., Tesuque, New Mexico, February 17, 1927. Rhodes Collection, Box 2, Huntington Library.

53. Rhodes to Ira Rich Kent, Tesuque, Santa Fe, New Mexico, March 10, 1927. Rhodes Collection, Box 2, Huntington Library.

54. Pingenot, *Siringo*, 116–17.

55. Ibid., 117.

56. Siringo to Neeta Marquis, November 5, 1926. MS in Marquis Papers, Huntington Library.

57. Siringo to Marquis, February 4, 1927. MS in Marquis Papers, Huntington Library. See also Pingenot, *Siringo*, 117.

58. Siringo to Marquis, March 23, 1927. MS in Marquis Papers, Huntington Library.

59. Luther Standing Bear, Brule Sioux author and film actor, was already a nationally known Indian leader, having brought a suit against the federal government for removing the Poncas from their reservation without just cause. General George Crook, who was sympathetic to the Poncas, allowed himself to be sued. In a landmark ruling that stated Indians could sue, Judge Elmer Scipio Dundy ruled in favor of Standing Bear and the Poncas. "Elmer Scipio Dundy," in Lamar, *NEAW*, 322–23, 606. See also "Luther Standing Bear," in Frederick E. Hoxie, ed., *Encyclopedia of North American Indians* (Boston: Houghton Mifflin Company, 1996), 607–8.

60. "Stirring Days When Six-shooters Ruled West Recalled," *Los Angeles Times*, March 26, 1927, II, p. 9. Pingenot, *Siringo*, 119–20. Also Estelle Lawton Lindsey, "Chat with Ex-Cowboy, Hailed as Great Literary Find, Recalls Wild West Days," *Los Angeles Evening Express*, April 11, 1927, sec. 3, pp. 1, 4.

61. Will Rogers to Siringo, March 27, 1927, HMC Records, HLHU, cited in Pingenot, *Siringo*, 121.

62. Basing his account on Houghton Mifflin Records, Pingenot's *Siringo*, pp. 121–22, 123–29, 130–33, is by far the most complete and accurate version of this last fight with the Pinkertons. The Houghton Mifflin Company Records, in the Houghton Library, Harvard University, contain an extensive correspondence between the firm and the Pinkerton lawyers.

63. Sawey, *Siringo*, 92–94. See also Siringo's postcard statement to friends, 2417 Grand Canal, Venice, Cal., Oct. 27, 1927 saying:

> Dear Friends:
>
> My revised edition of Riata and Spurs *is just off the press and will soon by in al [sic] leading Bookstores. It is an improvement over the first edition gotten out last April. In it are the lives of many bad-mad cowboys, such as John Wesley Hardin, Bill Longley, Ben Thompson, King Fisher, Clay Allison, Tom Horn and Sam Bass....*
>
> The Houghton-Mifflin Co., #2 Park Street, Boston, Mass, *will forward* Riata and Spurs, *post-paid for $3.*
>
> The Author
>
> Charles A. Siringo

Xerox in O. S. Clark Papers, Haley Collection, in Barker Historical Center, Austin, Tex.

64. Pingenot, *Siringo*, 101, 192.

65. Hart to Siringo, May 25, 1927, and Siringo to Hart, May 30, 1927. Hart Letters, CMNH (Los Angeles County Museum of Natural History).

66. Hart to Siringo, July 6, 1928, Hart Letters, CMNH.

67. Siringo to Renehan, May 6, 1926, Siringo Papers, Fray Angelico Chavez Library, Santa Fe, New Mexico. Also idem, May 7 and 8, June 14, and June 18; also Renehan to Siringo, June 15, 1926, enclosing a defense of Burns's *Billy the Kid* by his publisher, Doubleday. See also Pingenot, *Siringo*, 202, n. 10.

68. Pingenot, *Siringo*, 148.

69. Ibid., 149; See also copy of Rogers and Hart telegram in Box 5, Yale Media Design Studio Files, Beinecke Rare Book and Manuscript Library, Yale University, New Haven, Connecticut. Copy provided by Mrs. Carol Siringo McFarland, a granddaughter of Charlie Siringo.

70. Orlan Sawey, *Charles A. Siringo* (Boston: Twayne, 1980).

71. E. M. Rhodes, "He'll Make a Hand," *Sunset Magazine* 63 (June 1927): 23.

72. On a more practical basis one must acknowledge the persistence and dominance of ranching in the West, as attested to by Terry G. Jordan's classic, *North American Cattle-Ranching Frontiers: Origins, Diffusion, and Differentiation* (Albuquerque: University of New Mexico Press, 1993), chapter nine, "The Midwest Triumphant," 267–314.

73. William Kittredge, "Making Ourselves at Home," Essay in David Stanley and Elaine Thatcher, *Cowboy Poets & Poetry*, 362–69. The quotation is on 368–69.

   In 1986, fifty-six years after Siringo died, another history-minded Texas cowboy and songwriter, Don Edwards, produced his own *Songs of the Cowboy*, which he dedicated to Nathan Howard "Jack" Thorp (a Siringo admirer), and to eight others of the best song and ballad writers, among them Will James and Charles Badger Clark. Edwards's publications and his own career testify to the ongoing western lifestyle that boomed in Siringo's time but continues to thrive today. See Don Edwards, "Dedication," *Songs of the Cowboy* (Weatherford, Tex.: Sevenshoux Publishing, 1986).

Bibliography

ARCHIVAL AND MANUSCRIPT SOURCES

Eugene C. Barker, Texas History Center, University of Texas at Austin

"Papers and Letters of O. S. Clark" deposited in J. Evetts Haley, Panhandle-Plains Museum, July 1931. Xerox copies obtained from the Barker History Center (courtesy of Paul C. Stone).

Papers from the East Collection (relating to Jim East and Charles Siringo: letters, newspaper clippings.

Papers of Abel Head (Shanghai) Pierce.

Beinecke Rare Book and Manuscript Library

Western Americana Collection

Yale University Media Design Studio Files—collected by Howard R. Lamar, Philip Garvin, and David Laurance for the studio, 1975–1980, as research materials for a film biography of Charles A. Siringo. Six boxes deposited in Lamar papers (Beinecke) 2001.

Box 2–3: slides of South Texas, Siringo birthplace region; City of Matagorda, Texas, illustrations; Kansas cattle towns 1867–1885, photos; William Haywood Trial, Boise, Idaho, 1907, materials.

Box 4: photographs of Coeur d'Alene mining strikes, 1892, 1898; Haymarket riot scenes, 1886; Haywood Trial photographs, 1907; cattle ranching and roundup photographs from Amon Carter Museum, Fort Worth, Texas.

Box 5: William S. Hart and Will Rogers telegram on death of Siringo, October 1928; newspaper clippings of Steunenberg assassination, 1905; selections from Siringo–A. B. Renehan correspondence re: *Two Evil Isms*, 1914–1916.

Box 6: Photographs of Gem and Wallace, Idaho, 1890s; copy of Illinois Supreme Court Record of Pinkerton v. Charles A. Siringo testimony, April 20, 1915; excerpts from Governors' Papers: L. Bradford Prince, 1889–1893 (Xerox copies from New Mexico State Records Center and Archives, Santa Fe, New Mexico); copies of Siringo's expenses while on Ancheta case, 1891; Santa Fe newspaper accounts of Siringo's arrest and attempted extradition to Chicago to stand trial for libel, 1915.

Report of James H. Purdy on contents of four-hundred-page Renehan Collection to Philip Garvin; extensive selection of letters between Siringo and Renehan, 1923–1928 (Xerox copies from History Library, Museum of New Mexico, Santa Fe, New Mexico).

Type and typescript of Philip Garvin interview with J. Evetts Haley about Siringo, Canyon, Texas, October, 1975.

Nine Siringo letters to William E. Hawks, 1914–1915.

Pinkerton's National Detective Agency. A Registry of its Records in the Library of Congress. Prepared by Michael McEldering. Manuscript Division of Library of Congress, Washington, D.C., 2001. In addition to a history of the Pinkerton family, these records include accounts of Siringo lawsuits (container Number 61); Butch Cassidy and the Wild Bunch and associates, the Sundance Kid, etc. (containers 87, 88, 89, 90, 91, and 92–96; the murder of Governor Frank Steunenberg (containers 172–73); and Scrapbook of James McParland, 1903.

Copy of Registry in Western Americana Collection; courtesy of George A. Miles, Curator.

Fray Angelico Chavez History Library, Museum of New Mexico, Santa Fe, New Mexico

Charles Siringo Papers, 1896-1928 (AC 212). (These papers were originally listed as "Alois B. Renehan–Charles Siringo Correspondence" in the History Library, Museum of New Mexico, but are now classified as the Charles Siringo Papers.)

Houghton Library, Harvard University, Cambridge, Massachusetts

Charles A. Siringo File, Houghton Mifflin Company Records.

Huntington Library, San Marino, California

William S. Hart letters in Stuart Lake Collection.

Henry H. Knibbs–Charles F. Lummis Correspondence.

Neeta Marquis Collection, which contains six letters from Siringo.

Eugene Rhodes Collection, containing several letters to the Houghton Mifflin Company promoting Siringo and his last book, *Riata and Spurs*, in 1926 and 1927.

Matagorda County Historical Society and Museum, Bay City, Texas

Collections relating to Siringo identified by Mary Belle Ingram, Director, and Dr. Paul C. Stone, July 2001.

Arda Talbot Allen. *Miss Ella of the Deep South*. San Antonio, Texas: The Naylor Company, 1951.

"Biography and Personal Reminiscences of F. Cornelius, Sr., of Midfield, Matagorda County, Texas" (Xerox copy).

Clippings from local newspapers about Siringo, 1913, 1970, 1984.

Gayle Fritz. "Matagorda Bay Area, Texas: A Survey of the Archaeological and Historical Resources." Typescript for the University of Texas at Austin and Texas General Land Office, Research Report, No. 45 (1973).

John Columbus Maar. "The History of Matagorda County, Texas." M.A. thesis, University of Texas, August 1928.

Gail Renae Martin. "Early Settlement on Matagorda Peninsula." Typescript (n.d.).

Matagorda County, Texas Brand Book, vol. 1: brands filed by Antonio Siringo; Second Brand Book number 1, p. 386, registry of C. A. Siringo brand, "S2," May 19, 1873.

Jean W. Richardson. "Charles A. Siringo." Typescript (n.d.)

Claude A. Talley, Jr. "Geographic Factors in the Indianola–Matagorda Bay Area of Texas that Influenced the Development of the Southwest from 1840–1875." Victoria, Texas, March 1970, typescript.

Paul C. Stone interviews with Mary B. Ingram, Director, Matagorda County History Society.

Panhandle-Plains Museum, Canyon, Texas

Fifteen interviews relating to Siringo prepared by the Works Projects Administration. Typescripts in Haley Collection.

Thomas A. Frazier. "Charles Siringo: A Texas Cowboy." Undated article in Haley Papers.

J. Evetts Haley. "Jim East: Trail Hand and Cowboy." *Panhandle-Plains Historical Review* 4 (1931): 39–61.

———. "Charlie Siringo, Cowboy Chronicler." *Shamrock* (spring 1962): 5–7, 15.

Letters of J. Frank Dobie to Haley, March, 1929 to August 20, 1929.

Letter of J. Evetts Haley to Siringo, March 14, 1928.

Letter from Dr. Henry F. Hoyt to Siringo, Long Beach, California, June 9, 1921. Copy forwarded to Haley from Siringo.

O. W. Nolen. "Charlie Siringo, Old Time Cowboy Rancher, Detective, and Author." *The Cattleman* 38, vol. 7 (December 1951): 50–56.

Seaver Center for Western History Research

Natural History Museum of Los Angeles County, the William S. Hart Collection (General Collection #1012), which contains correspondence between Siringo and Hart.

REFERENCE WORKS

Dictionary of American Biography. Edited by Allen Johnson and Dumas Malone. Twenty vols. and index, 1928–1937. Supplements, 1944–Present. New York: Charles Scribner and Sons.

Encyclopedia of North American Indians. Edited by Frederick E. Hoxie. Boston: Houghton Mifflin Company, 1996.

A Literary History of the American West. Editor-in-Chief, J. Golden Taylor. Fort Worth: Texas Christian University Press, 1987.

Matagorda County Historical Commission. *Historic Matagorda County,* vols. I and II. Houston: D. Armstrong Company, Inc., 1986–1988.

New Encyclopedia of the American West. Editor-in-Chief, Howard R. Lamar. New Haven: Yale University Press, 1998.

The New Handbook of Texas in Six Volumes. Austin: Texas State Historical Association, 1996. A truly outstanding comprehensive source for the History of Texas.

The Trail Drivers of Texas. Originally compiled and edited by J. Marvin Hunter. Austin: University of Texas Press, 1985. Second printing 1986. Published under the direction of George W. Saunders. Introduction by B. Byron Price.

BOOKS BY CHARLES A. SIRINGO

A Texas Cowboy, or, Fifteen Years on the Hurricane Deck of a Spanish Pony, Taken from Real Life by Chas. A. Siringo, An Old Stove Up "Cow Puncher," Who Has Spent Nearly Twenty Years on the Great Western Cattle Ranches. Chicago: M. Umbdenstock and Co., 1885.

A Texas Cowboy. . . . Second edition, enlarged. Chicago: Siringo and Dobson, Publishers, 1886. Contains advice about ranching and horses.

A Texas Cowboy. . . . Introduction by J. Frank Dobie and bibliography of Siringo's writings. Drawings by Tom Lea. New York: William Sloan Associates, 1950.

A Texas Cowboy. . . . Paperback edition. Lincoln: University of Nebraska Press, 1979.

A Texas Cowboy. . . . Facsimile of 1885 edition. Washington, D.C.: Time-Life, 1980.

A Texas Cowboy, or, Fifteen Years on the Hurricane Deck of a Spanish Pony. Edited and with an introduction by Richard W. Etulain. New York: Penguin Books, 2000.

A Cowboy Detective: A True Story of Twenty-Two Years with a World-Famous Detective Agency (Chicago: W. B. Conkey Company, 1912).

Two Evil Isms, Pinkertonism and Anarchism, by a Cowboy Detective Who Knows, As He Spent Twenty-Two Years in the Inner Circle of Pinkerton's National Detective Agency. Chicago: Charles A. Siringo, Publisher, 1915.

Two Evil Isms. . . . Facsimile reprint with an introduction by Charles D. Peavy. Austin: Steck-Vaughn Company, 1967.

A Lone Star Cowboy: Being Fifty Years Experience in the Saddle as Cowboy, Detective and New Mexico Rancher, on Every Cow Trail in the Wooly Old West. Santa Fe, N.Mex.: Charles A. Siringo, 1919.

The Song Companion of a Lone Star Cowboy: Old Favorite Cow-Camp Songs. Santa Fe, N.Mex.: Chas. A. Siringo, 1919.

History of "Billy the Kid": The True Life of the Most Daring Young Outlaw of the Age. Santa Fe, N.Mex.: Chas. A. Siringo, 1920.

History of "Billy the Kid." Facsimile edition, with an introduction by Charles D. Peavy. Austin: Steck-Vaughn Company, 1967.

Riata and Spurs: The Story of a Lifetime Spent in the Saddle as Cowboy and Detective. Boston: Houghton Mifflin Company, 1927.

NEWSPAPERS

Caldwell Journal. April 16, 1885, p. 3, col. 4. Announcement of publication of *A Texas Cowboy.* April 23, 1885. Account of Siringo Cigar Store. September 6, 1885. Records sale of "confectionary and lunch business." December 24, 1885. Favorable review of *A Texas Cowboy.*

Caldwell Post Weekly. March 15, 1883, p. 3, col. 1, records Siringo's and Mamie Floyd's marriage.

Capital Evening News (Boise, Idaho). August 8, 1907, records Siringo's third marriage.

Chicago Evening News. April 3, 1886, contains critical review of *A Texas Cowboy.*

The Daily Tribune (Bay City, Texas). March 23, May 26 and 29, 1913, vol. 8, no. 151. Microfilm in Genealogy Room of the Bay City Public Library, which contains account of Siringo's fourth marriage to Ellen Partain. April 23, 1970, p. 5: "They were Great Old Days for Matagorda County Cowboy." March 7, 1984, Article by Anna Poole: "Charlie Siringo: Matagorda County's Most Prolific Writer—Penned Seven Books."

Idaho Daily Statesman. August 7, September 22, 1892. Coeur d'Alene Strike account. June 27, 1907, p. 8, account of Ethel Barrymore at Haywood trial. July 5, 1907, account of Haywood Trial.

Los Angeles Evening Express. April 11, 1927, pp. 1–2. "Ex-Cowboy, Hailed as Great Literary Find."

Los Angeles Times. March 26, 1927. Article on Siringo's *Riata and Spurs.*

New York Times Book Review. May 8, 1927. Review of *Riata and Spurs* by Owen P. White.

The Nation. July 13, 1927. Review of *Riata and Spurs* by J. Frank Dobie.

Secondary Sources

Abbott, E. C. "Teddy Blue" and Helena Huntington Smith. *We Pointed Them North: Recollections of a Cowpuncher.* Edited by Ron Tyler. Chicago: Lakeside Press, 1991.

Adams, Andy. *The Log of a Cowboy: Narrative of the Old Trail Days.* Introduction by Thomas McGuane. 1903; Repr. Boston: Houghton Mifflin Company, 2000.

Adams, Clarence Siringo. "Fair Trial at Encinoso." *True West* 13 (March–April 1966): 32–33, 50–51.

Adams, Ramon F., comp. *Six Guns and Saddle Leather: A Bibliography of Books and Pamphlets on Western Outlaws and Gunmen.* Privately printed, 1954; Rev. ed., 1969.

Adams, Ramon F. and Charles Britzman Homer. *Charles M. Russell, The Cowboy Artist: A Biography.* Pasadena, Calif.: Trail's End Publishing Co., Inc., 1948.

Adorno, Rolena, and Patrick Charles Pautz. *Alvar Nuñez Cabeza de Vaca.* Lincoln: University of Nebraska Press, 1999. 3 vols.

Amaral, Anthony. *Will James: The Gilt Edged Cowboy.* Los Angeles: The Westernlore Press, 1967.

Appleman, Roy E. *Charlie Siringo, Cowboy Detective.* Washington, D.C.: Potomac Corral, The Westerners, 1968.

Arnot, John. "My Recollections of Tascosa Before and After the Coming of the Law." *Panhandle-Plains Historical Review* 6 (1933).

Avrich, Paul. *The Haymarket Tragedy.* Princeton, N.J.: Princeton University Press, 1984.

Baker, Pearl. *The Wild Bunch at Robbers Roost.* New York: Abelard-Schuman, 1969; repr. 1971.

Ball, Eve. "Charlie Siringo and 'Eat Em Up Jake.'" *True West* 16 (May–June 1969): 36–37, 46–47.

Banker, Mark. "Beyond the Melting Pot and Multiculturalism: Cultural Politics in Southern Appalachia and Hispanic New Mexico." *Montana: The Magazine of Western History* 50 (summer 2000): 22–23.

Barker, Eugene C. *The Life of Stephen F. Austin, Founder of Texas, 1793–1836: A Chapter in the Westward Movement of the Anglo-American People.* Nashville: Cokesbury Press, 1925; repr. 1955, 1970.

———, ed. *The Austin Papers.* 4 vols. Washington, D.C.: Government Printing Office, 1924–1928.

Barr, Alwyn. "Texas Coastal Defense, 1861–1865." *Southwestern Historical Quarterly* XLV, No. 1 (July 1961).

Bay City Lions Club. "Historic Matagorda County in the Heart of the Rich Gulf Coast." Bay City, Tex.: n.d. Copy in Beinecke Library, Yale University.

Bieber, Ralph P., ed. *Historic Sketches of the Cattle Trade of the West and Southwest, 1874*, by Joseph McCoy. In *The Southwestern Historical Series* no. 7 (1940). Contains an excellent essay by Bieber on McCoy's life.

Birchard, Robert S. *King Cowboy: Tom Mix and the Movies*. Burbank, Calif.: Riverwood Press, 1993.

Botkin, B. A., ed. *A Treasury of American Folklore*. Foreword by Carl Sandburg. New York: Crown Publishers, 1944. See also 1980 edition, abridged with a new introduction by Joseph Leach.

Bouzereau, Laurent. *Ultraviolent Movies: From Sam Peckinpah to Quentin Tarantino*. New York: Citadel Press, 1996; rev. and updated, 2000.

Branch, Douglas. *The Cowboy and His Interpreters*. New York: Cooper Square Publishers, Inc., 1961.

Broehl, Wayne G, Jr. *The Molly Maguires*. Cambridge, Mass.: Harvard University Press, 1964.

Burton, Harley True. *A History of the LX Ranch*. Austin: Von Boeckman Jones, 1928. Repr. New York: Argonaut, 1966.

Carlson, Paul H., ed. *The Cowboy Way: An Exploration of History and Culture*. Lubbock: Texas Tech University Press, 2000.

Carlson, Peter. *Roughneck: The Life and Times of Bill Haywood*. New York: W. W. Norton, 1983.

Campbell, Randolph B. *An Empire for Slavery: The Peculiar Institution in Texas, 1821–1865*. Baton Rouge: Louisiana State University Press, 1989.

Cantrell, Gregg. *Stephen F. Austin: Impresario of Texas*. New Haven: Yale University Press, 1999.

Cary, Diana Serra. *The Hollywood Posse: The Story of a Gallant Band of Horsemen Who Made Movie History*. Norman: University of Oklahoma Press, 1995.

Clark, Badger. *Sun and Saddle Leather*. Sixth ed. Boston: Richard G. Badger, the Gorham Press, 1922.

Clark, Neil M. "Close Calls: An Interview with Charles A. Siringo, Daring Adventurer in the Old WILD WEST." *American Magazine* 107 (January 1929): 38–39, 130–31. (In Haley Collection.)

Collinson, Frank. *Life in the Saddle*. Norman: University of Oklahoma Press, 1963; repr. 1997. Excellent chapter on Fort Griffin, Texas.

Conlin, Joseph R. *Big Bill Haywood and the Radical Union Movement*. Syracuse, N.Y.: Syracuse University Press, 1969.

Cooke, John Byrne. *South of the Border*. New York: Bantam Books, 1989. (A novel about Siringo and Butch Cassidy.)

Corry, John. "Pinkerton's Biggest Wars: Only the Files Remain." *New York Times*, Saturday, July 19, 1975, pp. 25 and 38.

Covey, Cyclone, translator and annotator. *Cabeza de Vaca: Adventures in the Unknown Interior of America*. Albuquerque: University of New Mexico Press, 1990.

Cox, James. *Historical and Biographical Record of the Cattle Industry and the Cattlemen of Texas*. St. Louis: Woodward and Tiernan Printing Company, 1895.

Crouch, Barry A. *The Freedman's Bureau and Black Texans*. Austin: University of Texas Press, 1992.

Cusic, Don. *Cowboys and the Wild West: An A–Z Guide from the Chisholm Trail to the Silver Screen*. New York: Facts on File, Inc., 1994.

Dale, Edward Everett. *The Range Cattle Industry*. Norman: University of Oklahoma Press, 1930.

Dary, David. *Cowboy Culture: A Saga of Five Centuries*. New York: Alfred A. Knopf, 1981.

David, Henry. *The History of the Haymarket Affair: A Study in the American Social-Revolutionary and Labor Movements*. New York: Russell and Russell, 1964.

Day, Jack Hays. *The Sutton-Taylor Feud*. San Antonio: Murray, 1937.

Dearing, Frank V., ed. *The Best Novels and Stories of Eugene Manlove Rhodes*. With an introduction by J. Frank Dobie. Boston: Houghton Mifflin Company, 1949.

Dippie, Brian W. *Looking at Russell*. Fort Worth, Tex.: Amon Carter Museum, 1987.

Dobie, J. Frank. *Andy Adams: Cow Chronicler*. Dallas: Southern Methodist University, 1926.

———. *A Vaquero of the Brush Country*. New York: Grosset & Dunlap, 1929.

———. *Guide to Life and Literature of the Southwest*. Dallas: Southern Methodist University Press, 1952.

———. *James Cox and His Cattle Industry*. New York: Antiquarian Press, 1960.

Douglas, C. L. *Cattle Kings of Texas*. Austin: State House Press, 1989.

Durham, Philip, and Everett L. Jones. *Negro Cowboys*. New York: Dodd, Mead, 1965.

Dykstra, Robert R. *The Cattle Towns: A Social History of the Kansas Cattle Trading Centers*. New York: Alfred A. Knopf, 1968.

Dykstra, Robert R., and Jo Ann Manfra. "The Circle Dot Cowboy at Dodge City: History and Imagination in Andy Adams's *The Log of a Cowboy*." *WHQ* vol. 33, no. 1 (spring 2002): 19–40.

Eccles, W. J. *The Canadian Frontier, 1534–1760*. New York: Holt, Rinehart, 1969; repr. 1974.

Edwards, Don. *Songs of the Cowboy*. Weatherford, Tex.: Sevenshoux Publishing, 1986).

Emmett, Chris. *Shanghai Pierce: A Fair Likeness*. Norman: University of Oklahoma Press, 1953. Outstanding biography.

Everson, William K. *A Pictorial History of the Western Film*. Secaucus, N.J.: The Citadel Press, 1969.

Fahey, John. "Coeur d'Alene Confederacy." *Idaho Yesterdays* 12 (spring 1968).

Fehrenbach, T. R. *Lone Star: A History of Texas and the Texans.* New York: Macmillan Publishing Company, 1968 and 1985.

Fischer, John. *From the High Plains: An Account of the Hard Men, High-Spirited Women, and a Few Rascals—Who Settled the Last Frontier of the Old West.* New York: Harper & Row, Publishers, 1978. Has good coverage of Old Tascosa.

Galloway, B. P., ed. *The Dark Corner of the Confederacy.* Dubuque, Iowa: Kendall/Hurt Publishing Company, 1964; repr. 1972.

Gard, Wayne. *The Chisholm Trail.* Norman: University of Oklahoma Press, 1954.

Garrett, Pat F. *The Authentic Life of Billy the Kid.* Santa Fe: New Mexican Printing and Publishing Co., 1882.

Gatschet, Albert. *The Karankawa Indians: The Coast People of Texas.* Cambridge, Mass.: Peabody Museum of American Archaeology and Ethnology, 1891.

Gordon, Wally. "1976 Movie 'Siringo' Links Real and Celluloid Old West." *Albuquerque Journal,* Saturday, May 2, 1981, p. 13.

Gracey, David B., II. *Moses Austin: His Life.* San Antonio: Trinity University Press, 1987.

Green, Rena (Maverick), ed. *Samuel Maverick, Texan, 1803–1870: A Collection of Letters, Journals and Memoirs.* San Antonio: privately printed, 1952, i.e. 1953.

Greenslet, Ferris. *Under the Bridge.* Boston: Houghton Mifflin Company, 1943.

Haley, J. Evetts. "Jim East—Trail Hand and Cowboy." *Panhandle-Plains Historical Review* 4 (1931): 39–61.

———. *Charles Goodnight: Cowman and Plainsman.* Boston: Houghton Mifflin, 1936.

———. *George W. Littlefield, Texan.* Norman: University of Oklahoma Press, 1943.

———. *The XIT Ranch of Texas and the Early Days of the Llano Estacado.* Norman: University of Oklahoma Press, 1967.

Hammett, A. B. J. *The Empresario Martin de Leon.* Waco: Texas A & M University Press, 1973.

Hammond, John Hays. "Strong Men of the Wild West: Reminiscences and Reflections of the Law and Two Flags." *Scribner's Magazine* vol. LXXVII, no. 2 (February 1925): 115, 121–24, et. seq.

Hassrick, Peter H. *Charles M. Russell.* Norman: University of Oklahoma Press, 1999.

Haywood, William D. *Bill Haywood's Book.* New York: International, 1929.

Hess, Chester Newten. "Old Sleuth on the Range: An Appreciation of Charlie Siringo, Cowboy-Detective in the Days when Six-Shooters Ruled the West." *Touring Topics* (February 1929): 28–32.

———. "Sagebrush Sleuth: The Saga of Charlie Siringo." *The Cattleman* (January 1955): 36–37, 66–82.

Himmel, Kelly F. *The Conquest of the Karankawas and the Tonkawas, 1821–1859.* College Station: Texas A & M University Press, 1959.

Hoig, Stan. *Jesse Chisholm: Ambassador of the Plains.* Niwot: University of Colorado Press, 1991.

Horan, James D. *Desperate Men: Revelations from the Sealed Pinkerton Files.* New York: G. P. Putnam's Sons, 1949.

———. *The Pinkertons: The Detective Dynasty That Made History.* New York: Crown Publications, Inc., 1967. Second printing 1969.

Hough, Emerson. *North of '36.* New York: Grosset & Dunlap Publishers, 1923; repr. Curtis Publishing Company, 1925.

Hoyt, Henry F. *A Frontier Doctor.* Chicago: The Lakeside Press, 1979.

Hudson, Wilson. *Andy Adams: His Life and Writings.* Dallas: Southern Methodist University Press, 1964.

———. *Andy Adams: Storyteller and Novelist of the Great Plains.* Austin: Steck-Vaughn, 1967.

Hughes, R. J. *Rebellious Rangers: Rip Ford and the Old Southwest.* Norman: University of Oklahoma Press, 1964.

Hutchinson, W. H. *A Bar Cross Liar: Biography of Eugene Manlove Rhodes Who Loved the West.* Stillwater, Okla.: Redlands Press, 1955.

Jennings, N. A. *A Texas Ranger.* Edited by Ben Proctor Chicago: Lakeside Classics, 1992.

Jensen, Vernon H. *Heritage of Conflict: Labor Relations in the Nonferrous Metals Industry up to 1930.* New York: Greenwood Press, 1968.

Johansen, Dorothy O. and Charles M. Gates. *Empire of the Columbia: A History of the Pacific Northwest.* New York: Harper & Brothers, 1957.

Jordan, Terry G. *North American Cattle Frontiers: Origins, Diffusion, and Differentiation.* Albuquerque: University of New Mexico Press, 1993.

Josephy, Alvin M., Jr. *The Civil War in the American West.* New York: Alfred A. Knopf, 1991.

King, Murray E. *The Last of the Bandit Riders.* New York: Bonanza Books, 1938; repr. 1950.

Knibbs, Henry Herbert. *Cowboy Poetry: Classic Rhymes.* Compiled by Mason and Janice Coggin. Phoenix: Cowboy Mines Production, 1999.

Koszarski, Diane Kaiser. *The Complete Films of William S. Hart: A Pictorial Record.* New York: Dover Publications Inc., 1980.

Lamar, Howard R. *The Far Southwest, 1846–1912: A Territorial History.* Albuquerque: University of New Mexico Press, 2000.

———. "Rites of Passage: Young Men and Their Families in the Overland Trails Experience, 1843–1869." *Charles Redd Monographs in Western History*, no. 8. Edited by Thomas G. Alexander. Provo, Utah: Brigham Young University Press, 1978.

———. *The Trader on the American Frontier: Myth's Victim*. College Station: Texas A & M University Press, 1977.

Lamar, Howard R. and Sam Truett. "The Greater Southwest and California from the Beginning of European Settlement to the 1880s." In *The Cambridge History of the Native Peoples of the Americas*. Vol. I., part II. Edited by Bruce G. Trigger and Wilcomb E. Washburn. Cambridge: Cambridge University Press, 1996.

Lang, William L. *Centennial West: Essays on the Northern Tier States*. Seattle: University of Washington Press, 1991.

Larson, Robert W. *New Mexico's Quest for Statehood, 1846–1912*. Albuquerque: University of New Mexico Press, 1968.

———. *New Mexico Populism: A Study of Radical Protest in a Western Territory*. Boulder: Colorado Associated University Press, 1974.

Linn, John J. "Reminiscences of Fifty Years in Texas." In *Original Narratives of Texas History and Adventure*. A facsimile of original 1883 edition. Austin: The Steck Company, 1939.

Lubbock, Francis R. *Six Decades in Texas: Memoirs of Francis Richard Lubbock*. Austin: Ben Jones and Company, 1900.

Lukas, J. Anthony. *Big Trouble: Murder in a Small Western Town Sets off a Struggle for the Soul of America*. New York: Simon and Schuster, 1997. A truly exhaustive study of the Haywood Trial in Boise, Idaho.

McCan, Kerry. *Brindy Polaris: A Novel of the American West, 1866–1972*. Victoria, Tex.: Medio Press, 1996.

McCarty, John L. *Maverick Town: The Story of Old Tascosa*. Foreword by C. L. Sonnichsen. Norman: University of Oklahoma Press, 1946, 1968, 1988.

MacColl, E. Kimbark, and Harry H. Stein. *Merchants, Money, and Power: The Portland Establishment, 1843–1913*. Portland: Georgian Press, 1988.

McCoy, Joseph G. *Cattle Trade of the West and Southwest*. Kansas City, Mo.: Ramsey, Millett and Hudson, 1874.

McMurtry, Larry. *Lonesome Dove: A Novel*. New York: Simon and Schuster, 1985. A truly brilliant account of the Long Drive from Texas to Montana.

Magnusen, Richard G. *Coeur d'Alene Diary*. Portland, Ore.: Metropolitan Press, 1968.

Marks, Paula Mitchell. *Turn Your Eyes toward Texas: Pioneers Sam and Mary Maverick*. College Station: Texas A & M University Press, 1989.

Massey, Sara R. *Black Cowboys of Texas*. College Station: Texas A & M University Press, 2000.

Matagorda County Historical Commission. *Historic Matagorda County*. Vols. I and II. Houston: D. Armstrong Company, Inc., 1986–1988.

Matthews, Sallie Reynolds. *Interwoven: A Pioneer Chronicle*. College Station: Texas A & M University Press, 1936; new ed., 1999.

Memoirs of Mary A. Maverick: San Antonio's First American Woman. Arranged by Mary A. Maverick and her son, George Madison Maverick. San Antonio: Alamo Printing Company, 1921.

Metz, Leon C. *Pat Garrett: The Story of a Western Man.* Norman: University of Oklahoma Press, 1973.

Miller, Wilbur. *Revenuers and Moonshiners: Enforcing Federal Liquor Laws in the Mountain South, 1855–1900.* Chapel Hill: University of North Carolina Press, 1991.

Montoya, Maria. *Translating Property: The Maxwell Land Grant and the Conflict over Land in the American West, 1840–1900.* Berkeley: University of California Press, 2002.

Morn, Frank. *"The Eye That Never Sleeps": A History of the Pinkerton National Detective Agency.* Bloomington: Indiana University Press, 1982.

Moynihan, Ruth Barnes. "Children and Young People on the Overland Trail." *WHQ* 4 (July 1975): 279–94.

Murray, John A. *Cinema Southwest: An Illustrated Guide to the Movies and Their Locations.* Hong Kong: Midas Printing Co., 2002.

Nagel, Stony. "When Siringo Was Marked for Death." *True West* 18, no. 2 (November–December 1970): 31, 68–69.

Newcomb, William. *The Indians of Texas.* Austin: University of Texas Press, 1961.

Nolan, Frederick. *The Lincoln County War: A Documentary History.* Norman: University of Oklahoma Press, 1992.

———. *The West of Billy the Kid.* Norman: University of Oklahoma Press, 1998.

Oates, Stephen B., ed. *Rip Ford's Texas.* Austin: University of Texas Press, 1963.

O'Neal, Bill. *Henry Brown, The Outlaw-Marshal.* College Station, Tex.: Creative Publishing Co., 1980.

———. *Encyclopedia of Western Gunfighters.* Norman: University of Oklahoma Press, 1998.

———. *Historic Ranches of the Old West.* Austin: Eakin Press, 1997.

Otero, M. A. *My Life on the Frontier.* 2 vols. New York: The Press of the Pioneers, Inc., 1935–1939.

———. *The Real Billy the Kid.* New York: R. R. Wilson, 1936.

Parkman, Francis. *LaSalle and the Discovery of the Great West.* 1879. Repr. Boston: Little, Brown and Company, 1922.

Parsons, Chuck. *Phil Coe, Texas Gambler.* Wolf City, Tex.: Hemington, 1984.

Patterson, Richard. *Butch Cassidy: A Biography.* Lincoln: University of Nebraska Press, 1998. A crucial biography.

Pearson, Jim Berry. *The Maxwell Land Grant.* Norman: University of Oklahoma Press, 1961.

Peavy, Charles D. *Charles A. Siringo: A Texas Pícaro.* Austin: Steck-Vaughn Company, 1967.

Phipps, Stanley S. *From Bull Pen to Bargain Table: The Tumultuous Struggle of the Coeur d'Alene Miners for the Right to Organize, 1887–1942.* New York: Garland Publishing, 1988.

Pingenot, Ben E. "Charlie Siringo: New Mexico's Lone Star Cowboy." *Cattleman* 63 (November 1976): 56–57, 122–28.

———. *Siringo*. College Station: Texas A & M University Press, 1989. An outstanding biography of Siringo.

Rathjen, Frederick J. *The Texas Panhandle Frontier*. Lubbock: Texas Tech University Press, 1973; repr. 1998).

Reed, Ollie, Jr. "Cowboy Character." *The Albuquerque Tribune*, Saturday, June 30, 2001, Weekend Editor, p. 1, 4.

Rhodes, Eugene Manlove. "He'll Make A Hand." *Sunset Magazine* 63 (June 1927): 23, 89–91. A tribute to Siringo.

Rickles, Robert A. *The Karankawa Indians of Texas: An Ecological Study of Cultural Tradition and Change*. Austin: University of Texas Press, 1996.

Ridge, Martin, ed. *My Life East and West*. By William S. Hart. Chicago: The Lakeside Press, 1994.

Rile, Charlie. "The Trap Didn't Spring on Butch Cassidy?" *True West* (January–February 1969): 40–45.

Robertson, Pauline Durrett and R. L. Robertson. *Cowman's Country: Fifty Frontier Ranches in the Texas Panhandle, 1876–1887*. Amarillo, Tex.: Paramount Publishing Company, 1981. Has superb photographs and maps.

Romero, Jose Ymocencio, and Ernest L. Archambeau. "Spanish Sheepmen on the Canadian at Old Tascosa." *Panhandle-Plains Historical Review* 19 (1946).

Sackett, Samuel J. *Cowboys and the Songs They Sang*. New York: William R. Scott, Inc., 1967.

Sawey, Orlan. *Charles A. Siringo*. Boston: Twayne Publications, a division of G. K. Hall & Company, 1981.

———. "Charlie Siringo, Reluctant Propagandist." *Western American Literature* 7, no. 3 (fall 1972): 203–10.

Schwantes, Carlos A. "The History of Pacific Northwest Labor History." *Idaho Yesterdays* 28 (winter 1985): 23–35.

———. *The Pacific Northwest: An Interpretive History*. Lincoln: University of Nebraska Press, 1989.

———. *In Mountain Shadows: A History of Idaho*. Lincoln: University of Nebraska Press, 1991.

Seeligson, Lelia. "A History of Indianola." Compiled for the Indianola Historical Association, 1930. Xerox of printed copy (n.d.) in Matagorda Historical Society, courtesy of Paul C. Stone, July, 2001.

Sharpe, Ronna Lee and Tom Sharpe. "Some Folks Wouldn't Understand It: A Study of Henry Herbert Knibbs." In *Cowboy Poets and Poetry*. Edited by David Stanley and Elaine Thatcher. Urbana and Chicago: University of Illinois Press, 2000.

Sheers, Margaret. "The LX Ranch in Texas." *Panhandle-Plains Historical Review* 6 (1933). Reprinted in *The Cattleman* (May 1934): 23–28.

Sheffy, L. E. "British Pounds and British Purebreeds." *Panhandle-Plains Historical Review* 2 (1938): 59–60.

Sherwood, Morgan. "Alaska." In *Exploration of Alaska, 1865–1900.* New Haven: Yale University Press, 1965.

Skaggs, Jimmy M. *The Cattle Trailing Industry.* Lawrence, Kans.: University Press of Kansas, 1973.

Slatta, Richard W. *Cowboys of the Americas.* New Haven: Yale University Press, 1990.

Spence, Clark C. *Mining Engineers and the Lace Boot Brigade, 1849–1933.* New Haven: Yale University Press, 1970.

Starr, Kevin. *Inventing the Dream: California through the Progressive Era.* New York: Oxford University Press, 1985.

Stephens, A. Ray, and William M. Holmes. *Historical Atlas of Texas.* Norman: University of Oklahoma Press, 1989.

Streeter, Floyd B. *Ben Thompson.* New York: Fell, 1957.

———. *Prairie Trails and Cattle Towns: The Opening of the Old West.* New York: The Devin Adair Company, 1963.

Taliaferro, John. *Charles M. Russell: The Life and Legend of America's Cowboy Artist.* Boston: Little, Brown and Company, 1996.

Tatum, Stephen. *Inventing Billy the Kid: Visions of the Outlaw in America, 1881–1981.* Albuquerque: University of New Mexico Press, 1982.

Taylor, Lonn, and Ingrid Maar. *The American Cowboy.* Washington, D.C.: American Folklife Center, Library of Congress, 1983.

Taylor, Thomas Alvar. *Jesse Chisholm.* Bandera, Tex.: Frontier Times, 1939.

Tefertiller, Casey. *Wyatt Earp: The Life behind the Legend.* Foreword by Angus Cameron. New York: John Wiley and Sons, Inc., 1997.

Thorp, N. Howard (Jack). *Pardner of the Wind.* Lincoln: University of Nebraska Press, 1977. In collaboration with Neil M. Clark.

Thorp, R. W. "Famous Gun Men of the West." *Field and Stream* 35, no. 5 (September 1930): 28–29, 72. Based on interview with Siringo before his death in 1928 and on comments of other persons who knew him.

Tuska, Jon. *The Filming of the West.* Garden City, N.J.: Doubleday and Company, Inc., 1976.

———. *The American West in Film: Critical Approaches to the Western.* Westport, Conn.: Greenwood Press, 1985.

———. *Billy the Kid: His Life and Legend.* Westport, Conn.: Greenwood Press, 1994.

Twain, Mark. *The Adventures of Huckleberry Finn.* 1884. Repr. New York: Bantam Books, 1981.

Utley, Robert M. *Four Fighters of Lincoln County.* Albuquerque: University of New Mexico Press, 1986.

———. *High Noon in Lincoln: Violence on the Western Frontier.* Albuquerque: University of New Mexico Press, 1987.

———. *Billy the Kid: A Short and Violent Life.* Lincoln: University of Nebraska Press, 1989.

———. *Lone Star Justice: The First Century of the Texas Rangers.* New York: Oxford University Press, 2002.

Waller, Altina. *Feud: Hatfields, McCoys, and Social Change in Appalachia, 1860–1900*. Chapel Hill: University of North Carolina Press, 1988.

Webb, Walter Prescott. *The Great Plains*. New York: Grosset & Dunlap, 1929, and later printings.

Weber, David J. *The Spanish Frontier in North America*. New Haven: Yale University Press, 1992.

Weddle, Robert S., et al., eds. *LaSalle, the Mississippi and the Gulf: Three Primary Documents*. College Station: Texas A & M University Press, 1987.

———, ed. *Wilderness Manhunt: The Spanish Search for La Salle*. Austin: University of Texas Press, 1971.

Weinberger, Arthur, ed. *Attorney for the Damned*. New York: Simon and Schuster, 1957.

West, Elliott. *Growing Up with the Country: Childhood on the Far Western Frontier*. Albuquerque: University of New Mexico Press, 1989.

Westphall, Victor. *Thomas Benton Catron and His Era*. Tucson: University of Arizona Press, 1973.

Williams, John Alexander. *Appalachia: A History*. Chapel Hill: University of North Carolina Press, 2002.

Woolridge, Rockette L. "Here Come the Herds to Matagorda." *Texas Historian* (January 1975).

Wooster, Ralph H. "Notes on Texas' Largest Slaveholders, 1860." *The Southwestern Historical Journal Quarterly* 65, no. 1 (July 1961).

Worcester, Donald F. *The Chisholm Trail*. Lincoln: University of Nebraska Press, 1980.

Yagoda, Ben. *Will Rogers: A Biography*. New York: Knopf, 1993.

UNPUBLISHED ESSAYS AND LETTERS

Boudett, Michael. "Charlie Siringo and the Anarchists." Senior History Essay, Yale University, April, 1988.

Kent, Betty Siringo, to Philip Garvin, Canyon Park, California, April 15, 1991, acknowledging receipt of film on Siringo.

Lober, Douglas. "Caldwell, Kansas and the Cattletown Solution, 1879–1885." Senior History Essay, Yale University, May, 1982).

McFarland, Mrs. Carol Siringo, Whittier, California, to Howard Lamar, July 26, 1976.

McFarland, Mrs. William J., Whittier, California, to Howard Lamar, May 10, 1976.

Warburton, Sister Margaret Rose. "A History of the O'Connor Ranch, 1834–1939." Dissertation submitted to Faculty of Graduate School of Arts and Sciences, Catholic University, Washington, D.C. for a Master of Arts.

Index

Abilene, Kans., 108–9, 111
Adair, John G., 76
Adams, Andy, 124–26, 219
Adams, Jake, 119
Adams, Steve, 243–44
African-Americans, 30–31, 58
Ainsworth, Capt. John C., 174
Alaska, 232
Allen, Poole and Company, 49, 59
Alliance League, 166, 167
Allison, C. Leon, 178, 275
Allison, Robert Clay, 275–76
Altgeld, John Peter, 245
Ancheta, Joseph A., 158, 161–62
Anderson, G. M. "Broncho Billy,"
    284
Antrim, William. See Billy the Kid
Archuleta County, Colo., 141–45
Austin, James, 11
Austin, Moses, 8–9
Austin, Stephen F., 9–10
Averill, Jim, 197

Banks, Gen. Nathaniel P., 29
Barry, Pat, 148
Bartlett, John Russell, 20
Bates, Col. Joseph, 22

Bates, W. H. "Deacon", 67, 69,
    76–79
Beals, David Thomas, 67, 77–79
Bee, Brig. Gen. Hamilton P., 29–30
Big-foot Wallace (Frank Clifford),
    86, 87
Billy the Kid (William Bonney): biog-
    raphies of, 87, 88–89, 274, 279;
    and films, 301, 334; and the LX
    Ranch, 70, 81–83, 84–85
bison, 71, 112–13, 214, 279
Blair, Enos, 122
Boise, Idaho, 263
Bonney, William. See Billy the Kid
Borah, William E., 245–46, 259
Borden, Abel Pierce, 57
Borrego brothers, 167–68
Bowdre, Charles, 85, 274
Boyce, Edward, 187, 241
Bradley, Frederick Worthen, 174–75,
    241
Brady, William, 82
Breman, Eustace, 8
Brininstool, E. A., 289
Brown, Henry, 82, 120
Brown, R. E., 186
Brown's Park, Utah, 195–96
Bryan, David, 145

Bunker Hill and Sullivan Mine, 174, 176, 241
Burnet, David, 11
Burns Detective Agency, 266
Bush, Joe, 208
Butch Cassidy and the Sundance Kid (Hill), 192–93
Butte, Mont., 178
Byles, Frank, 124

Cabeza de Vaca, Alvar Nuñez, 6
Caldwell, Kans., 90, 113–22, 217, 218, 292
camels, 20
Caney Creek, 10–11, 18, 27, 29
Carey, Harry, 286
Carfrae, Joan, 138
Carpenter, E. L., 199–200
Carter, Charles L., 207–8
Carter, Fred, 184
Carver (Casey), Will, 209, 254
Cassidy, Butch, 192–95, 197–206, 254
Cassidy, George. *See* Butch Cassidy
Castle Gate, Utah, 199
Catron, Thomas, 158, 159, 165–68
cattle: during Civil War, 26, 30–32; and land acquisition, 52–53, 54; mavericks, 12–14, 60; open-range ranching, 2; pre–Civil War, 108–9; during Reconstruction, 36; rounding up, 60–61; rustling, 50–51, 197–98, 271–73; slaughtering, 62; and Texas tick fever, 57, 109, 111, 113; trails, 109–15
Chambers, Lon, 85–86, 87
Champion, Nate, 198
Chavez, Francisco, 162, 166, 167–68
Cherokee Strip, 114
Chisholm Trail, 96, 212; end of, 121; origin of, 36, 109; and Siringo, 63, 270, 271

Civil War, 21–24
Clark, Edward, 21
Clark, Orrie S., 275–76, 278
Clement, Erskine, 81, 87
Clement, Victor, 174, 175, 186
Clifford, Frank (Big-foot Wallace), 86, 87
Coe, Phil, 52
Coeur d'Alene mines, 177–87
Coghlan, Pat, 86, 87, 90
Cole, George T., 283–84
Colfax County, New Mex., 275
Colorado, 141–52
Comanche Indians, 71
comancheros, 73
Couch, William C., 115
A Cowboy Detective (Siringo), 266–67, 305
cowboys: African-American, 30–31, 58; and horses, 79; songs, 2, 279, 287; and western films, 284–87
Cox's Point, Tex., 18
Craftsville Post Office, Ky., 238
Crocker, William, 174
Crouse, Charlie, 195
Cruzan, Bill, 208
Currie, "Flat Nose" George, 201, 208

Dagner, James H., 113
Dalton, Emmett, 286
Darrow, Clarence, 244–47, 259, 269
Dawdy, Asa, 53
Debs, Eugene V., 187, 244
DeCrow's Point, 18
Dobie, J. Frank, 70
Dodge City, Kans., 112–13, 213, 214
Dubois, Wyo., 196
Duncan, John, 58
Dunkel, John, 228
Dutch Settlement, Tex., 4, 26–28

Eams, Superintendent, 147–48

Earp, Wyatt, 286–87

East, Jim, 70, 85, 274, 277–80

East, Nettie Boulding, 278

Elkins, Stephen, 166

Ellsworth, Kans., 111–12, 213

El Rancho Grande, 48–49, 50, 58, 94

Emory, Tom, 86

Engel, George, 132–33, 222

Esler, A. M., 186

Farr, Edward, 202

Farris, John, 81

Farwell, John V., 69

Fergusson, Harvey, 169

Fielden, Samuel, 132, 133, 136, 222, 245

Finch, John A., 178

Fischer, Adolph, 132–33, 222

Flat, George, 119

Folsom, New Mex., 202

Ford, Col. John S. "Rip", 29–30

Fort Elliot, Tex., 71

Fort Esperanza, Tex., 24, 26

Fort Griffin, Tex., 71, 97

Fort Harker, Kans., 112

Fort Worth Five, 254

French, William, 201–2

Frisco Mill (Idaho), 184, 226, 333

Gallegos, Sylvestre, 166

Galveston, Tex., 24–26

Garcia, Victoriano and Felipe, 163–64

Garrett, Pat, 85, 88, 104, 105, 274

Garvin, Philip, 228

Gelber, Jack, 228

Gem, Idaho, 178–85, 225

Gifford, George S., 57

Goodnight, Charles, 74–76, 279

Goss, A. D., 185

Grant, Sam, 64

Gray, John, 163

Green, James, 228

Greenow, Rose O'Neal, 141

Greenslet, Ferris, 293

Griffin, Black Jack, 181

Grimes, William Bradford "Bing", 47–48, 54

Gross, Charlie F., 111, 112

Hainer, Al, 196

Haley, J. Evetts, Sr., 70–71, 278

Hamilton, Thomas Jefferson, 52

Hammond, John Hays, 174, 294

Hardin, John Wesley, 52

Harriman, E. H., 201

Harris, Tom, 278

Hart, William S., 310; and Earp, 287; and Russell, 290–91; and Siringo, 3–4, 277, 284–85, 289, 291–92, 309

Hawkins, James Boyd, 18, 30

Hawks, William E., 292

Hawley, James, 245, 259

Haymarket Riot, 126–27, 129–34, 221, 222

Haywood, William D. (Big Bill), 258; and detectives, 230; and the Gem Mill, 137, 187, 188; on trial, 241, 244–47

Hazen Josiah, 201

Herrera, Juan José, 163

Herrera, Nicanor, 163

Herrera, Pablo, 161, 224

Hill, George Roy, 192–93

History of "Billy the Kid" (Siringo), 274

Hitt, Samuel N., 111, 112

Holcomb, Sol, 238

Hole-in-the-Wall gang (Wild Bunch), 200–201, 203, 206, 208

Hollicott, John, 87
Hollywood, Calif., 284–91
Holmes, Neptune, 56, 58
Horn, Tom, 197, 269
horses, 79, 196–97
Horsley, Albert E. *See* Orchard, Harry
Houghton Mifflin Publishing Company, 293–300
Houston, Sam, 21
Hoyt, Dr. Henry, *310*
Hoyt, Dr. Henry F., 82, 83, 276–77, 292
Hubbard, Charlie, 232–35
Hughes, Oliver, 181, 186
Hunnewell, Kans., 113
Hunt, Callie May, 209
Hurden, Bill, 55

Idaho, 178–85, 225, 226, 333
Idanha Hotel (Idaho), 263
Indianola (Indian Point), Tex., 19–21, 95
Indian Territory, 114

Jackson, Ky., 236
James, Will, 290, *308*
JA Ranch, 76
Johnson County, Wyo., 196–97, 198, 253
Jones, C. J. "Buffalo", 279
Joseph, Antonio, 165, 166, 167

Kansas, 111, 112–13, 115, *213*, 214
Karankawas, 6–8
Kelly, W. C., 119
Kentucky, 236–41
Ketchum, Sam, 202
Kid Curry, 201, 203, 206–8
Kilpatrick, Ben, 254
Knibbs, Henry Herbert, 287–91, *310*

Kountze, Herman, 52–53
Kuykendall, Wiley Martin, 54–56, 60–61

labor. *See* Coeur d'Alene mines; Haymarket Riot
Lacy, William Demetris, 50
Ladd, William S., *174*
Lamar, Howard, 228
land: acquisition, 12–14, 52–53, 54, 78; in Indian Territory, 115; land grants, 9, 160–61, 275
La Salle, Sieur de (Robert Cavelier), 7–8
Las Vegas, New Mex., 160, 167
Lavaca, Tex., 19
Lay, Elza, 198–202, 208–9
League, Hosea H., 11
Leussler, Harrison, *310*
Lewis, T. W., 199–200
Lincoln County, New Mex., 82, 88–89
Lingg, Louis, 131–32, 133, 222
Littlefield, Capt. George W., 66
Lloyd, Mamie, 90
Logan, Harvey "Kid Curry", 201, 203, 206–8, 254
Logan, Lonny, 207–8
A Lone Star Cowboy (Siringo), 273–74
The Lone Star (Harby), 16
Longabaugh, Harry (Sundance Kid), 199, 200, 203–4, 254, 255
Loving, Oliver, 74
Lowe, Jim, 201–2
Lummis, Charles F., 288
Lunn brothers, 51–52
LX Ranch, 78–79, 98

Magruder, Gen. John Bankhead, 24–26
Malone, Ida, 58

Marquis, Neeta, 297
Martinez, Felix, 161
Masterson, Bat, 215
Masterson, George, 214
Matagorda City, Tex., 11–12, 17–18, 19, 24–30
Matagorda County, Tex., 91
Matagorda Peninsula, 1, 9
mavericks, 12–14, 60
Maverick, Samuel, 12–14
Maxwell, Kate, 197
Maxwell Land Grant, 275
Maxwell, Pete, 85
McCarthy, Tom, 195
McClain, James, 64
McClellan, George B., 140–41
McCormick, Cyrus, 174
McCoy, Bill, 145–46
McCoy, Joseph G., 36, 108–9, 111, 112, 211
McCroskey, John, 58
McDonald, William C., 270, 271–72
McGinnis, William, 201–2
McParland, James, 224, 261; and the Haywood trial, 188, 243, 244, 246, 248–50; and the Molly Maguires, 140; as superintendent, 148
McSparrin, J. Clay, 57
Meeks, Henry "Bub", 199, 201, 203
Merril, Tom, 62–63
Mexico, 17
Middleton, John, 82
Miller, Elvira, 58
Millers Brothers 101 Ranch, 285–86
Miller, Stuart, 228
Mills, David O., 174
Mills, T. B., 161–62, 168
Mine Owners Protective Association (MOA), 175–77

miners: diversity of, 175–76; salting of mines, 148–52; "scabs", 179; unions, 177–79; wages, 176; Western Federation of Miners, 187–88
Mix, Tom, 285–86
Moffat, David, 195
Monihan, John, 178, 184, 185
Moore, Anthony, 63
Moore, John, 60
Moore, William C. (Outlaw Bill), 70, 79–81, 87, 99, 235
Morgan, Charles, 19–21, 41
Morgan Steamship Lines, 45, 49
Moyer, Charles H., 258; his arrest, 241, 244, 247; and the Gem Mill, 187, 188
Muckleroy Brothers, 62–63
Murray, Frank, 202

Neebe, Oscar, 132, 133, 136, 222, 245
Nevada, 203, 209
Newman, Paul, 192–93
New Mexico: Colfax County, 275; Folsom, 202; Las Vegas, 160, 167; Lincoln County, 82, 88–89; politics, 160–61, 165–69; and public schools, 158–59, 162
Nickelson, Johnny, 119
Noyer, Frank, 122
Nye, Thomas C. F. (Tom), 53–54

O'Brien, Thomas, 180, 186
O'Folliard (O'Phalliard), Tom, 82, 85, 274
Oklahoma Boomers, 115
Old Three Hundred, 9–10, 54–55
Orchard, Harry, 257, 260; in Caldwell, Idaho, 137, 242; his confession, 188, 243–44
Otero, Miguel A., 169

Palo Duro Canyon, Tex., 75–76

Parker, Cynthia Ann, 74

Parker, Dan, 205–6

Parker, George Leroy.
See Cassidy, Butch

Parsons, Albert, 131, 133, 222

Partain, Ellen, 268

Payne, David L., 115

Peareson, Dr. E. A., 22–23

Pelling, George, 152–55

Pelton, Dr. A. M., 293

Pettibone, George A., 258; and
the Gem Mill, 178–80,
183, 186, 188; on trial,
244, 247; and Two Evil
Isms (Siringo), 270

Pickett, Bill, 285

Pierce, Abel Head "Shanghai",
93; and Abilene, 111; during
Civil War, 48; El Rancho
Grande, 48–49, 50, 58, 94;
his employees, 53–59;
hiring Siringo, 42, 60;
and theLunn brothers,
51–52; his marriage, 50;
and Wichita, 112; his
youth, 46–48

Pierce, Jonathan Edwards, 48,
50–51, 267

Pinchot, Gifford, 294

Pinkerton, Allen, 137–41

Pinkerton National Detective
Agency, 223, 249, 251,
266–71, 299

Pinkerton, Robert, 236–37

Pinkerton, William, 135

Place, Etta, 199, 204, 255

Polk, Cal, 85

Poynton, Joe, 180, 186

Preston, Douglas A., 197, 199

Prince, L. Bradford, 160–68

Proctor, Fred C., 57–58

railroads: competition, 114; and
mining, 175, 176; and
Pinkerton operatives, 139–40;
and robberies, 201–2, 203, 204;
and Shanghai Pierce, 59

Railsback, Steve, 228, 229

ranching: and horses, 79; JA
Ranch, 76; LX Ranch, 78–79,
98; mavericks, 12–14, 60;
open-range, 2; pre-Civil
War, 108–9; sheep, 73; XIT
Ranch, 69, 70

Ray, Nick, 198

Read, Mrs. Will F., 158, 186

Redford, Robert, 192–93

Red River Indian War, 71

Reed, Simeon G., 173–74

Reilly, George W., 115

Renehan, Alois B., 266–67, 300–301

Rhodes, Eugene Manlove, 288,
294–96, 311

Riata and Spurs (Siringo), 293–301

Richardson, Edmund, 244

Robbers Roost, Utah, 195, 208

Robbins, Chester, 47

Robinson, John, 80

Rogers, Will, 285–86, 289–90, 291,
298–99, 307

Romero, Casimero, 73, 75

Rugeley, Edward S., Sr., 22

Rugeley, John, 18

Russell, Charles Marion, 290–91,
294, 307

salting of mines, 148–52

Sandoval, Agapito, 73

Santa Fe Ring, 159

Sayles, W. O., 204–10, 232–35, 252

Schell, Hiram, 232–35

Schnaubelt, Rudolph, 136

Schwab, Michael, 132, 133, 136,
222, 245

Selkirk, William, 11
Shawnee Trail, 109–10
Shea, Capt. D. R., 24
sheep ranching, 73
Shipley, Mrs. Kate, 179, 181–83, 228, 229
Shores, Cyrus W. "Doc", 205
Shultz, James W., 310
Silva, Vicente, 167
Siringo, Antonio, 4–5, 92
Siringo, Bridget, 5, 36–37
Siringo, Charlie, 92, 261, 262, 306, 309, 310; biographical film, 228; branding cattle, 61; and Butch Cassidy, 204–10; in Caldwell, Kans., 117–18, 217; in Chicago, 126–27, 135–37, 139; his children, 158, 216, 231–32, 267, 277, 296; and the Chisholm Trail, 63, 270, 271; and the Civil War, 23–24; and Coeur d'Alene, 177–87, 227; in Colorado, 141–52; A Cowboy Detective, 266–67, 305; his death, 301–4, 312; his family, 4–5, 65, 116–17; and the Haywood trial, 248–50; in Hollywood, 284, 291–301; his horse, 79, 83, 170; and Huck Finn, 39–41; in Kentucky, 236–41; A Lone Star Cowboy, 273–74; his marriages, 90, 117, 121, 153, 158, 216, 231–32, 265–66, 268; in Nevada, 152–55; in New Mexico, 158–64, 169–72, 224, 271–73; Riata and Spurs, 293–301; and Shanghai Pierce, 60–66; in St. Louis, 37–38; in the Texas Panhandle, 67, 80–90; and Treadwell Mill, 232–35; Two Evil Isms, 251, 256, 268–71
Siringo, Viola, 158, 216, 267, 277
Siringo, William Lee Roy, 231–32
slavery, 12, 30

Snyder, Philip, 153–54
songs, 2, 279, 287
Spanish, 6–7
Spies, August, 131, 133, 134, 222
Springer, New Mex., 72
Standing Bear, Luther, 298, 310, 346
Stark, Frank, 184–85
Steunenberg, Gov. Frank, 137, 188, 241–42, 257
St. John, Vincent, 243
Stone, Charles H., 113
Stover, Elias, 158
Sullivan, Daniel, 52, 53
Sundance Kid (Harry Longabaugh), 199, 200, 203–4, 254, 255
Sutton family, 51–52
Sweeney, Charles, 177

Tascosa, Tex., 71–72, 100, 101, 278
Taylor, E. M., 143
Taylor family, 51
Telluride, Colo., 195
Texas: during Civil War, 21–30; Cox's Point, 18; Dutch Settlement, 4, 26–28; Galveston, 24–26; Indianola (Indian Point), 19–21, 95; Matagorda City, 11–12, 17–18, 19, 24–30; Matagorda County, 91; Matagorda Peninsula, 1, 9; military forts, 24, 26, 71, 97; Palo Duro Canyon, 75–76; Panhandle frontier, 69–72, 97, 98, 102; tick fever, 57, 109, 111, 113
A Texas Cowboy (Siringo), 220
Thomas, Lillie, 231–32
Thompson, Ben J., 52
Thompson, Jim, 207–8
Thompson, Robert R., 174
Thornton, William T., 167–68
Thorp, Nathan Howard "Jack", 279
Tidehaven (Tres Palacios), 18

Tilton, Charles Nathan, 14
Tipton, Wyo., 203, 208, 254
Tone, Susan T., 55
Treadwell Mill, Alaska, 232
Tres Palacios (Tidehaven), 18
Tucker, Perry, 201
Tumbleweeds (Hart), 291–92
Tunstall, John, 88–89
Tuttle, W. C., 288, 310
Two Evil Isms (Siringo), 251, 256, 268–71

Upson, Ash, 88
Utah, 195–96, 199

Vásquez, Gen. Rafael, 17
Venture, Richard, 228

Wagner, Wyo., 204
Waite, Fred, 82
Walker, Joe, 208
Wallace, Idaho, 226
Ward, Leander, 62
Warner, Matt, 195–96, 198–99
Warren, Jennifer, 228, 229
Watson, Ellen "Cattle Kate", 197
Webb, Walter Prescott, 70
Webster, Tim, 141
Wentz, Dan, 236
Wentz, Dr. (Sr.), 236
Wentz, Edward, 236–37

Western Federation of Miners, 241
Western Trail, 111
White Caps (Gorras Blancas), 160–64
White, Mary, 64
Wichita, Kans., 112
Wightman, Elias R., 10–11
Wilcox, Wyo., 201
Wild Bunch (Hole-in-the-Wall gang), 200–201, 203, 206, 208
Williams, Doc, 148
Williams, John, 27–28
Wilson, John, 119
Winnemucca, Nev., 203, 209
Wolle, Adrián, 17
women, 197, 199
Wood, George, 119
Woods, George and Mag, 121, 122
Woodstock, C. E., 203
Word, Charles, 84
Wyoming: Dubois, 196; Stock Growers Association, 197–98; Tipton, 203, 208, 254; Wagner, 204; Wilcox, 201

XIT Ranch, 69, 70

Yeamans, Horace, 62

Zipprian, John, 5